CAMBRIDGE LIBRAR

C000125719

Books of enduring sch

Travel and Exploration

The history of travel writing dates back to the Bible, Caesar, the Vikings and the Crusaders, and its many themes include war, trade, science and recreation. Explorers from Columbus to Cook charted lands not previously visited by Western travellers, and were followed by merchants, missionaries, and colonists, who wrote accounts of their experiences. The development of steam power in the nineteenth century provided opportunities for increasing numbers of 'ordinary' people to travel further, more economically, and more safely, and resulted in great enthusiasm for travel writing among the reading public. Works included in this series range from first-hand descriptions of previously unrecorded places, to literary accounts of the strange habits of foreigners, to examples of the burgeoning numbers of guidebooks produced to satisfy the needs of a new kind of traveller - the tourist.

Journal of the Right Hon. Sir Joseph Banks

Sir Joseph Banks (1743–1820) was a British botanist and one of the most influential scientific patrons of the eighteenth century. After inheriting a fortune on the death of his father in 1761, Banks devoted his life to studying natural history. His fame following his participation in Captain Cook's epic voyage on the *Endeavour* between 1768 and 1771 led to his election as President of the Royal Society in 1778, a post which he then held until his death. This volume, first published in 1896, contains Banks' account of the voyage of the *Endeavour* across the Pacific Ocean. Edited by the great botanist Sir Joseph Hooker, it describes in fascinating detail the peoples, cultures and wildlife Banks encountered in Tahiti, New Zealand and Australia. Banks' aptitude as a natural historian and the crucial role he played in cataloguing and illustrating exotic wildlife during the expedition are emphasised in the work.

Cambridge University Press has long been a pioneer in the reissuing of out-of-print titles from its own backlist, producing digital reprints of books that are still sought after by scholars and students but could not be reprinted economically using traditional technology. The Cambridge Library Collection extends this activity to a wider range of books which are still of importance to researchers and professionals, either for the source material they contain, or as landmarks in the history of their academic discipline.

Drawing from the world-renowned collections in the Cambridge University Library, and guided by the advice of experts in each subject area, Cambridge University Press is using state-of-the-art scanning machines in its own Printing House to capture the content of each book selected for inclusion. The files are processed to give a consistently clear, crisp image, and the books finished to the high quality standard for which the Press is recognised around the world. The latest print-on-demand technology ensures that the books will remain available indefinitely, and that orders for single or multiple copies can quickly be supplied.

The Cambridge Library Collection will bring back to life books of enduring scholarly value (including out-of-copyright works originally issued by other publishers) across a wide range of disciplines in the humanities and social sciences and in science and technology.

Journal of the Right Hon. Sir Joseph Banks

*During Captain Cook's First Voyage
in H.M.S. Endeavour in 1768–71*

JOSEPH BANKS
EDITED BY JOSEPH DALTON HOOKER

CAMBRIDGE
UNIVERSITY PRESS

CAMBRIDGE UNIVERSITY PRESS

Cambridge, New York, Melbourne, Madrid, Cape Town,
Singapore, São Paolo, Delhi, Tokyo, Mexico City

Published in the United States of America by Cambridge University Press, New York

www.cambridge.org
Information on this title: www.cambridge.org/9781108029162

This edition first published 1896
This digitally printed version 2011

ISBN 978-1-108-02916-2 Paperback

JOURNAL

OF THE

RIGHT HON. SIR JOSEPH BANKS

Swan Electric Engraving Company.

The Right Honble Sir Joseph Banks. Bart. K.B. P.R.S.

From a portrait by Thomas Phillips. R.A in the possession of the Royal Society of London.

JOURNAL

OF

THE RIGHT HON.

SIR JOSEPH BANKS

BART., K.B., P.R.S.

DURING CAPTAIN COOK'S FIRST VOYAGE IN H.M.S.
ENDEAVOUR IN 1768-71 TO TERRA DEL FUEGO,
OTAHITE, NEW ZEALAND, AUSTRALIA,
THE DUTCH EAST INDIES,
ETC.

EDITED BY

SIR JOSEPH D. HOOKER

WITH PORTRAITS AND CHARTS

London

MACMILLAN AND CO., Ltd.

NEW YORK: THE MACMILLAN CO.

1896

TO

Rear-Admiral J. W. L. Wharton, C.B., F.R.S., &c. &c.

HYDROGRAPHER OF THE ADMIRALTY

MY DEAR ADMIRAL—Allow me to dedicate to you, as the able
Editor of Captain Cook's Journal of his first voyage round the world,
that of his fellow-voyager Sir Joseph Banks, in token of the great
assistance afforded me through your labour on the aforesaid work, and
as the efficient and accomplished tenant of an office for which I have
ever entertained a profound respect, that of Hydrographer of the
Admiralty.

Let me at the same time take the opportunity of coupling with
your name my tribute to the memory of three of your predecessors,
who honoured me with their friendship, and encouraged me in my
scientific career as an officer in the service to which you belong—
Admiral Sir F. Beaufort, Admiral Washington, and Captain Sir
F. Evans.

Believe me,

Very sincerely yours,

J. D. HOOKER.

THE CAMP, SUNNINGDALE,
May 1896.

PREFACE

MY principal motive for editing the Journal kept by Sir Joseph Banks during Lieutenant Cook's first voyage round the world is to give prominence to his indefatigable labours as an accomplished observer and ardent collector during the whole period occupied by that expedition, and thus to present him as the pioneer of those naturalist voyagers of later years, of whom Darwin is the great example.

This appears to me to be the more desirable, because in no biographical notice of Banks are his labours and studies as a working naturalist adequately set forth. Indeed, the only allusion I can find to their literally enormous extent and value is in the interesting letter from Linnæus to Ellis, which will be found on p. xl. In respect of Cook's first voyage this is in a measure due to the course pursued by Dr. Hawkesworth in publishing the account of the expedition, when Banks, with singular disinterestedness, placed his Journal in that editor's hands, with permission to make what use of it he thought proper. The result was that Hawkesworth[1] selected only such portions as would interest

---

[1] Dr. Hawkesworth devotes his "Introduction to the First Voyage" almost exclusively to the services which Banks rendered, and gratefully acknowledges that all such details as are not directly connected with navigation are extracted from the diary of that naturalist. But for the purpose of identifying the work of each observer this is insufficient, and barely does justice to the second of the two authors, who is in reality responsible for the greater portion of the book. In reference to Hawkesworth being employed as editor of Cook's Journal, the following passage is extracted

the general public, incorporating them with Cook's Journal, often without allusion to their author, and not unfrequently introducing into them reflections of his own as being those of Cook or of Banks. Fortunately the recent publication by Admiral Wharton of Cook's own Journal[1] has helped to rectify this, for any one comparing the two narratives can have no difficulty in recognising the source whence Hawkesworth derived his information.

Another motive for editing Banks's Journal is to emphasise the important services which its author rendered to the expedition. It needs no reading between the lines of the great navigator's Journal, to discover his estimation of the ability of his companion, of the value of his researches, and of the importance of his active co-operation on many occasions. It was Banks who rapidly mastered the language of the Otahitans and became the interpreter of the party, and who was the investigator of the customs, habits, etc., of these and of the natives of New Zealand. It was often through his activity that the commissariat was supplied with food. He was on various occasions the thief-taker, especially in the case of his hazardous expedition for the recovery of the stolen quadrant, upon the use of which, in observing the transit of Venus across the sun's disc, the success of the expedition so greatly depended. And, above all, it is to Banks's forethought and at his own risk that an Otahitan man and boy were taken on board, through whom Banks directed, when in New Zealand, those inquiries into the customs of its inhabitants, which are the founda-

from Prior's *Life of Malone* :—" Hawkesworth, the writer, was introduced by Garrick to Lord Sandwich, who, thinking to put a few hundred pounds into his pocket, appointed him to revise and publish Cook's Voyages. He scarcely did anything to the MSS., yet sold it to Cadell and Strahan, the printer and bookseller, for £6000. . . ."

[1] *Captain Cook's Journal during his First Voyage round the World in H.M. Bark "Endeavour,"* 1768-71, with Notes and Introduction by Captain W. J. L. Wharton, R.N., F.R.S., Hydrographer of the Admiralty.

tion of our knowledge of that interesting people. And
when it is considered that the information obtained was at
comparatively few points, and those on the coast only, the
fulness and accuracy of the description of the New Zea-
landers, even as viewed in the light of modern knowledge,
are very remarkable. Nor should it be forgotten that it was
to the drawings made by the artists whom Banks took in
his suite that the public is indebted for the magnificent
series of plates that adorn Hawkesworth's account of the
voyage. Still another motive is, that Banks's Journal gives
a life-like portrait of a naturalist's daily occupation at sea
and ashore nearly one hundred and thirty years ago ; and thus
supplements the history of a voyage which, for extent and importance of geographic and hydrographic results, was unique
and " to the English nation the most momentous voyage of
discovery that has ever taken place " (Wharton's *Cook*, Preface), and which has, moreover, directly led to the prosperity
of the Empire; for it was owing to the reports of Cook and
Banks, and, it is believed, to the representations of the latter
on the advantages of Botany Bay as a site for a settlement,
that Australia was first colonised.

The following brief history of the Journal itself is interesting. On Sir J. Banks's death without issue in 1820,
his property and effects passed to the Hugessen (his wife's)
family, with the exception of the library, herbarium, and
the lease of the house in Soho Square. These were left to
his librarian, the late eminent botanist, Robert Brown, F.R.S.,
with the proviso that after that gentleman's death, the
library and herbarium were to go to the British Museum.
Banks's papers and correspondence, including the Journal
of the voyage of the *Endeavour*, were then placed by the
trustees in Mr. Brown's hands, with the object of his writing a Life of Banks, which he had agreed to do. Age and
infirmities, however, interfered with his prosecution of this

work, and at his suggestion the materials were transferred with the same object to my maternal grandfather, Dawson Turner, F.R.S.,[1] an eminent botanist and antiquarian, who had been a friend of Banks. Mr. Turner at once had the whole faithfully transcribed, but for which precaution the Journal would as a whole have been irretrievably lost, as the sequel will show. Beyond having copies of the manuscript made, Mr. Turner seems to have done nothing towards the Life, and after a lapse of some years the originals were returned, together with the copies, to Mr. Knatchbull Hugessen, who placed them in the hands of the late Mr. Bell, Secretary of the Royal Society, in the hopes that he would undertake to write the Life. For their subsequent wanderings and the ultimate fate of many portions, I am indebted to Mr. Carruthers, F.R.S., late Keeper of the Botanical Collections at the British Museum, who has favoured me with the following interesting letter concerning them :—

BRITISH MUSEUM (NATURAL HISTORY),
CROMWELL ROAD, SOUTH KENSINGTON, S.W.,
14th July 1893.

DEAR SIR JOSEPH—Since I saw you about the Journal of Sir Joseph Banks in Captain Cook's Voyage, I have been making further inquiries regarding the original document.

The Banksian Journal and correspondence were sent to the Botanical Department, after correspondence with Mr. Knatchbull Hugessen, to remain in my keeping till the death of Lady Knatchbull, when it would become the property of the trustees. I was instructed to deposit it in the Manuscript Department. This was in October 1873. Some time thereafter I persuaded Mr. Daydon Jackson to look at the correspondence with the view of preparing a biography of Banks. This he agreed to do. I wrote to Mr. Bell, who informed me in a letter written 14th February 1876, that he had tried to get Lord

---

[1] It was when on a visit to my grandfather in 1833 that I first saw the original Journal in Banks's handwriting. It was then being copied, and I was employed to verify the copies of the earlier part by comparison with the original. I well remember being as a boy fascinated with the Journal, and I never ceased to hope that it might one day be published.

Stanhope to undertake the biography, when he found that he could
not himself face it, and thereafter Mr. Colquhoun and then Mr. John
Ball, F.R.S. I obtained from the box, by leave from Mr. Bond, then
Keeper of MSS., in the beginning of 1876, the transcripts made for
Mr. Dawson Turner by his two daughters, which have remained under
my care in the Botanical Department.

The story of the originals after I parted with them is a distressing
one. Some seven or eight years ago Lord Brabourne claimed the
letters as his property. Mr. Maunde Thompson remonstrated, and
told him that they were to remain in the museum till the death of
Lady Knatchbull, and then they were to become the property of the
trustees. Lord Brabourne would not accept this view, but claimed
them as his own, and carried off the box and its contents. They were
afterwards offered to the museum for sale, but the price offered by
the Keeper of the MSS. was not satisfactory, and the whole collection was broken up into lots, 207, and sold by auction at Sotheby's
on 14th April 1886. The Journal of Cook's voyage was lot 176,
and was described in the catalogue as " Banks's (Sir Joseph) Journal
of a Voyage to the Sandwich Islands and New Zealand, from March
1769 [1] to July 1771, in the autograph of Banks." It was purchased
by an autograph dealer, John Waller, for £7 : 2 : 6. Mr. Britten has
gone to Waller's to inquire after the Journal. Waller did not
specially remember that purchase, and he does not believe he has
got the manuscript. So where it is now no one knows.[2] As you
will see, the earlier portion of the Journal was missing in the lot sold.
Waller bought in all 57 lots. The letters were broken up and sold
as autographs ; those that he purchased and did not know, like
those of Brass, Nelson, Alex. Anderson, etc., and were of no money
value, he would probably at once destroy, so he told Mr. Britten. So
now all is gone—for whether the letters are preserved by autograph
collectors, or were at once thrown into the wastepaper basket, they
are equally lost to science. The 207 lots realised in all £182 : 19s. !

The result is that the Journal and letters transcribed for Dawson
Turner, and now here, are the only ones available. I am thankful
they have been saved out of the catastrophe.

Your transcriber is diligently at work.—I am, faithfully yours,

                                        WM. CARRUTHERS.

---

[1] That is some time after leaving Rio, and before arriving at Otahite.

[2] I have since ascertained that the Journal came into the possession of
J. Henniker Heaton, Esq., M.P., who informs me that he disposed of it to
a gentleman in Sydney, N.S.W.

It will be seen from the above that the present work
owes its existence to the copy of the original made by the
Miss Turners, and of which I was permitted by the Trustees of the British Museum to have a transcript made for
publication.   In doing this I have largely exercised my
duties as editor in respect of curtailments.   The Journal
was literally a diary, to which may truly be applied the
motto *nulla dies sine linea*, and contains nearly double
the quantity of matter here reproduced.   The omitted portions are chiefly observations on the wind and weather;
extracts from the ship's log, which find their proper place
in Cook's Journal; innumerable notices of birds and marine
animals that were of constant recurrence; and lists of
plants and animals, many with MS. names that have since
been superseded.

Owing also to the Journal being a diary written up
from day to day, and in no way revised for publication, the
grammar and orthography are in the original very loose,
and I have therefore corrected the language to accord with
modern requirements; the only exceptions being in the
case of native words, such as *Otahite, tattowing, kangooroo*,
etc., of which the spelling is consistent throughout, and
which consequently really represent Banks's own impres-
sion of the native pronunciation of such words.

It remains gratefully to record my obligations to the
Trustees of the British Museum, for permission to tran-
scribe the Journal, and to the Officers of the Natural
History Department, Sir W. Flower, Mr. Carruthers, and
Mr. Murray, and to Mr. E. R. Sykes, an acute malacologist,
for aid in the endeavour to determine some of the animals
designated by MS. names in the Journal.   My friend Mr.
B. D. Jackson, Sec.L.S., author of the article on Banks in
the *Dictionary of National Biography*, has kindly supplied
me with information for the Life of Banks, and has con-

tributed that of Solander. My son, Reginald H. Hooker, has aided me in the revision of the Journal and in the press work, and has drawn up the notices of the earlier voyagers and naturalists to whom reference is made by Banks. Lastly, I have cordially to thank the Presidents and Councils of the Royal and Linnean Societies respectively, for permission to reproduce in photography the admirable portraits of Banks and Solander which adorn their meeting-rooms.

J. D. HOOKER.

THE CAMP, SUNNINGDALE,
   May 1896.

CONTENTS

CHAPTER I

ENGLAND TO RIO DE JANEIRO

CHAPTER II

RIO DE JANEIRO

CHAPTER III

RIO TO TERRA DEL FUEGO

CHAPTER IV

TERRA DEL FUEGO TO OTAHITE

CHAPTER V

OTAHITE

CHAPTER VI

OTAHITE TO OHETEROA

b

CHAPTER X

GENERAL ACCOUNT OF NEW ZEALAND

CHAPTER XI

NEW ZEALAND TO AUSTRALIA (ENDEAVOUR RIVER)

CHAPTER XII

AUSTRALIA (ENDEAVOUR RIVER) TO TORRES STRAITS

CHAPTER XIII

CHAPTER XIV

CHAPTER XV

CHAPTER XVI

SAVU ISLAND TO BATAVIA

CHAPTER XVII

DESCRIPTION OF BATAVIA

CHAPTER XVIII

BATAVIA TO CAPE OF GOOD HOPE

CHAPTER XIX

CAPE OF GOOD HOPE TO ENGLAND

PORTRAITS

CHARTS

BIOGRAPHICAL SKETCHES

SIR JOSEPH BANKS [1]

THE name of Sir Joseph Banks is pre-eminent amongst the many distinguished scientific men who adorned the long reign of George the Third, and his career practically coincides with the reign of that monarch, closing in the same year. The hold he has always had on popular estimation is perhaps less due to his high position in the royal favour, or his long tenancy of the presidential chair of the Royal Society, than to the prominent part he took in the voyage of H.M.S. *Endeavour* under Lieutenant Cook, and his contributions to Hawkesworth's account of it. Cook's story is that of a sailor, and his account of his discoveries is rendered more attractive by the introduction of passages from the more graphic pages of Banks's Diary: it is these passages which attracted so much attention in the narrative drawn up by Dr. Hawkesworth. Cook's own Journal, recently published by Admiral Wharton, shows this very clearly, and the naturalist's own record of their discoveries and adventures is now for the first time given to the public.

Joseph Banks was born in Argyle Street, London, on 2nd February 1743 (o.s.). He was the son of William Banks (sometime Sheriff of Lincolnshire and M.P. for Peterborough), of Revesby Abbey, Lincolnshire, a gentleman of some fortune, due to his father's successful practice of medicine in that

---

[1] No adequate Life of Sir Joseph Banks having as yet appeared, the compiler of the following notes is indebted mainly for his information to Weld's *History of the Royal Society*, Sir John Barrow's *Sketches of the Royal Society and the Royal Society Club*, to Mr. B. Daydon Jackson's article on Banks in the *Dictionary of National Biography*, and to scattered incidental notices.

county. At the age of nine he was sent to Harrow, and four years later was transferred to Eton, where he displayed an extreme aversion from study, especially of Greek and Latin, and an inordinate love of all kinds of energetic sports. It was while he was here that he was first attracted to the study of botany, and having no better instructor he paid some women—" cullers of simples," as Sir Joseph himself afterwards called them—who were employed in gathering plants, for which he paid them sixpence for each article they collected and brought to him. During his holidays he found on his mother's dressing-table an old torn copy of Gerard's *Herbal*, having the names and figures of some of the plants with which he had formed an imperfect acquaintance ; and he carried it back with him to school. While at Eton he made considerable collections of plants and insects. He also made many excursions in company with the father of the great Lord Brougham, who describes him as a fine-looking, strong, and healthy boy, whom no fatigue could subdue, and no peril daunt.

He left Eton when seventeen to be inoculated for the small-pox, and on his recovery he went up to Oxford, entering as a gentleman commoner at Christ Church. Prior to this, however, after his father's death in 1761, he had resided with his mother at Chelsea, where he had availed himself of the then famous botanical garden of the Apothecaries' Company. He found himself unable to get any teaching in botany at Oxford, but obtaining leave, he proceeded to Cambridge and returned with Israel Lyons,[1] the astronomer and botanist, under whom a class was formed. In December 1763 he left Oxford with an honorary degree, and coming of age in the year following, found himself possessed of an ample fortune, which enabled him to devote himself entirely to the study of natural science. At this time also he formed a friendship with Lord Sandwich, a neighbouring landowner, both being devoted to hunting and other field sports. The two are credited with having formed a project

---

[1] Afterwards calculator for the Nautical Almanac, and, owing to the influence of Banks, astronomer to Captain Phipps' Polar Voyage in 1773.

to drain the Serpentine, in order to obtain some light on the fishes it contained.

In May 1766 he was elected F.R.S., at the early age of twenty-three, and in the summer of that year accompanied his friend Lieutenant Phipps (afterwards Lord Mulgrave) to Newfoundland, where he investigated the Flora of that then botanically unknown island, returning next year by way of Lisbon. His journal of the trip is preserved in manuscript in the British Museum. After his return home, he became acquainted with Dr. Solander, of whom a brief notice is appended, and with whom he was closely connected until the death of the latter.

Shortly after the accession of George III., several ships had been sent to the Southern Seas in the interest of geographical science. Commodore Byron sailed in 1764, Captains Wallis and Carteret in 1766, and these had no sooner returned than the Government resolved to fit out an expedition to the island of Tahiti, or, as it was then called, Otahite, under Lieutenant James Cook, in order to observe the transit of Venus in 1769. Mr. Banks decided to avail himself of this opportunity of exploring the unknown Pacific Ocean, and applied to his friend Lord Sandwich, then at the head of the Admiralty, for leave to join the expedition. At his own expense, stated by Ellis to be £10,000, he furnished all the stores needed to make complete collections in every branch of natural science, and engaged Dr. Solander, four draughtsmen or artists, and a staff of servants (or nine in all) to accompany him.

The adventures of Banks and his companions on this voyage in the *Endeavour* are told in the diary which is the main object of this volume. It will be enough here to point out his untiring activity, whether in observing or collecting animals and plants, investigating and recording native customs and languages, bartering for necessaries with the inhabitants, preventing the pillaging to which the expedition was frequently subjected, or in the hazardous chase of the stolen quadrant in the interior of Otahite.

In July 1771 the travellers returned with an immense

amount of material, the botanical part of which was for the most part already described, and needed but little to prepare it for the press. The descriptive tickets, which had been drawn up by Solander, were arranged in systematic order in what are still known as " Solander cases," and transcribed fairly by an amanuensis for publication. About 700 plates were engraved on copper in folio at Banks's expense, and a few prints or proofs were taken, but they were never published. Five folio books of neat manuscript, and the coppers, rest in the hands of the trustees of the British Museum. The question arises, why were they never utilised ? The descriptions were ready long before Solander's death, although the plants collected in Australia do not seem to have been added to the fair copies, and the plates were mainly outlines. This has always been regarded as an insoluble problem, but the following extracts from a letter written by Banks very shortly before Solander died, may be accepted as evidence of his intention to publish. The letter from which the extract is taken is undated, and takes the shape of a draft without any name, but it is a reply to a letter addressed to Banks by Hasted, who was then collecting materials for the second edition of his history of the county of Kent.

Botany has been my favourite science since my childhood ; and the reason I have not published the account of my travels is that the first from want of time necessarily brought on by the many preparations for my second voyage was entrusted to Dr. Hawkesworth, and since that I have been engaged in a botanical work, which I hope soon to publish, as I have near 700 folio plates prepared ; it is to give an account of all such new plants discovered in my voyage round the world, somewhat above 800.

Hasted's letter, to which this is an answer, was dated 25th February 1782, little more than two months before Solander's death (alluded to on a subsequent page), an event which has generally been accepted as determining the fate of the intended publication.

But we must now go back a few years. In 1772 preparations were made for a second expedition under Cook in the *Resolution*, with the object of ascertaining the existence, or the contrary, of an Antarctic continent, and Lord Sandwich invited Banks to accompany it as naturalist, to which he readily consented. Towards this new venture he made elaborate preparations, on a scale for which even his ample fortune did not suffice, for he had to raise money to complete his outfit.[1] Various surmises or explanations have been advanced to account for Banks's abandonment of his intention to proceed on this voyage; amongst others it has been said that Cook raised difficulties concerning the accommodation; and it is stated that Banks's equipment would have necessitated the addition of a poop-deck on the vessel destined for the voyage, which would have materially interfered with its sailing powers. But the reason given by Sir John Barrow, who was for many years Secretary of the Admiralty, is no doubt the correct one. He states (*Sketches of the Royal Society*, p. 26) that " such a system was adopted by the Navy Board to thwart every step of his proceedings, especially on the part of its chief, the Comptroller of the Navy, Sir Hugh Palliser, whereby his patience was worn out, and his indignation so far excited as to cause him, though reluctantly, to abandon this enterprise altogether." It may be incidentally mentioned that the great chemist Priestley, whom Banks had invited to join the expedition (on advantageous terms, including a provision for his family), was also objected to, in his case on account of religious principles, by the Board of Longitude. Although thus bitterly disappointed, Banks nevertheless used his utmost endeavour to promote the objects of the voyage; and that there was no personal bitterness between Banks and Cook seems certain from the following extract from a hasty note by Solander to Banks after Cook's return :—

Two o'clock, Monday, 14th August 1775.

This moment Captain Cook is arrived. I have not yet had an opportunity of conversing with him, as he is still in the Board-room

---

[1] The last few cases of specimen bottles prepared for this voyage were not utilised until they were transferred by Robert Brown to the editor of this "Journal," when the latter was preparing to accompany Captain James Ross on his voyage to the Antarctic Ocean in 1839.

giving an account of himself and company.   He looks as well as ever.

Captain Cook desires his best compliments to you ; he expressed himself in the most friendly manner towards you that could be ; he said, " Nothing could have added to the satisfaction he has had in making this tour, but having had your company."   He has some birds in spr. v. [spirits of wine] for you, etc. etc.

Thus baulked of their design, Banks and Solander set out on a scientific expedition to Iceland in a vessel specially chartered for them at a cost of £100 a month.   They sailed on the 12th July 1772, and on the way Banks carried out an intention he had formed to visit Staffa, to which he was the first to draw the attention of scientific men, sending a complete description, with drawings and measurements, to Thomas Pennant, who inserted it in his *Tour to the Highlands of Scotland*.   They spent a month in Iceland, exploring Mount Hecla, the geysers, and other remarkable features of the island.   Banks made copious observations, which Dr. Troil, one of the party, and afterwards Archbishop of Upsala, included in his interesting account of the island, without, however, according to Barrow, doing full justice to the exertions of Banks and his companions, whom he dismisses with a too vague and general eulogium.   Banks also afterwards placed his MS. journal at the disposal of Sir William Hooker, whom he had advised to visit the island for scientific purposes, and who made copious use of it, with due acknowledgment, in his *Tour in Iceland*.

Banks always continued to take a keen interest in the Icelanders, and his humanity " was of signal service to these poor creatures ; for when, some years afterwards, they were in a state of famine, the benevolence and powerful interest of this kind-hearted man brought about the adoption of measures which absolutely saved the inhabitants from starvation.   We were at war with Denmark, and had captured the Danish ships, and no provisions could be received into Iceland.   Clausen, a merchant, was sent to England to implore the granting of *licences* for ships to enter the island, and through the active intervention of Sir Joseph, who, as a Privy Councillor, was an honorary member of the Board of Trade, the indulgence was granted" (Barrow, *loc. cit.* p. 29).

That Banks contemplated a voyage to the North Pole appears from a statement by Barrow that he announced such an intention at a meeting of the Batavian Society at Rotterdam in 1773, when he desired to be put in possession of such discoveries and observations as had been made by the Dutch, promising to acquaint them with any discoveries he might make in the course of such a voyage.

On his return from Iceland, Banks settled in Soho Square, where he accumulated a magnificent library (as well as at Revesby Abbey) and large collections, the whole being arranged in the most methodical manner. These business-like habits formed a marked feature in everything he undertook throughout his life, as to which interesting testimony is afforded by Barrow, who, during a visit shortly before Banks's death, was shown his papers and correspondence carefully assorted and labelled. In this he received considerable assistance from his successive librarians, Solander and Dryander.

On the resignation of Sir John Pringle in November 1778, Banks was chosen to succeed him as President of the Royal Society, an honour for which he had incontestable claims, in his many sacrifices to science in all climates during the voyages to Newfoundland, round the world with Cook, and to Iceland, in his ardent love of natural science, his many accomplishments, his wealth and social position, his habitual intercourse with the king and with the heads of public departments whose influence was greatest for the furtherance of scientific research, and, above all, perhaps, in the disinterestedness with which he placed his collections and library at the disposal of all applicants of merit, and in the expenditure of his wealth.

Notwithstanding all these claims on the votes of the Fellows of the Society, Banks was not destined to retain tranquil possession of the Presidency, and two or three circumstances, arising out of the zeal with which he discharged his duties, made him several enemies. One of these causes was his action with regard to the election of Fellows. Owing to the absence of any scrutiny of the claims of the candidates proposed for the Fellowship, Banks announced his intention of performing this office himself, and of making known his views concerning each proposal to the Council and Fellows. This measure, which created considerable dissatisfaction amongst a certain section of the Fellows, was nevertheless necessary, owing to the recent election of numerous candidates of no scientific merit whatever. " D'Alembert, in allusion to the extreme prodigality with which the honours of the Fellowship were distributed, was in use to ask jocularly any person going to England, if he desired to be made a Member, as he could easily obtain it for him, should he think it any honour. . . . Upon this subject Lord Brougham says: 'Two principles were laid down by him [Banks]; first, that any person who had successfully cultivated science, especially by original investigations, should be admitted, whatever might be his rank or fortune ; secondly, that men of wealth, or station, disposed to promote, adorn, and patronise science, should, but with due caution and deliberation, be allowed to enter ' " (Weld's *History of the Royal Society*).

A crisis was, however, brought about by the following circumstance. The Council, under the influence, it is said, of the President, passed a resolution recommending that the Foreign Secretary should reside in London ; and this measure was followed by the resignation of Dr. Hutton, then Foreign Secretary, and Professor at Woolwich, who, it was complained, had neglected his duties as secretary of the Society. Dr. Horsley, afterwards Bishop of St. Asaph, attacked the President in very bitter terms, lamenting that the chair which had been filled by Newton should be thus lowered in dignity, and predicting all kinds of disasters as the direct consequence of electing a naturalist as President. He induced several influential members to follow him, but when the fact became clear, as it soon did, that he desired the reversion of the chair for himself, his influence declined ; he withdrew from the Society with a few intimates, and

Banks remained in undisputed possession of the chair till his death in 1820.

The excellent qualities of the President whom this victory kept in the chair were clearly exhibited by the temper with which he regarded the opposition. The sketch of his character (says Barrow) given by Lord Brougham is true to the life: "He showed no jealousy of any rival, no prejudice in anybody's favour rather than another's. He was equally accessible to all for counsel and help. His house, his library, his whole valuable collections, were at all times open to men of science, while his credit both with our own and foreign Governments, and, if need were, the resource of his purse, were ever ready to help in the prosecution of their inquiries."

One of the earliest official acts of the new President was a proof of the estimation in which he held his late fellow-voyager Cook. On the death of the latter in 1779, Banks proposed to the Council that a medal should be struck as a mark of the high sense entertained by the Society of the importance of his extensive discoveries in different parts of the globe, the cost being defrayed by subscription among the Fellows. The medal, designed by L. Pingo, bears a portrait of the great navigator in profile on the obverse, with a representation of Britannia pointing to the south pole of a globe on the reverse.

Amongst other noteworthy services rendered by Banks in his capacity as President of the Royal Society, the following may be mentioned. In 1784 the Council obtained the permission of George III. to commence a geodetical survey under General Roy: this served as the basis of the Ordnance Survey. In the following year he made successful application to the king to guarantee the cost (amounting to £4000) of Sir William Herschel's 40-foot telescope. He served on a committee of the Society appointed, at the instance of the Secretary of State, to ascertain the length of the pendulum vibrating seconds of time at various localities in Great Britain. In 1817 the Council at his suggestion recommended Government to fit out an Arctic expedition:

as a result, two were sent, the one under Captain John
Ross in search of the North-West Passage ; the other, which
included Franklin, to sail northwards by the east coast of
Greenland.

He was on several occasions invited to stand for Parliament, but always declined, preferring to devote his entire
time to his duties as President of the Royal Society, and
to the innumerable functions it entailed.

It is sometimes said that Banks viewed with strong
disapproval the formation of other societies for the pursuit
of natural science.   This was certainly so in the case of the
Astronomical Society, which he considered would seriously
decrease the importance of that over which he himself
presided.   But this was only because he conceived the
objects of the former association to be so intimately connected with those of the Royal Society that there would
not be sufficient scope for both.   On the other hand, he
was one of the founders of the Linnean Society in 1788,
and took an even more prominent part in the formation of
the Royal Institution in 1799.

In March 1779 he married Dorothea, daughter of
William Western Hugessen, Esq., of Provender, Kent.   In
1782 Solander died, and from that time onward Banks
became more and more absorbed in the duties of the Royal
Society, and acted as chief counsellor in all scientific matters
to the king.   In this capacity he had virtual control of the
Royal Gardens at Kew, then under the cultural care of
the elder Aiton, where were raised the plants produced by
seeds brought home by himself, and so many of the novelties
described in l'Héritier's *Sertum Anglicum*, Aiton's *Hortus
Kewensis*, and other botanical works.   It was due to his
indefatigable exertions and representations that the Royal
Gardens at Kew were raised to the position of the first in
the world, and that collectors were sent to the West Indies,
the Cape Colonies, and Australia, to send home living plants
and seeds, and herbaria, for the Royal Gardens.   He kept
Francis Bauer (who, and his brother Ferdinand, were the most
accomplished botanical artists of the century) at Kew con-

stantly occupied in making drawings of Australian and other plants, keeping him in liberal pay, and leaving him a legacy in his will.

He was the first to bring indiarubber into notice, and early advocated the cultivation of tea in India. He established botanic gardens in Jamaica, St. Vincent, and Ceylon, besides giving invaluable support to Colonel Kyd in the foundation of the garden at Sibpur, near Calcutta.

He was a keen agriculturist, and amongst his very few published writings one is on Blight Mildew and Rust, another on the introduction of the Potato, and a third on the Apple Aphis. The Horticultural Society was founded in 1804, and Banks is named as one of the persons to whom the Charter was granted in 1809. The esteem in which he was held by this Society is shown by their electing him an honorary member, and by their instituting, after his death, a Banksian medal.

Services of an international character were rendered by him when, in the course of war, the collections of foreign naturalists had been captured by British vessels; on no less than eleven occasions were they restored to their former owners through the direct intervention of Banks with the Lords of the Admiralty and Treasury. The disinterestedness of such a course will be at once understood when it is remembered that these collections, some of them of inestimable value (now at the Jardin des Plantes at Paris), would otherwise have contributed to the aggrandisement of his own magnificent museum. "He even sent as far as the Cape of Good Hope to procure some chests belonging to Humboldt; and it is well known that his active exertions liberated many scientific men from foreign prisons. He used great exertions to mitigate the captivity of the unfortunate Flinders, and it was principally by his intercession that our Government issued orders in favour of La Perouse" (Weld's *History of the Royal Society*).

Great as his services to science are known to have been, these will never be fully realised till his correspondence in the British Museum and elsewhere shall have been thoroughly searched. That they were not confined to natural history is evident. He was an assiduous promoter of the Association for the Exploration of Tropical Africa, and it was under his auspices that Mungo Park, Clapperton, and others were sent out. He was one of a committee to investigate the subject of lightning conductors. His letters to Josiah Wedgwood show his keen appreciation not only of the work of the great potter, but of his other ingenious contrivances; among the mass of papers left by him on his death was an illustrated dissertation on the history and art of the manufacture of porcelain by the Chinese. He took a deep interest in the coinage, and was in close communication with Matthew Boulton on questions of minting. On applying for information on this latter point to Dr. Roberts-Austen, that gentleman informed the editor that, though not officially an officer of the Mint, Banks had probably served on some departmental or Parliamentary commissions charged with mint questions; and further, that he had presented the mint with a really fine library, embracing all the books it possessed relating to numismatics and coinage questions generally, together with a valuable collection of coins. In reference to this, the editor has also found, on looking over some Banksian MS. in the British Museum, that these included a draft code of regulations for the conduct of the officers of the Mint.

His interest in manufactures was also constant; could his letters be brought together, a flood of light would thereby be thrown upon the progress of arts and sciences in Europe during his long tenure of the presidency of the Royal Society.

As an instance of his zeal for science may be mentioned the interest he took in Sir Charles Blagden's experiments to determine the power of human beings to exist in rooms heated to an excessive temperature. Sir Joseph Banks was one of the first who plunged into a chamber heated to the temperature of 260° Fahr., and was taken out nearly exhausted. It may be mentioned that Sir Francis Chantrey once remained two minutes in a furnace at a temperature of 320°.

For a man of his distinction the dignities which were conferred upon him by royal favour seem disproportionate. He was created a Baronet in 1781, a Knight of the Bath in 1795, and two years subsequently was sworn of the Privy Council. In 1802 he was chosen one of the eight foreign members of the French Académie des Sciences, in Paris.

To the last his house, library, and museum were open to all scientific men, of whatever nationality, and the services of his successive librarians, Solander, Dryander, and Brown, cannot be over-estimated. His Thursday breakfasts and Sunday soirées in Soho Square made his house the centre of influential gatherings of an informal kind; curiosities of every description were brought by visitors and exhibited, and each new subject, book, drawing, animal, plant, or mineral, each invention of art or science, was sure to find its way to Sir Joseph's house. It was at one of these parties that he strongly recommended the acquisition of the Linnean Library and collections to James Edward Smith, a young Norwich physician, and an ardent botanist. This was the turning-point of Smith's life, and led to the foundation of the Linnean Society, which held its meetings for many years, during the lifetime of Robert Brown, in Banks's house in Soho Square, where the Linnean collections were placed previous to the Society's removal to apartments provided by Government in Burlington House.

Sir Joseph Banks became latterly a great martyr to the gout, " which grew to such an intensity as to deprive him entirely of the power of walking, and for fourteen or fifteen years previous to his death, he lost the use of his lower limbs so completely as to oblige him to be carried, or wheeled, as the case might require, by his servants in a chair : in this way he was conveyed to the more dignified chair of the Royal Society, and also to the [Royal Society] Club—the former of which he very rarely omitted to attend, and not often the latter; he sat apparently so much at his ease, both at the Society and in the Club, and conducted the business of the meetings with so much spirit and dignity, that a stranger would not have supposed that he was often suffering at the time, nor even have observed an infirmity, which never disturbed his uniform cheerfulness.

" As the gout increased his difficulty of locomotion, Sir Joseph found it convenient to have some spot to retire to in the neighbourhood of London, and fixed upon a small villa near Hounslow Heath, called Spring Grove, consisting of some woods and a good garden laid out with ornamental shrubs and flower-beds, and neatly kept under the inspection of Lady and Miss Banks" (his sister) [Barrow, *loc. cit.* pp. 40-42]. Since his death the building has been pulled down and replaced by a mansion now in the possession of A. Pears, Esq.

The last occasion on which Banks took the chair at the Royal Society was on 16th March 1820. In May, declining health led him to announce his resignation of the Presidency, which he had held for over forty-one years ; but the universal desire which was expressed, both by the Council of the Society and by the king himself, that he would retain the office, induced him to withdraw his resignation. He died, however, very shortly afterwards at Spring Grove, on the 19th June 1820, leaving a widow but no lineal issue.

He was buried at Heston, Middlesex, in which parish Spring Grove is situated. The church has since been rebuilt, and now covers the spot where he was buried. A tablet with a simple inscription marks as nearly as possible the place where his body lies. By his will he expressly desires that his body be interred in the most private manner in the church or churchyard of the parish in which he should happen to die, and entreats his dear relatives to spare themselves the affliction of attending the ceremony, and earnestly requests that they will not erect any monument to his memory.

In July of the same year the Council of the Royal Society resolved to erect a full-length marble statue of Sir Joseph Banks, to be executed by Mr. (afterwards Sir Francis) Chantrey. A sum of £2000 was subscribed, of which £525 was paid to the sculptor, the surplus being devoted to an engraving of the statue, copies of which were distributed to various institutions and individuals. The monument now stands in the Natural History Department of the British Museum.

Amongst public notices of Sir Joseph Banks after his death, the best known are Cuvier's *Éloge* delivered before the French Academy, and Sir Everard Home's Hunterian Oration.

The lease of his house in Soho Square, and an annuity of £200, were left to Robert Brown, to whom were also bequeathed his library and natural history collections, with reversion to the British Museum. On condition of being appointed keeper of the botanical department, Brown made over the whole in 1828, reserving to himself the fullest use of the collections during his life, and accepting the duty of preparing a Life of Banks, as told in the preface to this "Journal."

Considering the eminence of Banks's position in the scientific world, it is surprising to find how little he wrote. The following are the most important of his publications—

"A short Account of the cause of the Disease in Corn, called by farmers the Blight, the Mildew, and the Rust."—Nicholson, *Journ.* x. (1805), pp. 225-234; Tilloch, *Phil. Mag.* xxi. (1805), pp. 320-327; *Ann. Bot.* ii. (1806), pp. 51-61. Also as a separate publication, 1805, 8vo, 15 pp. 1 tab.; and reprinted in Curtis, *Practical Observations on the British Grasses*, 1824, pp. 151-166, t. 1.

"An attempt to ascertain the time when the Potato (*Solanum tuberosum*) was first introduced into the United Kingdom; with some Account of the Hill Wheat of India" (1805).—*Hortic. Soc. Trans.* i. 1812, pp. 8-12.

"Some Hints respecting the proper Mode of inuring tender Plants to our Climate," *l.c.* pp. 21-25.

"On the Forcing-houses of the Romans, with a List of Fruits cultivated by them now in our Gardens," *l.c.* pp. 147-156.

"On ripening the second Crop of Figs that grow on the new Shoots," *l.c.* pp. 252-254.

"Notes relative to the first appearance of the *Aphis lanigera*, or the Apple Tree Insect, in this Country" (1812), *l.c.* ii. pp. 162-170.

"Observations on the nature and formation of the Stone incrusting the Skeletons which have been found in the Island of Guadeloupe, with some account of the origin of those Skeletons" (1818).—*Trans. Linn. Soc.* xii. (1818), pp. 53-61.

He also published various papers in *Archæologia*.

To the labours of J. Dryander (who succeeded Solander as Banks's secretary and librarian, and who was on his death succeded by Robert Brown in 1810) is due the publication of the catalogue of Banks's library. It is entitled " Catalogus Bibliothecæ historico-naturalis Josephi Banks . . . auctore Jono Dryander," 5 vols. 8vo, 1798-1800. In it are enumerated the works of upwards of 6000 authors, with analyses of their writings, arranged according to the subjects treated. This work has never been superseded.

The name of Banks is commemorated botanically in the Australian genus *Banksia*, so named in his honour by the younger Linnæus.

DR. SOLANDER

This sketch cannot be concluded without some notice of the career of Banks's first librarian, and companion during Cook's voyage, Daniel Carl Solander. He was the son of a country clergyman, and born in Norrland, Sweden, on the 28th February 1736. He studied at the University of Upsala, took the degree of M.D., and became a pupil of Linnæus, who recommended him to go to England. He left Upsala in 1759, being warmly commended by his botanical professor to the eminent naturalist John Ellis, F.R.S., but was detained in the south of Sweden by sickness for nearly a year, only reaching our shores in July 1760. In the following October he was strongly recommended by Peter Collinson, F.R.S., to the notice of the trustees of the British Museum, but no permanent employment was the result of this appeal. In the autumn of 1762 Linnæus procured for him the offer of the botanical professorship at St. Petersburg, but after consultation with his English friends, Solander decided to decline the appointment, for " many reasons," which are not given. The chief one seems to have been that at this time he was engaged in classifying and cataloguing in the British Museum, with prospect of advancement. A few months later he was appointed assistant in

Swan Electric Engraving Company.

Dr Daniel Solander, F.L.S.

From a portrait in the possession of the Linnean Society of London.

that institution, and in 1764 elected a Fellow of the Royal Society. It was in 1767 that he first made the acquaintance of Banks, who, when he had in the following year resolved to accompany Cook to the Pacific, induced Solander to go with him. His situation in the Museum was kept open for him, a deputy being put in to act during his absence with Banks.

An extract from a letter from Ellis to Linnæus gives a clear idea of the arrangements made for the journey :—

I must now inform you that Joseph Banks, Esq., a gentleman of £6000 per annum estate, has prevailed on your pupil, Dr. Solander, to accompany him in the ship that carries the English astronomers to the new-discovered country in the South Sea [1] . . . where they are to collect all the natural curiosities of the place, and, after the astronomers have finished their observations on the transit of Venus, they are to proceed under the direction of Mr. Banks, by order of the Lords of the Admiralty, on further discoveries. . . . No people ever went to sea better fitted out for the purpose of natural history, nor more elegantly. They have got a fine library of natural history : they have all sorts of machines for catching and preserving insects ; all kinds of nets, trawls, drags, and hooks for coral fishing ; they have even a curious contrivance of a telescope by which, put into the water, you can see the bottom at a great depth, where it is clear. They have many cases of bottles with ground stoppers, of several sizes, to preserve animals in spirits. They have the several sorts of salts to surround the seeds ; and wax, both bees'-wax and that of the *Myrica ;* besides, there are many people whose sole business it is to attend them for this very purpose. They have two painters and draughtsmen, several volunteers who have a tolerable notion of natural history ; in short, Solander assured me this expedition would cost Mr. Banks £10,000. . . . About three days ago I took my leave of Solander, when he assured me he would write to you and to all his family, and acquaint them with the particulars of this expedition. I must observe to you that his places are secured to him, and he has promises from persons in power of much better preferment on his return. Everybody here parted from him with reluctance, for no man was ever more beloved, and in so great esteem with the public from his affable and polite behaviour.

On his return from the South Seas, Dr. Solander was installed under Banks's roof in Soho Square as his secretary and librarian ; and at the British Museum he was advanced to the post of under-librarian. A short time after his return

[1] The Society Islands.

the project of a second voyage was mooted, as already mentioned on p. xxvii. How this idea was received by Linnæus, the following extracts from his correspondence with Ellis will show :—

I have just read, in some foreign newspapers, that our friend Solander intends to revisit those new countries, discovered by Mr. Banks and himself, in the ensuing spring. This report has affected me so much as almost entirely to deprive me of sleep. How vain are the hopes of man ! Whilst the whole botanical world, like myself, has been looking for the most transcendent benefits to our science, from the unrivalled exertions of your countrymen, all their matchless and truly astonishing collection, such as has never been seen before, nor may ever be seen again, is to be put aside untouched, to be thrust into some corner, to become perhaps the prey of insects and of destruction.

I have every day been figuring to myself the occupations of my pupil Solander, now putting his collection in order, having first arranged and numbered his plants, in parcels, according to the places where they were gathered, and then written upon each specimen its native country and appropriate number. I then fancied him throwing the whole into classes, putting aside and naming such as were already known ; ranging others under known genera, with specific differences, and distinguishing by new names and definitions such as formed new genera, with their species. Thus, thought I, the world will be delighted and benefited by all these discoveries ; and the foundations of true science will be strengthened, so as to endure through all generations !

I am under great apprehension that, if this collection should remain untouched till Solander's return, it might share the same lot as Forskål's Arabian specimens at Copenhagen. . . . Solander promised long ago, while detained off the coast of Brazil, in the early part of his voyage, that he would visit me after his return, of which I have been in expectation. If he had brought some of his specimens with him, I could at once have told him what were new ; and we might have turned over some books together, and he might have been informed or satisfied upon many subjects, which after my death will not be so easily explained.

I have no answer from him to the letter I enclosed to you, which I cannot but wonder at. You, yourself, know how much I have esteemed him, and how strongly I recommended him to you.

By all that is great and good, I entreat you, who know so well the value of science, to do all that in you lies for the publication of these new acquisitions, that the learned world may not be deprived of them. . . .

Again the plants of Solander and Banks recur to my imagination.

When I turn over Feuillée's figures, I meet with more extraordinary things among them than anywhere else. I cannot but presume therefore, as Peru and Chili are so rich, that in the South Sea Islands, as great abundance of rarities have remained in concealment, from the beginning of the world, to reward the labours of our illustrious voyagers. I see these things now but afar off. . . .

When I ponder upon the insects they have brought, I am overwhelmed at the reported number of new species. Are there many new genera ? . . .

When I think of their *Mollusca*, I conceive the new ones must be very numerous. These animals cannot be investigated after death, as they contract in dying. Without doubt, as there were draughtsmen on board, they would not fail to afford ample materials for drawing.

Do but consider, my friend, if these treasures are kept back, what may happen to them. They may be devoured by vermin of all kinds. The house where they are lodged may be burnt. Those destined to describe them may die. Even you, the promoter of every scientific undertaking in your country, may be taken from us. All sublunary things are uncertain, nor ought anything to be trusted to treacherous futurity. I therefore once more beg, nay I earnestly beseech you, to urge the publication of these new discoveries. I confess it to be my most ardent wish to see this done before I die. To whom can I urge my anxious wishes but to you, who are so devoted to me and to science ?

Remember me to the immortal Banks and Solander.

The writer clearly recognised the dangers of that dilatoriness which evidently formed a marked feature in the character of Solander; he had repeatedly complained of his pupil's neglect in writing, not only to him, but to his mother. This was the subject of reproach even before the great expedition, but it seems to have been intensified afterwards, for after Solander's death, letters from his mother addressed to him were found actually unopened !

The closing scene came with startling suddenness. Sir Joseph Banks was out of town, and to that fact we owe the following details from the pen of Dr. (afterwards Sir Charles) Blagden, an intimate acquaintance.

SOHO SQUARE,
Wednesday, 8th May 1782, 2.30 P.M.

Soon after breakfast this morning Dr. Solander began to find himself much indisposed, and in a short time the symptoms of a palsy of the left side began to appear. I was conversing with him at the time, and as soon as the stroke became certain, dispatched a messenger for Mr. Hunter, whilst Professor Linnæus [1] went to call Dr. Heberden and Dr. Pitcairne. All these gentlemen have been with him, and the necessary remedies prescribed. I dare not say what the event will be, but am not without hopes, notwithstanding the extreme danger with which you know all paralytic strokes are attended. It was found impossible to move him; Lady Banks has therefore been so kind as to order an apartment for him in her house, and I shall quit him as little as possible, particularly not to-night. You may judge of the affliction of every one here. I am so much affected myself that I know not what to say to you, but that I am most affectionately yours,

C. BLAGDEN.

It is a striking testimony of the regard in which Solander was held, that the foremost physicians of the day should be summoned to his side at the moment of attack, and that the son and successor of his botanical preceptor should be one of the messengers in search of medical aid. All efforts were unavailing to prolong his life, for he died at Soho Square on the 16th of the same month.

He is stated to have been a short, fair man, somewhat stout, with small eyes, and a good-humoured expression of countenance. The genus *Solandra* is his botanical memorial, named after him by his fellow-countryman, Swartz. A full-length portrait of him, by an unknown artist, in the possession of the Linnean Society (to which body it was given by R. A. Salisbury), is here reproduced.

[1] Carl von Linné, son of the eminent naturalist.

NATURALISTS AND VOYAGERS MENTIONED
IN THE JOURNAL

ANSON, George, Lord (1697-1762), entered the navy in 1712, and was in 1740 sent to the Pacific in command of a squadron. Reaching his destination by way of South America, he captured the " Spanish galleon," and brought it to England, returning by the Cape of Good Hope in 1744. His " Voyage round the World " was published in 1748. In 1746 he was appointed to the command of the Channel Fleet, and was raised to the peerage in 1747. In 1751 he became First Lord of the Admiralty, having virtually performed all the duties of that office for two or three years previously.

BASTER, Job (1711-75), a Dutch naturalist, who published many works on natural history, including a treatise on the classification of plants and animals (1768), and " Opuscula subseciva " (1759-65), consisting of miscellaneous observations on animals and plants, referring more especially to seeds and embryos.

BIRON, C., author of " Curiosités de la Nature et de l'Art, apportées de deux Voyages des Indes, en Occident, 1698-99 ; en Orient, 1701-2 ; avec une Relation abrégée des deux Voyages " (1703).

BOUGAINVILLE, Louis Antoine de (1729-1811), was successively lawyer, soldier, secretary to the French Embassy in London, and officer under Montcalm in Canada. In 1765 he persuaded the inhabitants of St. Malo to fit out an expedition to colonise the Falkland Islands, but upon these being claimed by the Spaniards, Bougainville was sent out in 1766, in command of the frigate *Boudeuse*, with a consort, to transfer them to the latter country. After accomplishing this mission he proceeded through the Straits of Magellan and fell in with Otahite (to which he gave the name of *Cythère*, but which had been previously seen by Quiros and Wallis), the Navigators, and the New Hebrides (Quiros' Terra del Espiritu Santo). Endeavouring to steer due west at about the 15th degree of south latitude, he was, when still out of sight of land, brought up by reefs (outside the Great

Barrier Reef). Turning northwards he sailed, by the Louisiade Archipelago and New Guinea, to the Moluccas, returning to France in 1769 *via* Batavia and Mauritius.

Bougainville was accompanied on this voyage by a naturalist, Philibert Commerson, whose servant, Jean Bary, passed for a man until her sex was recognised by the Tahitians. Otourrou, a Tahitian whom Bougainville took with him to France, died of small-pox at Madagascar while being conveyed back to his native country. The genus *Bougainvillea* was so named by Commerson in honour of the navigator, who was the first Frenchman to circumnavigate the globe. Bougainville afterwards commanded various vessels in the American War.

BRISSON, Mathurin Jacques (1723-1806), French naturalist and physicist, author of "Le règne animal" (1756), and "Ornithologie" (1760), and various works on physics.

BROSSE or BROSSES, Charles de (1709-77), first President of the Parliament of Burgundy, author of "Histoire des Navigations aux Terres Australes" (1756).

BROWNE, Patrick (1720?-1790), a physician who studied natural history, more particularly botany, and after a voyage to the West Indies published the "Civil and Natural History of Jamaica" (1756). He also compiled more or less local catalogues of birds, fishes, and plants.

BUFFON, Georges Louis Leclerc, Comte de (1707-88), French naturalist and writer. Upon being appointed Director of the King's Garden at Paris, in 1739, he conceived the idea of compiling a natural history of creation, and devoted the following fifty years of his life to carrying out this project, with the help of other naturalists. His "Histoire naturelle" (published at various periods from 1749 to 1788) treats of the theory of the earth, nature of animals, man, viviparous quadrupeds, birds, and minerals. The task was continued after his death by Lacépède.

BYRON, Vice-Admiral John (1723-86), was the second son of the fourth Lord Byron, and grandfather of the poet. He accompanied Anson on his voyage to the Pacific as a midshipman on board the *Wager*, which was wrecked on the coast of Chile in 1741 : some years later he published the details of his adventures (1768). In 1764 he was appointed to the *Dolphin*, with orders to explore the South Seas. He left England in company with the *Tamar*, and, passing through the Straits of Magellan, stood across the Pacific, but following a course already known, made no discoveries of any importance. With a great deal of scurvy on board he reached the Ladrones, and returned home in 1766. [Otahite was rediscovered on the *Dolphin's* second voyage by Wallis, *q.v.*]   Byron was afterwards (1769-72) Governor of Newfoundland, and had command of the West Indian Fleet in 1778-79.

CANTON, John (1718-72), F.R.S., electrician, was the first English-man who successfully repeated Franklin's experiments.   He invented an electroscope and an electrometer.   The Copley Medal of the Royal Society was awarded him in 1751.

COOK, Captain James (1728-79), the son of an agricultural labourer, was born at Marton in Yorkshire.   He served several years in the merchant service, but volunteered for the navy in 1755, enter-ing on the *Eagle* under Captain Hugh Palliser.   It was owing to the influence of the latter that Cook, who had previously surveyed the St. Lawrence river, was afterwards appointed " Marine Surveyor to the coast of Newfoundland and Labrador."   He published his results as directions for navigating these coasts (1766-68).

The Admiralty having at the instance of the Royal Society resolved to despatch an expedition to observe the transit of Venus in the Pacific, Cook was appointed Lieutenant and placed in command of the *En-deavour* (1768) : this voyage is described in the following pages.

On his return in 1771, Cook was immediately promoted to the rank of Commander and sent again to the Pacific with the *Resolution* and *Adventure*, the primary object of the expedition being to verify the existence or non-existence of an antarctic continent.   He left Plymouth in 1772, and proceeded to the Cape of Good Hope, whence sailing in a south-easterly direction, he was the first to cross the Antarctic circle.   After revisiting New Zealand, Otahite, and New Zealand again (when the *Resolution* and *Adventure* parted company), he sailed to the south, and reached his highest latitude (71°·10) in January 1774.   After touching at Easter Island he explored the New Hebrides and discovered New Caledonia, whence he returned home by New Zealand, Cape Horn, and South Georgia, reaching Plymouth in July 1775.

Apart from the geographical discoveries, and finally setting at rest the question of a habitable southern continent, this voyage was, even more than the first, remarkable for the fact that Cook kept his crew absolutely free from scurvy, and lost only a single man during the whole of the three years.   Cook's demonstration of the possibility of maintaining the health of crews during long periods is one of his greatest titles to fame.   He gave an account of his methods for the prevention of scurvy to the Royal Society in 1776, and the Copley Medal was in the same year awarded to him, in recognition of his services to the maritime world and to humanity in this connection.

Having been promoted to the rank of Captain, he offered to take command of an expedition to the North Pacific in search of a North-west Passage.   He left England on this, his third voyage, in July

1776, in the *Resolution*, his consort, the *Discovery*, joining him at the Cape of Good Hope. The two ships visited Van Diemen's Land and New Zealand, and spent 1777 among the islands of the South Pacific. Going north, he discovered the Sandwich Islands (1778), and surveyed the west coast of North America as far as Icy Cape (thus passing through the Behring Straits). Thence, finding further advance impossible, he returned to the Sandwich Islands, anchoring in Karakakoa Bay. The natives at first proved friendly, but quarrels afterwards arose, and Cook, going on shore to recover a stolen boat, was killed (14th February 1779), no attempt at a rescue being made.

COWLEY, Captain, buccaneer, fell in with "Pepys" Island, which was afterwards recognised to be one of the Falklands, about the year 1683. He sailed round the world in 1683-86, keeping a Journal from which the account of his voyage in Callander's "Terra Australis Cognita" is taken.

DALRYMPLE, Alexander (1737-1808), went out as a writer in the East India Company's service in 1752, and undertook several voyages for the Company, particularly to the Sulu Islands and to China. In 1767 he published an "Account of Discoveries in the South Pacific Ocean before 1764," and later a "Historical Collection of South Sea Voyages" (1770-71), besides pamphlets on Indian affairs. He was appointed the first Hydrographer to the Admiralty in 1795, but was dismissed in 1808, and died the same year.

DAMPIER, William (1652-1715), buccaneer, captain in the navy, and hydrographer, made several voyages to the South Seas. In one of these he left Virginia in 1683 and went by way of South America to the East Indies, where he spent some time in trading. He returned to England in 1691 and published his "Voyage Round the World" (1697). On a later voyage he sailed under directions from the Admiralty along the northern coast of New Holland and visited New Guinea (1699-1701). His narrative of this expedition, entitled "Voyage to New Holland in the year 1699" (published 1703-9), is remarkable for the information it contains on the natural history, etc., of Australia. He was again in the South Seas in 1703-7 and in 1708, upon which last occasion he rescued Alexander Selkirk, whom he had himself left there on the former voyage, from the island of Juan Fernandez.

"DOLPHIN," the first vessel in the English navy sheathed with copper: 1st voyage, see *Byron*; 2nd voyage (to Otahite), see *Wallis*.

EDWARDS, George, F.R.S. (1694-1773), naturalist, Librarian to the Royal College of Physicians. He was the author of a "History of Birds" (1743-64), one volume of which is remarkable for being dedicated to God.

FERNANDEZ, Juan (died 1576), Spanish navigator, appears to have been constantly employed as pilot off the coasts of South America. He discovered the islands bearing his name about 1572, and in 1576 reported another large island or continent, which has not been identified.

FOTHERGILL, John, M.D., F.R.S. (1712-80), was a Quaker, and the first graduate of Edinburgh to be admitted as a licentiate of the College of Physicians (1744). He was greatly interested in botany, and possessed a magnificent botanical garden at Upton, near Stratford, where he kept many draughtsmen. He also made large collections of shells and insects. His " Hortus Uptonensis " was published amongst his " Works " after his death in 1783-84.

FRÉZIER, Amédée François (1682-1773), engineer and traveller, born at Chambéry, was descended from the Scotch Frasers. He was sent out by the French king in 1711 to examine the Spanish colonies in South America, and on his return in 1714 published his " Relation d'un Voyage de la Mer du Sud aux côtes du Chili et du Pérou " (1716). He was afterwards Director of Fortifications of Brittany, and was the author of several works on architecture.

HASSELQUIST, Fredrik (1722-52), Swedish naturalist and pupil of Linnæus. He spent three years (1749-52) travelling in Palestine and Egypt, and made large collections of fishes, reptiles, insects, plants, and minerals, studying also Arab manuscripts, coins, and mummies. He died at Smyrna, and his collections passed into the hands of Linnæus, who published Hasselquist's journal and observations under the title of " Iter Palestinum " (1757).

HISTOIRE des Navigations aux Terres Australes, see *Brosse.*

HULME, Nathaniel, F.R.S. (1732-1807), was Physician to the Charter-house.

LE MAIRE, Jacob (died 1616), Dutch navigator, left Holland in company with William Cornelissen Schouten (died 1625) in 1615, in the *Concorde,* with the view of determining the position of the southern point of South America, in defiance of the regulations of the Dutch East India Company, which attempted to close the routes to India, either by the Cape of Good Hope or the Straits of Magellan. Le Maire and Schouten discovered Staten Island and Cape Horn, which they doubled, and thence proceeded to Batavia, passing along the north-east coast of New Guinea. On their arrival at Batavia, their ship was seized and they were sent to Holland, but Le Maire died before reaching Europe. Schouten published an account of the voyage in 1618.

L'Hermite, Jacques (died 1624), Dutch Admiral, was sent out in 1623 by the States-General in command of eleven vessels (the *Nassau* fleet, so named after Prince Maurice of Nassau) to attack Peru. The expedition did not meet with much success, and L'Hermite himself died at Callao. He appears to have previously served under the Dutch East India Company.

Marcgrav, George (1610-44), German physician and traveller, accompanied Piso (*q.v.*) and the Prince of Nassau to Brazil in 1636, where he travelled for six years. The results of his discoveries are embodied with those of Piso in the "Historia naturalis Brasiliæ" (1648). He afterwards went to the coast of Guinea and there died.

Maskelyne, Nevil, F.R.S. (1732-1811), was sent by the Royal Society to St. Helena to observe the transit of Venus in 1761, but the phenomenon was obscured by clouds. He was afterwards Astronomer-Royal (1765); and to him we owe the "Nautical Almanac," the publication of which he superintended for forty-five years. In 1769 he observed the transit of Venus from Greenwich. Later, in 1784, Maskelyne strongly supported Dr. Charles Hutton against Sir Joseph Banks, then President, during the dissensions in the Royal Society (see p. xxx.)

M'Bride, David (1726-78), medical writer, advocated the use of fresh wort or infusion of malt as a preventive of scurvy at sea, a specific adopted by Banks on this voyage. It was, however, soon after superseded by Lind's lemon juice.

Narbrough, Admiral Sir John (1640-88), was sent out to the South Seas in 1669. Passing through the Straits of Magellan, he sailed as far as Valdivia and then returned home. He was present at the battle of Solebay (1672), and after some years of service, died at Saint Domingo, whither he had gone, at the instance of the Government, to search for treasure.

Nassau Fleet. See *L'Hermite.*

Oldenland, Henry Bernhard, Dutch naturalist, author of "Catalogi duo plantarum Africanarum" in the "Thesaurus Zeylanicus" (1737).

Osbeck, Pehr (1723-1805), Swedish naturalist and traveller. He studied natural history, and on the recommendation of Linnæus was appointed chaplain to a vessel of the Swedish East India Company, in which he visited China, and, on the return voyage, Ascension. Osbeck published his observations under the title of "Journal of a voyage to the East Indies, 1750-52, with observations on the natural history, language, manners, and domestic economy of foreign peoples" (1757).

PALLAS, Peter Simon (1741-1811), traveller and naturalist, was born at Berlin, and in 1767, at the invitation of the Empress Catherine, accepted the professorship of Natural History at St. Petersburg. He went to Siberia in 1768 to observe the transit of Venus, and spent the following six years travelling there, penetrating to the frontiers of China. He remained in Russia till 1810, when he returned to Berlin. He was an indefatigable naturalist, and published many works on natural history, of which the greater part deal with the flora, fauna, and ethnology of the Russian possessions.

PENNANT, Thomas, LL.D. (1726-98), Scotch naturalist and antiquary. He was the author of "British Zoology" (1766); "Synopsis of Quadrupeds" (1771), afterwards enlarged and published as the "History of Quadrupeds" (1781); "Genera of Birds" (1773), etc. He was a constant correspondent of Gilbert White of Selborne.

PISO, William (17th century), Dutch naturalist and doctor, accompanied Prince Maurice of Nassau as his physician on his voyage to Brazil in 1636, taking with him two young German savants, Marcgrav (q.v.) and Kranitz. The observations which he and Marcgrav made were published in 1648 under the title of "Historia naturalis Brasiliæ." He was the first to introduce into Europe and to describe ipecacuanha and its medicinal properties.

QUIROS, Pedro Fernandez de (died 1614), Spanish navigator, accompanied Mendana in 1595 to the Solomon and Santa Cruz Islands. On the death of Mendana, Quiros brought the remains of the fleet to Manilla, and then returned by South America to Madrid. Obtaining permission to search for the supposed Southern Continent, he set out again from Lima in 1605, and discovered "Dezana," afterwards called Osnaburg Island. In the following year he discovered Otahite, which he named "Sagittaria." Proceeding westwards he then discovered "Terra del Espiritu Santo," one of the New Hebrides. From this point he turned back to Mexico, and died at Panama in 1614.

REMBRANTZ VON NIEROP, Dirk (1610-82), Dutch astronomer and mathematician, published, besides several works on mathematics and astronomy, a short account of Tasman's voyage.

ROGGEWEEN, Jacob (1659-1729), Dutch navigator, was at one time counsellor of the Court of Justice at Batavia. In his voyage round the world he started from Holland in 1721, reached the Falkland Islands, and sailed south as far as $62\frac{1}{2}$° S. lat., then went to Chile, Juan Fernandez, Easter Island (of which he was the discoverer), New Britain and Batavia. An account of his voyage was published in 1728.

RUMPHIUS or RUMPF, George Eberhard (1627-1702), German doctor and botanist. He went out to the Dutch possessions in the

d

East Indies about 1654, and entered the Company's service. He was made Consul at Amboyna, where he resided until his death, making large collections there and in the adjacent islands. Notwithstanding that he became totally blind in 1669, he was the author of several works on natural history, which, however, were not published until after his death, notably the "Herbarium Amboinense" (1741-55), "Herbarii Amboinensis Auctuarium" (1755), supplementing the former work, "D'Amboinische Rariteitkammer" (1704), and "Thesaurus imaginum piscium, testaceorum, et cochlearum" (1711).

SHARP, Captain Bartholomew (17th century), made several buccaneering voyages to the South Seas, chiefly off the coast of South America and Darien. He kept a journal, and published an account of his voyages in 1684.

SHELVOCKE, George (18th century), buccaneer, although he had been long in the navy, went out in command of the *Speedwell* (privateer) in 1719-22 to the South Seas. He was wrecked on Juan Fernandez, but built a craft out of the remains of the wreck, and reached Peru ; he thence sailed to Formosa. After three years of constant fighting and adventures, he reached England and published his "Voyage round the World by way of the Great South Sea" (1726).

SLOANE, Sir Hans, Bart. (1660-1753), botanist and physician. He went to Jamaica in 1687, collecting 800 plants there, and afterwards published an account of his travels (1707-25), and a "Catalogue of the Plants of Jamaica" (1696). He became Secretary to the Royal Society in 1693, and edited its Transactions for twenty years. He was appointed Physician-General to the army, and was the first medical practitioner to be created a baronet (1716). He was elected President of the College of Physicians in 1719, and of the Royal Society in 1727, retaining the latter dignity until 1740. He was an indefatigable collector, and his library and collections, which he by will directed should be offered to the nation for £20,000, were in 1759 opened to the public as the British Museum.

TASMAN, Abel Jansen (*cir.* 1602-59), Dutch navigator. In 1639 he was sent by Van Diemen to the Philippines and Japan ; and in 1642 the same Governor directed him to investigate the south of New Holland. He fell in with Van Diemen's Land, without discovering it to be an island, and thence sailed across to New Zealand, which he called Staten Land. Anchoring in Massacre Bay, he lost three men, killed by the natives (whence the name), and then coasted along the west coast of North Island. After leaving this he reached the Friendly Islands, returning to Batavia by the north coast of New Guinea. In 1644 he undertook a third voyage to the north coast of New Holland and discovered the Gulf of Carpentaria. He died at Batavia in 1659.

TORRES, Luis Vaez de, commanded the *Almiranta*, the second ship on Quiros' expedition. After accompanying Quiros to "Sagittaria" (Otahite), the ships were separated at Terra del Espiritu Santo, and Torres, sailing westwards, passed through the straits between Australia and New Guinea in 1606. In connection with the fire thrown by the natives of this latter country when Banks landed there (see p. 326), it is interesting to find that Torres records that "among the weapons used by them were hollow bamboo sticks, which they filled with lime, and by throwing it endeavoured to blind their enemies," also that he "met with Mahometans who had swords and firearms" (Burney, *History of Discoveries in the South Seas*). Cook and Banks were unaware of the previous discovery, by Torres, of these straits.

VALENTIJN, François (1656-1727), Dutch traveller, was for many years pastor of the Protestant Church at Amboyna. He was the author of "Oudt en Nieuw Oost-Indie" (1724-26), and of various theological works, including a Malay version of the Bible.

WALLIS, Captain Samuel (died 1795), was sent out in command of the *Dolphin* on Byron's return in 1766. In company with the *Swallow*, he left England in August 1766, but was separated from his consort in a gale after emerging from the Straits of Magellan. He rediscovered Otahite (already seen by Quiros in 1606) in June 1767, one year before Bougainville. He named it King George III. Island. After a month's stay he left the island for Batavia, and finally reached England in May 1768. Hawkesworth published an account of this voyage in 1773. It was Wallis who recommended Otahite as a station for observing the transit of Venus in 1769. Wallis retired from active service in 1772, and was in 1780 appointed an extra commissioner of the navy. (For the first voyage of the *Dolphin*, see *Byron*.)

OFFICERS OF THE "ENDEAVOUR"

JAMES COOK, Lieutenant in Command.

ZACHARY HICKS, Lieutenant, died 25th May 1771.

JOHN GORE, Lieutenant.

ROBERT MOLINEUX, Master, died 17th April 1771.

RICHARD PICKERSGILL, Master's Mate (Master, 16th April 1771).

CHESTER CLERKE, Master's Mate.

FRANCIS WILKINSON, A.B. (Master's Mate, 20th August 1768).

JOHN BOOTIE, Midshipman, died 4th February 1771.

JONATHAN MONKHOUSE, Midshipman, died 6th February 1771.

PATRICK SAUNDERS, Midshipman.

ISAAC SMITH, A.B. (Midshipman, 24th May 1770; Master's Mate, 27th May 1771).

JOS. MAGRA, A.B. (Midshipman, 27th May 1771).

ISAAC MANLEY, Master's Servant (Midshipman, 5th February 1771).

WILLIAM B. MONKHOUSE, Surgeon, died 5th November 1770.

WILLIAM PERRY, Surgeon's Mate (Surgeon, 6th November 1770).

RICHARD ORTON, Clerk.

CHARLES GREEN, Astronomer, died 27th January 1771.

MR. BANKS'S STAFF

DANIEL CARL SOLANDER, Naturalist.

JOHN REYNOLDS, Artist, died 18th December 1770.

SYDNEY PARKINSON, Artist, died 26th January 1771.

ALEXANDER BUCHAN, Artist, died 17th April 1769.

HERMAN SPORING, died 24th January 1771.

JAMES ROBERTS, Servant.

PETER BRISCOE, Servant.

THOMAS RICHMOND, Negro Servant
GEORGE DOLLIN, Negro Servant
} Frozen to death, 16th February 1769.

The total on board (including a seaman pressed at Madeira) was 95; of these, 38 were lost by death during the voyage.

CHAPTER I

ENGLAND TO RIO DE JANEIRO

AUG. 25—NOV. 13, 1768

Departure—Birds and marine animals—Species of *Dagysa*—Madeira—Dr. Heberden—Madeira mahogany—Wine-making—Vines—Carts—Vegetable productions—Convent—Chapel wainscoted with bones—General account of Madeira—Peak of Teneriffe—Marine animals—Cross the Equator—Climate of tropics—Luminous animals in the water—Trade winds—Brazilian fishermen—Sargasso weed—Rio harbour.

25th August 1768. Plymouth.—After having waited in this place ten days, the ship and everything belonging to me being all that time in perfect readiness to sail at a moment's warning, we at last got a fair wind; and this day at three o'clock in the evening weighed anchor and set sail, all in excellent health and spirits, perfectly prepared (in mind at least) to undergo with cheerfulness any fatigues or dangers that may occur in our intended voyage.

26th. Saw this evening a shoal of those fish which are particularly called *Porpoises* by the seamen, probably the *Delphinus Phocœna* of Linnæus, as their noses are very blunt.

28th. In some sea water which was on board to season a cask, observed a very minute sea-insect, which Dr. Solander described by the name of *Podura marina.* Took several specimens of *Medusa pelagica*, whose different motions in swimming amused us very much; among the appendages to this animal we found also a new species of *Oniscus.* We took also another animal, quite different from any we had ever seen; it was of an angular figure, about three inches

B

long and one thick, with a hollow passing quite through it; on one end was a brown spot, which might be the stomach of the animal. Four of these, the whole number that we took, adhered together when taken by their sides; so that at first we imagined them to be one animal: but upon being put into a glass of water, they very soon separated, and swam briskly about.

31st. Observed about the ship several of the birds called by the seamen Mother Carey's Chickens, *Procellaria pelagica,* Linn., which were thought by them to be a sure presage of a storm, as indeed it proved.

2nd September. The casting-net brought up two kinds of animals, different from any before taken. They came up in clusters, both sorts indifferently in each cluster, although there were much fewer of a horned kind than of the other: they seemed to be two species of one genus, but are not at all reducible to any hitherto described.

3rd. We were employed all day in describing the animals taken yesterday: we found them to be of a new genus, and of the same as that taken on the 28th of August; we called the genus *Dagysa,* from the likeness of one species to a gem.

4th. Employed in fishing with the casting-net. We were fortunate in taking several specimens of *Dagysa saccata* adhering together, sometimes to the length of a yard or more, and shining in the water with very beautiful colours; but another insect we took to-day was possessed of more beautiful colouring than anything in nature I have ever seen, hardly excepting gems. It is of a new genus, called *Carcinium,* of which we took another species, having no beauty to boast of; but the first, which we called *opalinum,* shone in the water with all the splendour and variety of colours that we observe in a real opal. It lived in a glass of salt water, in which it was put for examination, several hours, darting about with great agility, and at every motion showing an almost infinite variety of changeable colours. Towards the evening of this day a new phenomenon appeared: the sea was almost covered with a small species of crab (*Cancer depurator,* Linn.),

floating upon the surface of the water, and moving with tolerable agility, as if the surface and not the bottom of the
ocean were their proper station.

   5th. I forgot to mention yesterday that two birds were
caught in the rigging, which had probably come from Spain,
as we were not then distant more than five or six leagues
from that country.   This morning another was caught and
brought to me, but so weak that it died in my hand almost
immediately.   All three were of the same species, and not
described by Linnæus; we called them *Motacilla velificans*,
as they must be sailors who would venture themselves
aboard a ship which is going round the world.   To balance
to some extent our good fortune, now become too prevalent,
a misfortune happened this morning, almost the worst which
our enemies could have wished.   The morning was calm,
and Richmond employed in searching for what should
appear on the surface of the water; a shoal of *Dagysæ* was
observed, and he, eager to take some of them, threw the
casting-net, fastened only to his wrist; the string slipped
from him, and the net at once sunk into the deep, never
more to torment its inhabitants.   This left us for some time
entirely without a resource ; plenty of animals came past
the ship, but all the nets were in the hold, stowed under so
many other things that it was impossible even to hope that
they may be got out to-day at least.   However, an old hoop-
net was fastened to a fishing-rod, and with it one new
species of *Dagysa* was caught: it was named *lobata*.

   6th. Towards the middle of the day the sea was almost
covered with *Dagysæ* of different kinds, among which two
entirely new ones were taken (*rostrata* and *strumosa*), but
neither were observed hanging in clusters, as most of the
other species had been ; whether from the badness of the
new machine, or the scarcity of the animals, I cannot say.

   It is now time to give some account of the genus of
Dagysa, of which we have already taken six species, all
agreeing very well in many particulars, but chiefly in this
very singular one, that they have a hole at each end, communicating by a tube often as large as the body of the

animal, by the help of which they swim with some degree of activity when separated from each other. Several sorts are most generally seen joined together, *gemmæ* more particularly, which adhere in irregularly-shaped clusters of some hundreds; in the midst of these were generally found a few specimens of *cornuta*, from which circumstance we may judge that they are very nearly allied. It seems singular that no naturalist should have taken notice of these animals, as they abound so much where the ship now is, not twenty leagues from the coast of Spain. From hence, however, great hopes may be formed that the inhabitants of the deep have been but little examined, and as Dr. Solander and myself will have probably greater opportunity in the course of this voyage than any one before us, it is a very encouraging circumstance that so large a field of natural history has remained almost untrod until now, and that we may be able from this circumstance alone (almost unthought of when we embarked in the undertaking) to add considerable lights to the science which we so eagerly pursue.

This evening a large quantity of *Carcinium opalinum*, which may be called the *opal insect*, came under the ship's stern, making the very sea appear of uncommon beauty, their colours appearing with vast brightness even at the depth of two or three fathoms, though they are not more than three lines long and one broad.

7th. On examining the *Dagysæ* which were taken yesterday several small animals were found lodged in the hollow parts of their bodies, and some in the very substance of their flesh, which seems to be their food, as many of the *Dagysæ* were full of scars, which had undoubtedly been the lodgment of these animals some time before. Upon a minute inspection they proved to be animals not to be classed under Linnæus's genera, though nearly related to *Oniscus*, from which circumstance the name of *Onidium* was given to the new genus, and to them was added an animal taken on the 28th of August, and mentioned by the name of *Oniscus macrophthalmus*.

In one particular these insects differ from any hitherto

described, and in that they all three agree, viz. in having two eyes joined together under one common membrane without the least distinction or division between them, which circumstance alone seems a sufficient reason for constituting a new genus.

10*th.* To-day for the first time we dined in Africa, and took leave of Europe for heaven alone knows how long, perhaps for ever; that thought demands a sigh as a tribute due to the memory of friends left behind, and they have it, but two cannot be spared, 'twould give more pain to the sigher than pleasure to those sighed for. 'Tis enough that they are remembered : they would not wish to be too much thought of by one so long to be separated from them, and left alone to the mercy of winds and waves.

12*th.* At ten to-night came to an anchor in Funchiale Bay, Madeira.

13*th*–18*th.* The product boat [1] (as it is called by English sailors) from the officers of health, whose leave must be obtained before any ship's crew can land, came on board about eleven, and we immediately went on shore in the town of Funchiale, the capital of the island, situate in latitude 32° 40′ N. It is so called from the fennel which grows in plenty upon the rocks in its neighbourhood, and is called *funcho* in Portuguese. Here we immediately went to the house of the English consul, Mr. Cheap, one of the first merchants in the place, where we were received with uncommon marks of civility, he insisting upon our taking possession of his house, and living entirely with him during our stay, which we did, and were by him furnished with every accommodation that we could wish for. Leave was procured by him for us to search the island for whatever natural productions we might find worth noticing ; people were also employed to procure for us fish and shells ; horses and guides were obtained for Dr. Solander and myself to carry us to any part of the island which we might choose to visit. But our very short stay, which was only five days, made it impossible to go to any distance ; so we

---

[1] *i.e.* the *pratique* boat.

contented ourselves with collecting as much as we could in the neighbourhood of the town, never going above three miles from it during our whole stay.

The season of the year was undoubtedly the worst for both plants and insects, being that of the vintage, when nothing is green in the country, except just on the verge of small brooks, by which their vines are watered; we made shift, however, to collect specimens of several plants, etc.

The five days which we remained upon the island were spent so exactly in the same manner that it is by no means necessary to divide them. I shall therefore only say that in general we got up in the morning, went out on our researches, returned to dine, and went out again in the evening. On one day, however, we had a visit from the Governor, of which we had notice beforehand, and were obliged to stay at home; so that this unsought honour lost us very nearly the whole day, a very material part of the short time we were allowed to stay upon the island. We, however, contrived to revenge ourselves upon his Excellency by means of an electrical machine which we had on board; for, upon his expressing a desire to see it, we sent for it ashore, and shocked him fully as much as he chose.

While here we were much indebted to Dr. Heberden, the chief physician of the island, and brother to the physician of that name at London. He had for many years been an inhabitant of the Canaries, and of this island, and had made several observations, chiefly philosophical; some, however, were botanical, describing the trees of the island. Of these he immediately gave us a copy, together with such specimens as he had in his possession, and indeed spared no pains to get for us living specimens of such as could be procured in flower.

We tried here to learn what species of wood it is which has been imported into England, and is now known to cabinet-makers by the name of Madeira mahogany, but without much success, as we could not learn that any wood had been exported from the island by that name. The wood, however, of the tree called here *Vigniatico, Laurus indicus*,[1] Linn., bids fair to be the thing, it being of a fine grain and brown like mahogany, from which it is difficult to distinguish it, as is well shown at Dr. Heberden's house, where, in a book-case, *vigniatico* and mahogany were placed close by each other, and were only to be known asunder by the first being of not quite so dark a colour as the other.

As much of the island as we saw showed evident signs of a volcano having some time or other possibly produced the whole, for we saw no one piece of stone which did not clearly show signs of having been burnt, some very much, specially the sand, which was absolutely cinders. Indeed, we did not see much of the country, but we were told that the whole resembled the specimen we saw of it.

When first approached from seaward the land has a very beautiful appearance, the sides of the hills being entirely covered with vineyards almost as high as the eye can distinguish. This gives a constant appearance of verdure, although at this time nothing but the vines remain green, the grass and herbs being entirely burnt up, except near the rills by which the vines are watered and under the shade of the vines themselves. But even there very few species of plants were in perfection, the greater part being burnt up.

The people here in general seem to be as idle, or rather uninformed, a set, as I ever yet saw; all their instruments, even those with which their wine, the only article of trade in the island, is made, are perfectly simple and unimproved. In making wine the grapes are put into a square wooden vessel, of dimensions depending upon the size of the vineyard to which it belongs, into which the servants get (having taken off their stockings and jackets), and with their feet and elbows squeeze out as much of the juice as they can; the stalks, etc., are then collected, tied together with a rope, and put under a square piece of wood which is pressed down by a lever, to the other end of which is fastened a stone that may be raised up at pleasure by a

[1] *Persea indica,* Spreng.

screw.   By this means and this only they make their wine,
and by this probably Noah made his when he had newly
planted the first vineyard after the general destruction of
mankind and their arts, although it is not impossible that
he might have used a better, if he remembered the methods
he had seen before the flood.

It was with great difficulty that some (and not as yet all)
of them were persuaded not long ago to graft their vines,
and by this means bring all the fruit of a vineyard to be of
one sort.   Formerly the wine had been spoiled by various
inferior kinds of vines, which were nevertheless suffered to
grow, and taken as much care of as the best, because they
added to the quantity of the wine.   Yet they were perfectly
acquainted with the use of grafting, and constantly practised
it on their chestnut trees, by which means they were brought
to bear much sooner than they would have done had they
been allowed to remain unimproved.

Wheeled carriages I saw none of any sort or kind;
indeed their roads are so intolerably bad, that if they had
any they could scarcely make use of them.   They have,
however, some horses and mules wonderfully clever in
travelling upon these roads, notwithstanding which they
bring every drop of wine to town upon men's heads in
vessels made of goat-skins.   The only imitation of a carriage
which they have is a board slightly hollowed in the middle,
to one end of which a pole is tied by a strap of white
leather, the whole machine coming about as near the perfection of an European cart as an Indian canoe does to a boat;
with this they move the pipes of wine about the town.   I
suppose they would never have made use even of this had
not the English introduced vessels to contain the wine,
which were rather too large to be carried by hand, as they
used to do everything else.

A speech of their late Governor is recorded here, which
shows in what light they are looked upon even by the
Portuguese (themselves, I believe, far behind all the rest of
Europe, except possibly the Spaniards).   " It was very
fortunate," said he, " that the island was not Eden, in which

Adam and Eve dwelt before the fall, for had it been so, the inhabitants here would never have been induced to put on clothes; so much are they resolved in every particular to follow exactly the paths of their forefathers."

Indeed, were the people here only tolerably industrious, there is scarcely any luxury which might not be produced that either Europe or the Indies afford, owing to the great difference of climate observable in ascending the hills. This we experienced on a visit to Dr. Heberden, who lives about two miles from the town; we left the thermometer when we set out at 74°, and found it there at 66°. The hills produce almost spontaneously vast quantities of walnuts, chestnuts, and apples, but in the town you find some few plants natives of both the Indies, whose flourishing state puts it out of all doubt, that were they taken any care of, they might have any quantity of them. Of such they have the banana (*Musa sapientum*, Linn.) in great abundance, the guava (*Psidium pyriferum*, Linn.) not uncommon, and the pine-apple (*Bromelia Ananas*, Linn.)—of this I saw some very healthy plants in the provision-garden, the mango (*Mangifera indica*, Linn.)—one plant also of this in the same garden bearing fruit every year, and the cinnamon (*Laurus Cinnamomum*, Linn.)—very healthy plants of which I saw on the top of Dr. Heberden's house at Funchiale, which had stood there through the winter without any kind of care having been taken of them. These, without mentioning any more, seem very sufficient to show that the tenderest plants might be cultivated here without any trouble; yet the indolence of the inhabitants is so great, that even that is too much for them. Indeed, the policy here is to hinder them as much as possible from growing anything themselves except what they find their account in taking in exchange for corn, though the people might with much less trouble and expense grow the corn themselves. What corn does grow here (it is not much) is of a most excellent quality, large-grained and very fine. Their meat also is very good, mutton, pork, and beef more especially, which was agreed by all of us to be very little inferior to our own, though *we Englishmen* value ourselves not a little on our peculiar excellence in that production. The fat of this was white, like the fat of mutton, but the meat brown and coarse-grained as ours, though much smaller.

The town of Funchiale is situated at the bottom of the bay, very ill-built, though larger than the size of the island seems to deserve. The houses of the better people are in general large, but those of the poorer sort very small, and the streets very narrow and uncommonly ill-paved. The churches here have abundance of ornaments, chiefly bad pictures, and figures of their favourite saints in laced clothes. The Convent of the Franciscans, indeed, which we went to see, had very little ornament; but the neatness with which those fathers kept everything was well worthy of commendation, especially their infirmary, the contrivance of which deserves to be particularly noticed. It was a long room; on one side were windows and an altar for the convenience of administering the sacrament to the sick, on the other were the wards, each just capable of containing a bed, and lined with white Dutch tiles. To every one of these was a door communicating with a gallery which ran parallel to the great room, so that any of the sick might be supplied with whatever they wanted without disturbing their neighbours.

In this convent was a curiosity of a very singular nature: a small chapel whose whole lining, wainscot and ceiling, was entirely composed of human bones, two large thigh bones being laid crossways, with a skull in each of the openings. Among these was a very singular anatomical curiosity: a skull in which one side of the lower jaw was perfectly and very firmly fastened to the upper by an ossification, so that the man, whoever he was, must have lived some time without being able to open his mouth; indeed it was plain that a hole had been made on the other side by beating out his teeth, and in some measure damaging his jawbone, by which alone he must have received his nourishment.

I must not leave these good fathers without mentioning a thing which does great credit to their civility, and at the same time shows that they are not bigots in their religion.

We visited them on Thursday evening, just before their supper-time; they made many apologies, that they could not ask us to sup, not being prepared; " but," said they, " if you will come to-morrow, notwithstanding that it is a fast with us, we will have a turkey roasted for you."

There are here besides friaries, three or four houses of nuns. To one of these (Saint Clara) we went, and indeed the ladies did us the honour to express great pleasure in seeing us there. They had heard that we were great philosophers, and expected much from us: one of the first questions that they asked was when it would thunder; they then desired to know if we could put them in a way of finding water in their convent, of which it seems they were in want. Notwithstanding that our answers to their questions were not quite so much to the purpose as they expected, they did not at all cease their civilities; for while we stayed, which was about half an hour, I am sure that there was not a fraction of a second in which their tongues did not go at an uncommonly nimble rate.

It remains now that I should say something of the island in general, and then take my leave of Madeira till some other opportunity offers of visiting it again, for the climate is so fine that any man might wish it was in his power to live there under the benefits of English laws and liberty.

The hills here are very high, much higher than any one would imagine; Pico Ruievo, the highest, is 5068 feet,[1] which is much higher than any land that has been measured in Great Britain. The whole island, as I hinted before, has probably been the production of a volcano, notwithstanding which its fertility is amazing: all the sides of the hills are covered with vines to a certain height, above which are woods of chestnut and pine of immense extent, and above them forests of wild timber of kinds not known in Europe, which amply supply the inhabitants with whatever they may want. Among these, some there were whose flowers we were not able to procure, and consequently could

---

[1] 6059 feet by more recent measurement.

not settle their genera, particularly those called by the Portuguese *mirmulano* and *pao branco*,[1] both which, and especially the first, from the beauty of their leaves, promise to be a great ornament to our European gardens.

The inhabitants here are supposed to number about 80,000, and from the town of Funchiale (its custom-house I mean) the King of Portugal receives £20,000 a year, after having paid the Governor and all expenses of every kind, which may serve to show in some degree of what consequence this little island is to the Crown of Portugal. Were it in the hands of any other people in the world its value might easily be doubled from the excellence of its climate, capable of bearing any kind of crop, a circumstance of which the Portuguese do not take the least advantage.

The coin current here is entirely Spanish, for the balance of trade with Lisbon being in disfavour of this island, all the Portuguese money naturally goes there, to prevent which Spanish money is allowed to pass; it is of three denominations, pistereens, bitts, and half bitts, the first worth about a shilling, the second 6d., the third 3d. They have also copper Portuguese money, but it is so scarce that I did not in my stay there see a single piece.[2]

18*th*. This evening got under weigh.

20*th*. Took with the casting-net a most beautiful species of *Medusa* of a colour equalling, if not exceeding, the finest ultramarine; it was described and called *Medusa azurea*.

23*rd*. A fish was taken which was described and called *Scomber serpens;* the seamen said they had never seen it before, except the first lieutenant, who remembered to have taken one before just about these islands. Sir Hans Sloane[3] in his passage out to Jamaica also took one of these fish, and gives a figure of it (vol. i. t. i. f. 2).

24*th*. This morning the Pike [of Teneriffe] appeared very plainly, and immensely high above the clouds, as may well

---

[1] Probably *Apollonias canariensis*, Nees ; and *Oreodaphne fœtens*, Nees.

[2] Here Banks has a list of 18 Madeiran fish and 299 plants.

[3] For notes on the naturalists and travellers mentioned throughout the Journal, see pp. xliii.-li.

be imagined by its height, which Dr. Heberden of Madeira, who has been himself upon it, gave as 15,396 feet.[1] The Doctor also says that though there is no eruption of visible fire from it, yet that heat issues from the chinks near the top so strongly, that a person who puts his hand into these is scalded. From him we received, among many other favours, some salt which he supposes to be true natron or nitrum of the ancients, and some exceedingly pure native sulphur, both which he collected himself on the top of the mountain, where large quantities, especially of the salt, are found on the surface of the earth.

25th. Wind continued to blow much as it has done, so we were sure we were well in the *trade*. Now for the first time we saw flying-fish, whose beauty, especially when seen from the cabin window, is beyond imagination, their sides shining like burnished silver. Seen from the deck they do not appear to such advantage, as their backs, which are dark-coloured, are then presented to view.

27th. About one this morning a flying-fish, the first that had been taken, was brought into the cabin; it flew aboard, chased, I suppose, by some other fish, or may be because he did not see the ship; at breakfast another was brought, which had flown into Mr. Green the astronomer's cabin.

28th. Three birds were to-day about the ship: a swallow, to all appearance the same as our European one, and two *Motacillæ*; about nightfall one of the latter was taken. About eleven a shoal of porpoises came about the ship, and the fizgig was soon thrown into one of them, but would not hold.

29th. Employed in drawing and describing the bird taken yesterday; called it *Motacilla avida*. While the drawing was in hand, it became very familiar, so much so that we had a brace made for it in hopes of keeping it alive; as flies were in amazing abundance on board the ship, we had no fear but that the bird would have a plentiful supply of provision.

About noon a young shark was seen from the cabin

---

[1] 12,300 feet by more recent measurement.

windows following the ship. It immediately took a bait and was hauled on board. It proved to be the *Squalus carcharias*, Linn., and assisted us in clearing up much confusion, which almost all authors had made about that species. With it came on board four sucking-fish, *Echeneis remora*, Linn., which were preserved in spirits. Although it was twelve o'clock before the shark was taken, we made shift to have a part of him stewed for dinner, and very good meat he was, at least in the opinion of Dr. Solander and myself, though some of the seamen did not seem to be fond of him, probably from some prejudice founded on the species sometimes feeding on human flesh.

30th. This evening another *Motacilla avida* was brought to us ; it differed scarcely at all from the first taken, except that it was somewhat larger ; its head, however, gave us some material, by supplying us with nearly twenty specimens of ticks, which differed but little from *Acarus ricinus*, Linn. ; it was, however, described, and called *Acarus motacillæ*.

1st October. Bonitos were in great plenty about the ship. We were called up early to see one that had been struck and found it to be the *Scomber pelamis*, Linn., a drawing being made of it. I confess, however, that I was a good deal disappointed, expecting to find the animal much more beautiful than it proved, though its colours were extremely lively, especially the blue lines on the back (which equalled at least any ultramarine), yet the name, and the accounts I had heard from all who had seen them, made me expect an animal of much greater variety of colour. This consisted merely of blue lines on the back, crossing each other, a changeable gold and purple on the sides, and white with black lines on the bottom of the sides and belly. After having examined and drawn the animal, we proceeded to dissect it, and in the course of the operation were much pleased by the infinite strength we observed in every part of him, especially the stomach, the coats of which were uncommonly strong, especially about the sphincter, or extremity by which the digested meat is discharged ; this I suppose is intended to crush and render useful the scales and bones of fishes which this animal must continually swallow without separating them from the flesh. From the outside of its scales we took a small animal which seemed to be a louse (if I may so call it), as it certainly stuck to him, and preyed upon the juices which it extracted by suction, probably much to his disquiet: it proved to be *Monoculus piscinus*, Linn. Baster has given a figure of it in his " Opera Subseciva," but has by some unlucky accident mistaken the head for the tail. Inside the fish were also found two animals which preyed upon him; one *Fasciola pelami*, Mss., in his very flesh, though near the membrane which covers the intestines; the other *Sipunculus piscium*, Mss., in the stomach.

2nd. This morning two swallows were about the ship, though we must now be sixty leagues at least from any land; at night one of them was taken, and proved to be *Hirundo domestica*, Linn.

4th. I went out in a boat and took *Dagysa strumosa*, *Medusa porpita*, which we had before called *azurea*, *Mimus volutator*[1] and a *Cimex*, which runs upon the water here in the same manner as *C. lacustris* does in our ponds in England. Towards evening two small fish were taken under the stern; they were following a shirt which was towing, and showed not the least signs of fear, so that they were taken with a landing-net without the smallest difficulty. They proved to be *Balistes monoceros*, Linn.

7th. Went out in the boat, and took what is called by the seamen a Portuguese man-of-war, *Holothuria physalis*,[2] Linn., also *Medusa velella*, Linn., *Onidium spinosum*, Mss., *Diodon erinaceus*, Mss., *Dagysa vitrea*, Mss., *Helix ianthina*, Linn., *violacea*, Mss., and *Procellaria oceanica*, Mss. The *Holothuria* proved to be one of the most beautiful sights I had ever seen; it consisted of a small bladder, in shape much like the air-bladder of a fish, from the bottom of which descended a number of strings of bright blue and red, some three or four feet in length; if touched,

---

[1] This cannot be identified.

[2] The Portuguese man-of-war is now known as *Physalia*, and is classed among the *Cœlenterata*.

these stung the person who touched them in the same manner as nettles, only much more severely. On the top of this bladder was a membrane which he turned either one way or the other to receive the wind; this was veined with pink, in an uncommonly beautiful manner; in short, the whole was one of the most beautiful sights I have seen among the mollusca, though many of them are beautiful.

The floating shells, *Helix ianthina*[1] and *violacea*, from their particularity, also deserve mention. They are to be found floating on the top of the water by means of a small cluster of bubbles filled with air, composed of a tenacious slimy substance, not easily parting with its contents; these keep them suspended on the surface of the water, and serve as a nidus for their eggs: it is probable that they never go down to the bottom, or willingly come near any shore, as the shell is of so brittle a construction that few sea-water snails are so thin.

Every shell contains within it about a teaspoonful of liquid, which it freely discharges on being touched; this is of a most beautiful red purple colour, and easily dyes linen clothes; it may be well worth inquiry whether or not this is the *purpura*[2] of the ancients, as the shell is certainly found in the Mediterranean. We have not yet taken a sufficient quantity of the shells to try the experiment, perhaps we shall soon.

Procellaria oceanica differs very little from *P. pelagica*, Linn., but from his place of abode so far south, and some small difference in plumage, it is more than likely that he is different in species.

9th. Found two new species of *Lepas* (*vittata* and *midas*) on the stern of the ship; they were both sticking to the bottom, in company with *L. anatifera*, of which there was great abundance.

10th. Took plenty of *Helix ianthina* and some few of *violacea*. Shot the black-toed gull of Pennant; it had not

---

[1] These two species are not *Helices*, but belong to the genus *Ianthina*.

[2] The purple of the ancients has since been proved to have been derived from a species of *Murex* or of *Purpura*.

yet been described according to Linnæus's system, so called
it *Larus crepidatus*. Its food here seems to be chiefly
Helices, on account of its dung being of a lively red colour,
much like that which was procured from the shells.

12*th*. A shark, *Squalus carcharias*, Linn., taken this morning, and with it two pilot fish. I went out in the boat
and took several blubbers. The pilot fish, *Gasterosteus ductor*,
Linn., is certainly as beautiful a fish as can be imagined; it
is of a light blue, with cross streaks of darker colour. It is
wonderful to see them about a shark, swimming round it
without expressing the least signs of fear; what their
motive for doing so is, I cannot guess, as I cannot find
that they get any provision by it, or any other emolument,
except possibly that the company of the shark keeps them
free from the attacks of dolphins or other large fish of
prey, who would otherwise devour them.

The blubbers taken to-day were *Beroe labiata* and *mar-
supialis*, Mss., the first of which made a pretty appearance
in the water by reason of its swimmers, which line its side
like fringes, and are of a fine changeable colour; and
Callirrhoe bivia, Mss., the most lifeless lump of jelly I
have seen; it scarcely seems to be possessed of life, but for
one or two motions we saw it make.

13*th*. A shark taken, but not one pilot fish attended
it, which is rather uncommon, as they are seldom without
a shoal of from ten to twenty. At noon I went in the
boat, and took the Sallee man, *Phyllodoce velella*, Linn., which
is a sailor, but inferior in size to the Portuguese man-of-
war, yet not without its beauty, chiefly from the charming
blue of the lower side. Its sail is transparent, but not
movable, so it trusts itself to the mercy of the winds,
without being able to turn to windward, as the Portuguese
man-of-war perhaps can. We saw several of these latter
to-day, and observed many small fish under their tentacula,
which seemed to shelter there, as if with its stings it could
defend them from large enemies.

15*th*. I had the good fortune to see a bird of the shearwater kind, which I shot; it proved not to have been

described. It was about as large as the common kind, but differed from it in being whiter, especially about the face. We named it *Procellaria crepidata*, as its feet were like those of the gulls shot last week, black on the outside, but white near the legs. A large shoal of fish were all this day under the ship's stern, playing about, but refusing to take bait. We contrived to take one of them with a fizgig: it was in make and appearance like a carp, weighing nearly two pounds. Its sides were ornamented with narrow lines, and its fins almost entirely covered with scales : called it *Chætodon cyprinaceus*.

16*th*. I had the opportunity of seeing a phenomenon I had never before met with, a lunar rainbow which appeared about ten o'clock, very faint, and almost or quite without colour, so that it could be traced by little more than an appearance resembling shade on a cloud.

18*th*. This evening, trying, as I have often (foolishly no doubt) done, to exercise myself by playing tricks with two ropes in the cabin, I got a fall which hurt me a good deal, and alarmed me the more as the blow was on my head, and two hours after it I was taken with sickness at my stomach, which made me fear some ill consequence.

19*th*. To-day, thank God, I was much better, and eased of all apprehensions.

21*st*. To-day the cat killed our bird, *Motacilla avida*, which had lived with us ever since the 29th September entirely on the flies which it caught for itself : it was hearty and in high health, so that it might have lived a great while longer had fate been more kind.

25*th*. This morning about eight o'clock we crossed the equinoctial line in about 33° W. from Greenwich, at the rate of four knots, which our seamen said was uncommonly good, the thermometer standing at 79°. (The thermometers used in this voyage are two of Mr. Bird's making, after Fahrenheit's scale, and seldom differ by more than a degree from each other, and that only when they are as high as 80°, in which case the mean reading of the two instruments is set down.) This evening the ceremony of ducking the

ship's company was performed, as is always customary on
crossing the line, when those who have crossed it before
claim a right of ducking all that have not. The whole
of the ceremony I shall describe.

About dinner-time a list was brought into the cabin
containing the names of everybody and thing aboard the ship
(in which the dogs and cats were not forgotten); to this
was fixed a signed petition from the ship's company desiring
leave to examine everybody in that list, that it might be
known whether or not they had crossed the line before.
This was immediately granted, everybody being called upon
the quarter-deck and examined by one of the lieutenants
who had crossed the line : he marked every name either to
be ducked or let off as their qualifications directed. Captain
Cook and Dr. Solander were on the black list, as were I
myself, my servants, and dogs, for all of whom I was obliged
to compound by giving the duckers a certain quantity of
brandy, for which they willingly excused us the ceremony.

Many of the men, however, chose to be ducked rather
than give up four days' allowance of wine, which was the
price fixed upon, and as for the boys they are always ducked,
of course, so that about twenty-one underwent the ceremony.

A block was made fast to the end of the main-yard, and
a long line reved through it, to which three pieces of wood
were fastened, one of which was put between the legs of the
man who was to be ducked, and to this he was tied very
fast, another was for him to hold in his hands, and the
third was over his head, lest the rope should be hoisted too
near the block, and by that means the man be hurt. When
he was fastened upon this machine the boatswain gave the
command by his whistle, and the man was hoisted up as
high as the cross-piece over his head would allow, when
another signal was made, and immediately the rope was let
go, and his own weight carried him down; he was then
immediately hoisted up again, and three times served in
this manner, which was every man's allowance. Thus
ended the diversion of the day, for the ducking lasted until
almost night, and sufficiently diverting it certainly was to

see the different faces that were made on this occasion, some grinning and exulting in their hardiness, whilst others were almost suffocated, and came up ready enough to have compounded after the first or second duck, had such a proceeding been allowable.

Almost immediately after crossing the tropic the air had sensibly become much damper than usual, though not materially hotter: the thermometer in general stood from 80° to 82°. The nearer we approached to the calms, the damper everything grew; this was very perceptible even to the human body, but more remarkable was its effect upon all kinds of furniture. Everything made of iron rusted so fast that the knives in people's pockets became almost useless, and the razors in cases did not escape; all kinds of leather became mouldy, portfolios and trunks covered with black leather were almost white. Soon afterwards this mould adhered to almost everything; all the books in my library became mouldy, so that they had to be wiped to preserve them.

About this time we came into the calms, which we met with earlier than usual: the thermometer was then at 83°, and we suffered from the heat and damp together. Bathing, however, kept me in perfect health, although many of the ship's company were ill of bilious complaints, which, however, were but of short duration. This continued till we got the S.E. trade, when the air became cooler, but the dampness continued yet: to that I chiefly attribute the ill-success of the electrical experiments, of which I have written an account in separate papers, that the different experiments may appear at one view.[1]

The air, during the whole time since we crossed the tropic, and indeed for some time before, has been nearly of the same temperature throughout the twenty-four hours, the thermometer seldom rising more than a degree during the time the sun is above the horizon; the cabin windows have been open without once being shut ever since we left Madeira.

29th. This evening the sea appeared uncommonly beautiful,

---

[1] An account of these will be found at the end of the volume.

flashes of light coming from it, perfectly resembling small flashes of lightning, and these so frequent that sometimes eight or ten were visible at the same moment; the seamen were divided in their accounts, some assuring us that it proceeded from fish, who made the light by agitating the salt water, as they called it, in their darting at their prey; while others said that they had often seen them to be nothing more than blubbers (*Medusæ*). This made us very eager to procure some of them, which at last we did by the help of the landing-net; they proved to be a species of *Medusa*, which when brought on board appeared like metal violently heated, emitting a white light. On the surface of this animal was fixed a small *Lepas* of exactly the same colour and almost transparent, not unlike thin starch in which a small quantity of blue is dissolved. In taking these animals three or four species of crabs were also obtained, of which one very small kind gave fully as much light as a glow-worm in England, though the creature was not so large by nine-tenths. Indeed, the sea this night seemed to abound with light in an unusual manner, as if every inhabitant of it furnished its share; as might have been the case, although none retained that property after being brought out of the water except the two above mentioned.

30th. Employed in examining the things caught last night, which being taken by the light of our lamps (for the wind which blows in at the windows always open will not suffer us to burn candles) we could hardly then distinguish into genera, much less into species. We had the good fortune to find that they were all quite new, and named them *Medusa pellucens, Lepas pellucens, Clio, Cancer fulgens,* and *Cancer amplectens,* but we had the misfortune to lose two more species of crabs through the glass in which they were contained falling overboard. Two other species of crabs were taken, one of which was very singular.

31st. Find that the crabs taken yesterday were both new; called them *vitreus* and *crassicornis.*

5th November. That the trade blows toward the northward upon the coast of Brazil has been observed long ago, although

I question whether our navigators are yet sufficiently apprised of it.   Piso, in his *Natural History of the Brazils*, says that the winds along shore are constantly to the northward from October to March, and to the southward from March to October.   Dampier also, who certainly had as much experience as most men, says the same thing, advising ships outward bound to keep to the westward, where they are almost certain to find the trade more easterly than in mid-channel, where it is sometimes due south, or within half a point of it, as we ourselves experienced.

6*th*. Towards evening the colour of the water was observed to change, upon which we sounded and found ground at thirty-two fathoms.   The lead was cast three times between six and ten without finding a foot's difference in the depth or quality of the bottom, which was encrusted with coral. We supposed this to be the tail of a great shoal laid down in all our charts by the name of Abrolhos, on which Lord Anson struck soundings on his outward bound passage.

7*th*. About noon long ranges of a yellowish colour appear upon the sea, many of them very large, one (the largest) might be a mile in length and three or four hundred yards in width.   The seamen in general affirmed roundly that they were the spawn of fishes, and that they had often seen the same appearance before.   Upon taking up some of the water thus coloured, we found it to be caused by innumerable small atoms, each pointed at the end, and of a yellowish colour, none of them above a quarter of a line in length. In the microscope they appeared to be fasciculi of small fibres interwoven one within the other, not unlike the *nidi* of some *Phryganeæ*, which we call caddises ; what they were, or for what purpose designed, we could not even guess, nor so much as distinguish whether their substance was animal or vegetable.

8*th*. At daybreak to-day we made the land, which proved to be the Continent of South America, in latitude 21° 16′. About ten we saw a fishing-boat, whose occupants told us that the country formed part of the captainship of Espirito Santo.

Dr. Solander and I went on board this boat, in which were eleven men (nine of whom were blacks), who all fished with lines. We bought the chief part of their cargo, consisting of dolphins, two kinds of large pelagic scombers, sea bream, and the fish called in the West Indies Welshman, for which they made us pay nineteen shillings and sixpence. We had taken Spanish silver with us, which we imagined was the currency of the country; we were therefore not a little surprised that they asked us for English shillings, and preferred two, which we by accident had, to the pistereens, though after some words they took them also. The business of the people seemed to consist in going a good distance from land and catching large fish, which they salted in bulk, in the middle of their boat, which was arranged for that purpose. They had about two quintals of fish, laid in salt, which they offered for sale for sixteen shillings, and would doubtless have taken half the money had we been inclined to buy them; but fresh provisions were all we wanted, and the fresh fish which we bought served for the whole ship's company.

Their provisions for the sea consisted of a cask of water and a bag of the flour of cassada, which they call *Farinha de Pao*, or wooden flour, a very proper name for it, as indeed it tastes more like powdered chips than anything else.

Their method of drinking from their cask was truly primitive and pleased me much: the cask was large, as broad as the boat, and exactly fitted a place made for it in the ballast; they consequently could not get at the bottom of it to put in a tap by which the water might be drawn out. To remedy this difficulty they made use of a cane about three feet long, hollow, and open at each end, this the man who wanted to drink desired his neighbour to fill for him, which he did by putting it into the cask, and laying the palm of his hand over the uppermost end, prevented the water from running out of the lower, to which the drinker applied his mouth, and the other man taking away his hand, let the liquor run into the drinker's mouth till he was satisfied.

Soon after we came on board, a *Sphinx* was taken, which proved to be quite new, and a small bird, *Tanagra Jacarini*, Linn.; it seemed, however, from Linnæus's description, as well as Edwards' and Brisson's, that neither of them had seen the bird, which was in reality a *Loxia nitens*.

The fish brought on board proved to be *Scomber amia*, *S. falcatus, Coryphœna, Hippurus ?, Sparus pagrus* and *Sciœna rubens;* the second and last not being before described, we called them by these names.

10*th*. Species of seaweed now came floating by the ship. It proved to be *Sargasso, Fucus natans,*which is generally supposed to increase upon the surface of the sea in the same manner as duckweed (*Lemna*) does on fresh-water, without having any root; this, however, plainly showed that it had been rooted in the coral rock on the bottom, as two specimens particularly had large lumps of the coral still adhering to them. Among the weed were some few animals, but scarcely worth mentioning: one *Balistes,* but quite a fry, so young that it was impossible to refer it to its species; also a worm, which proved to be *Nereis pelagica*.

12*th*. This morning we were abreast of the land, which proved, as we thought last night, to be the island just within Cape Frio, called in some maps the Isle of Frio. About noon we saw the hill called the Sugar Loaf, which is just by the harbour's mouth, but it was a long way off yet, so we had no hopes of reaching it 'this night.

The shore from Cape Frio to this place has been one uninterrupted beach of the whitest colour I ever saw, which they tell me is a white sand.

In the course of this evening we approached very near the land, and found it very cold, to our feelings at least: the thermometer at ten o'clock stood at $68\frac{1}{4}°$, which gave us hopes that the country would be cooler than we should expect from the accounts of travellers, especially M. Biron, who says that no business is done here from ten to two on account of the intense heat.

13*th*. This morning the harbour of Rio Janeiro was right ahead, about two leagues off, but it being quite calm

we made our approach very slowly. The sea was inconceivably full of small *vermes*, which we took without the
least difficulty : they were almost all new, except *Beroe
labiata, Medusa radiata, fimbriata, crystallina,* and a *Dagysa.*
Soon after a fishing-boat came aboard and sold us three
scombers, which proved to be new, and were called *S.
salmoneus.* His bait was *Clupea chinensis,* of which we also
procured specimens.

CHAPTER II

RIO DE JANEIRO

Nov. 13—Dec. 7, 1768

Obstacles to landing — Viceroy memorialised — Boat's crew imprisoned — Vegetation, etc. — Ship fired at — Leave Rio harbour — Description of Rio — Churches — Government — Hindrances to travellers — Population — Military — Assassinations — Vegetables — Fruits — Manufactures — Mines — Jewels — Coins — Fortifications — Climate.

13th November.[1] As soon as we were well in the river, the captain sent his first lieutenant, Mr. Hicks, with a midshipman, to get a pilot: the boat returned, however, without the officers, but with a Portuguese subaltern. The coxswain informed us that the lieutenant was detained until the captain should go off. A ten-oared boat, containing about a dozen soldiers, then came off and rowed round the ship, no one in it appearing to take the slightest notice of us. A quarter of an hour later another boat came off, on board which was a *Disembargador* and a colonel of a Portuguese regiment. The latter asked many questions, and at first seemed to discourage our stay, but ended by being extremely civil, and assuring us that the Governor would give us every assistance in his power. The lieutenant, he said, was not detained, but had not been allowed on shore on account of the *practica*, but that he would be sent on board immediately.

14th. Captain Cook went on shore this morning. He returned with a Portuguese officer with him in the boat,

---

[1] This account, from the 13th to the 24th November inclusive, of the treatment of Captain Cook at Rio, has been much condensed from the original "Journal."

also an Englishman, Mr. Forster, a lieutenant in the Portuguese service. We were informed that we could not have a house nor sleep on shore, and that no person except the captain and such common sailors as were required on duty would be permitted to land ; we, the passengers, were particularly objected to. In spite of this we attempted to go on shore in the evening, under excuse of a visit to the Viceroy, but were stopped by the guard-boat. The captain went ashore to remonstrate with the Viceroy, but the latter said that he was acting under the King of Portugal's orders.

15*th* and 16*th*. The captain vainly remonstrated with the Viceroy against our being forbidden to land, and particularly against the sentinel placed in his boat, which was done, he was told, as an honour.

17*th*. The captain and I drew up written memorials complaining of his Excellency's behaviour, which to us, as a King's ship, was almost a breach of duty.

18*th*. Answers to our memorials were received : the captain is told that he had no reason to complain, as he had only received the usual treatment customary in all the ports of Brazil ; as for me, I am informed that as I have not brought proper credentials from the court at Lisbon, it is impossible that I can be permitted to land.

19*th*. We sent answers to his Excellency's memorials. The lieutenant who took them had orders not to suffer a guard to be put into his boat ; the guard-boat let him pass, but the Viceroy, on hearing of it, ordered sentinels to be put on the boat. The lieutenant refused to go on board unless they were taken out, whereupon he was sent on board in a guard-boat and his crew arrested. He reported that the men in our pinnace had not made the least resistance, but that they had notwithstanding been treated very roughly, being struck by the soldiers several times. The guard brought back the letters unopened.

This evening, by some mismanagement, our long-boat broke adrift, carrying with her my small boat. The yawl was sent after her, and managed to take her in tow, but in

spite of all the efforts of the crew, the boats soon drifted
out of sight. The yawl came back at two in the morning
with the news that the other two boats were lost. We
were, however, glad to find the men safe, for they had been
in considerable danger.

20*th.* The yawl was sent ashore to seek assistance in
recovering our long-boat : it returned with our pinnace and
its crew, and a boat of the Viceroy, which had orders to
assist us in searching for our boats.

The crew of the pinnace declared that they had been
confined in a loathsome dungeon, where their company was
chiefly blacks who were chained. The coxswain purchased
a better apartment for seven petacks (about as many
English shillings). At dark the pinnace returned with both
the boats and all their contents.

21*st.* Letters arrived from the Viceroy ; in mine he told
me very politely that it was not in his power to permit me
to go ashore. In the captain's he raises some doubts about
our ship being a King's ship.[1]

23*rd.* An answer to the captain's last memorial accuses
him of smuggling.

24*th.* Dr. Solander went into the town as surgeon of the
ship to visit a friar who had desired that the surgeon might
be sent to him : he received civilities from the people.

26*th.* I myself went ashore this morning before daybreak, and stayed until dark night. While I was ashore I
met several of the inhabitants, who were very civil to me,
taking me to their houses, where I bought of them stock for
the ship tolerably cheap : a middlingly fat porker for eleven
shillings, a Muscovy duck for something under two shillings, etc.

The country, where I saw it, abounded with vast variety
of plants and animals, mostly such as had not been described
by our naturalists, as so few have had an opportunity of
coming here ; indeed, no one even tolerably curious that I

---

[1] "The build and general appearance of the *Endeavour* not being that of
a man-of-war, the Portuguese authorities entertained suspicions regarding her
true character, which is not altogether surprising, considering the times."—
Wharton's *Cook*, p. 22, footnote.

know of has been here since Marcgrav and Piso about 1640 ; so it is easy to guess the state in which the natural history of such a country must be.

To give a catalogue of what I found would be a trouble very little to the purpose, as every particular is mentioned in the general catalogues of this place. I cannot, however, help mentioning some which struck me the most, and consequently gave me particular pleasure. These were chiefly the parasitic plants, especially *Renealmiæ* (for I was not fortunate enough to see one *Epidendrum*) and the different species of *Bromelia*, many not before described. *Karratas* I saw here growing on the decayed trunk of a tree sixty feet high at least, which it had so entirely covered that the whole seemed to be a tree of *Karratas*. The growth of the *Rhizophora*[1] also pleased me much, although I had before a very good idea of it from Rumphius, who has a very good figure of the tree in his *Herb. Amboin.* [v. iii. tab. 71, 72]. Add to these that the whole country was covered with the beautiful blossoms of *Malpighiæ, Bannisteriæ, Passifloræ,* not forgetting *Poinciana* and *Mimosa sensitiva,* and a beautiful species of *Clusia,* of which I saw great plenty ; in short, the wildest spots here were varied with a greater quantity of flowers, as well as more beautiful ones, than our best-devised gardens ; a sight infinitely pleasing for a short time, though no doubt the eye would soon tire with a continuance of it.

The birds of many species, especially the smaller ones, sat in great abundance on the boughs, many of them covered with most elegant plumage. I shot *Loxia brasiliensis,* and saw several specimens of it. Insects also were here in great quantity, many species very fine, but much more nimble than our European ones, especially the butterflies, almost all which flew near the tops of the trees, and were very difficult to come at, except when the sea breeze blew fresh, which kept them low down among the trees where they might be taken. Humming-birds I also saw of one species, but could not shoot them.

[1] Mangrove tree.

The banks of the sea, and more remarkably all the edges of small brooks, were covered with innumerable quantities of small crabs (*Cancer vocans*, Linn.), one hand of which is very large. Among these were many whose two hands were remarkably small and of equal size; these my black servant told me were the females of the other, and indeed all I examined, which were many, proved to be females, but whether they were really of the same species as *C. vocans*, I cannot determine on so short an acquaintance.

I saw but little cultivation, and small pains seemed to be taken with that. Most of it was grass land, on which were many lean cattle; and lean they might well be, for almost all the species of grass which I observed here were creepers, and consequently so close to the ground that though there might be upon them a sufficient bite for horses or sheep, yet how horned cattle could live at all appeared extraordinary to me.

I also saw their gardens, or small patches in which they cultivate many sorts of European garden stuffs, such as cabbages, peas, beans, kidney beans, turnips, white radishes, pumpkins, etc., but all much inferior to ours, except perhaps the last. They also grow water-melons and pine-apples, the only fruits which I have seen them cultivate; the first are very good, but the pines were much inferior to those I have tasted in Europe; I have hardly had one which could be reckoned of average quality, many were worse than some I have seen sent away from table in England, where nobody would eat them. Though in general very sweet, they have not the least flavour. In these gardens grow also yams, and mandihoca or cassada, which supplies the place of bread, for as our European bread corn will not grow here, all the flour they have is brought from Portugal at great expense, too great even for the middle-class people to purchase, much less the poorer.

27th. On the boats returning from watering, we were told that men had been sent out yesterday in search of some of our people who were ashore without leave; we concluded that this referred either to Dr. Solander or myself, which

made it necessary for us to go no more ashore while we
stayed.

1st December. We learnt that Mr. Forster had been taken
into custody, charged with smuggling. The real cause, we
believe, was that he had shown some countenance to his
countrymen, as we heard at the same time that five or six
Englishmen residing in the town, and a poor Portuguese,
who used to assist our people in bringing things to the boats,
had also been put into prison without any reason being
given.

2nd. This morning, thank God, we have got all we
want from these illiterate, impolite gentry, so we got up
our anchor and sailed to the point of Ilhoa dos Cobras,
where we were to lie and wait for a fair wind, which should
come every night from the land. A Spanish brig from
Buenos Ayres with letters for Spain arrived about a week
ago; her officers were received ashore with all possible
civility, and allowed to take a house without the least
hesitation. The captain, Don Antonio de Monte negro y
Velasco, with great politeness offered to take our letters to
Europe. Of this very fortunate circumstance we availed
ourselves, and sent our letters on board this morning.

5th. We attempted to tow down with our boats, and
came nearly abreast of Santa Cruz, their chief fortification,
when to our great surprise the fort fired two shots at us,
one of which went just over our mast; we immediately
brought to, and sent ashore to inquire the reason; we were
told that no order had come down to allow us to pass, and
that without such no ship was ever suffered to go below that
fort. We were now obliged to send to town to know the
reason of such extraordinary behaviour; the answer came
back about eleven that it was a mistake, for the brigadier
had forgotten to send the letter, which had been written
some days ago. It was, however, sent by the boat, and we
had leave to proceed. We now began to weigh our anchor,
which had been dropped in foul ground, when we were fired
upon, but it was so fast in a rock that it could not be got
up while the land breeze blew, which to-day continued

almost till four in the evening. As soon as the sea breeze came we filled our sails, and carrying the ship over the anchor, tripped it, but were obliged to sail back almost as far as we had towed the ship in the morning.

This day and yesterday the air was crowded in an uncommon manner with butterflies, chiefly of one sort, of which we took as many as we pleased on board the ship; their quantity was so large that at some times I may say many thousands were in view at once in almost any direction you could look, the greater part of them far above our mast-heads.

6th. No land breeze to-day, so we are confined in our disagreeable situation without a possibility of moving; many curses were this day expended on his Excellency.

7th. Weighed and stood out to sea. As soon as we came to Santa Cruz the pilot desired to be discharged, and with him our enemy the guard-boat went off, so we were left our own masters, and immediately resolved to go ashore on one of the islands in the mouth of the harbour. There was a great swell, but we made shift to land on one called Raza, on which we gathered many species of plants and some insects. *Alströmeria Salsilla* was here in tolerable plenty, and *Amaryllis mexicana.* We stayed until about four o'clock, and then came aboard the ship heartily tired, for the desire of doing as much as we could in a short time had made us all exert ourselves, though exposed to the hottest rays of the sun just at noon-day.

Now we are got fairly to sea, and have entirely got rid of these troublesome people, I cannot help spending some time in describing them, though I was not myself once in their town; yet my intelligence coming from Dr. Solander, and Mr. Monkhouse, our surgeon, a very sensible man, who was ashore every day to buy our provisions, I think cannot err much from truth.

The town of Rio Janeiro, the capital of the Portuguese dominions in America, is situate on the banks of the river of that name, and both are so called, I apprehend, from the Roman Saint Januarius, according to the Spanish and

Portuguese custom of naming their discoveries from the saint on whose feast they are made.

It is regular and well built after the fashion of Portugal, every house having before its window a lattice of wood, behind which is a little balcony. In size it is much larger than I could have expected, probably little inferior to any of our country towns in England, Bristol or Liverpool not excepted. The streets are all straight, intersecting each other at right angles, and have this peculiar convenience that the greater number lie in one direction, and are commanded by the guns of their citadel, called St. Sebastian, which is situate on the top of a hill overlooking the town.

It is supplied with water from the neighbouring hills by an aqueduct upon two stories of arches, said in some places to be very high; the water is conveyed into a fountain in the great square immediately opposite the governor's palace. This is guarded by a sentry, who has sufficient work to keep regularity and order among so many as are always in waiting here. Water is laid on in some other part of the town, but how it is brought there I could not hear; the water there is said to be better than the fountain, which is exceedingly indifferent, so much so as not to be liked by us, though we had been two months at sea, in which time our water was almost continually bad.

The churches are very fine, with more ornaments even than those in Europe, and all the ceremonies of their religion are carried on with more show; their processions in particular are very extraordinary. Every day one or other of the parishes has a solemn procession with all the insignia of its church, altar, and host, etc., through the parish, begging for whatever can be got, and praying in all forms at every corner of a street. While we were there one of the largest churches in the town was being rebuilt, and for that reason the parish had leave to walk through the whole city, which was done once a week, and much money collected for the carrying on of the edifice. At this ceremony all boys under a certain age were obliged to

D

attend, nor were gentlemen's sons ever excused; each of these was dressed in a black cassock with a short red cloak reaching half-way down the shoulders, and carried in his hand a lantern hung on the end of a pole about six or seven feet long. The light caused by this (for there were always at least 200 lanterns) is greater than can be imagined; I myself, who saw it out of the cabin windows, called my messmates, imagining that the town was on fire.

Besides this travelling religion, any one walking through the streets has opportunity enough to show his attachment to any saint in the calendar, for every corner and almost every house has before it a little cupboard in which some saint or other keeps his residence; and lest he should not see his votaries in the night, he is furnished with a small lamp which hangs before his little glass window. To these it is very customary to pray and sing hymns with all the vociferation imaginable, as may be imagined when I say that I and every one in the ship heard it very distinctly every night, though we lay at least half a mile from the town.

The government of this place seems to me to be much more despotic even than that of Portugal, although many precautions have been taken to render it otherwise. The chief magistrates are the Viceroy, the Governor of the town, and a Council, whose number I could not learn, but only that the viceroy had in this the casting vote. Without the consent of this council nothing material should be done, yet every day shows that the viceroy and governor at least, if not all the rest, do the most unjust things without consulting any one; putting a man into prison without giving him a hearing, and keeping him there till he is glad at any rate to get out, without asking why he was put in, or at best, sending him to Lisbon to be tried there without letting his family here know where he is gone, as is very common. This we experienced while here, for every one who had interpreted for our people, or who had only assisted in buying provisions for them, was put into jail, merely, I suppose, to show us their power. I should, however, except from this one John Burrith, an officer in their customs, a man who has been here thirteen years, and has become so completely Portuguese that he is known by no other name than Don John; he was of service to our people, though what he did was so clogged with a suspicious fear of offending the Portuguese as rendered it disgustful. It is necessary for any one who should come here to know his character, which is mercenary, though contented with a little, as the present given to him demonstrated; it consisted of one dozen of beer, ten gallons of brandy, ten pieces of ship's beef, and as many of pork. This was what he himself asked for, and sent on board the keg for the spirit, and with this he was more than satisfied.

They have a very extraordinary method of keeping people from travelling; to hinder them, I suppose, from going into any district where gold or diamonds may be found, as there are more of such districts than they can possibly guard. There are certain bounds beyond which no man must go; these vary every month at the discretion of the viceroy, sometimes they are few, sometimes many leagues from the city. Every man must in consequence of this come to town to know where the bounds are, for if he is taken by the guards, who constantly patrol on their limits, he is infallibly put in prison, even if he is within them, unless he can tell where they are.

The inhabitants are very numerous; they consist of Portuguese, negroes, and Indians, aborigines of the country. The township of Rio, whose extent I could not learn, but was only told that it was but a small part of the capitanea, or province, is said to contain about 37,000 whites, and about 17 negroes to each white, which makes their number 629,000, and the number of inhabitants in all 666,000. As for the Indians, they do not live in this neighbourhood, though many of them are always here doing the king's work, which they are obliged to do by turns, for small pay, and for which purpose they came from their habitations at a distance. I saw many of them, as our guard-boat was constantly rowed by them; they are of a light copper colour,

with long, lank, black hair. As to their policy, or manner
of living when at home, I could not learn anything.

The military here consist of twelve regiments of
regulars, six Portuguese and six Creoles, and as many of
provincial militia, who may be assembled upon occasion.
To the regulars the inhabitants show great deference, for as
Mr. Forster told me, if any of the people did not pull off
their hats when they meet an officer, he would immediately
knock them down, which custom renders the people remarkably civil to strangers who have at all a gentlemanlike
appearance. All the officers of these regiments are expected
to attend three times a day at " Sala " or the viceroy's
levée, where they formally ask for commands, and are
constantly answered " there is nothing new." This policy
is intended, as I have been told, to prevent them from going
into the country, which it most effectually does.

Assassinations are, I fancy, more frequent here than in
Lisbon, as the churches still take upon themselves to give
protection to criminals. One accident of the kind happened
in the sight of S. Evans, our coxswain, a man whom I can
depend upon. He saw two people talking together, to all
appearance in a friendly manner, when one suddenly drew
a knife, stabbed the other twice, and ran away pursued by
some negroes who likewise saw the act. What the further
event of this was I could not learn.

Of the country I know rather more than of the town, as
I was ashore one whole day. In that time I saw much
cleared ground, but chiefly of an indifferent quality, though
doubtless there is much that is very good, as the sugar and
tobacco which is sent to Europe from hence plainly testify ;
but all that I saw was employed in breeding cattle, of which
they have great plenty, though their pastures are the worst
I ever saw on account of the shortness of the grass. Consequently the beef sold in the market, though tolerably
cheap, is so lean that an Englishman can hardly eat it. I
likewise saw great plantations of *Jatropha Manihot*, which is
called in the West Indies *Cassada*, and here *Farinha de Pao*
or wooden meal, a very proper name, for the cakes they make

with it taste as if they were made of sawdust. Yet it is the only bread which is eaten here, for European bread is sold at nearly the rate of a shilling a pound, and is exceedingly bad on account of the flour, which is generally heated in its passage from Europe.

The country produces many more articles, but as I did not see them or hear them mentioned, I shall not set them down, though doubtless it is capable of producing anything that our West Indian islands do; notwithstanding this they have neither coffee nor chocolate, but import both from Lisbon.

Their fruits, however, I must not pass over in silence. Those that were in season during our stay were pine-apples, melons, water-melons, oranges, limes, lemons, sweet lemons, citrons, plantains, bananas, mangos, mamme-apples, acajou-apples and nuts, *Jambosa*,[1] another sort which bears a small black fruit, cocoanuts, palm nuts of two kinds, palm berries. Of these I must separately give my opinion, as no doubt it will seem strange to some that I should assert that I have eaten many of them, and especially pine-apples, better in England than any I have met with here. I begin, then, with the pines, as the fruit from which I expected the most, they being, I believe, natives of this country, though I cannot say I have seen or even heard of their being at this time wild anywhere in this neighbourhood. They are cultivated much as we do cabbages in Europe, or rather with less care, the plants being set between beds of any kind of garden stuff, and suffered to take their chance : the price of them in the market is seldom above, and generally under a *vintain*, which is three halfpence.

All that Dr. Solander and myself tasted we agreed were much inferior to those we had eaten in England, though in general they were more juicy and sweet, yet they had no flavour, but were like sugar melted in water. Their melons are still worse, to judge from the single specimen we had, which was perfectly mealy and insipid ; their water-melons, however, are very good, for they have some little flavour or at least a degree of acid, which ours have not. Oranges are

---

[1] *Eugenia jambos*, Linn.

large and very juicy; we thought them good, doubtless better
than any we had tasted at home, but probably Italy and
Portugal produce as good, had we been there in the time of
their being in perfection.   Lemons and limes are like ours;
sweet lemons are sweetish and without flavour.   Citrons
have a faint sickly taste, otherwise we liked them.   Mangoes
were not in perfection, but promised to be a very fine fruit;
they are about the size of a peach, full of a yellow melting
pulp, not unlike that of a summer peach, with a very grateful
flavour; but the one we had was spoilt by a taste of turpentine,
which I am told does not occur in the ripe fruit.   Bananas
are in shape and size like a small thick sausage, covered
with a thick yellow rind, which is peeled off, and the fruit
within is of a consistence which might be expected of a
mixture of butter and flour, but a little slimy; its taste is
sweet with a little perfume.   Acajou or casshew is shaped
like an apple, but larger; the taste is very disagreeable,
sourish and bitter: the nut grows at the top of it.   Plantains differ [from bananas] in being longer and thinner and
less luscious in taste.   Both these fruits were disagreeable
to most of our people, but after some use I became tolerably
fond of them.   Mamme-apples are bigger than an English
codlin, and are covered with a deep yellow skin: the pulp
is very insipid, or rather disagreeable, and full of small
round seeds covered with a thick mucilage, which continually
clogs the mouth.   *Jambosa* is the same as I saw at
Madeira, a fruit calculated more to please the smell than
the taste; the other kind is small and black, and resembles
much our English bilberries in taste.   Cocoanuts are so
well known in England that I need only say I have tasted
as good there as any I met with here.   Palm nuts are of
two sorts, one long and shaped like dates, the other round;
both are roasted before their kernels are eatable, and even
then they are not so good as cocoanuts.   Palm berries
appear much like black grapes; they are the fruit of *Bactris
minor*, but have scarcely any pulp covering a very large stone,
and what there is has nothing but a light acid to recommend

it.   There are also the fruits of several species of prickly

pear, which are very insipid, and one peach also proved
very bad.

Though this country should produce many and very
valuable drugs, we could not find any in the apothecary's
shops except *Pareira Brava* and *Balsam Capivi*, both of
which we bought at excessively cheap prices, and very good
of the sort. I fancy the drug trade is chiefly carried on to
the northward, as is that of dyeing woods ; at least we could
hear nothing of them here.

For manufactures, I know of none carried on here
except that of cotton hammocks, which are used by the
people to be carried about in, as we do sedan-chairs.
These hammocks are made chiefly by the Indians. But
the chief riches of the country come from the mines, which
are situated far up the country ; indeed, no one could tell me
how far, for even the situation of them is concealed as
carefully as possible, and troops are continually employed
in guarding the roads that lead to them ; so that it is
next to impossible for any one to get a sight of them,
except those who are employed there. No one at least
would attempt it from mere curiosity, for everybody who is
found on the road without being able to give a good account
of himself is hanged immediately. From these mines a
great quantity of gold undoubtedly comes, but it is purchased
at a vast cost of lives ; 40,000 negroes are annually imported on the king's account for this purpose, and notwithstanding this the year before last they died so fast that
20,000 more were obliged to be drafted from the town of
Rio.

Precious stones are also found here in very large
quantities, so large that they do not allow more than a
certain quantity to be collected in a year. A troop of
people is sent into the country where they are found, and
ordered to return when they have collected a certain
quantity, which they sometimes do in a month, more or less ;
they then return, and after that it is death for any one to
be found in the country on any pretence whatever until the
following year. Diamonds, topazes of several different

qualities, and amethysts, are the stones most usually found.
Of the first I did not see any, but was told that the viceroy
had by him large quantities, and would sell them on the
King of Portugal's account, but in that case they would not
be at all cheaper than those in Europe.   I bought a few
topazes and amethysts as specimens ;   the former were
divided into three sorts of very different value, called here
pinga d'agua qualidade premeiro and *segondo*, and *chrystallos
ormerillos.*   They were sold, large and small, good and bad
together, by octaves, or the eighth part of an ounce : the
first sort 4s. 9d., the second 2s. 4d., the third 3d. ; but
it was smuggling in the highest degree to have anything to
do with them.

Formerly there were jewellers here who cut stones, but
about fourteen months ago orders came from the King of
Portugal that no more stones should be wrought here
except on his account.   The jewellers were immediately
ordered to bring all their tools to the viceroy, and from that
time to this have not been suffered to do anything for their
support ; there are, however, a number of slaves who cut
stones for the King of Portugal.

The coin current here is either that of Portugal, especially
thirty-six shilling pieces, or coin made here, which is much
debased, particularly the silver.   These are called petacks, of
which there are two sorts, one of less value than the other,
easily distinguishable by the number of reis marked on
them, but they are little used.   They also have copper coins
like those in Portugal of five and ten rey pieces.   Two of
the latter are worth three halfpence; forty petacks are worth
thirty-six shillings.

The harbour of Rio de Janeiro is certainly a very good
one : the entrance is not wide, but the sea breeze which
blows every morning makes it easy for any ship to go in
before the wind, and when you get abreast of the town it
increases in breadth prodigiously, so that almost any number
of ships might lie in five or six fathoms of water with an
oozy bottom.   It is defended by many works, especially the
entrance, where it is narrow, and where is their strongest

fortification, Santa Cruz, and another opposite it. There is also a platform mounting about twenty-two guns, just under the Sugar-loaf on the seaside, but it seems entirely calculated to hinder the landing of an enemy in a sandy bay, from whence there is a passage to the back part of the town, which is entirely undefended, except that the whole town is open to the guns of the citadel, St. Sebastian, as I said before. Between Santa Cruz and the town are several small batteries of five or ten guns, and one fairly large one called Berga Leon. Immediately before the town is the Ilhoa dos Cobras, an island fortified all round, which seems incapable of doing much mischief owing to its immense size; at least it would take more men to defend it, even tolerably, in case of an attack, than could possibly be spared from a town totally without lines or any defence round it. Santa Cruz, their chief fortification, on which they most rely, seems quite incapable of making any great resistance if smartly attacked by shipping. It is a stone fort, mounting many guns indeed, but they lie tier above tier, and are consequently very open to the attack of a ship which may come within two cable lengths or less; besides, they have no supply of water but what they obtain from a cistern, in which they catch the rain, or, in times of drought, which they supply from the adjacent country. This cistern they have been obliged to build above ground, lest the water should become tainted by the heat of the climate, which a free access of air prevents; consequently should a fortunate shot break the cistern, the defenders would be reduced to the utmost necessity.

I was told by a person who certainly knew, and I believe meant to inform me rightly, that a little to the southward, just without the south head of the harbour, was a bay in which boats might land with all facility without obstruction, as there is no kind of work there, and that from this bay it is not above three hours' march to the town, which is approached from the back, where it is as defence-less as the landing-place; but this seems incredible. Yet I am inclined to believe it of these people, whose chief policy consists in hindering people as much as possible from looking about them. It may therefore be, as my informer said, that the existence of such a bay has been but lately discovered; indeed, were it not for that policy, I could believe anything of their stupidity and ignorance. As an example of this, the governor of the town, Brigadier-General Don Pedro de Mendozay Furtado, asked the captain of our ship whether the transit of Venus, which we were going to observe, were not the passing of the North Star to the South Pole, as he said he had always understood it to be.

The river, and indeed the whole coast, abounds with greater variety of fish than I have ever seen; seldom a day passed in which we had not one or more new species brought to us. Indeed the bay is the most convenient place for fishing I have ever seen, for it abounds with islands between which there is shallow water and proper beaches for drawing the seine. The sea also without the bay is full of dolphins, and large mackerel of several sorts, who very readily bite at the hooks which the inhabitants tow after their boats for that purpose. In short, the country is capable, with very little industry, of producing infinite plenty, both of necessaries and luxuries: were it in the hands of Englishmen we should soon see its consequence, as things are tolerably plentiful even under the direction of the Portuguese, whom I take to be, without exception, the laziest as well as the most ignorant race in the whole world.

The climate here is, I fancy, very good. During our whole stay the thermometer was never above 83°, but we had a good deal of rain, and once it blew very hard. I am inclined to think that this country has rather more rain than those in the same northern latitude are observed to have, not only from what happened during our short stay, but from Marcgrav, who gives us meteorological observations on this climate for three years. It appears that it rained here in those years almost every other day throughout the year, but more especially in May and June, when it rained almost without ceasing.[1]

---

[1] Here follows, in the manuscript, a list of 316 plants collected by Banks near Rio de Janeiro.

CHAPTER III

Birds — Christmas — Insects floating at sea — "Baye sans fond " — *Cancer gregarius—Fucus giganteus*—Penguins—Terra del Fuego—Staten Island —Vegetation—Winter's bark, celery—Fuegians—Excursion inland — Great cold and snow-storm—Sufferings of the party—Death of two men from cold—Return to ship—Shells—Native huts—General appearance of the country—Animals—Plants—Scurvy grass, celery—Inhabitants and customs—Language—Food—Arms—Probable nomadic habits—Dogs —Climate.

8th December. Soon after daybreak a shark appeared, which took the bait very readily. While we were playing him under the cabin window he cast something out of his mouth which either was, or appeared very like, his stomach; this it threw out and drew in again many times. I have often heard from seamen that they can do it, but never before saw anything like it.

11th. This morning we took a shark, which cast up its stomach when hooked, or at least appeared to do so. It proved to be a female, and on being opened six young ones were taken out of her, five of which were alive, and swam briskly in a tub of water. The sixth was dead, and seemed to have been so for some time.

13th. At night a squall, with thunder and lightning, which made us hoist the lightning chain.

22nd. Shot one species of Mother Carey's chickens and two shearwaters; both proved new, *Procellaria gigantea* and *sandalecta.* The Carey was one but ill-described by Linnæus, *Procellaria fregata.* While we were shooting, the people were employed in bending the new set of sails for Cape Horn.

23rd. Killed another new *Procellaria* (*æquorea*) and many of the sorts we had seen yesterday. Caught *Holothuria angustata*, and a species of floating *Helix*, much smaller than those under the line, and a very small *Phyllodoce velella*, sometimes not so large as a silver penny, yet I believe it was the common species. In the evening I went out again, and killed an albatross, *Diomedea exulans*, measuring nine feet one inch between the tips of his wings, and struck one turtle (*Testudo caretta*).

25th. Christmas Day : all good Christians, that is to say, all good hands, got abominably drunk, so that all through the night there was scarce a sober man in the ship. Weather, thank God, very moderate, or the Lord knows what would have become of us.

27th. The water has been discoloured all day, the depth being fifty fathoms. All this day I have noticed a singular smell from windward, though the people in the ship did not take notice of it ; it was like rotten seaweed, and at times very strong.

During the whole of the gale which was blowing to-day we had many *Procellariæ* about the ship—at some times immense numbers. They seemed perfectly unconcerned at the weather, or the height of the sea, but continued, often flapping, near the surface of the water as if fishing.

29th. We observed now some feathers and pieces of reed floating by the ship, which made us get up the hoave-net to see what they were. Soon after some drowned *Carabi* and *Phalænæ* came past, which we took, as well as many other specimens, by means of the hoave. A large *Sphinx* was also taken (lat. 41° 48′).

30th. Water very white, almost of a clay colour : sounded forty-seven fathoms. Plenty of insects passed by this morning, many especially of the *Carabi*, alive, some *Grylli*, and one *Phalæna*. I stayed in the main chains from eight till twelve, dipping for them with the hoave, and took vast numbers. In the evening many *Phalænæ* and two *Papiliones* came flying about the ship : of the first we took about twenty, but the last would not come near enough, and at last flew away ; they appeared large. Both yesterday and to-day we also took several ichneumons flying about the rigging. All the seamen say that we cannot be less than twenty leagues from the land, but I doubt *Grylli*, especially, coming so far alive, as they must float all the way upon the water. The sailors ground their opinion chiefly on the soundings, the bottom being continuously of sand of different colours, which, had we been nearer the land, would have been intermixed with shells. Their experience of this coast must, however, be slight.

Lat. 42° 31'. A sea-lion was entered in the log-book as being seen to-day, but I did not see it. I saw, however, a whale, covered with barnacles as the seamen told me. It appeared of a reddish colour, except the tail, which was black like those to the northward.

31st. No insects seen to-day; the water changed to a little better colour. On looking over the insects taken yesterday I find thirty-one land species, all so like in size and shape to those of England that they are scarcely distinguishable from the latter; probably some will turn out identically the same. We ran among them 160 miles by the log, without reckoning any part of last night, though they were seen till dark. We must be now nearly opposite to " Baye sans fond," [1] near which place Mr. Dalrymple supposes that there is a passage quite through the continent of America. It would appear by what we have seen that there is at least a very large river, probably at this time much flooded, although it is doubtful whether even that could have so great an effect (supposing us to be twenty leagues from the land) as to render the water almost of a clay colour, and to bring insects such as *Grylli* and an *Aranea*, which never fly twenty yards. I lament much not having tasted the water at the time, which never occurred to me, but probably the difference of saltness would have been hardly perceptible to the taste, and my hydrostatic balance being broken I had no other method of trying it.

2nd January 1769. Met with some small shoals of red

_____
[1] Probably the Gulf of San Mathias.

lobsters, which have been seen by almost every one passing through these seas ; they were, however, so far from colouring the sea red, as Dampier and Cowley say they do, that I may affirm that we never saw more than a few hundreds of them at a time.   We called them *Cancer gregarius.*

3rd. This evening many large bunches of seaweed floated by the ship, and we caught some of it with hooks.   It was of immense size, every leaf four feet long, and the stalk about twelve.   The footstalk of each leaf was swelled into a long air-vessel.   Mr. Gore tells me that he has seen this weed grow quite to the top of the water in twelve fathoms ; if so, the swelled footstalks are probably the trumpet-grass or weed of the Cape of Good Hope.   We described it, how-ever, as it appeared, and called it *Fucus giganteus.*[1]

5th. In some of the water taken up we observed a small and very nimble insect of a conical figure, which moved with a kind of whorl of legs or tentacula round the base of the cone.   We could not find any *Nereides,* or indeed any other insect than this, in the water, but were not able to prove that he was the cause of the lightness of the water, which was much observed hereabouts, so we deferred our observations on the animal until the morning.

7th. We now for the first time saw some of the birds called *penguins* by the southern navigators : they seem much of the size and not unlike *Alca pica,* but are easily known by streaks upon their faces and their remarkably shrill cry, different from that of any sea-bird I am acquainted with.   We saw also several seals, but much smaller than those I have seen in Newfoundland, and black ; they gener-ally appeared in lively action, leaping out of the water like porpoises, so much so that some of our people were deceived by them, mistaking them for fish.

During a gale which had lasted yesterday and to-day we observed vast numbers of birds about us.   *Procellariæ* of all kinds we have before mentioned ; gray ones and another kind, all black, *Procellaria æquinoctialis ?* Linn.   We could not discern whether or not their beaks were yellow.

[1] *Macrocystis pyrifera,* Ag.

There were also plenty of albatrosses. Indeed, I have observed a much greater quantity of birds upon the wing in gales than in moderate weather, owing perhaps to the tossing of the waves, which must render swimming very uneasy. They must be more often seen flying than when they sit upon the water.

The ship has been observed to go much better since her shaking in the last gale of wind; the seamen say that it is a general observation that ships go better for being, as they say, loosened in their joints, so much so that in a chase it is often customary to knock down stanchions, etc., to make the ship as loose as possible.

10th. Seals plentiful to-day, also a kind of bird, different from any we have before seen. It was black, and a little larger than a pigeon, plump like it, and easily known by its flapping its wings quickly as it flies, contrary to the custom of sea-birds in general. This evening a shoal of porpoises of a new species swam by the ship; they are spotted with large dabs of white, with white under the belly: in other respects, as swimming, etc., they are like common porpoises, only they leap rather more nimbly, sometimes lifting their whole bodies out of the water.

11th. This morning at daybreak we saw the land of Terra del Fuego. By eight o'clock we were well in with it. Its appearance was not nearly so barren as the writer of Lord Anson's voyage has represented it. We stood along shore, about two leagues off, and could see trees distinctly through our glasses. We observed several smokes, made probably by the natives as a signal to us.

The hills seemed to be high, and on them were many patches of snow, but the sea-coast appeared fertile, the trees especially being of a bright verdure, except in places exposed to the south-west wind, which were distinguishable by their brown appearance. The shore itself was sometimes beach and sometimes rock.

12th. We took *Beroe incrassata, Medusa limpidissima, plicata* and *obliquata, Alcyonium anguillare* (probably the thing that Shelvocke mentions in his *Voyage Round the*

World, p. 60), and *A. frustrum, Ulva intestinalis,* and *Corallina officinalis.*

14*th.* Staten Land is much more craggy than Terra del Fuego, though the view of it in Lord Anson's voyage is exaggerated. The Captain stood into a bay just within Cape St. Vincent [Staten Island]; and while the ship stood off and on, Dr. Solander and I went ashore. I found about a hundred plants, though we were not ashore above four hours. Of these I may say every one was new, and entirely different from what either of us had before seen.

The country about this bay is, in general, flat. Here is, however, good wood, water, and great quantities of fowl. In the cod of the bay is a flat covered with grass, where much hay might be made. The bay itself is bad, affording but little shelter for shipping, and in many parts of it the bottom is rocky and foul. This, however, may be always known in these countries by the beds of *Fucus giganteus,* which constantly grow upon the rock, and are not seen upon sand or ooze. These weeds grow to an immense length. We sounded upon them, and found fourteen fathoms of water. As they seem to make a very acute angle with the bottom in their situation in the water, it is difficult to guess how long they may be, but probably they are not less than half as long again as the depth of the water, which makes their length 126 feet; a wonderful length for a stalk not thicker than a man's thumb.

Among other things the bay affords, there is plenty of Winter's bark,[1] easily known by its broad leaf, like a laurel, of a light green colour, bluish underneath. The bark is easily stripped off with a bone or stick, as oaks are barked in England. Its virtues are so well known that of them I shall say little, except that it may be used as a spice even in culinary matters, and is found to be very wholesome. Here is also plenty of wild celery (*Apium antiscorbuticum*)[2] and scurvy grass (*Cardamine antiscor-*

---

[1] *Drimys Winteri,* Forst.

[2] *Apium prostratum,* Thou. A variety of the European celery, and as wholesome.

butica),[1] both which are as pleasant to the taste as any herbs of the kind found in Europe, and, I believe, possess as much virtue in curing the scurvy.

The trees here are chiefly of one sort, a kind of birch, *Betula antarctica*,[2] with very small leaves. It has a light white wood, and cleaves very straight. The trees are sometimes between two and three feet in diameter, and run thirty or forty feet in the bole; possibly they might, in cases of necessity, supply top-masts. There are also great quantities of cranberries, both white and red (*Arbutus rigida*).[3] Inhabitants I saw none, but found their huts in two places, once in a thick wood, and again close by the beach. They are most unartificially made, conical, but open on one side, where were marks of fire, which last probably served them instead of a door.

15th. By dinner we came to an anchor in the Bay of Good Success [Terra del Fuego]: several Indians[4] were in sight near the shore.

After dinner, went ashore on the starboard side of the bay, near some rocks, which made the water smooth and the landing good. Before we had walked a hundred yards, many Indians made their appearance on the other side of the bay, at the end of a sandy beach which forms the bottom of the bay, but on seeing our numbers to be ten or twelve they retreated. Dr. Solander and I then walked forward a hundred yards before the rest, and two of the Indians advanced also, and sat down about fifty yards from their companions. As soon as we came up they rose, and each of them threw a stick he had in his hand away from him and us: a token, no doubt, of peace. They then walked briskly towards the others, and waved to us to follow, which we did, and were received with many uncouth signs of friendship. We distributed among them a number of beads and ribbons, which we had brought ashore for that purpose,

---

[1] Closely allied to the common English weed, *Cardamine hirsuta*, Linn.

[2] The *Betula* of Banks is a species of beech, *Fagus betuloides*, Mirb.

[3] *Pernettya mucronata*, Gaudich.

[4] Banks constantly uses the term *Indians* to denote the natives of a country, throughout the "Journal."

and at which they seemed mightily pleased, so much so that when we embarked again on our boat three of them came with us and went aboard the ship. One seemed to be a priest or conjuror, at least we thought so by the noises he made, possibly exorcising every part of the ship he came into, for when anything new caught his attention, he shouted as loud as he could for some minutes, without directing his speech either to us or to any one of his countrymen. They ate bread and beef which we gave them, though not heartily, but carried the largest part away with them. They would not drink either wine or spirits, but returned the glass, though not before they had put it to their mouths and tasted a drop. We conducted them over the greater part of the ship, and they looked at everything without any remarks of extraordinary admiration, unless the noise which our conjuror did not fail to repeat at every new object he saw might be reckoned as such.

After having been aboard about two hours, they expressed a desire to go ashore, and a boat was ordered to carry them. I went with them, and landed them among their countrymen, but I cannot say that I observed either the one party curious to ask questions, or the other to relate what they had seen, or what usage they had met with; so after having stayed ashore about half an hour, I returned to the ship, and the Indians immediately marched off from the shore.

16*th*. This morning very early Dr. Solander and I, with our servants and two seamen to assist in carrying baggage, and accompanied by Messrs. Monkhouse and Green, set out from the ship to try to penetrate as far as we could into the country, and, if possible, gain the tops of the hills, which alone were not overgrown with trees. We entered the woods at a small sandy beach a little to the westward of the watering-place, and continued pressing through pathless thickets, always going uphill, until three o'clock, before we gained even a near view of the places we intended to go to. The weather had all this time been vastly fine, much like a sunshiny day in May, so that neither heat nor cold was troublesome to us, nor were there any insects to molest us, which made me think the travelling much better than what I had before met with in Newfoundland.

Soon after we saw the plains we arrived at them, but found to our great disappointment that what we took for swathe was no better than low bushes of birch reaching to about a man's middle. These were so stubborn that they could not be bent out of the way, but at every step the leg must be lifted over them; on being placed again on the ground it was almost sure to sink above the ankle in bog. No travelling could possibly be worse than this, which seemed to last about a mile, beyond which we expected to meet with bare rock, for such we had seen from the tops of the lower hills as we came. This I in particular was infinitely eager to arrive at, expecting there to find the alpine plants of a country so curious. Our people, though rather fatigued, were yet in good spirits, so we pushed on, intending to rest ourselves as soon as we should arrive on the level ground.

We proceeded two-thirds of the way without the least difficulty, and I confess that I thought, for my own part, that all difficulties were surmounted, when Mr. Buchan fell into a fit. A fire was immediately lit for him, and with him all those who were most tired remained behind, while Dr. Solander, Mr. Green, Mr. Monkhouse and myself advanced for the alp, which we reached almost immediately, and found, according to expectation, plants which answered to those we had found before, as in Europe alpine ones do to those which are found on the plains.

The air was very cold, and we had frequent snow-blasts. I had now given over all thought of reaching the ship that night, and thought of nothing but getting into the thick of the wood, and making a fire, which, as our road lay all down-hill, seemed very easy to accomplish. So Messrs. Green and Monkhouse returned to the other people, and appointed a hill for our general rendezvous, from whence we should proceed and build our wigwam. The cold now increased apace; it might be nearly eight o'clock, though the daylight was still exceedingly good, so we proceeded to the nearest valley, where the short birch, the only thing we now dreaded,

could not be half a mile across.   Our people seemed well,
though cold, and Mr. Buchan was stronger than we could
have expected.   I undertook to bring up the rear and see
that no one was left behind.   We got about half-way very
well, when the cold seemed to have at once an effect infinitely beyond what I have ever experienced.   Dr. Solander
was the first to feel it : he said he could not go any farther,
but must lie down, though the ground was covered with
snow, and down he lay, notwithstanding all I could say to
the contrary.   Richmond, a black servant, now also lay
down, and was much in the same way as the Doctor.   At
this juncture I despatched five in advance, of whom Mr.
Buchan was one, to make ready a fire at the very first convenient place they could find, while I myself, with four more,
stayed behind to persuade the Doctor and Richmond to
come on if possible.   With much persuasion and entreaty
we got through the greater part of the birch, when they both
gave out.   Richmond said that he could not go any farther,
and when told that if he did not he must be frozen to death,
only answered that there he would lie and die ; the Doctor,
on the contrary, said that he must sleep a little before he
could go on, and actually did so for a full quarter of an
hour, after which time we had the welcome news of a fire
being lit about a quarter of a mile ahead.   I then undertook
to make the Doctor proceed to it, and, finding it impossible
to make Richmond stir, left two hands with him who seemed
the least affected by the cold, promising to send two to
relieve them as soon as I should reach the fire.   With
much difficulty I got the Doctor to it, and as soon as two
men were properly warmed sent them out in hopes that
they would bring Richmond and the others.   After staying
about half an hour they returned, bringing word that they
had been all round the place shouting and hallooing, but
could not get any answer.   We now guessed the cause of
the mischief : a bottle of rum, the whole of our stock, was
missing, and we soon concluded that it was in one of their
knapsacks, and that the two who were left in health had
drunk immoderately of it, and had slept like the other.

For two hours now it had snowed almost incessantly, so that we had little hopes of seeing any of the three alive; about midnight, however, to our great joy, we heard a shouting, on which I and four more went out immediately, and found it to be the seaman, who had walked, almost starved to death, from where he lay. I sent him back to the fire and proceeded by his direction to find the other two. Richmond was upon his legs, but not able to walk; the other lay on the ground as insensible as a stone. We immediately called all hands from the fire, and attempted, by all the means we could contrive, to bring them down, but found it absolutely impossible. The road was so bad, and the night so dark, that we could scarcely ourselves get on, nor did we without many falls. We would then have lit a fire upon the spot, but the snow on the ground, as well as that which continually fell, rendered this plan as impracticable as the other, and to bring fire from the other place was also impossible from the quantity of snow which fell every moment from the branches of the trees. We were thus obliged to content ourselves with laying out our unfortunate companions upon a bed of boughs and covering them over with boughs as thickly as possible, and thus we left them, hopeless of ever seeing them again alive, which, indeed, we never did.

In this employment we had spent an hour and a half, exposed to the most penetrating cold I ever felt, as well as to continual snow. Peter Brisco, another servant of mine, began now to complain, and before we came to the fire became very ill, but got there at last almost dead with cold.

Now might our situation be called terrible: of twelve, our original number, two were already past all hopes, one more was so ill that, though he was with us, I had little hopes of his being able to walk in the morning, and another seemed very likely to relapse into his fits, either before we set out or in the course of our journey. We were distant from the ship, we did not know how far; we knew only that we had spent the greater part of a day in walking through pathless woods: provision we had none but one vulture, which had been shot on the way, and at the shortest allowance could not furnish half a meal; and, to complete our misfortunes, we were caught in a snowstorm in a climate we were utterly unacquainted with, but which we had reason to believe was as inhospitable as any in the world, not only from all the accounts we had heard or read, but from the quantity of snow which we saw falling, though it was very little after midsummer, a circumstance unheard of in Europe, for even in Norway or Lapland snow is never known to fall in the summer.

17*th.* The morning now dawned and showed us the earth as well as the tops of the trees covered with snow; nor were the snow squalls at all less frequent; we had no hopes now but of staying here as long as the snow lasted, and how long that would be God alone knew.

About six o'clock the sun came out a little, and we immediately thought of sending to see whether the poor wretches we had been so anxious about last night were yet alive; three of our people went, but soon returned with the melancholy news of their being both dead. The snow continued to fall, though not quite so thickly as before. About eight o'clock a small breeze of wind sprang up, and with the additional power of the sun began (to our great joy) to clear the air, and soon after the snow commenced to fall from the tops of the trees, a sure sign of an approaching thaw. Peter continued very ill, but said he thought himself able to walk; Mr. Buchan, thank God, was much better than I could have expected; so we agreed to dress our vulture, and prepare to set out for the ship as soon as the snow should be a little more melted. The vulture was skinned and cut into ten equal shares, every man cooking his own share, which furnished about three mouthfuls of hot meat, the only refreshment we had had since our cold dinner yesterday, and all we were to expect till we should reach the ship.

About ten we set out, and after a march of three hours, arrived at the beach fortunate in having met with much better roads on our return than in going out, as well as

being nearer to the ship than we had any reason to hope for.
From the ship we found that we had made a half-circle
round the hills instead of penetrating, as we thought we
had done, into the inner part of the country. With what
pleasure we congratulated each other on our safety no one
can tell who has not been in such circumstances.

18th. Peter was very ill to-day, and Mr. Buchan not at
all well; the rest of us, thank God, in good health, though
not yet recovered from our fatigue.

20th. This morning was very fine, so much so that we
landed without any difficulty at the bottom of the bay and
spent our time very much to our satisfaction in collecting
shells and plants. Of the former we found some very
scarce and fine, particularly limpets; of several species of
these we observed (as well as the shortness of our time
would permit) that the limpet with a longish hole at the
top of his shell is inhabited by an animal very different
from that which has no such hole. Here were also some
fine whelks, one particularly with a long tooth, and an
infinite variety of *Lepades, Sertulariæ, Onisci,* etc., in much
greater variety than I have anywhere seen. But the
shortness of our time would not allow us to examine
them, so we were obliged to content ourselves with taking
specimens of as many of them as we could in so short a
time scrape together.

We returned on board to dinner, and afterwards went
about two miles into the country to visit an Indian town, of
which some of our people had given us news. We arrived
there in about an hour, walking through a path which I
suppose was their common road, though it was sometimes
up to our knees in mud. The town itself was situated upon
a dry knoll among the trees, which had not been at all
cleared; it consisted of not more than twelve or fourteen
huts or wigwams of the most unartificial construction imaginable; indeed, nothing bearing the name of a hut could possibly be built with less trouble. A hut consisted of a few
poles set up and meeting together at the top in a conical
figure, and covered on the weather side with a few boughs

and a little grass ; on the lee side about one-eighth part of
the circle was left open, and against this opening a fire was
made.   Furniture, I may justly say, they had none ; a little,
a very little, dry grass laid round the edges of the circle
furnished both beds and chairs, and for dressing the shell-
fish (the only provision I saw them make use of) they had
no one contrivance but broiling them upon the coals.   For
drinking, I saw in a corner of one of their huts a bladder of
some beast full of water ; in one side of this near the top
was a hole through which they drank by elevating a little the
bottom, which made the water spring up into their mouths.

In these few huts, and with this small share, or rather
none at all, of what we call the necessaries and conveniences
of life, lived about fifty men, women, and children, to all
appearance contented with what they had, not wishing for
anything we could give them except beads.   Of these they
were very fond, preferring ornamental things to those which
might be of real use, and giving more in exchange for a
string of beads than they would for a knife or a hatchet.

Notwithstanding that almost all writers who have mentioned this island have imputed to it a want of wood, we
plainly distinguished, even at the distance of some leagues,
that the largest part of the country, particularly near the
sea-coast, was covered with wood, which observation was
verified in both the bays we put into.   In either of these
firing might be got close by the beach in any quantity, and
also trees, which to all appearance might be fit for repairing
a vessel, or even in cases of necessity for making masts.

The hills are high, though not to be called mountains ;
the tops of these, however, are quite bare, and on them
patches of snow were frequently to be seen, yet the time of
the year when we were there answered to the beginning of
July in England.   In the valleys between these, the soil
has much the appearance of fruitfulness, and is in some
places of considerable depth ; at the bottom of almost every
one of these runs a brook, the water of which in general has
a reddish cast like that which runs through turf bogs in
England ; it is very well tasted.

Quadrupeds I saw none in the island, unless the seals and sea-lions, which were often swimming about in the bay, might be called such; but Dr. Solander and I, when we were on the top of the highest hill reached by us, observed the footsteps of a large beast imprinted on the surface of a bog, but could not with any probability guess of what kind it might be.

Land birds were very few, I saw none larger than an English blackbird, except hawks and a vulture; but water-fowl are much more plentiful. In the first bay we were in I might have shot any quantity of ducks or geese, but would not spare the time from gathering plants; in the other we shot some, but the Indians in the neighbourhood had made them shy, as well as much less plentiful; at least so we found.

Fish we saw few, nor could we with our hooks take any fit to eat: shell-fish, however, are in the greatest abundance, limpets, mussels, clams, etc., but none of them delicate, yet such as they were we did not despise them.

Insects are very scarce, and not one species hurtful or troublesome: during the whole of our stay we saw neither gnat nor mosquito, a circumstance which few, if any, uncleared countries can boast of.

Of plants there are many species, and those truly the most extraordinary I can imagine; in stature and appearance they agree a good deal with the European ones, only in general are less specious, white flowers being much more common among them than any other colour; but, to speak of them botanically, probably no botanist has ever enjoyed more pleasure in the contemplation of his favourite pursuit than did Dr. Solander and I among these plants. We have not yet examined many of them, but what we have, have proved in general so entirely different from any before described, that we are never tired of wondering at the infinite variety of creation, and admiring the infinite care with which Providence has multiplied her productions, suiting them no doubt to the various climates for which they were designed. Trees are not numerous: a birch,

(*Betula antarctica*),[1] a beech (*Fagus antarctica*), and winter's
bark (*Winterana aromatica*),[2] are all worth mentioning, the
two first for timber, the other for its excellent aromatic
bark, so much valued by physicians.   Of other plants we
could not ascertain the virtues, not being able to converse
with the Indians, who may have experienced them; but
the scurvy grass, *Cardamine antiscorbutica*, and wild celery,
Apium antarcticum, may easily be known to contain anti-
scorbutic properties, capable of being of great service to
ships which may in future touch here.   Of these two, therefore, I shall give a short description.   *Scurvy grass* is found
plentifully in damp places near springs, in general everywhere near the beach, especially at the watering-place in
the Bay of Good Success.   When young and in its greatest
perfection it lies flat on the ground, having many bright
green leaves standing in pairs opposite each other, with an
odd one, in general the fifth, at the end.   When older it
shoots up in stalks sometimes two feet high, at the top of
which are small white blossoms, which are succeeded by
long pods.   The whole plant much resembles what is called
Lady's-smock in England, only that the flowers are much
smaller.   *Wild celery* greatly resembles the celery in our
gardens, only that the leaves are of a deeper green; the
flowers, as in ours, stand in small tufts at the top of the
branches, and are white.   It grows plentifully near the
beach, generally on soil which is just above the spring tides,
and is not easily mistaken, as the taste resembles celery or
parsley, or rather is between both.   These herbs we used
plentifully while we stayed here, putting them in our soup,
etc., and derived the benefit from them which seamen in
general find from a vegetable diet after having been long
deprived of it.

   The inhabitants we saw here seemed to be one small
tribe of Indians, consisting of not more than fifty of all

---

[1] Both the beech and birch are species of *beech* (*Fagus*): one, *F. betuloides*,
Mirb. (the birch of Banks), is an evergreen; the other, *F. antarctica*, Forst, is
deciduous-leaved.

[2] *Drimys Winteri*, Forst.

ages and sexes. They are of a reddish colour, nearly resembling that of rust of iron mixed with oil; the men are largely built, but very clumsy, their height being from five feet eight inches to five feet ten inches, and all very much of the same size. The women are much smaller, seldom exceeding five feet. Their clothes are nothing more than a kind of cloak of guanaco or seal skin, thrown loosely over their shoulders, and reaching nearly to their knees; under this they have nothing at all, nor anything to cover their feet, except a few who had shoes of raw seal hide drawn loosely round their instep like a purse. In this dress there is no distinction between men and women, except that the latter have their cloak tied round their waist with a kind of belt or thong.

Their ornaments, of which they are extremely fond, consist of necklaces, or rather solitaires, of shells, and bracelets, which the women wear both on their wrists and legs, the men only on their wrists; but to compensate for this the men have a kind of wreath of brown worsted which they wear over their foreheads, so that in reality they are more ornamented than the women.

They paint their faces generally in horizontal lines, just under their eyes, and sometimes make the whole region round their eyes white, but these marks are so much varied that no two we saw were alike. Whether they were marks of distinction or mere ornaments I could not at all make out. They seem also to paint themselves with something like a mixture of grease and soot on particular occasions, for when we went to their town there came out to meet us two who were daubed with black lines in every direction, so as to form the most diabolical countenance imaginable. These two seemed to exorcise us, or at least make a loud and long harangue, which did not seem to be addressed to us or any of their countrymen.

Their language is guttural, especially in particular words, which they seem to express much as an Englishman when he hawks to clear his throat. But they have many words which sound soft enough. During our stay among them I could learn but two of their words : *halléca*, which signifies beads, at least so they always said when they wanted them, instead of the ribbons or other trifles which I offered them ; and *oouda*, which signifies water, for so they said when we took them ashore from the ship and by signs asked where water was ; they at the same time made the sign of drinking and pointed to our casks, as well as to the place where we put them ashore, where we found plenty of water.

Of civil government I saw no signs ; no one seemed to be more respected than another ; nor did I ever see the least appearance of quarrelling between any two of them. Religion also they seemed to be without, unless those people who made the strange noises I have mentioned before were priests or exorcists ; but this is merely conjectural.

Their food, so far as we saw, was either seals or shell-fish. How they took the former we never knew, but the latter were collected by the women, whose business it seemed to be to attend at low water with a basket in one hand, a stick with a point and a barb in the other, and a satchel on their backs. They loosened the limpets with the stick, and put them into the basket, which, when full, was emptied into the satchel.

Their arms consisted of bows and arrows, the former neatly enough made, the latter more neatly than any I have seen, polished to the highest degree, and headed either with glass or flint ; this was the only neat thing they had, and the only thing they seemed to take any pains about.

That these people have before had intercourse with Europeans was very plain from many instances, first, from the European commodities, of which we saw sail-cloth, brown woollen cloth, beads, nails, glass, etc., especially the last (which they used for pointing their arrows in considerable quantity), and also from the confidence they immediately put in us at our first meeting, though well acquainted with our superiority, and from the knowledge they had of the use of our guns, which they very soon showed by making signs to me to shoot a seal. They

probably travel and stay but a short time at a place, so at
least it would seem from the badness of their houses, which
seem all built to stand but for a short time; from their
having no kind of household furniture but what has a
handle, adapted either to be carried in the hand or on the
back; from the thinness of their clothing, which seems little
calculated even to bear the summers of this country, much
less the winters; from their food of shell-fish, which must
soon be exhausted at any one spot; and from the deserted
huts we saw in the first bay we came to, which had plainly
been inhabited but a short time previously, probably this
spring.　Boats they had none with them, but as they were
not sea-sick or particularly affected when they came on
board our ship, possibly they might have been left at some
bay or inlet, which passes partly, but not entirely, through
this island from the Straits of Magellan, from which place
I should be much inclined to believe these people have
come, as so few ships before ours have anchored upon any
part of Terra del Fuego.

Their dogs, which I forgot to mention before, seem also
to indicate a commerce at some time or other with Europeans,
they being all of the kind that bark, contrary to what has
been observed of (I believe) all dogs natives of America.

The weather here has been very uncertain, though in
general extremely bad; every day since the first more or less
snow has fallen, and yet the thermometer has never been
below 38°.　Unseasonable as this weather seems to be in
the middle of summer, I am inclined to think it is generally
so here, for none of the plants appear at all affected by it,
and the insects which hide themselves during a snow blast
are, the instant it is fair again, as lively and nimble as the
finest weather could make them.[1]

[1] Here follows a list of 104 phanerogamic and 41 cryptogamic plants
collected in Terra del Fuego.

CHAPTER IV

Leave Terra del Fuego—Cape Horn—Albatross and other birds, etc.—Multiplication of *Dagysa*—Cuttlefish—Cross the line drawn by the Royal Society between the South Sea and the Pacific Ocean—Tropic birds—Occultation of Saturn—Freshness of the water taken on board at Terra del Fuego—Speculations respecting a southern continent—Marine animals—Suicide of a marine—Scurvy—Lemon juice—Lagoon Island—King George III. Island—Means adopted for preventing the scurvy—Preserved cabbage.

21st January 1769. Sailed this morning, the wind foul; but our keeping-boxes being full of new plants, we little regarded any wind, provided it was but moderate enough to let the draughtsmen work, who, to do them justice, are now so used to the sea that it must blow a gale of wind before they leave off.

25th. Wind to-day north-west; stood in with some large islands, but we could not tell for certain whether we saw any part of the mainland. At some distance the land formed a bluff head, within which another appeared, though but faintly, farther to the southward. Possibly that might be Cape Horn, but a fog which overcast it almost immediately after we saw it, hindered our making any material observations upon it; so that all we can say is, that it was the southernmost land we saw, and does not answer badly to the description of Cape Horn given by the French, who place it upon an island, and say that it is two bluff headlands (vide *Histoire des Navigat. aux terres australes*, tom. i. p. 356).

1st February. Killed *Diomedea antarctica*, *Procellaria lugens* and *turtur*. The first, or black-billed albatross, is much like the common one, but differs in being scarcely half as large, and having a bill entirely black. *Procellaria lugens*, the southern shearwater, differs from the common kind in being smaller and of a darker colour on the back, but is easily distinguished by the flight, which is heavy, and by two fasciæ or streaks of white, which are very conspicuous when it flies, under its wings. *Procellaria turtur*, Mother Carey's dove, is of the petrel kind, about the size of a Barbary dove, of a light silvery blue upon the back, which shines beautifully as the bird flies. Its flight is very swift and it remains generally near the surface of the water. More or less of these birds have been seen very often since we left the latitude of Falkland's Island, where in a gale of wind we saw immense quantities of them.

3rd. Shot *Diomedea exulans*, an albatross, or alcatrace, much larger than those seen to the northward of the Straits of Le Maire, and often quite white on the back between the wings, though certainly the same species; *D. antarctica*, lesser black-billed albatross; *D. profuga*, lesser albatross, with a party-coloured bill differing from the last in few things except the bill, the sides of which were yellow, with black between them.

4th. I had been unwell these three or four days, and to-day was obliged to keep the cabin with a bilious attack, which, although quite slight, alarmed me a good deal, as Captain Wallis had such an attack in the Straits of Magellan, which he never got the better of throughout the whole voyage.

5th. I was well enough to eat part of the albatrosses shot on the 3rd; they were so good that everybody commended and ate heartily of them, although there was fresh pork upon the table. To dress them, they are skinned overnight, and the carcases soaked in salt water until morning, then parboiled, and, the water being thrown away, stewed well with very little water, and when sufficiently tender served up with savoury sauce.

9th. This morning some seaweed floated past the ship, and my servant declares that he saw a beetle fly over her. I do not believe he would deceive me, and he certainly knows what a beetle is, as he has these three years been often employed in taking them for me.

15th. Went in the boat and killed *Procellaria velox, Nectris munda* and *fuliginosa*, which two last are a new genus between *Procellaria* and *Diomedea :* this we reckon a great acquisition to our bird collection.

17th. Saw several porpoises without any " pinna dorsalis," black on the back, white under the belly and on the nose. We saw also an albatross different from any other I have seen, it being black all over, except the head and bill, which were white.

21st. A bird not seen before attended the ship ; it was about the size of a pigeon, black above and light-coloured underneath. It darted swiftly along the surface of the water in the same manner as I have observed the *Nectris* to do, of which genus it is probably a species.

26th. Albatrosses began to be much less plentiful than they have been (lat. 41° 8′).

3rd March. Killed *Procellaria velox, velificans, sordida, melanopus, lugens, agilis,* and *Diomedea exulans.* The albatross was very brown, exactly the same as the first I killed, which, if I mistake not, was nearly in the same latitude on the other side of the continent. Caught *Holothuria obtusata, Phyllodoce velella,* exactly the same as those taken on the other side of the continent, except in size, which in these did not exceed that of an English sixpence. *Dagysa vitrea* was also the same as that taken off Rio de Janeiro ; now, however, we had an opportunity of seeing its extraordinary manner of breeding. The whole progeny, fifteen or twenty in number, hung in a chain from one end of the mother, the oldest only, or the largest, adhering to her, and the rest to each other.

Among a large quantity of birds I had killed (sixty-two in all) I found two *Hippoboscæ*, or forest flies, both of one species, and different from any described. More than probably these

belonged to the birds, and came off with them from the land.
I found also this day a large *Sepia*, or cuttlefish, lying in the
water, just dead, but so pulled to pieces by the birds that
its species could not be determined. Only this I know,
that of it was made one of the best soups I ever ate. It
was very large; and its arms, instead of being like the
European species, furnished with suckers, were armed with
a double row of very sharp talons, resembling in shape those
of a cat, and like them, retractable into a sheath of skin,
from whence they might be thrust at pleasure.

The weather has now become pleasantly warm, and the
barnacles on the ship's bottom seem to regenerate, very
few of the old ones remaining alive, but young ones without
number, scarcely bigger than lentils.

5th. It now begins to be very hot; thermometer 70°,
and damp, with prodigious dews at night, greater than any
I have felt. This renews our uncomfortably damp situation,
everything beginning to mould, as it did about the equinoctial line in the Atlantic.

7th. No albatrosses have been seen since the 4th, and
for some days before that we had only now and then a
single one in sight, so we conclude that we have parted with
them for good and all.

11th. A steady breeze had blown during the last three
days, and there was no sea at all; from whence we concluded that we had passed the line drawn between the Great
South Sea and the Pacific Ocean by the Council of the
Royal Society; notwithstanding we are not yet within the
tropics.

13th. I saw a tropic bird for the first time hovering over
the ship, but flying very high: if my eyes did not deceive
me it differed from that described by Linnæus (*Phaëton
aetherius*), in having the long feathers of his tail red. The
servants with a dipping net took *Mimus volutator* and
Phyllodoce velella, both exactly the same as those we saw in
the Atlantic Ocean (lat. 30° 45', long. 126° 23' 45").

15th. This night there was an occultation of Saturn by
the moon, which Mr. Green observed, but was unlucky in

F

having the weather so cloudy that the observation was good for little or nothing.

16*th.* Our water which had been taken on board at Terra del Fuego has remained until this time perfectly good without the least change, which I am told is very rare, especially when, as in our case, water is brought from a cold climate into a hot one; ours, however, has stood it without any damage, and drinks as brisk and pleasant as when first taken on board, or better, for the red colour it had at first has subsided, and it is now as clear as any English spring water.

20*th.* When I look on the charts of these seas, and mark our course, which has been nearly straight at N.W. since we left Cape Horn, I cannot help wondering that we have not yet seen land. It is, however, some pleasure to be able to disprove that which only exists in the opinions of theoretical writers, as are most of those who have written anything about these seas without having themselves been in them. They have generally supposed that every foot of sea over which they believed no ship to have passed to be land, although they had little or nothing to support that opinion, except vague reports, many of them mentioned only as such by the authors who first published them. For instance, the *Orange Tree*, one of the Nassau fleet, having been separated from her companions, and driven to the westward, reported on her joining them again that she had twice seen the Southern continent; both these places are laid down by Mr. Dalrymple many degrees to the eastward of our track, yet it is probable that he put them down as far to the westward as he thought it possible that the *Orange Tree* could have gone.

To strengthen these weak arguments another theory has been started, according to which as much of the South Sea as its authors call land must necessarily be so, for otherwise this world would not be properly balanced, since the quantity of earth known to be situated in the northern hemisphere would not have a counterpoise in this. The number of square degrees of their land which we have already changed into water sufficiently disproves this, and teaches me at least, that till we know how this globe is fixed in that place which has been since its creation assigned to it in the general system, we need not be anxious to give reasons how any one part of it counterbalances the rest.

21st. Took *Turbo fluitans*, floating on the water in the same manner as *Helix ianthina, Medusa porpita*, exactly like that taken on the other side of the continent, and a small *Cimex*, which had also been taken before. This last appears to be a larva; if so, it is probably of some animal that lives under water, as I saw many, but none that appeared perfect.

On *Phaëton erubescens* were plenty of a very curious kind of *Acarus phaëtonis*, which either was or appeared to be viviparous. Besides what was shot to day, there were seen man-of-war birds (*Pelecanus aquilus*), and a small bird of the *Sterna* kind, called by the seamen egg-birds; they were white with red beaks, and about the size of *Sterna hirundo*. Of these I saw several just at nightfall, flying very high and following one another, all standing towards the N.N.W.; probably there is land in that direction, as we were not far from the spot where Quiros saw his southernmost islands, Incarnation and St. John Baptist.

24th. The officer of the watch reported that in the middle watch the water, from being roughish, became suddenly as smooth as a mill pond, so that the ship, from going only four knots, at once increased to six, though there was little or no more wind than before. A log of wood also which was seen by several people to pass the ship made them believe that there was land to windward. When I came on deck at eight o'clock the signs were all gone. I saw, how-ever, two birds which seemed to be of the *Sterna* kind, both very small, one quite white and the other quite black, which from their appearance could not venture far from land.

To-day by our reckoning we crossed the tropic.

25th. This evening one of our marines threw himself overboard, and was not missed until it was much too late even to attempt to recover him. He was a very young man, scarcely twenty-one years of age, remarkably quiet and industrious, and, to make his exit more melancholy, was driven to the rash resolution by an accident so trifling that it must appear incredible to everybody who is not well acquainted with the powerful effects that shame can work upon young minds.

This day at noon he was sentry at the cabin door, and while he was on that duty, one of the captain's servants, being called away in a hurry, left a piece of sealskin in his charge, which it seems he was going to cut up to make tobacco pouches, some of which he had promised to several of the men. The poor young fellow had several times asked him for one, and when refused had told him that since he refused him so trifling a thing, he would, if he could, steal one from him. This he put into practice as soon as the skin was given into his charge, and was of course found out immediately, as the other returned and took the piece he had cut off from him, but declared that he would not complain to the officers for so trifling a cause. In the meantime the fact came to the ears of his fellow-soldiers, thirteen in number, who stood up for the honour of their corps so highly that before night they drove the young fellow almost mad by representing his crime in the blackest colours as a breach of trust of the worst description. A theft committed by a sentry on duty they made him think a most inexcusable crime, especially when the thing stolen had been given into his charge. The sergeant particularly declared that if the person aggrieved would not complain, he would himself do so, for people should not suffer scandal from the ill-behaviour of one. This affected the young man much, and he went to his hammock; soon after the sergeant called him on deck; he got up, and slipping past the sergeant, went forward; it was dusk, and the people were not convinced that he had gone overboard till half an hour after the event.

31st. Myself not quite so well; a little inflammation in my throat, and swelling of the glands.

1st April. Somewhat better to-day. As my complaint

has something in it that puts me in mind of the scurvy, I took up the lemon-juice put up by Dr. Hulme's direction, and found that that which was concentrated by evaporating six gallons into less than two has kept as well as anything could do. The small cag, in which was lemon-juice with one-fifth of brandy, was also very good, though a large part of it had leaked out by some fault in the cag: this, therefore, I began to make use of immediately, drinking very weak punch made with it for my common liquor.

4th. At ten this morning my servant, Peter Briscoe, saw land which we had almost passed by; we stood towards it, and found it to be a small island (Lagoon Island) about a mile and a half or two miles in length; those who were upon the topmast-head perceived it to be nearly circular, and to have a lagoon or pool of water in the middle, which occupied by far the largest part of the island. About noon we were close to it, within a mile or thereabouts, and distinctly saw inhabitants, of whom we counted twenty-four; they appeared to us through our glasses to be tall and to have very large heads, or possibly much hair upon them; eleven of them walked along the beach abreast of the ship, each with a pole or pike as long again as himself in his hand. Every one of them was stark naked, and appeared of a brown copper colour; as soon, however, as the ship had fairly passed the island they retired higher up on the beach and seemed to put on some clothes, or at least cover themselves with something which made them appear of a light colour.

The island was covered with trees of many different verdures: the palms or cocoanut trees we could plainly distinguish, particularly two that were amazingly taller than their fellows, and at a distance bore a great resemblance to flags. The land seemed very low; though at a distance several parts of it had appeared high, yet when we came near them they proved to be clumps of palms. Under the shade of these were the houses of the natives, in spots cleared of all underwood, so that pleasanter groves cannot be imagined, at least so they appeared to us, whose eyes had so long been unused to any other object than water and sky.

After dinner, land was again seen, with which we came up at sunset ; it proved a small island, not more than three-quarters of a mile in length, but almost round.   We ran within less than a mile of it, but saw no signs of inhabitants, or any cocoanut trees, or indeed any that bore the least resemblance to palms, though there were many sorts of trees, or at least many varieties of verdure.

In the neighbourhood of both this and the other island were many birds, man-of-war birds, and a small black sort of *Sterna* with a white spot on its head, which the seamen called noddies, but said that they were much smaller than the West Indian noddies.

While we were near the island a large fish was taken with a towing-line baited with a piece of pork rind cut like a swallow's tail ; the seamen called it a king-fish (*Scomber lanceolatus*).

9*th*. It is now almost night, and time for me to wind up the clue of my this day's lucubrations ; so, as we have found no island, I shall employ the time and paper which I had allotted to describe one in a work which I am sure will be more useful, if not more entertaining, to all future navigators, by describing the method which we took to cure cabbage in England.   This cabbage we have eaten every day since we left Cape Horn, and have now good store remaining ; as good, to our palates at least, and fully as green and pleasing to the eye as if it were bought fresh every morning at Covent Garden Market.   Our steward has given me the receipt, which I shall copy exactly—false spelling excepted.

Take a strong iron-bound cask, for no weak or wooden-bound one should ever be trusted in a long voyage.   Take out the head, and when the whole is well cleaned, cover the bottom with salt ; then take the cabbage, and, stripping off the outside leaves, take the rest leaf by leaf till you come to the heart, which cut into four.   Lay these leaves and heart about two or three inches thick upon the salt, and sprinkle salt freely over them ; then lay cabbage upon the salt, *stratum super stratum*, till the cask is full.   Then lay on the head of the cask with a weight which, in five or six

days, will have pressed the cabbage into a much smaller
compass.   After this, fill up the cask with more cabbage, as
before directed, and head it up.

N.B.—The cabbage should be gathered in dry weather,
some time after sunrise, so that the dew may not be upon it.
Halves of cabbages are better for keeping than single leaves.

10*th.* Weather very hazy and thick: about nine it cleared
up a little, and showed us Osnaburg Island, discovered by
the *Dolphin* in her last voyage.   About one o'clock land
was seen ahead in the direction of George's Land ; it was,
however, so faint that very few could see it.

11*th.* Up at five this morning to examine a shark
caught yesterday evening : it proves to be a blue shark
(*Squalus glaucus*).   To-day we caught two more, which were
the common gray shark (*Squalus carcharias*), on one of
which were some sucking-fish (*Echeneis remora*).   The seamen tell us that the blue shark is the worst of all to eat ;
indeed, its smell is abominably strong, so as we have two of
the better sort it was hove overboard.

As I am now on the brink of going ashore after a long
passage, thank God, in as good health as man can be, I shall
fill a little paper in describing the means which I have taken
to prevent the scurvy in particular.

The ship was supplied by the Admiralty with sour-crout,
of which I eat constantly, till our salted cabbage was opened,
which I preferred : as a pleasant substitute, wort was served
out almost constantly, and of this I drank a pint or more
every evening, but all this did not check the distemper so
entirely as to prevent my feeling some small effect of it.
About a fortnight ago my gums swelled, and some small
pimples rose on the inside of my mouth, which threatened
to become ulcers ; I then flew to the lemon juice, which had
been put up for me according to Dr. Hulme's method,
described in his book, and in his letter, which is inserted
here.[1]   Every kind of liquor which I used was made sour

---

[1] To J. BANKS, Esq., Burlington Street.—Sir—The vessels containing the
orange and lemon juice, sent by Dr. Fothergill, were to be marked, that
you might know their contents ; but lest in the hurry of sending them that

with the lemon juice No. 3, so that I took nearly six ounces a day of it; the effect of this was surprising, in less than a week my gums became as firm as ever, and at this time I am troubled with nothing but a few pimples on my face, which have not deterred me from leaving off the juice entirely.

circumstance should have been neglected, I will take the liberty to explain them.

The case No. 1 contains six gallons of lemon juice evaporated down to less than two gallons. The large cask, No. 2, contains seven gallons of orange juice and one gallon of brandy. The small cask, No. 3, contains five quarts of lemon juice and one of brandy.

When you come to make use of the juice which is in the casks, do not open the bung-hole, but draw it off at the end of the cask by means of a wooden cock, and make a vent-hole with a peg in it at the top of the cask; and always observe this method when you draw off the juice you keep in casks. It would not be amiss if you were to take out with you several wooden cocks, lest any should be lost or broken; and perhaps two or three strong iron-bound casks, holding ten gallons apiece, might be very useful for taking in a quantity of orange, lemon or lime juice, when you touch at any place abroad where those fruits grow. Besides the juices I would recommend to you to carry out a quantity of molasses, and two or three pounds of the best Chio and Strasburg turpentine, in order to brew beer with for your daily drink when your water becomes bad. So small a quantity of molasses as two gallons, or two gallons and a half, are said to be sufficient for making an hogshead of tolerably good beer, and this method of brewing beer at sea will be peculiarly useful in case you should have stinking water on board; for I find by experiments that the smell of stinking water will be entirely destroyed by the process of fermentation. I sincerely wish you and your companions a most prosperous voyage and a safe return to old England, loaded with all the honours you so justly deserve,—and am, sir, your most humble servant,

N. HULME.

HATTON GARDEN, *August* 1, 1768.

CHAPTER V

OTAHITE

APRIL 13—JULY 12, 1769

Reception by natives—Peace offerings and ceremonies—Thieving—Natives fired upon—Death of Mr. Buchan, the artist—Lycurgus and Hercules—Tents erected—An honest native—Flies—Music—A foreign axe found—Thefts—Names of the natives—The *Dolphin's* queen—Quadrant stolen—Dootahah made prisoner—Visit to Dootahah—Wrestling—Tubourai offended—Natives at divine service—Cask stolen—Natives swimming in surf—*Imao*—Transit of Venus—Nails stolen by sailors—Mourning—Previous visit of foreign ships—Banks takes part in a native funeral ceremony—Travelling musicians—Canoes seized for thefts—Dogs as food—Circumnavigation of the island—Image of man made of basketwork—Gigantic buildings (*marai*)—Battlefield—Return to station—Breadfruit—Excursion inland—Volcanic nature of the island—Seeds planted—Dismantling the fort—Banks engages a native to go to England.

13th. This morning early we came to an anchor in Port-royal by King George-the-Third's Island. Before the anchor was down we were surrounded by a large number of canoes, the people trading very quietly and civilly, chiefly for beads, in exchange for which they gave cocoanuts, breadfruit both roasted and raw, some small fish and apples. They had one pig with them which they refused to sell for nails upon any account, but repeatedly offered it for a hatchet; of these we had very few on board, so thought it better to let the pig go than to give one of them in exchange, knowing, on the authority of those who had been here before, that if we did so they would never lower their price.

As soon as the anchors were well down the boats were hoisted out, and we all went ashore, where we were met by some hundreds of the inhabitants, whose faces at least gave

evident signs that we were not unwelcome guests, although
at first they hardly dared approach us; after a little while
they became very familiar. The first who approached us
came creeping almost on his hands and knees, and gave us
a green bough, the token of peace; this we received, and
immediately each of us gathered a green bough and carried
it in our hands. They marched with us about half a mile,
then made a general halt, and scraping the ground clean from
the plants that grew upon it, every one of the chiefs threw
his bough down upon the bare place, and made signs that
we should do the same. The marines were drawn up, and,
marching in order, dropped each a bough upon those that
the Indians had laid down; we all followed their example,
and thus peace was concluded. We then walked into the
woods followed by the whole train, to whom we gave beads
and small presents. In this manner we proceeded for
four or five miles, under groves of cocoanut and bread-
fruit trees, loaded with a profusion of fruit, and giving the
most grateful shade I have ever experienced. Under these
were the habitations of the people, most of them without
walls; in short, the scene that we saw was the truest picture
of an Arcadia of which we were going to be kings that the
imagination can form.

Our pleasure in seeing this was, however, not a little
allayed by finding in all our walk only two hogs, and not
one fowl. Those of our crew who had been with the
Dolphin told us that the people whom we saw were only of
the common sort, and that the bettermost had certainly
removed: as a proof of this they took us to the place where
the Queen's palace had formerly stood, and of which there
were no traces left. We, however, resolved not to be dis-
couraged at this, but to proceed to-morrow morning in
search of the place to which these superior people had removed, in hopes of making the same peace with them as
with our friends the blackguards.

14th. Several canoes came to the ship, including two in
which were people who, by their dress and appearance,
seemed to be of a rank superior to those whom we had seen

yesterday. These we invited to come on board, and in coming into the cabin each singled out his friend: one took the captain, and the other chose myself. Each took off a large part of his clothes, and dressed his friend with what he took off; in return for this we presented them with a hatchet and some beads apiece. As they made many signs to us to go to the places where they lived, to the south-west of where we lay, the boats were hoisted out, and, taking them with us, we immediately proceeded according to their directions.

After rowing about a league, they beckoned us on shore, and showed us a long house where they gave us to understand that they lived: here we landed and were met by some hundreds of the inhabitants, who conducted us into the long house. Mats were spread, and we were desired to sit down fronting an old man whom we had not before seen. He immediately ordered a cock and a hen to be brought, which were presented to Captain Cook and myself. We accepted the present; a piece of cloth was then presented to each of us, perfumed, not disagreeably, after their manner, as they took great pains to make us understand. My piece was eleven yards long by two wide. For this I made return by presenting him with a large laced silk neck-cloth I had on, and a linen pocket handkerchief: these he immediately put on and seemed much pleased. After this ceremony was over we walked freely about several large houses, attended by the ladies, who showed us all kinds of civilities.

We now took leave of our friendly chief, and proceeded along shore for about a mile, when we were met by a throng of people, at the head of whom appeared another chief. We had learned the ceremony we were to go through, namely, to receive the green bough always brought to us at every fresh meeting, and to ratify the peace of which it was the emblem, by laying our hands on our breasts and saying *Taio*, which I imagine signifies friend. The bough was here offered and accepted, and every one of us said *Taio*; the chief then made signs that if we chose to eat, he had victuals ready:

we accordingly dined heartily on fish and bread-fruit with plantains, etc., dressed after their method. Raw fish was offered to us, which it seems they themselves eat. The adventures of this entertainment I much wish to record particularly, but am so much hurried by attending the Indians ashore almost all day long, that I fear I shall scarcely understand my own language when I read it again.

Our chief's own wife (ugly enough in conscience) did me the honour with very little invitation to squat down on the mats close by me; no sooner had she done so than I espied among the common crowd a very pretty girl with a fire in her eyes that I had not before seen in the country. Unconscious of the dignity of my companion I beckoned to the other, who, after some entreaties, came and sat on the other side of me. I was then desirous of getting rid of my former companion, so I ceased to attend to her, and loaded my pretty girl with beads and every present I could think pleasing to her: the other showed much disgust, but did not quit her place, and continued to supply me with fish and cocoanut milk.

How this would have ended is hard to say; it was interrupted by an accident which gave us an opportunity of seeing much of the people's manners. Dr. Solander and another gentleman who had not been in as good company as myself found their pockets had been picked: one had lost a snuff-box, the other an opera-glass. Complaint was made to the chief, and to give it weight I started up from the ground, and striking the butt end of my gun, made a rattling noise which I had before used in our walk to frighten the people and keep them at a distance. Upon this every one of the common sort (among whom was my pretty girl) ran like sheep from the house, leaving us with only the chief, his three wives, and two or three better dressed than the rest, whose quality I do not guess at. The chief then took me by the hand to the other end of the house where lay a large quantity of their cloth; this he offered to me piece by piece, making signs that if it would make amends, I might take any part or all. I put

it back, and by signs told him that I wanted nothing but
our own, which his people had stolen: on this he gave me
into the charge of my faithful companion his wife, who had
never budged an inch from my elbow. With her I sat
down on the mat, and conversed by signs for nearly half an
hour, after which time the chief came back bringing the
snuff-box and the case of the opera-glass, which, with vast
pleasure in his countenance, he returned to the owners; but
his face changed when he was shown that the case was
empty. He then took me by the hand and walked along
shore with great rapidity about a mile; on the way he re-
received a piece of cloth from a woman which he carried in
his hand. At last we came to a house in which we were
received by a woman: to her he gave the cloth and told us
to give her some beads. The cloth and beads were left on
the floor by us, and she went out and returned in about a
quarter of an hour, bringing the glass in her hand, with a
vast expression of joy on her countenance, for few faces have
I seen with more expression in them than those of these
people. The beads were now returned with a positive
resolution of not accepting them, and the cloth was as
resolutely forced upon Dr. Solander as a recompense for his
loss; he then made a present of beads to the lady. Our
ceremonies ended, we returned to the ship, admiring a
policy, at least equal to any one we had seen in civilised
countries, exercised by people who have never had any
advantage but mere natural interest uninstructed by the
example of any civilised country.

15th. This morning we landed at the watering-place,
bringing with us a small tent, which we set up. Whilst
doing this we were attended by some hundreds of the natives,
who showed a deference and respect to us which much
amazed me. I drew a line before them with the butt end
of my musket, and made signs to them to sit down without
it. They obeyed instantly, and not a man attempted to set
a foot within it. Above two hours were thus spent, and
not the least disorder being committed, we proposed to
walk into the woods and see if to-day we might not find

more hogs, etc., than when we had last visited them, supposing it probable that some at least had been driven away
on our arrival. This in particular tempted us to go, with
many other circumstances, although an old man (an Indian
well known to the *Dolphin's* crew) attempted by many signs
to hinder us from going into the woods; the tent was left
in charge of a midshipman with the marines, thirteen in
number. We marched away, and were absent about two hours.
Shortly before we came back we heard several musket shots.
Our old man immediately called us together, and, by waving
his hand, sent away every Indian who followed us except
three, every one of whom took in their hands a green bough;
on this we suspected that some mischief had happened at
the tent, and hastened home with all expedition. On our
arrival we found that an Indian had snatched a sentry's
musket from him unawares and run off. The midshipman
(may be) imprudently ordered the marines to fire, which
they did, into the thickest of the flying crowd, some hundreds
in number, and pursuing the man who had stolen the musket,
killed him. Whether any others were killed or hurt no
one could tell. No Indian was now to be seen about the
tent except our old man, who with us took all pains to
reconcile them again before night. By his means we got
together a few of them, and explaining to them that the
man who had suffered was guilty of a crime deserving of
death (for so were we forced to make it), we retired to the
ship, not well pleased with the day's expedition, guilty, no
doubt, in some measure of the death of a man whom the
most severe laws of equity would not have condemned to
so severe a punishment.

16*th*. No canoes about the ship this morning, indeed we
could not expect any, as it is probable that the news of our
behaviour yesterday was now known everywhere, a circumstance which doubtless will not increase the confidence of
our friends the Indians. We were rather surprised that
the *Dolphin's* old man, who seemed yesterday so desirous of
making peace, did not come on board to-day. Some few
people were upon the beach, but very few in proportion to

what we saw yesterday. At noon went ashore, the people rather shy of us, as we must expect them to be, till by good usage we can gain anew their confidence.

Poor Mr. Buchan, the young man whom I brought out as landscape and figure painter, was yesterday attacked by an epileptic fit; he was to-day quite insensible, and our surgeon gives me very little hopes of him.

17th. At two this morning Mr. Buchan died; about nine everything was made ready for his interment, he being already so much changed that it would not be practicable to keep him even till night. Dr. Solander, Mr. Sporing, Mr. Parkinson, and some of the officers of the ship, attended his funeral. I sincerely regret him as an ingenious and good young man, but his loss to me is irretrievable; my airy dreams of entertaining my friends in England with the scenes that I am to see here have vanished. No account of the figures and dresses of the natives can be satisfactory unless illustrated by figures; had Providence spared him a month longer, what an advantage would it have been to my undertaking, but I must submit.

Our two friends, the chiefs of the west, came this morning to see us. One I shall for the future call Lycurgus, from the justice he executed on his offending subjects on the 14th; the other, from the large size of his body, I shall call Hercules. Each brought a hog and bread-fruit ready dressed as a present, for which they were presented in return with a hatchet and a nail apiece. Hercules's present is the largest; he seems indeed to be the richest man.

In the afternoon we all went ashore to measure out the ground for the tents, which done, Captain Cook and Mr. Green slept ashore in a tent erected for that purpose, after having observed an eclipse of one of the satellites of Jupiter.

18th. The Indians brought down such great provision of cocoanuts and bread-fruit to-day that before night we were obliged to leave off buying, and acquaint them by signs that we should not want any more for two days. Everything was bought for beads, a bead about as large as a pea purchasing four or six bread-fruits and a like number of cocoanuts. My tents were got up before night, and I slept ashore in them for the first time. The lines were guarded by many sentries, but no Indian attempted to come near them during the whole night.

19*th*. This morning Lycurgus and his wife came to see us and brought with them all their household furniture, and even houses to be erected in our neighbourhood, a circumstance which gave me great pleasure, as I had spared no pains to gain the friendship of this man, who seemed more sensible than any of his fellow-chiefs we have seen. His behaviour in this instance makes us sure of having gained his confidence at least.

Soon after his arrival he took me by the hand and led me out of the lines, signing that I should accompany him into the woods, which I did willingly, as I was desirous of knowing how near us he intended to settle. I followed him about a quarter of a mile, when we arrived at a small house, or rather the awning of a canoe set up on the shore, which seemed to be his temporary habitation. Here he unfolded a bundle of their cloths and clothed me in two garments, one of red cloth, the other of a very pretty matting, after which we returned to the tents. He ate pork and bread-fruit which was brought him in a basket, using salt-water instead of sauce, and then retired into my bed-chamber and slept about half an hour.

About dinner-time Lycurgus's wife brought a handsome young man of about twenty-two to the tents, whom they both seemed to acknowledge as their son; at night he and another chief, who had also visited us, went away to the westward, but Lycurgus and his wife went towards the place I was at in the morning, which makes us not doubt of their staying with us for the future.

20*th*. Rained hard all this day, at intervals so much so that we could not stir at all: the people, however, went on briskly with the fortification in spite of weather. Lycurgus dined with us, he imitated our manners in every instance, already holding a knife and fork more handily than a Frenchman could learn to do in years. In spite of the rain some provisions are brought to the market, which is kept just without the lines.

21*st*. Several of our friends at the tents this morning; one from his grim countenance we have called Ajax, and at one time thought to be a great king. He had in his canoe a hog, but chose rather to sell it in the market than give it to us as a present, which we accounted for by his having in the morning received a shirt in return for a piece of cloth; this may have made him fear that had he given the hog it might have been taken into the bargain, a proceeding very different from that of our friend Lycurgus, who seems in every instance to place a most unbounded confidence in us.

22*nd*. Our friends as usual come early to visit us, Hercules with two pigs, and a *Dolphin's* axe which he wished to have repaired, as it accordingly was. Lycurgus brought a large fish, an acceptable present, as that article has always been scarce with us. Trade brisk to-day; since our new manufacture of hatchets has been set on foot we get some hogs, though our tools are so small and bad that I only wonder how they can stand one stroke.

The flies have been so troublesome ever since we have been ashore, that we can scarcely get any business done; they eat the painter's colours off the paper as fast as they can be laid on, and if a fish has to be drawn, there is more trouble in keeping them off than in the drawing itself.

Many expedients have been thought of, but none succeed better than a mosquito-net covering table, chair, painter and drawings, but even that is not sufficient. A fly-trap was necessary within this to attract the vermin from eating the colours. For this purpose tar and molasses were mixed yesterday together, but this did not succeed, for the plate which had been smeared with it was left outside the tent to clean, and one of the Indians noticing this took the opportunity, when he thought no one was observing him, of taking some of this mixture up into his hand. I saw him, and was curious to know for what use it was intended: the gentleman had a large sore on his body, to which this clammy

G

liniment was applied, but with what result I never took the trouble to inquire.

Hercules to-day gave us a specimen of the music of this country; four people performed upon flutes, which they sounded with one nostril, while they stopped the other with their thumbs: to these four others sang, keeping very good time, but during half an hour they played only one tune, consisting of not more than five or six notes; more I am inclined to think they have not upon their instruments, which have only two stops.

23rd. Mr. Green and myself went to-day a little way upon the hills in order to see how the roads were. Lycurgus went with us, but complained much at the ascent, saying that it would kill him. We found as far as we went, possibly three miles, exceedingly good paths, and at the end of our walk we met boys bringing wood from the mountains, which we look upon as a proof that the journey will be very easy whenever we attempt to go higher.

We had this evening some conversation about an axe which was brought in the morning by Hercules to be ground. It was very different from our English ones, and several gentlemen were of opinion that it was French. Some went so far as to give it as their opinion that some other ship had been here since the *Dolphin*. The difficulty, however, appeared to be easily solved by supposing axes to have been taken in the *Dolphin* for trade, in which case old ones of any make might have been bought, for many such I suppose there are in every old iron shop in London.

25th. I do not know by what accident I have so long omitted to mention how much these people are given to thieving. I will make up for my neglect to-day, however, by saying that great and small, chiefs and common men, all are firmly of opinion that if they can once get possession of anything it immediately becomes their own. This we were convinced of the very second day we were here; the chiefs were employed in stealing what they could in the cabin, while their dependents took everything that was loose about the ship, even the glass ports not escaping them, of

which they got off with two. Lycurgus and Hercules were
the only two who had not yet been found guilty; but they
stood in our opinion but upon ticklish ground, as we could
not well suppose them entirely free from a vice their countrymen were so much given to.

Last night Dr. Solander lent his knife to one of
Lycurgus's women, who forgot to return it; this morning
mine was missing. I resolved to go to Lycurgus, and ask
him whether or not he had stolen it, trusting that if he had
he would return it. On taxing him with it, he denied
knowing anything concerning it. I told him I was resolved
to have it returned; on this a man present produced a rag
in which were tied up three knives. One was Dr. Solander's,
the other a table-knife, and the third no one claimed. With
these he marched to the tents to make restitution, while I
remained with the women, who much feared that he would
be hurt. Arrived there, he restored the two knives to the
proper owners, and began immediately to search for mine in
all the places where he had ever seen it. One of my
servants seeing what he was about brought it to him; he
had, it seems, laid it aside the day before without my
knowledge. Lycurgus then burst into tears, making signs
with my knife that if he was ever guilty of such an action
he would submit to have his throat cut. He returned
immediately to me with a countenance sufficiently upbraid-
ing me for my suspicions; the scene was immediately
changed, I became the guilty and he the innocent person.
A few presents and staying a little with him reconciled him
entirely; his behaviour, however, has given me a much
higher opinion of him than of his countrymen.

27th. Lycurgus and a friend of his (who ate most
monstrously, and was accordingly christened Epicurus) dined
with us. At night they took their leave and departed; but
Lycurgus soon returned with fire in his eyes, seized my
arm, and signed to me to follow him. I did, and he
soon brought me to a place where was our butcher, who, he
told me by signs, had either threatened or attempted to cut
his wife's throat with a reaping-hook he had in his hand.

I signed to him that the man should be punished to-morrow
if he would only clearly explain the offence, which made
him so angry that his signs were almost unintelligible. He
grew cooler, and showed me that the butcher had taken
a fancy to a stone hatchet lying in his house; this he offered
to purchase for a nail; his wife who was there, refused to
part with it, upon which he took it up and, throwing down
the nail, threatened to cut her throat if she attempted to
hinder him. In evidence of this the hatchet and nail were
produced, and the butcher had so little to say in his defence
that no one doubted of his guilt; after this we parted and
he appeared satisfied, but did not forget to put me in
mind of my promise that the butcher should to-morrow be
punished.

This day we found that our friends had names, and they
were not a little pleased to discover that we had them
likewise. For the future Lycurgus will be called *Tubourai
Tamaide*, his wife *Tamio*, and the three women who commonly
came with him, *Terapo*, *Teraro*, and *Omie*. As for our
names, they make so poor a hand at pronouncing them that
I fear we shall each be obliged to take a new one for
the occasion.

After breakfast Jno. Molineux came ashore, and the
moment he entered the tent, fixed his eyes upon a woman
who was sitting there, and declared that she had been the
queen when the *Dolphin* was here. She also instantly acknowledged him as a person whom she had seen before. Our
attention was now entirely diverted from every other object
to the examination of a personage we had heard of so much
of in Europe; she appeared to be about forty, tall, and very
lusty, her skin white and her eyes full of meaning; she
might have been handsome when young, but now few or no
traces of it were left.

As soon as her Majesty's quality was known to us, she
was invited to go on board the ship, where no presents were
spared that were thought to be agreeable to her in consideration of her services to the *Dolphin*. Among other things
a child's doll was given to her, of which she seemed very

fond; on her landing she met Hercules (whom for the future
I shall call by his real name *Dootahah*), and showed him her
presents. He became uneasy, and was not satisfied till he
also had got a doll, which he now seemed to prefer to a
hatchet; after this, however, dolls were of no value.

29th. My first business this morning was to see that the
butcher was punished, as I promised Tubourai and Tamio,
and of which they had not failed to remind me yesterday,
when the crowd of people who were with us had prevented
its being carried out. I took them on board the ship,
where Captain Cook immediately ordered the offender to be
punished; they stood quietly and saw him stripped and
fastened to the rigging, but as soon as the first blow was
given, interfered with many tears, begging that the punishment might cease, a request which the captain would not
comply with.

At night I visited Tubourai, as I often did by candle-
light, and found him and all his family in a most melancholy
mood; most of them shed tears, so that I soon left them
without being at all able to find out the cause of their grief.
An old man had prophesied to some of our people that in
four days we should fire our guns; this was the fourth night,
and the circumstance of Tubourai crying over me, as we
interpreted it, alarmed our officers a good deal; the sentries
are therefore doubled, and we sleep to-night under arms.

30th. A very strict watch was kept last night, as
intended, and at two in the morning I myself went round
the point, finding everything perfectly quiet. Our little
fortification is now complete; it consists of high breastworks
at each end; the front palisades and the rear guarded by
the river, on the bank of which we placed casks full of
water: at every angle is mounted a swivel, and two carriage-
guns pointed in the two directions by which the Indians
might attack us out of the woods. Our sentries are also
as well relieved as they could be in the most regular
fortification.

About ten, Tamio came running to the tents; she seized
my hand and told me that Tubourai was dying, and that I

must go instantly with her to his house. I went and found him leaning his head against a post. He had vomited, they said, and he told me he should certainly die in consequence of something our people had given him to eat, the remains of which were shown me carefully wrapped up in a leaf. This upon examination I found to be a chew of tobacco which he had begged of some of our people, and trying to imitate them in keeping it in his mouth, as he saw them do, had chewed it almost to powder, swallowing his spittle. I was now master of his disease, for which I prescribed cocoanut milk, which soon restored him to health.

1st May. In walking round the point, I saw a canoe which I supposed to have come from a distance, as she had a quantity of fresh water in her in bamboos. In every other respect she is quite like those we have seen; her people, however, are absolute strangers to us.

2nd. This morning the astronomical quadrant, which had been brought ashore yesterday, was missed, a circumstance which alarmed us all very much. After some time, we ascertained from Tubourai that it was in the hands of an Indian; so we set out together. At every house we passed Tubourai inquired after the thief by name, and the people readily told which way he had gone, and how long ago it was since he passed by, a circumstance which gave us great hopes of coming up with him. The weather was excessively hot, the thermometer before we left the tents was 91°, which made our journey very tiresome. At times we walked, at times we ran, when we imagined (as we sometimes did) that the chase was just before us, till we arrived at the top of a hill about four miles from the tents: from this place Tubourai showed us a point about three miles off, and made us understand that we were not to expect the instrument till we got there. We now considered our situation: no arms among us but a pair of pocket-pistols, which I always carried, going at least seven miles from our fort, where the Indians might not be quite so submissive as at home, going also to take from them a prize for which they had ventured their lives; all this considered, we thought it proper that while Mr. Green and myself proceeded, the midshipman should return, and desire Captain Cook to send a party of men after us, telling him at the same time that it was impossible that we could return till night. This done we proceeded, and at the very spot Tubourai had mentioned, were met by one of his people bringing part of the quadrant in his hand: we now stopped, and many Indians gathered about us rather rudely; the sight of one of my pistols, however, instantly checked them, and they behaved with all the order imaginable, though we quickly had some hundreds surrounding a ring we had marked out on the grass. The box was now brought to us, and some of the small matters such as reading glasses, etc., which in their hurry they had put into a pistol-case. This I knew belonged to me; it had been stolen from the tents with a horse-pistol in it, which I immediately demanded, and had immediately restored. Mr. Green began to overlook the instrument to see if any part, or parts, were wanting; several small things were, and people were sent out in search of them, some of whom returned, and others did not: the stand was not there, but that, we were informed, had been left behind by the thief, and we should have it on our return, an answer which, coming from Tubourai, satisfied us. Nothing else was wanting but what could easily be repaired, so we packed up all in grass as well as we could, and proceeded homewards. After walking about two miles we met Captain Cook with a party of marines coming after us, all not a little pleased at the event of our excursion.

The captain on leaving the tents left orders, both for the ship and shore, that no canoes should be suffered to go out of the bay, but that nobody's person should be seized or detained, as we rightly guessed that none of our friends had any hand in the theft. These orders were obeyed by the first lieutenant, who was ashore; but the second aboard, seeing some canoes going along shore, sent a boat to fetch them back. The boatswain commanding it did so, and with them brought Dootahah; the rest of the crew leaped overboard. Dootahah was sent ashore prisoner; the first

lieutenant of course could not do less than confine him, to
the infinite dissatisfaction of the Indians. This we heard
from them two miles before we reached the tents. On our
return Tubourai, Tamio, and every Indian that we let in,
joined in lamenting over Dootahah with many tears. I
arrived about a quarter of an hour before the captain, during
which time this scene lasted. As soon as he came he
ordered him to be instantly set at liberty, which done he
walked off sulkily enough, though at his departure he
presented us with a pig.

3rd. No kind of provisions brought to market to-day.

5th. At breakfast - time two messengers came from
Dootahah to remind the captain of his promise [given yester-
day] to visit him ; accordingly the boat set out, carrying the
captain, Dr. Solander, and myself. We arrived in about an
hour, *Eparre*, his residence, being about four miles from the
tents. An immense throng of people met us on the shore,
crowding us very much, though they were severely beaten for
so doing by a tall good-looking man, who laid about him most
unmercifully with a long stick, striking all who did not get
out of his way without intermission, till he had cleared for
us a path to Dootahah, who was seated under a tree, attended
by a few grave-looking old men. With him we sat down,
and made our presents, consisting of an axe and a gown of
broadcloth made after their fashion, and trimmed with
tape ; with these he seemed mightily satisfied. Soon after
this Oborea [the queen] joined us, and with her I retired to
an adjacent house where I could be free from the suffocating
heat, occasioned by so large a crowd of people as was
gathered about us. Here was prepared for our diversion an
entertainment quite new to us, a wrestling match, at which
the other gentlemen soon joined us. A large courtyard
railed round with bamboo about three feet high was the
scene of the diversion ; at one end of this Dootahah was
seated, and near him were seats for us, but we rather chose
to range at large among the spectators, than confine ourselves to any particular spot.

The diversion began by the combatants, some of them

at least, walking round the yard with a slow and grave pace, every now and then striking their left arms very hard, by which they caused a deep and very loud noise, and which it seems was a challenge to each other, or to any one of the company who chose to engage in the exercise. Within the house stood the old men ready to applaud the victor, and some few women who seemed to be here out of compliment to us, as much the larger number absented themselves upon the occasion.

The general challenge being given as above, the particular soon followed it, any man singling out his antagonist by joining the finger-ends of both hands level with the breast, and moving the elbows up and down; if this was accepted, the challenged immediately returned the signal, and both instantly put themselves in an attitude to engage. This they very soon did, striving to seize each other by the hands, hair, or the cloth round the waist, for they had no other dress. They then attempted to seize each other by the thigh, which commonly decided the contest, by the fall of him who was thus taken at a disadvantage; if this was not soon done, they always parted either by consent, or their friends interfered in less than a minute, in which case both began to clap their arms, and seek anew for an antagonist, either in each other or some one else. When any one fell, the whole amusement ceased for a few moments, while the old men in the house gave their applause in a few words which they repeated together in a kind of tune. This lasted about two hours, during all which time the man whom we observed at our first landing continued to beat the people who did not keep at a proper distance; we understood that he was some officer belonging to Dootahah, and was called his *Tomite*.

The wrestling over, the gentlemen informed me that they understood that two hogs and a large quantity of bread-fruit, etc., were cooking for our dinner; news which pleased me very well, as I was by this time sufficiently prepared for the repast. I went out and saw the ovens in which they were buried; these the Indians readily showed me, telling me at the same time that they would soon be ready, and how good a dinner we should have. In about half an hour all was taken up, but Dootahah began to repent of his intended generosity (he thought, I suppose, that a hog would be looked upon as no more than a dinner, and consequently no present made in return); he therefore changed his mind, and ordering one of the pigs into the boat, sent for us, who soon collected together, and getting our knives prepared to fall to, saying that it was civil of the old gentleman to bring the provisions into the boat, where we could with ease keep the people at a proper distance. His intention was, however, very different from ours, for instead of asking us to eat, he asked to go on board of the ship, a measure we were forced to comply with, and row four miles with the pig growing cold under our noses before he would give it to us. On board, however, we dined upon this same pig, and his Majesty ate very heartily with us. After dinner we went ashore. The sight of Dootahah reconciled to us acted like a charm upon the people, and before night, bread-fruit and cocoanuts were brought for sale in tolerable quantity.

10*th.* This morning Captain Cook planted divers seeds which he had brought with him in a spot of ground turned up for the purpose; they were all bought of Gordon at Mile End, and sent in bottles sealed up. Whether or no that method will succeed, the event of this plantation will show.

We have now got the Indian name of this island, *Otahite,* so therefore for the future I shall call it. As for our own names the Indians find so much difficulty in pronouncing them that we are forced to indulge them in calling us what they please, or rather what they say when they attempt to pronounce them. I give here the list: Captain Cook is *Toote,* Dr. Solander *Torano,* Mr. Hicks *Hete,* Mr. Gore *Toarro,* Mr. Molineux *Boba* (from his Christian name Robert), Mr. Monkhouse *Mato,* I myself *Tapane.* In this manner they have names for almost every man in the ship.

11*th.* Cocoanuts were brought down so plentifully this

morning that by half-past six I had bought 350. This made it necessary to lower the price of them, lest so many being brought at once we should exhaust the country, and want hereafter; notwithstanding which I had before night bought more than a thousand at the rate of six for an amber-coloured bead, ten for a white one, and twenty for a fortypenny nail.

13th. Going on shore I met Tubourai near his house. I stopped with him; he took my gun out of my hand, cocked it, and holding it up in the air, drew the trigger. Fortunately for him it flashed in the pan. Where he had obtained so much knowledge of the use of a gun I could not conceive, but I was sufficiently angry that he should attempt to exercise it upon mine, as I had upon all occasions taught him and the rest of the Indians that they could not offend me more than by merely touching it. I scolded him severely, and even threatened to shoot him. He bore all patiently, but the moment I had crossed the river he and his family moved bag and baggage to their other house at Eparre. This step was no sooner taken than I was informed of it by the Indians about the fort. Not willing to lose the assistance of a man who had upon all occasions been particularly useful to us, I resolved to go this evening and bring him back. Accordingly as soon as dinner was over I set out, accompanied by Mr. Molineux. We found him sitting among a large circle of people, himself and many of the rest with most melancholy countenances, some in tears. One old woman on our coming into the circle struck a shark's tooth into her head several times till it foamed with blood, but her head seemed to have been so often exercised with this expression of grief that it had become quite callous, for though the crown of it was covered with blood, enough did not issue from the wounds to run upon her cheeks. After some few assurances of forgiveness Tubourai agreed to return with us, in consequence of which resolution a double canoe was put off, in which we all returned to the tents before supper-time, and as a token of renewal of friendship both he and his wife slept in my tent all night.

14*th*. Our friends Dootahah, Oborea, Otheothea, etc., at the tents this morning as usual. It being Sunday, Captain Cook proposed that divine service should be celebrated, but before the time most of our Indian friends had gone home to eat. I was resolved, however, that some should be present that they might see our behaviour, and we might if possible explain to them (in some degree at least) the reasons of it. I went, therefore, over the river, and brought back Tubourai and Tamio, and having seated them in the tent, placed myself between them. During the whole service they imitated my motions, standing, sitting, or kneeling as they saw me do ; and so much understood that we were about something very serious, that they called to the Indians without the fort to be silent. Notwithstanding this they did not, when the service was over, ask any questions, nor would they attend at all to any explanation we attempted to give them. We have not yet seen the least traces of religion among these people, maybe they are entirely without it.

15*th*. In the course of last night one of the Indians was clever enough to steal an iron-bound cask. It was indeed without the fort, but so immediately under the eye of the sentry that we could hardly believe the possibility of such a thing having happened. The Indians, however, acknowledged it, and seemed inclined to give intelligence, in consequence of which I set off in pursuit of it, and traced it to a part of the bay where they told me it had been put into a canoe. It was not of sufficient consequence to pursue with any great spirit, so I returned home. At night Tubourai made many signs that another cask would be stolen before morning ; and thinking, I suppose, that we did not sufficiently regard them, came with his wife and family to the place where the cask lay, and said that they themselves would take care that no one should steal them. On being told this I went to them, and explaining to them that a sentry was this night put over these particular casks, they agreed to come and sleep in my tent, but insisted on leaving a servant to assist the sentry in case the thief came, which he did about midnight. He was seen by the sentry, who fired at him, on which he retreated most expeditiously.

18*th.* The apples[1] now begin to be ripe, and are brought in large quantities very cheap; so that apple-pies are a standing dish with us.

29*th.* We saw the Indians amuse or exercise themselves in a manner truly surprising. It was in a place where the shore was not guarded by a reef, as is usually the case, consequently a high surf fell upon the shore, and a more dreadful one I have not often seen; no European boat could have landed in it, and I think no European who had by any means got into it could possibly have saved his life, as the shore was covered with pebbles and large stones. In the midst of these breakers ten or twelve Indians were swimming. Whenever a surf broke near them they dived under it with infinite ease, rising up on the other side; but their chief amusement was being carried on by an old canoe; with this before them they swam out as far as the outermost beach, then one or two would get into it, and opposing the blunt end to the breaking wave, were hurried in with incredible swiftness. Sometimes they were carried almost ashore, but generally the wave broke over them before they were half-way, in which case they dived and quickly rose on the other side with the canoe in their hands. It was then towed out again, and the same method repeated. We stood admiring this very wonderful scene for fully half an hour, in which time no one of the actors attempted to come ashore, but all seemed most highly entertained with their strange diversion.

30*th.* Carpenters employed to-day in repairing the long-boat, which is eaten in a most wonderful manner; every part of her bottom is like a honey-comb, some of the holes being an eighth of an inch in diameter, such progress has this destructive insect made in six weeks.

31*st.* The day of observation now approaches. The weather has for some days been fine, though in general,

---

[1] *Spondias dulcis,* Forst.

since we have been upon the island, we have had as much
cloudy as clear weather, which makes us all not a little
anxious for the success. In consequence of hints from
Lord Morton, the captain resolved to send a party to the
eastward and another to Imao, an island in sight of us,
thinking that in case of thick weather one or the other
might be more successful than those at the observatory. I
resolve to go on the Imao expedition.

1st June. The boat was not ready until after dinner,
when we set out: we rowed most of the night, and came
to a grappling just under the island of Imao.

2nd. Soon after daybreak we saw an Indian canoe, and
upon hailing her she showed us an inlet through the reef
into which we pulled, and soon fixed upon a coral rock
about 150 yards from the shore as a very proper situation
for our observatory. It was about eighty yards long and
twenty broad, and had in the middle a patch of white sand
large enough for our tents. The second lieutenant and
people therefore immediately set about fixing them, while
I went upon the main island to trade with the inhabitants
for provisions, of which I soon bought a sufficient supply.
Before night our observatory was in order, the telescopes
all set up, and tried, etc., and we went to bed anxious for the
events of to-morrow. The evening having been very fine
gave us great hopes of success.

3rd. Various were the changes observed in the weather
during the course of last night; some one or other of us
was up every half-hour, and constantly informed the rest
that it was either clear or hazy. At daybreak we rose, and
soon after had the satisfaction of seeing the sun rise as clear
and bright as we could wish. I then wished success to the
observers, Messrs. Gore and Monkhouse, and repaired to the
island, where I could do the double service of examining the
natural produce and buying provision for my companions
who were engaged in so useful a work. Tarroa, the king
of the island, came to pay me a visit. After the first
internal contact was over, I went back to the observatory,
carrying with me Tarroa, his sister Nuna, and some of their

chief attendants; we showed them the planet upon the sun, and made them understand that we had come on purpose to see it. I spent the rest of the day in examining the produce of the island, and found it very nearly similar to that of Otahite. The people, indeed, were exactly the same. Many of them we had often seen at Otahite, and every one knew well what kind of trade we had and the value it bore in that island. The hills in general came nearer to the water, and the plains were consequently smaller and less fertile than in Otahite. The low point near which we lay was composed entirely of sand and coral; here neither bread-fruit nor any other useful vegetables would grow; the land was covered with *Pandanus sectorius*, with which grew several plants we had not seen at Otahite. Among them was *Iberis*,[1] which Mr. Gore tells me is the plant called by the voyagers scurvy grass, and which grows plentifully upon all the low islands.

4*th*. What with presents and trade our stock of provisions was so large that we were obliged to give away a large quantity; this done we put off, and before night arrived at the tents, where we had the great satisfaction to find that the observation there had been attended with as much success as Mr. Green and the captain could wish, the day having been perfectly clear, without so much as a cloud intervening. We also heard the melancholy news that a large part of our stock of nails had been purloined by some of the ship's company during the time of the observation, when everybody who had any degree of command was ashore. One of the thieves was detected, but only seven nails out of one hundredweight were found upon him, and he bore his punishment without impeaching any of his accomplices. This loss is of a very serious nature, as these nails, if circulated by the people among the Indians, will greatly lessen the value of iron, our staple commodity.

5*th*. During our absence at Imao an old woman of some consequence died, and was placed not far from the fort to rot above ground, as is the custom of the island. I went

[1] *Lepidium piscidium*, Forst.

this morning to see her. A small square was neatly railed
in with bamboo, and in the midst of it a canoe awning set
up upon two posts; in this the body was laid, covered with
fine cloth. Near this was laid fish, meat, etc. for the gods,
not for the deceased, but to satisfy the hunger of the deities
lest they should eat the body, which Tubourai told us they
would certainly do, if this ceremony were neglected. In
the front of the square was a kind of stile, or place lower
than the rest, where the relatives of the deceased stood
when they cried or bled themselves. Under the awning
were numberless rags containing the blood and tears they
had shed. Within a few yards were two occasional houses;
in one of them some of the relations, generally a good
many, constantly remained; in the other the chief male
mourner resided, and kept a very remarkable dress in
which he performed a ceremony. Both dress and ceremony
I shall describe when I have an opportunity of seeing it in
perfection, which Tubourai promises me I shall soon have.

This day we kept the King's birthday, which had been
delayed on account of the absence of the two observing
parties. Several of the Indians dined with us and drank
his Majesty's health by the name of *Kilnargo*, for we could
not teach them to pronounce a word more like King George.
Tupia (Oborea's right-hand man, who was with her when
the *Dolphin* was here), to show his loyalty, got most
enormously drunk.

6*th.* In walking into the woods yesterday, I saw in the
hands of an Indian an iron tool, made in the shape of the
Indian adzes, but very different, I am sure, from anything
that had been carried out or made either by the *Dolphin* or
this ship. This excited my curiosity, the more so as I
was told that it did not come out of either of those ships,
but from two others which came here together. This was
a discovery not to be neglected. With much difficulty
and labour I at last got the following account of them, viz.
that in their month of *Pepare* (which answers to our January
1768), two Spanish ships came here, commanded by a man
whom they called *To Otterah;* that they lay eight days in a

bay called *Hidea*, some leagues to the eastward of *Matavie*, where our ship now lies; that during their stay they sent tents ashore, and some slept in them; that they were chiefly connected with a chief whose name was Orette, and whose younger brother they carried away with them, promising to return in nine months; that they had on board their ships a woman; and that on their departure they stood to the westward as long as they were seen from the island. I was very particular in these inquiries, as the knowledge got by them may be of some consequence. The methods by which I gained this account would be much too tedious to mention. One of my greatest difficulties was to determine the nationality of the ships: for this purpose I pointed to our colours and asked whether the two ships had the same or not. "No," was the answer, when the question was thoroughly understood. I then opened a large sheet of flags, and asked which of them they had. Tubourai looked steadfastly over them, and at last pitched upon the Spanish ensign, and to that he adhered, although we tried him over and over again.[1]

9th. Yesterday and to-day the *Heiva no Metua*, or chief mourner, walked. My curiosity was raised by his most singular dress, and being desirous of knowing what he did during his walk, I asked Tubourai, at the same time desiring leave to attend him to-morrow, which was readily granted upon my consenting to act a character.

Bread-fruit has for some time been scarce with us; about ten days ago, when there had been a great show of fruit, the trees were thinned all at once, and every one was employed in making *mahie* for about a week. Where the bread-fruit we now have comes from we cannot tell, but we have more than the woods around us can supply us with; probably our consumption has thinned the trees in this neighbourhood, as the *Dolphin*, which came here about this time, found great plenty during the whole of her stay. If this is the case, what we now get may be brought from

---

[1] As will appear later (see p. 370), the ships were French, under Bougainville.

some neighbouring place, where the trees are not yet exhausted.

10th. This evening, according to my yesterday's engagement, I went to the place where the *Metua* lay; there I found Tubourai, Tamio, Hoona, the *Metua's* daughter, and a young Indian prepared to receive me. Tubourai was the *Heiva*, the three others and myself were to be *Nineveh*. Tubourai put on his most fantastical though not unbecoming dress. I was next prepared by stripping off my European clothes and putting on a small strip of cloth round my waist, the only garment I was allowed to have. They then began to smut me and themselves with charcoal and water, the Indian boy was completely black, the women and myself as low as our shoulders; we then set out. Tubourai began by praying twice, once near the corpse, and again near his own house. We then proceeded towards the fort; it was necessary, it seems, that the procession should visit that place, but they dare not do it without our sanction, indeed it was not until they had received many assurances of our consent that they ventured to perform any part of their ceremonies.

To the fort then we went, to the surprise of our friends and affright of the Indians who were there, for they everywhere fly before the *Heiva*, like sheep before a wolf; we soon left it and proceeded along shore towards a place where above a hundred Indians were collected together. We, the *Ninevehs*, had orders from the *Heiva* to disperse them; we ran towards them, but before we came within a hundred yards of them they dispersed every way, running to the first shelter and hiding themselves under grass or whatever else would conceal them. We now crossed the river into the woods and passed several houses, all deserted; not another Indian did we see during the half-hour that we spent in walking about. We (the *Ninevehs*) then came to the *Heiva* and said *imatata* (there are no people), after which we repaired home; the *Heiva* undressed, and we went into the river and scrubbed one another until it was dark, before the blacking came off.

12*th*. In my morning's walk to-day I met a company of travelling musicians; they told me where they should be at night, so after supper we all repaired to the place. There was a large concourse of people round the band, which consisted of two flutes and three drums, the drummers accompanying their music with their voices. They sang many songs, generally in praise of us, for these gentlemen, like Homer of old, must be poets as well as musicians. The Indians seeing us entertained with their music, asked us to sing them an English song, which we most readily agreed to, and received much applause, so much so that one of the musicians became desirous of going to England to learn to sing. These people, by what we can learn, go about from house to house, the master of the house and the audience paying them for their music in cloth, meat, beads, or anything else which the one wants and the other can spare.

13*th*. Mr. Monkhouse, our surgeon, met to-day with an insult from an Indian, the first that has been met with by any of us; he was pulling a flower from a tree which grew on a burial-ground, and was consequently, I suppose, sacred, when an Indian came behind him and struck him; Mr. Monkhouse caught and attempted to beat him, but was prevented by two more, who, coming up, seized hold of his hair and rescued their companion, after which they all ran away.

14*th*. I lay in the woods last night, as I very often do; at daybreak I was called up by Mr. Gore and went with him shooting. We did not return till night, when we saw a large number of canoes in the river behind the tents. It appears that last night an Indian was clever enough to steal a coal-rake out of the fort without being perceived; in the morning it was missed, and Captain Cook being resolved to recover it, and also to discourage such attempts for the future, went out with a party of men and seized twenty-five of their large sailing canoes which had just come in from Tethurva, a neighbouring island, with a supply of fish. The coal-rake was upon this soon brought back, but Captain Cook thought he had now an opportunity of recovering all the things which had been stolen; he therefore proclaimed to every one that the boats should not stir until all the things were brought back. A list of the articles was immediately drawn up and read several times to the Indians, who at once promised that everything should be returned. Great application was made to me on my arrival that some of the boats might be released. I did not until I got to the fort understand the reason of their detention, but when I did nothing appeared plainer than that no one of them should on any account be given up from favour, but that the whole should be kept till the things were restored—if ever they were—which I much doubted, as the canoes did not belong to the people who had the articles. I confess, that had I taken a step so violent, I would have seized either the persons of the people who had stolen from us (most of whom we either knew, or shrewdly suspected), or at least their goods, instead of those of people who were entirely unconcerned in the affair, and had not probably interest enough with their superiors (to whom all valuable things are carried) to procure the restoration demanded.

17th. Mr. Gore and myself went to Eparre to shoot ducks, little thinking what the consequence of our expedition would be ; for before we had half filled our bags we had frightened away Dootahah and all his household with their furniture. It was no small diversion to us to find his Majesty so much more fearful than his ducks.

20th. This morning early Oborea and some others came to the tents, bringing a large quantity of provisions as a present, among the rest a very fat dog. We had lately learnt that these animals were eaten by the Indians, and esteemed more delicate food than pork ; now therefore was an opportunity of trying the experiment. The dog was immediately given over to Tupia, who, finding that it was a food that we were not accustomed to, undertook to stand butcher and cook. He killed the animal by stopping his breath, holding his hands fast over his mouth and nose, an operation which took more than a quarter of an hour : he then proceeded to dress him much in the same manner as we would do a pig, singeing him over the fire and scraping

him clean with a shell.   He then opened him with the same
instrument, and taking out his entrails, pluck, etc., sent
them to the sea, where they were most carefully washed and
put into cocoanut shells with what blood he had found in
him.   The stones were now laid, and the dog, well covered
with leaves, laid upon them; in about two hours he was
dressed, and in another quarter of an hour completely eaten.
A most excellent dish he made for us, who were not much
prejudiced against any species of food.   I cannot, however,
promise that an European dog would eat as well, as these in
Otahite scarcely in their lives touch animal food; cocoanut
kernel and bread-fruit, yams, etc., being what their masters
can best afford to give them, and what indeed from custom
I suppose they prefer to any other food.

24*th*. The market has been totally stopped ever since
the boats were seized, nothing being offered for sale but a
few apples; our friends, however, are liberal in presents, so
that we make-shift to live without expending our bread,
which last, and spirits, are our most valuable articles.   Late
in the evening Tubourai and Tamio returned from Eparre,
bringing with them several presents, among the rest a large
piece of thick cloth, which they desired that I would carry
home to my sister *Opia*, and for which they would take no
kind of return.   They are often very inquisitive about our
families, and remember anything that is told them very
well.

26*th*. At three o'clock this morning Captain Cook and
myself set out to the eastward in the pinnace, intending, if it
was convenient, to go round the island.[1]

28*th*. We saw an English goose and a turkey-cock,
which they told us had been left by the *Dolphin*, both of
them immensely fat and as tame as possible, following the
Indians everywhere, who seemed immensely fond of them.

29*th*. We saw a singular curiosity: a figure of a man
made of basket-work, roughly but not ill designed.   It was

---

[1] The circumnavigation of the island presents few interesting features
beyond what was noticed on the 28th and 29th; any differences in customs
are recorded in Chapter VII. ("General Account of the South Sea Islands").

seven feet high, and too bulky in proportion to its height; the whole was neatly covered with feathers—white to represent skin, and black to represent hair, and tallow on the head, where were three protuberances which we should have called horns, but the Indians called them *tata ete* (little men). The image was called by them *Manne.* They said it was the only one of the kind in Otahite, and readily attempted to explain its use, but their language was totally unintelligible, and seemed to refer to some customs to which we are perfect strangers. Several miles farther on we went ashore again, though we saw nothing remarkable but a burying-ground, whose pavement was unusually neat. It was ornamented by a pyramid about five feet high, covered entirely with the fruits of *Pandanus odorus* and *Cratæva gynandra.* In the middle, near the pyramid, was a small image of stone very roughly worked, the first instance of carving in stone that I have seen among these people. This they seemed to value, as it was protected from the weather by a kind of shed built purposely over it. Near it were three human skulls, laid in order, very white and clean, and quite perfect.

We afterwards took a walk towards a point on which we had from afar observed trees of *etoa* (*Casuarina equiseti-folia*), from whence we judged that there would be some *marai* in the neighbourhood; nor were we disappointed, for we had no sooner arrived there than we were struck with the sight of a most enormous pile, certainly the masterpiece of Indian architecture in this island, and so all the inhabitants allowed. Its size and workmanship almost exceed belief. Its form was similar to that of *marais* in general, resembling the roof of a house, not smooth at the sides, but formed into eleven steps, each of these four feet in height, making in all 44 feet; its length was 267 feet, its breadth 71 feet. Every one of these steps was formed of white coral stones, most of them neatly squared and polished; the rest were round pebbles, but these, from their uniformity of size and roundness, seemed to have been worked. Some of the coral stones were very large, one I measured was $3\frac{1}{2}$ by $2\frac{1}{2}$ feet.

The foundation was of rock stone, likewise squared; the corner-stone measured 4 feet 7 inches by 2 feet 4 inches. The building made part of one side of a spacious area walled in with stone; the size of this, which seemed to be intended for a square, was 118 by 110 paces, and it was entirely paved with flat paving-stones. It is almost beyond belief that Indians could raise so large a structure without the assistance of iron tools to shape their stones or mortar to join them; which last appears almost essential, as most of them are round: but it is done, and almost as firmly as an European workman would have done it, though in some things they seem to have failed. The steps for instance, which range along its greatest length, are not straight; they bend downward in the middle, forming a small segment of a circle. Possibly the ground may have sunk a little under the immense weight of such a great pile; such a sinking, if it took place regularly, would have this effect. The labour of the work is prodigious, the quarried stones are but few, but they must have been brought by hand from some distance; at least we saw no signs of a quarry near it, though I looked carefully about me. The coral must have been fished up from under the water, where indeed it is most plentiful, but usually covered with at least three or four feet of water, and generally with much more. The labour of forming the blocks when obtained must also have been at least as great as that employed in getting them. The natives have not shown us any way by which they could square a stone except by means of another, which must be a most tedious process, and liable to many accidents through tools breaking. The stones are also polished as well and as truly as stones of the kind could be by the best workman in Europe; in that particular they excel, owing to the great plenty of a sharp coral sand which is admirably adapted to the purpose, and which is found everywhere upon the sea-shore in this neighbourhood.

About a hundred yards to the west of this building was another court or paved area, in which were several *Ewhattas*, a kind of altar raised on wooden pillars about seven feet high; on these they offer meat of all kinds to the gods. We have thus seen large hogs offered; and here were the skulls of above fifty of them, besides those of dogs, which the priest who accompanied us assured us were only a small fraction of what had been here sacrificed. This *marai* and apparatus for sacrifice belonged, we were told, to Oborea and Oamo.

The greatest pride of an inhabitant of Otahite is to have a grand *marai;* in this particular our friends far exceed any one in the island, and in the *Dolphin's* time the first of them exceeded every one else in riches and respect. The reason of the difference of her present appearance, I found by an accident which I now relate. Our road to the *marai* lay by the seaside, and everywhere under our feet were numberless human bones, chiefly ribs and vertebræ. So singular a sight surprised me much, and I inquired the reason. I was told that in the month called by them *Owarahew* last, which answers to our December 1768, the people of *Tiarreboo* made a descent here and killed a large number of people, whose bones we now saw; that upon this occasion Oborea and Oamo were obliged to flee for shelter to the mountains; that the conquerors burnt all the houses, which were very large, and took away all the hogs, etc.; that the turkey and goose which we had seen were part of the spoils, as were the jaw-bones which we had also seen; these had been carried away as trophies, and are used by the Indians here in exactly the same manner as the North Americans do scalps.

30th. At night we came to *Otahourou*, the very place at which we were on the 28th of May; here we were among our intimate friends, who expressed the pleasure they had in entertaining us, by giving us a good supper and good beds, in which we slept the better for being sure of reaching Matavie [where the ship lay] to-morrow night at the farthest. Here we learned that the bread-fruit (a little of which we saw just sprouting upon the trees) would not be fit to eat in less than three months.

2nd July. All our friends crowded this morning to see

us, and tell us that they were rejoiced at our return; nor were they empty-handed, most of them brought something or other. The canoes were still in the river, and Captain Cook, finding that there was no likelihood now of any of the stolen goods being restored, resolved to let them go as soon as he could. His friend Potattow solicited for one, which was immediately granted, as it was imagined that the favour was asked for some of his friends; but no sooner did he begin to move the boat than the real owners and a number of Indians opposed him, telling him and his people very clamorously that it did not belong to them. He answered that he had bought it of the captain, and given a pig for it; the people were by this declaration satisfied, and had we not luckily overheard it, he would have taken away this boat, and probably soon after have solicited for more. On being detected he became so sulky and ashamed, that for the rest of the day neither he nor his wife would open their mouths, or look straight at any of us.

3rd. This morning very early Mr. Monkhouse and myself set out, resolving to follow the course of the valley down which our river comes, in order to see how far up it was inhabited, etc. etc. When we had got about two miles up it, we met several of our neighbours coming down with loads of bread-fruit upon their backs: we had often wondered from whence our small supply of bread-fruit came, as there was none to be seen upon the flats. They soon explained the mystery, showing us bread-fruit trees planted on the sides of the hills, and telling us at the same time that when the fruit in the flats failed, these, which had been by them planted upon the hills to preserve the succession, were ready for use. The quantity was much less than in the lowlands, and not by any means sufficient to supply the whole interval of scarcity. When this was exhausted they were obliged to live on *ahee* nuts, plantains, and *vae* (or wild plantain), which grows very high up in the mountains. How the *Dolphin's* men, who were here much about this time, came to find so great plenty of bread-fruit upon the trees, is a mystery to me, unless perhaps the season of this fruit alters. As for their

having met with a much larger supply of hogs, fowls, etc.,
than we have done, I can most readily account for that, as
we have found by constant experience that these people
may be frightened into anything. They have often described
to us the terror which the *Dolphin's* gun caused them, and
when we ask how many people were killed, they number
names upon their fingers, some ten, some twenty, some
thirty, and then say *worrow worrow*, the same word as is.
used for a flock of birds or a shoal of fish. The *Dolphin's*
journals often serve to confirm this opinion. "When," say
they, "towards the latter end of our time provisions were
scarce, a party of men were sent towards Eparre to get
hogs, etc., an office which they had not the smallest difficulty in performing, for the people, as we went along the
shore, drove out their hogs to meet us, and would not
allow us to pay anything for them."

About a mile farther on we found houses fairly plentiful
on each side of the river, the valley being all this way three
or four hundred yards across. We were now shown a house
which proved the last we saw; the master offered us cocoanuts, and we refreshed ourselves. Beyond this we went
maybe six miles (it is difficult to guess distances when roads
are bad as this was, for we were generally obliged to travel
along the course of the river). We passed by several hollow
places under stones where, we were told, that people who
were benighted slept. At length we arrived at a place
where the river was banked on each side with steep rocks;
and a cascade which fell from them made a pool so deep,
that the Indians said we could not go beyond it—they never
did. Their business lay below the rocks, on each side of the
plains, above which grew great plenty of *vae*. The avenues
to these were truly dreadful, the rocks were nearly perpendicular, one being nearly a hundred feet in height, with its
face constantly wet and slippery from the water of numberless springs. Directly up the face of even this was a road,
or rather a succession of long pieces of bark of *Hibiscus
tiliaceus*, which served as a rope to take hold of and scramble
up from ledge to ledge, though upon these very ledges none

but a goat or an Indian could have stood. One of these ropes was nearly thirty feet in length; our guides offered to help us up this pass, but rather recommended one lower down, a few hundred yards away, which was much less dangerous. We did not choose to venture on it, as the sight which was to reward our hazard was nothing but a grove of *vae* trees, such as we had often seen before.

In the whole course of this walk the rocks were almost constantly bare to the view, so that I had a most excellent opportunity of searching for any appearance of minerals, but saw not the smallest sign of any. The stones everywhere showed manifest signs of having been at some time or other burnt, indeed I have not yet seen a specimen of stone in the island that has not the visible marks of fire upon it; small pieces indeed of the hatchet stone may be without them, but I have pieces of the same kind burnt almost to a pumice : the very clay upon the hills shows manifest signs of fire. Possibly the island owes its origin to a volcano, which now no longer burns, or, theoretically speaking, for the sake of those authors who balance this globe by a proper weight of continent placed near these latitudes, this necessary continent may have been sunk by dreadful earthquakes and volcanoes two or three hundred fathoms under the sea, the tops of the highest mountains only remaining above the water in the shape of islands : an undoubted proof being that such a thing now exists, to the great support of their theory, which, were it not for this proof, would have been already totally demolished by the course our ship made from Cape Horn to this island.

4th. I employed myself in planting a large quantity of the seeds of water-melons, oranges, lemons, limes, etc., which I had brought from Rio de Janeiro; they were planted on both sides of the fort in as many varieties of soil as I could choose. I have very little doubt of the former, especially, coming to perfection, as I have given away large quantities of seed among the natives; I planted some also in the woods. The natives now continually ask me for seeds, and have already shown me melon plants of their raising which had taken perfectly well. The seeds that Captain Cook sowed have proved so bad that not one has come up, except the mustard; even the cucumbers and melons have failed, owing probably to their having been packed in small bottles sealed down with rosin.

7th. The carpenters were this morning employed in taking down the gates and palisades of our little fortification to make us firewood for the ship, when one of the Indians made shift to steal the staple and hook of the great gate. We were immediately apprised of the theft, to the great affright of our visitors, of whom the bell-tent was full; their fears were, however, presently quieted, and I (as usual) set out on my ordinary occupation of thief-catching. The Indians most readily joined me, and away we set full cry, much like a pack of fox-hounds; we ran and walked, and walked and ran, for, I believe, six miles with as little delay as possible, when we learnt that we had very early in the chase passed our game, who was washing in a brook when he saw us coming, and hid himself in the rushes. We returned to the place, and by some intelligence which some of our people got, found a scraper which had been stolen from the ship and was hid in those very rushes; with this we returned, and Tubourai soon after brought the staple.

12th. This morning Tupia came on board; he had expressed his intention of going with us to England, a circumstance which gives me much satisfaction; he is certainly a most proper man, well born, chief *Tahowa* or priest of this island, consequently skilled in the mysteries of their religion; but what makes him more than anything desirable is his experience in the navigation of these people and knowledge of the islands in these seas. He has told us the names of above seventy, at most of which he has himself been. The captain refuses to take him on his own account; in my opinion sensibly enough, as the Government will never in all human probability take any notice of him. I therefore have resolved to take him; thank Heaven, I have a sufficiency, and I do not know why I may not keep him as a curiosity as well as my neighbours do lions and tigers at a larger expense than he will ever probably put me to. The amusement I shall have in his future conversation, and the benefit which will be derived by this ship, as well as any other which may in the future be sent into these seas, will, I think, fully repay me. As soon as he had made his mind known, he said he would go ashore and return in the evening, when he would make a signal for a boat to be sent off for him. He took with him a miniature picture of mine to show his friends, and several little things to give them as parting presents.

CHAPTER VI

OTAHITE TO OHETEROA

JULY 13—AUGUST 14, 1769

Departure from Otahite—Huahine—Ulhietea—God-houses—Boats and boat-houses—Otahah—Bola-Bola—Return to Ulhietea—Reception by natives —Dancing—Pearls—The King of Bola-Bola—Native drama—Oheteroa —Dress—Arms.

13*th July.* About ten this morning we sailed from Otahite, leaving our friends, some of them at least, I really believe, personally sorry for our departure. Our nearest friends came on board at this critical time, except only Tubourai and Tamio; we had Oborea, Otheothea, Taysa, Nuna, Tuanne, Matte, Pottatow, Polothearia, etc., on board. When the anchor was weighed they took their leaves tenderly enough, not without plenty of tears, though entirely without that clamorous weeping made use of by the other Indians, several boats of which were about the ship, shouting out their lamentations, as vying with each other, not who should cry most, but who should cry loudest, a custom we had often condemned in conversation with our particular friends, as savouring more of affected than real grief.

Tupia, who after all his struggles stood firm at last in his resolution of accompanying us, parted with a few heart-felt tears, so I judge them to have been by the efforts I saw him make to hide them. He sent by Otheothea his last present, a shirt, to *Potamia*, Dootahah's favourite; he and I went then to the topmast-head, where we stood a long time waving to the canoes as they went off, after which he came down and showed no further signs of seriousness or concern.

15*th*. Our Indian often prayed to *Tane* for a wind, and as often boasted to me of the success of his prayers, which I plainly saw he never began till he perceived a breeze so near the ship that it generally reached her before his prayer was finished.

16*th*. This morning we were very near the island of Huahine; some canoes very soon came off, but appeared very much frightened; one, however, came to us bringing a chief and his wife, who on Tupia's assurance of our friendship came on board. They resembled the Otahite people in language, dress, tattow, in short, in everything. Tupia has always said that the people of this island and Ulhietea will not steal, in which they indeed differ much from our late friends if they only keep up to their character.

Soon after dinner we came to an anchor in a very small bay, called by the natives Owalle, and immediately went ashore. As soon as we landed Tupia squatted down on the ground, and ranging us on one side and the Indians on the other, began to pray to the chief who stood opposite to him, answering him in a kind of response; this lasted about a quarter of an hour, in which time he sent at different intervals two handkerchiefs and some beads he had prepared for the purpose for *Eatua ;* these were sent among many messages which passed backwards and forwards with plantains, etc. In return for this present to their gods, which it seems was very acceptable, we had a hog given for our *Eatua*, which in this case will certainly be our stomachs.

17*th*. We found the productions here almost exactly the same as at Otahite—upon the hills the rocks and slag were burnt if anything more than they were in that island. The people also were almost exactly like our late friends, but rather more stupid and lazy, in proof of which I need only say that we should have gone much higher up the hills than we did if we could have persuaded them to accompany us; their only excuse was the fear of being killed by the fatigue. Their houses are very neat, and their boat-houses particularly very large: one of these I measured was fifty good paces in length, ten in breadth, and twenty-four feet in height.

The Gothic arch of which it consisted was supported on one side by twenty-six, and on the other by thirty pillars, or rather clumsy thick posts of about two feet high and one thick; most of these were carved with the heads of men, boys, or other devices, as the rough fancy and rougher workmanship of these stone-hatchet-furnished gentry suggested and executed. The flats were filled with very fine bread-fruit trees and an infinite number of cocoanuts, upon which latter the inhabitants seem to depend much more than those of Otahite; we saw, however, large spaces occupied by lagoons and salt swamps, upon which neither bread-fruit nor cocoanut would thrive.

18*th.* This morning we went to take a further view of a building which we had seen yesterday, and admired a good deal, taking with us Tupia's boy Tayeto (he himself was too much engaged with his friends to have time to accompany us). The boy told us that the building was called *Ewharre no Eatua,* or the house of the god, but could not explain at all the use of it. It consisted of a chest whose lid was nicely sewed on, and very neatly thatched over with palm-nut leaves; the whole was fixed on two poles by little arches of very neatly carved wood. These poles seemed to be used in carrying it from place to place, though when we saw it, it was supported upon two posts. One end of the chest was open, with a round hole within a square one; this was yesterday stopped up with a piece of cloth, which, lest I should offend the people, I left untouched; but to-day the cloth, and probably the contents of the chest, were removed, as there was nothing at all in it.

Trade to-day does not go on with any spirit; the people, when anything is offered them, will not rely on their own judgment, but take the opinion of twenty or thirty people about them, a proceeding which takes up much time.

19*th.* This morning trade was rather better; we obtained three very large hogs and some pigs by producing hatchets, which had not been before given, and which we had hoped to have had no occasion for in an island not hitherto seen by Europeans.

Huahine differs scarcely at all from Otahite, either in its productions or in the customs of the people. In all our researches here we have not found above ten or twelve new plants; there were, indeed, a few insects and a species of scorpion which we had not seen at Otahite. This island seems, however (this year, at least), to be a month more forward than the other, as the ripeness of the cocoanuts, now full of kernel, and the new bread-fruit, some of which is fit to eat, fully evinces. Of the cocoanut kernels they make a food, called *poe*, by scraping them fine and mixing them with yams, also scraped; these are then put into a wooden trough, and hot stones laid among them. By this means a kind of oily hasty-pudding is made, which our people relished very well, especially when fried.

The men here are large and stout; one we measured was six feet three inches high and well made. The women are very fair, more so than at Otahite, though we saw none so handsome. Both sexes seemed to be less timid, as well as less curious; the firing of a gun frightened them, but they did not fall down, as our Otahite friends generally did. On one of their people being taken in the act of stealing, and seized by the hair, the rest did not run away, but coming round, inquired into the cause, and, seemingly at least, approving of the justice, recommended a beating for the offender, which was immediately put into practice.

When they first came on board the ship they seemed struck with sights so new, and wondered at everything that was shown to them, but did not seem to search or inquire for matters of curiosity even so much as the people of Otahite did, although the latter had before seen almost everything we had to show them.

20th. At noon to-day we came to anchor at Ulhietea, in a bay called by the natives Oapoa, the entrance of which is very near a small islet called Owhattera. Some Indians soon came on board, expressing signs of fear. There were two canoes, each of which brought a woman, I suppose, as a mark of confidence, and a pig as a present. To each of these ladies was given a spike-nail and some beads, with which they seemed much pleased. Tupia, who has always expressed much fear of the men of Bola-Bola, says that they have conquered this island, and will to-morrow come down and fight with us; we therefore lose no time in going ashore, as we are to have to-day to ourselves.

On landing Tupia repeated the ceremony of praying, as at Huahine, after which an English Jack was set up on shore, and Captain Cook took possession of this and the other three islands in sight, viz. Huahine, Otahah, and Bola-Bola, for the use of His Britannic Majesty. After this we walked together to a great *marai*, called *Tapodeboatea*, whatever that may signify. It is different from those of Otahite, consisting merely of walls of coral stones (some of an immense size) about eight feet high, filled up with smaller ones, and the whole ornamented with many planks set up on end, and carved throughout their entire length. In the neighbourhood of this we found the altar or *Ewhatta*, upon which lay the last sacrifice, a hog of about eighty pounds weight, which had been put up there whole, and very nicely roasted. Here were also four or five *Ewharre no Eatua*, or god-houses, which were made to be carried on poles; one of these I examined by putting my head into it. Within was a parcel about five feet long and one thick, wrapped up in mats. These I tore with my fingers till I came to a covering of mat made of plaited cocoanut fibres, which it was impossible to get through, so I was obliged to desist, especially as what I had already done gave much offence to our new friends. In an adjoining long house, among several other things such as rolls of cloth, etc., was standing a model of a canoe about three feet long, upon which were tied eight human lower jaw-bones. Tupia told us that it was the custom of these islanders to cut off the jaw-bones of those whom they had killed in war. These were, he said, the jaw-bones of Ulhietea people, but how they came here, or why tied thus to a canoe, we could not understand; we therefore contented ourselves with conjecturing that they were placed there as a trophy won back from the men of Bola-Bola, their mortal enemies. Night now

came on apace, but Dr. Solander and I walked along shore
a little way, and saw an *Ewharre no Eatua*, the under part of
which was lined with a row of jaw-bones. These, we were
told, were also those of Ulhietea men. We saw also cocoanut trees, the stems of which were hung round with nuts,
so that no part could be seen; these, we were told, were
put there to dry a little, and be prepared for making *poe*.
A tree of *Ficus prolixa* was in great perfection; the trunk,
or rather congeries of small roots, being forty-two paces in
circumference.

21*st*. Dr. Solander and I walked out this morning and
saw many boat-houses like that described at Huahine
(p. 111); on these the inhabitants were at work, making
and repairing the large canoes called by them *Pahie*, at
which business they worked with incredible cleverness,
although their tools were as bad as possible. I will first
give the description and dimensions of one of their boats,
and then their method of building. Her extreme length
from stem to stern, not reckoning the bending up of both
those parts, 51 feet; breadth in the clear at the top forward,
14 inches, amidships 18, aft 15; in the bilge forward 32
inches, amidships 35, aft 33; depth amidships, 3 feet 4
inches; height above the ground, 3 feet 6 inches; her head
raised, without the figure, 11 inches; her stern, 8 feet 9
inches; the figure, 2 feet. Alongside of her was lashed
another like her in all respects, but smaller in proportion,
being only 33 feet in her extreme length. The form of
these canoes can be better shown by a drawing than by
any description; the annexed may
serve to give some idea of a section: *a a* is the first seam, *b b* the
second, *c c* the third. The first
stage, or keel under *a a*, is made
of trees hollowed out like a
trough. For this purpose they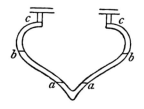
choose the longest trees they can find, so that two or three
form the bottom of their largest boat (some of which are
much larger than that described here, as I make a rule to

describe everything of this kind from the commonest size). The next stage, under *b b*, is formed of straight planks about 4 feet long, 15 inches broad, and 2 inches thick. The third stage, under *c c*, is made, like the bottom, of trunks of trees hollowed out into its bilging form. The last stage, above *c c*, is formed also out of the trunks of trees, so that the moulding is of one piece with the plank. This work, difficult as it would be to an European with his iron tools, they perform without iron and with amazing dexterity. They hollow out with their stone axes as fast, at least, as our carpenters could do, and dubb, though slowly, with prodigious nicety. I have seen them take off the skin of an angular plank without missing a stroke, the skin itself scarce one-sixteenth part of an inch in thickness. Boring the holes through which their sewing is to pass seems to be their greatest difficulty. Their tools are made of the bones of men, generally the thin bone of the upper arm; these they grind very sharp and fix to a handle of wood, making the instrument serve the purpose of a gouge, by striking it with a mallet made of hard black wood. With them they would do as much work as with iron, were it not that the brittle edge of the tool is very liable to be broken. When they have prepared their planks, etc., the keel is laid on blocks and the whole canoe put together much in the same manner as we do a ship, the sides being supported by stanchions and all the seams wedged together before the last sewing is put on, so that they become tolerably tight, considering that they are without caulking.

With these boats they venture themselves out of sight of land: we saw several of them at Otahite which had come from Ulhietea; and Tupia has told us that they undertake voyages of twenty days; whether this is true or false I do not affirm. They keep the boats very carefully under such boat-houses as are described on p. 111.

22nd. We saw a double *pahie* such as that described yesterday, but much longer. She had upon her an awning supported by pillars, which held the floor at least four feet above the deck or upper surface of the boats. We saw also a trough for making *Poe poe*, or sour paste, carved out of hard black stone such as their hatchets are made of; it was 2 feet 7 inches long and 1 foot 4 broad, very thick and substantial, and supported by four short feet, the whole neatly finished and perfectly polished, though quite without ornaments. To-day, as well as yesterday, every one of us who walked out saw many jaw-bones fixed up in houses, as well as out-of-doors, which confirmed what we had been told of their taking these bones instead of scalps.

24th. The captain attempted to go out of the reef by another passage situated between the two islets of Opourourou and Taumou. Whilst the ship was turning to windward within the reef she narrowly escaped going ashore; the quartermaster in the chains called out two fathoms, but as the ship drew at least fourteen feet, it was impossible that such a shoal could be under her keel, so that either the man was mistaken, or the ship went along the edge of a coral rock, many of which are here as steep as a wall.

Soon after this we came to an anchor, and I went ashore, but saw nothing except a small marai, ornamented with two sticks about five feet long, each hung with as many jaw-bones as possible, and one having a skull stuck on its top.

28th. Dr. Solander and I went ashore on the island of Otahah. We went through a large breach in the reef situate between two islands called Toahattu and Whennuaia, within which we found very spacious harbours, particularly in one bay, which was at least three miles deep. The inhabitants as usual, so that long before night we had purchased three hogs, twenty-one fowls, and as many yams and plantains as the boat would hold; indeed, of these last we might have had any quantity, and a more useful refreshment they are to us, in my opinion, even than the pork. They have been for this week past boiled, and served instead of bread; every man in the ship is fond of them, and with us in the cabin they agree much better than the bread-fruit did. But what makes any refreshment of this kind more acceptable is that our bread is at present so full of vermin that, notwithstanding all possible care, I have sometimes had

twenty at a time in my mouth, every one of which tasted
as hot as mustard.

The island itself seemed more barren than Ulhietea,
though the produce was very similar, but bread-fruit was
less plentiful than plantains and cocoanuts. The people
were exactly the same, so much so that I did not observe
one new custom worth mention. They were not very
numerous, but flocked from all quarters to the boat where-
ever she went, bringing with them whatever they had to
sell. Here, as well as in the rest of the islands, they paid
us the same compliment as they are used to pay to their
own kings, uncovering their shoulders and lapping their
garments round their breasts. Here particularly they were
so scrupulously observant of it that a man was sent with us
who called out to every one we met, telling him who we
were and what they should do.

29*th*. We are this morning close under the island of
Bola-Bola, whose high craggy peak appears, on this side at
least, totally inaccessible to man ; round it is a large quantity
of low land, which seems very barren. Tupia tells us that
between the shore and the mountain is a large salt lagoon,
a certain sign of barrenness in this climate.

31*st*. Tupia to-day shows us a large breach in the reef
of Otahah, through which the ship might conveniently pass
into a large bay, where he says there is good anchorage.
We have now a very good opinion of Tupia's pilotage,
especially since we observed him at Huahine send a man
to dive down to the heel of the ship's rudder; this the man
did several times, and reported to him the depth of water
the ship drew, since when he had never suffered her to go
in less than five fathoms without being much alarmed.

2*nd August*. Dr. Solander and I have spent this day ashore
[on Ulhietea], and been very agreeably entertained by the
reception we have met with from the people, though we
were not fortunate enough to meet with one new plant.
Every one seemed to fear and respect us, but nobody to
mistrust us in the smallest degree. Men, women, and
children came crowding after us, but no one showed us

the least incivility; on the contrary, wherever there was
dirt or water to pass over they strove who should carry us
on their backs.   On arriving at the houses of the principal
people we were received with a ceremony quite new to us;
the people, who generally followed us, rushed into the
houses before us, leaving, however, a lane sufficiently wide
for us to pass through.   When we came in, we found them
ranged on either side of a long mat spread upon the ground,
at the farther end of which sat one or more very young
women or children, neatly dressed, who, without stirring,
expected us to come up to them and make them presents,
which we did with no small pleasure, for prettier or better
dressed children we had nowhere seen.   One of these
Tettuas, as they were called, was about six years old, her
apron or gown was red, and round her head was wound a
large quantity of *tamou* (plaited hair), an ornament they
value more than anything they have; she sat at the farthest
end of a mat thirty feet long, on which no one of the
spectators presumed to set a foot, notwithstanding the
crowd.   She was leaning upon the arm of a well-looking,
well-dressed woman of about thirty, possibly her nurse.
We walked up to her, and as soon as we approached she
stretched out her hand to receive the beads we were to give.
Had she been a princess-royal of England giving her hand
to be kissed, no instructions could have taught her to do it
with a better grace; so much is untaught nature superior
to art, that I have seen no sight of the kind that has struck
me half so much.

Grateful possibly for the presents we had made to these
girls, the people on our return tried every method to oblige
us, particularly in one house where the master ordered one
of his people to dance for our amusement, which he did thus.
He put upon his head a large cylindrical basket about four
feet long and eight inches in diameter, on the front of which
was fastened a facing of feathers bending forwards at the
top and edged round with sharks' teeth and the tail feathers
of tropic birds.   With this on he danced, moving slowly,
and often turning his head round, sometimes swiftly throwing

the end of his head-dress, or *whow*, so near the faces of the spectators as to make them start back, which was a joke that seldom failed to make everybody laugh, especially if it happened to one of us.

We had also an opportunity of seeing the inside of the *Ewharre no Eatua*, so often mentioned : there were three of them, much ornamented with jaw-bones, and very full of bundles wrapped up in their cloth ; these the people opened after some persuasion, and in them we found complete skulls, with their lower jaw-bones in their proper places; perhaps these were the skulls of those of the victorious party who died in battle, and the jaw-bones fastened on the outside were those of the conquered, but for this conjecture I had no authority from the Indians, who seemed to avoid as much as possible any questions upon the subject.

3rd. Went along shore in the opposite direction to that we took yesterday, intending to spend most of our time in purchasing stock, which we have always found the people ready to part with at their houses, and selling cheaper than at the market. In the course of our walk we met a set of strolling dancers, called by the Indians *heiva*, who detained us two hours, and during all that time entertained us highly indeed. The party consisted of three drums, two women dancers and six men ; these Tupia tells us go round the island, as we have seen the little *heivas* do at Otahite, but differ from those in that most of the members of the *heiva* here are important people, of which assertion we had in the case of one of the women an undoubted proof.

The women had on their heads a quantity of *tamou*, or plaited hair, which was rolled, and flowers of gardenia were stuck between the interstices, making a head-dress truly elegant. Their shoulders, arms, and breasts as low as their arms were bare, below this they were covered with black cloth, and under each shoulder was placed a bunch of black feathers much as our ladies' nosegays or bouquets. On their hips rested a quantity of cloth plaited very full, which reached almost up to their arms, and fell down below into long petticoats, reaching below their feet, which they managed with as much dexterity as our opera dancers could have done; these plaits were brown and white alternately, but the petticoats were all white. In this dress they advanced sideways, keeping excellent time to the drums, which beat briskly and loud: they soon began to shake their hips, giving the folds of cloth that lay upon them a very quick motion, continued during the whole dance. They sometimes stood, sometimes sat, and sometimes rested on their knees and elbows, generally moving their fingers with a quickness scarcely to be imagined.

One of these girls had in her ear three pearls, one very large but so foul that it was worth scarce anything; the other two were as large as a middling pea, and of a clear water as well as a good shape. For these I offered at different times any price the owner would have, but she would not hear of parting with them; I offered once the price of four hogs down and anything she would ask beside. They have always set a value upon their pearls, if tolerably good, almost equal to our valuation, supposing them (as they always are, however) not spoiled by the drilling.

Between the dances of the women (for they sometimes rested) the men acted a kind of interlude, in which they spoke as well as danced; we were not, however, sufficiently versed in their language to be able to give an account of the drama.

4th. We had often heard Tupia speak of lands belonging to him which had been taken away by the Bola-Bola men. These, he tells us now, are situated in the very bay where the ship lies. On going ashore this morning, the inhabitants confirmed what he had told us, and showed us several different *whennuas*, which, they all acknowledged, belonged of right to him. The greater number of the people here are, it seems, the so-much-feared Bola-Bola men, and we were told that to-morrow Opoony, the king of that island, will come to visit us. We are much inclined to receive him civilly, as we have met with so civil a reception from his subjects.

We saw the game which the Indians call *erowhaw*. It

consists of nothing more than pitching a kind of light lance, headed with hard wood, at a mark. Of this amusement they seem to be very fond, but none that we then saw excelled in doing it, not above one in twelve striking the mark, which was the bole of a plantain tree about twenty yards distant.

5th. Went in the boat to the southward with the captain, etc.; saw two inlets in the reef, and good harbours within them. They were both situate close to islands, having one on each side of them; indeed, in general, I have seen breaches in reefs wherever there are islands upon them. The people along shore were very poor, so much so that after all our day's work we did not procure either hog or fowl, nor, indeed, did we see either.

6th. Yesterday Opoony, the king of Bola-Bola, sent his compliments and a present of hogs and fowls to the king of the ship, sending word also that he would in person wait upon him to-day. We therefore all stayed at home in hopes of the honour of his Excellency's visit. We were disappointed in our expectations, but not disagreeably, for instead of his Majesty came three handsome, lively girls, who stayed with us the morning, and took off all regret for the want of his Majesty's company.

In the evening we all went to see the great king, and thank him for his civilities. The king of the Tata-toas, or clubmen, who have conquered this island, and are the terror of all others, we expected to see young, lively, handsome, etc. etc., but were disappointed when we were led to an old, decrepit, half-blind man, who seemed to have scarce reason enough left to send hogs, much less gallantry enough to send ladies.

7th. We learned from Opoony yesterday that his chief residence was at Otahah: to this place he proposed to accompany us to-day. Captain Cook and Dr. Solander went upon the expedition, while I stayed at home. They proceeded with Opoony and all his train, and many canoes, to a bay in Otahah called Obooto-booto, his Majesty's chief residence. Here the houses were very large and good, and the canoes also finer than any the gentlemen had before seen. Such a prelude made them expect much from the owners—a boat-load of hogs was the least they thought of, especially as they had plenty of Spartan money to pay for them ; but, alack ! the gentlemen who had fatigued themselves with building their houses chose to refresh themselves with eating the hogs, so that after the whole day was spent a small number only were procured in proportion to what were expected.

Took Mr. Parkinson to the *heiva* that he might sketch the dresses. The dancing was exactly the same as I had seen before, except that another woman was added to the former two. The interludes of the men were varied ; they gave us five or six which resembled much the drama of an English stage dance. Their names and relationships, as they are chiefly one family, are : (1) *Tiarree no Horaa*, a king or chief. (2) *Whannooutooa*, wife to 1. (3) *Otoobooi*, sister to 2. (4) *Orai*, elder brother to 2. (5) *Tettuanne*, younger brother to 2. (6) *Otehammena*, dancing girl. (7) *Ouratooa*, do. (8), *Mattehea*, father to 1. (9) *Opipi*, mother to 1.

8*th*. Dr. Solander and I went along shore to gather plants, buy hogs, or anything else that might occur. We took our course towards the *heiva*, and at last came up with it. It has gradually moved from very near us till now it is two leagues off. Tupia tells us that it will in this manner move gradually round the island. Our friends received us, as usual, with all manner of civility, dancing, and giving us, after the amusement, a very good dinner, as well as offering us a quantity of their cloth as a present, which we should have accepted had we not been full-stocked with it before. We now understood a little more of the interludes than formerly. I shall describe one as well as I can. The men were divided into two parties, differing in the colour of their clothes, one brown, the other white. The chief of the browns gives a basket of meat to his servants that they might take care of it. The whites represent thieves who constantly attempt to steal it, dancing all the time. Several different expedients they make use of without success, till at last they find the watchmen asleep; they then go gently up to them, and lifting them off from the basket, which for security they have placed in their middle, they go off with their prize. The others awake and dance, but seem to show little regret for their loss, or indeed hardly to miss the basket at all.

9th. We resolved to sail as soon as the people left off bringing provisions, which about noon they did, and we again launched out into the ocean in search of what chance and Tupia might direct us to.

13th. Many albecores have been about the ship all this evening. Tupia took one, and had not his rod broken, would probably have taken many. He used an Indian fish-hook made of mother-of-pearl, so that it served at the same time for hook and bait.

At noon to-day, high land in sight, which proves to be an island which Tupia calls Oheteroa.

14th. The island of Oheteroa was to all appearance more barren than anything we have seen in these seas, the chief produce seeming to be *etoa* (from the wood of which the people make their weapons); indeed, everywhere along shore where we saw plantations, the trees were of this kind. It is without a reef, and the ground in the bay we were in was so foul and coralline, that although a ship might come almost close to the shore, she could not possibly anchor.

The people seemed strong, lusty, and well made, but were rather browner than those we have left behind; they were not tattowed like them, but had instead black marks about as broad as my hand under their armpits, the sides of which marks were deeply indented. They had also smaller circles round their arms and legs. Their dress was indeed most singular, as well as the cloth of which it was made. It consisted of the same materials as the inhabitants of the other islands make use of, and was generally dyed of a very bright deep yellow; upon this was spread in some cases a composition, either red or of a dark lead colour, which covered it like oil colour or varnish. Upon

this again were painted stripes in many different patterns
with infinite regularity, much in the same way as lustring
silks in England, all
the straight lines upon
them being drawn with
such accuracy that we
were almost in doubt
whether or not they

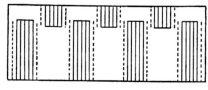

were stamped on with some kind of press. The red cloth was
painted in this manner with black, the lead-coloured with
white. Of this cloth, generally the lead-coloured, they had
on a short jacket that reached about down to their knees, and
made of one piece, with a hole through which they put their
heads, the sides of which hole differed from anything I have
seen, being stitched with long stitches. This was tied round
their bodies by a piece of yellow cloth which passed behind
their necks and came across the breasts in two broad stripes
crossing each other; it was then collected round the waist
in the form of a belt, under which was another of the red
cloth, so that the whole made a very gay and warlike
appearance. Some had on their heads caps, as described
above, of the tails of tropic birds, but these did not become
them so well as a piece of white or lead-coloured cloth,
which most of them had wound on their heads like a small
turban.

Their arms consisted of long lances made of the *etoa*, or
hard wood, well polished and sharpened at one end; of these
some were nearly twenty feet long, and scarcely as thick as
three fingers; they had also clubs or pikes of the same
wood about seven feet long, well polished, and sharpened
at one end into a broad point. How expert they may
be in the use of these we cannot tell, but the weapons
themselves seem intended more for show than use, as the
lance was not pointed with stings of sting-rays, and their
clubs or pikes, which must do more execution by their
weight than their sharpness, were not more than half as
heavy as the smallest I have seen in the other islands.
Defensive weapons I saw none; they, however, guarded

themselves against such weapons as their own by mats folded and laid upon their breasts under their clothes.

Of the few things we saw among the people, every one was ornamented in a manner infinitely superior to anything we had hitherto seen. Their cloth was of a better colour, as well as nicely painted; their clubs were better cut and polished; the canoe which we saw, though very small and narrow, was nevertheless very highly carved and ornamented. One thing particularly in her seemed to be calculated rather as an ornament for something that was never intended to go into the water, and that was two lines of small white feathers placed on the outside of the canoe, and which were, when we saw them, thoroughly wet with the water.

We have now seen seventeen islands in these seas, and have landed on five of the most important; of these the language, manners, and customs agreed most exactly. I should therefore be tempted to conclude that those islands which we have not seen do not differ materially at least from the others. The account I shall give of them is taken chiefly from Otahite, where I was well acquainted with their policy, as I found them to be a people so free from deceit that I trusted myself among them almost as freely as I could do in my own country, sleeping continually in their houses in the woods without so much as a single companion. Whether or not I am right in judging their manners and customs to be general among these seas, any one who gives himself the trouble of reading this journal through can judge as well as I myself.

CHAPTER VII

GENERAL ACCOUNT OF THE SOUTH SEA ISLANDS

Description of the people—Tattowing—Cleanliness—Clothing—Ornaments and head-dress—Houses—Food—Produce of the sea—Fruits—Animals —Cooking—*Mahai*-making—Drinking salt-water—Meals—Women eat apart from the men—Pastimes—Music—Attachment to old customs— Making of cloth from bark—Dyes and dyeing—Mats—Manufacture of fishing-nets—Fish-hooks—Carpentry, etc.—Boats and boat-building— Fighting, fishing, and travelling *ivahahs*—Instability of the boats— Paddles, sails, and ornaments — *Pahies* — Predicting the weather — Astronomy—Measurement of time and space—Language—Its resemblance to other languages—Diseases—Medicine and surgery—Funeral ceremonies —Disposal of the dead—Religion—Origin of mankind—Gods—Priests— Marriage—*Marais*—Bird-gods—Government—Ranks—Army and battles —Justice.

ALL the islands I have seen are very populous along the whole length of the coast, where are generally large flats covered with a great many bread-fruit and cocoanut trees. There are houses scarcely fifty yards apart, with their little plantations of plantains, the trees from which they make their cloth, etc. But the inland parts are totally uninhabited, except in the valleys, where there are rivers, and even there there are but a small proportion of people in comparison with the numbers who live upon the flats.

These people are of the larger size of Europeans, all very well made, and some handsome, both men and women; the only bad feature they have is their noses, which are in general flat, but to balance this their teeth are almost without exception even and white to perfection, and the eyes of the women especially are full of expression and fire. In colour they differ very much; those of inferior rank who are obliged in the exercise of their profession, fishing especially, to be much exposed to the sun and air, are of a dark brown, while those of superior rank, who spend most of their time in their houses under shelter, are seldom browner (the women particularly) than that kind of brunette which many in Europe prefer to the finest red and white. Complexion, indeed, they seldom have, though some I have seen show a blush very manifestly; this is perhaps owing to the thickness of their skin, but that fault is in my opinion well compensated by their infinite smoothness, much superior to anything I have met with in Europe.

The men, as I have before said, are rather large. I have measured one 6 feet $3\frac{1}{2}$ inches. The superior women are also as tall as Europeans, but the inferior sort are generally small. Their hair is almost universally black and rather coarse, this the women wear always cropped short round their ears; the men, on the other hand, wear it in many various ways, sometimes cropping it short, sometimes allowing it to grow very long, and tying it at the top of their heads or letting it hang loose on their shoulders, etc. Their beards they all wear in many different fashions, always, however, plucking out a large part of them and keeping what is left very clean and neat. Both sexes eradicate every hair from under their armpits, and they looked upon it as a great mark of uncleanliness in us that we did not do the same.

During our stay in these islands I saw some, not more than five or six, who were a total exception to all I have said above. They were whiter even than we, but of a dead colour, like that of the nose of a white horse; their eyes, hair, eyebrows, and beards were also white; they were universally short-sighted, and always looked unwholesome, the skin scurfy and scaly, and the eye often full of rheum. As no two of them had any connection with one another, I conclude that the difference of colour, etc., was totally accidental, and did not at all run in families.

So much for their persons. I shall now mention their methods of painting their bodies, or *tattow* as it is called in their language. This they do by inlaying black under their skins, in such a manner as to be indelible. Every one is thus marked in different parts of his body, according maybe to his humour, or different circumstances of his life. Some have ill-designed figures of men, birds or dogs ; but they more generally have a **Z**, either plain—as is generally the case with the women on every joint of their fingers and toes and often round the outside of their feet—or in different figures such as squares, circles, crescents, etc., which both sexes have on their arms and legs ; in short, they have an infinite diversity of figure in which they place this mark. Some of them we were told had significations ; but these we never learnt to our satisfaction. Their faces are generally left without any marks ; I did not see more than one instance to the contrary. Some few old men had the greater part of their bodies covered with large patches of black, which ended in deep indentations, like coarse imitations of flame ; these we were told were not natives of Otahite, but came from a low island called Noonoora. Although they vary so much in the application of the figures—I have mentioned that both the quantity and situation seem to depend entirely upon the humour of each individual—yet all the islanders I have seen (except those of Oheteroa) agree in having their buttocks covered with a deep black. Over this most have arches, which are often a quarter of an inch broad, drawn one above the other as high as their short ribs, and neatly worked on their edges with indentations, etc. These arches are their great pride : both men and women show them with great pleasure, whether as a mark of beauty, or a proof of their perseverance and resolution in bearing pain I cannot tell. The pain in doing this is almost intolerable, especially the arches upon the loins, which are so much more susceptible to pain than the fleshy buttocks.

The colour they use is lamp black prepared from the smoke of a kind of oily nut, used by them instead of candles. This is kept in cocoanut shells, and occasionally mixed with water for use. Their instruments for pricking this under the skin are made of flat bone or shell ; the lower part of

K

which is cut into sharp teeth, numbering from three to twenty, according to the purposes it is to be used for; the upper end is fastened to a handle. The teeth are dipped into the black liquor, and then driven by quick sharp blows, struck upon the handle with a stick used for that purpose, into the skin, so deeply that every stroke is followed by a small quantity of blood, or serum at least, and the part so marked remains sore for many days before it heals.

I saw this operation performed on the 5th of July on the buttocks of a girl about fourteen years of age; for some time she bore it with great resolution, but afterwards began to complain; and in a little time grew so outrageous that all the threats and force her friends could use could hardly oblige her to endure it. I had occasion to remain in an adjoining house an hour at least after this operation began, and yet went away before it was finished, in which time only one side was blacked, the other having been done some weeks before.

It is performed between the ages of fourteen and eighteen, and so essential is it that I have never seen one single person of years of maturity without it. What can be a sufficient inducement to suffer so much pain is difficult to say; not one Indian (though I have asked hundreds) would ever give me the least reason for it. Possibly superstition may have something to do with it, nothing else in my opinion could be a sufficient cause for so apparently absurd a custom. As for the smaller marks upon the fingers, arms, etc., they may be intended only for beauty; our European ladies have found the convenience of patches, and something of that kind is more useful here where the best complexions are much inferior to theirs in England; and yet whiteness is esteemed the first essential in beauty.

They are certainly as cleanly a people as any under the sun; they all wash their whole bodies in running water as soon as they rise in the morning, at noon, and before they sleep at night. If they have not such water near their houses, as often happens, they will go a good way to it. As for their lice, had they the means only they would certainly be as free from them as any inhabitants of so warm a climate could be. Those to whom combs were given proved this, for those with whom I was best acquainted kept themselves very clean during our stay by the use of them. Eating lice is a custom which none but children, and those of the inferior people, can be charged with. Their clothes also, as well as their persons, are kept almost without spot or stain; the superior people spend much of their time in repairing, dyeing, etc., the cloth, which seems to be a genteel amusement for the ladies here as it is in Europe.

Their clothes are either of a kind of cloth made of the bark of a tree, or mats of several different sorts; of all these and of their manner of making them I shall speak in another place; here I shall only mention their method of covering and adorning their persons, which is most diverse, as they never form dresses, or sew any two pieces together. A piece of cloth, generally two yards wide and eleven long, is sufficient clothing for any one, and this is put on in a thousand different ways, often very genteelly. Their formal dress however is, among the women, a kind of petticoat, *parou*, wrapped round their hips, and reaching to about the middle of their legs; and one, two, or three pieces of thick cloth, about two and a half yards long and one wide, called *tebuta*, through a hole in the middle of which they put their heads, and suffer the sides to hang before and behind, the open edges serving to give their arms liberty of movement. Round the ends of this, about as high as their waists, are tied two or three large pieces of thin cloth, and sometimes one or two more thrown loosely over their shoulders, for the rich seem to take the greatest pride in wearing a large quantity of cloth. The dress of the men differs but little from this, their bodies are rather more bare, and instead of the petticoat they have a piece of cloth (*maro*) passed between their legs and round their waists, which gives them rather more liberty to use their limbs than the women's dress will allow. Thus much of the richer people; the poorer sort have only a smaller allowance of cloth given them from the tribes or families to which they belong, and must use that to the best advantage.

It is no uncommon thing for the richest men to come to see us with a large quantity of cloth rolled round the loins, and all the rest of the body naked ; though the cloth wrapped round them was sufficient to have clothed a dozen people. The women at sunset always bared their bodies down to the waist, which seemed to be a kind of easy undress to them ; as it is to our ladies to pull off any finery that has been used during the course of the day, and change it for a loose gown or capuchin.

Both sexes shade their faces from the sun with little bonnets of cocoanut leaves, which they make occasionally in a very few minutes ; some have these made of fine matting, but that is less common. Of matting they have several sorts ; some very fine, which is used in exactly the same manner as cloth for their dresses, chiefly in rainy weather, as the cloth will not bear the least wet.

Ornaments they have very few. They are very fond of earrings, but wear them only in one ear. When we arrived they had their own earrings made of shell, stone, berries, red peas, and some small pearls, of which they wore three tied together; but our beads very quickly supplied their place. They are also very fond of flowers, especially of the Cape jasmine, of which they have great plenty planted near their houses. These they stick into the holes of their ears and into their hair, if they have enough of them, which is but seldom. The men wear feathers, often the tails of tropic birds stuck upright in their hair. They have also a kind of wig made upon one string, of the hair of men or dogs, or of cocoanut, which they tie under their hair at the back of the head. I have seen them also wear whimsical garlands made of a variety of flowers stuck into a piece of the rind of plantain, or of scarlet peas stuck upon a piece of wood with gum, but these are not common. But their great pride in dress seems to be centred in what they call *tamou*, which is human hair plaited scarcely thicker than common thread ; of this I may easily affirm that I have seen pieces above a mile [1]

---

[1] 21st January 1772, measured one 6144 feet, another 7294 feet. (*Note by Banks.*)

in length, worked on end without a single knot; and I have seen five or six of such pieces wound round the head of one woman, the effect of which, if done with taste, was most becoming. Their dancing dresses I have described in the island of Ulhietea; and that of the *Heiva* I shall when I come to their mourning ceremonies. They have also several others suited to particular ceremonies which I had not an opportunity of seeing, although I was desirous of doing so, as the singular taste of those I did see promised much novelty, at least, if not something worth imitation, in whatever they take pains with.

I had almost forgotten the oil (*monoe* it is called in their language) with which they anoint their heads, a custom more disagreeable to Europeans than any other among them. This is made of cocoanut oil, in which some sweet woods or flowers are infused. It is most commonly very rancid, and consequently the wearers of it smell most disagreeably; at first we found it so, but very little custom reconciled me, at least, completely to it.

The houses, or rather dwellings, of these people are admirably adapted to the continual warmth of the climate. They do not build them in villages or towns, but separate each from the other, according to the size of the estate the owner of the house possesses. They are always in the woods; and no more ground is cleared for each house than is just sufficient to hinder the dropping off the branches from rotting the thatch with which they are covered, so that you step from the house immediately under shade, and that the most beautiful imaginable. No country can boast such delightful walks as this; for the whole plains where the people live are covered with groves of bread-fruit and cocoanut trees without underwood. These are intersected in all directions by the paths which go from one house to the other, so that the whole country is one shade, than which nothing can be more grateful in a climate where the sun has so powerful an influence. The houses are built without walls, so that the air, cooled by the shade of the trees, has free access in whatever direction it happens to blow. I shall describe one of the middle size, which will give an idea of all the rest, as they differ scarcely at all in fashion.

Its length was 24 feet, breadth 11 feet, extreme height $8\frac{1}{2}$ feet, height of the eaves $3\frac{1}{2}$ feet; it consisted of nothing more than a thatched roof of the same form as in England, supported by three rows of posts or pillars, one on each side, and one in the middle. The floor was covered some inches deep with soft hay, upon which here and there were laid mats for the convenience of sitting down. This is almost the only furniture, as few houses have more than one stool, the property of the master of the family, and constantly used by him; most are entirely without the stool. These houses serve them chiefly to sleep in, and make their cloth, etc.; they generally eat in the open air under the shade of the nearest tree, if the weather is not rainy. The mats which serve them to sit upon in the daytime are also their beds at night; the cloth which they wear in the day serves for covering; and a little wooden stool, a block of wood, or bundle of cloth, for a pillow. Their order is generally this: near the middle of the room sleep the master of the house and his wife, and with them the rest of the married people; next to them the unmarried women; next to them again, at some small distance, the unmarried men; the servants (*toutous*) generally lie in the open air, or if it rains, come just within shelter.

Besides these, there is another much larger kind of house. One in our neighbourhood measured in length 162 feet, breadth $28\frac{1}{2}$ feet, height of one of the middle row of pillars 18 feet. These are conjectured to be common to all the inhabitants of a district, raised and kept up by their joint labour. They serve, maybe, for any meetings or consultations, or for the reception of any visitors of consequence, etc. Such we have also seen used as dwelling-houses by the most important people. Some of them were much larger than this which I have here described.

In the article of food these happy people may almost be said to be exempt from the curse of our forefathers; scarcely can it be said that they earn their bread by the sweat of their brow, when their chief sustenance, bread-fruit, is procured with no more trouble than that of climbing a tree and pulling it down. Not that the trees grew here spontaneously, but, if a man in the course of his life planted ten such trees (which, if well done, might take the labour of an hour or thereabouts), he would as completely fulfil his duty to his own as well as future generations, as we, natives of less temperate climates, can do by toiling in the cold of winter to sow, and in the heat of summer to reap, the annual produce of our soil; which, when once gathered into the barn, must again be re-sowed and re-reaped as often as the colds of winter or the heats of summer return to make such labour disagreeable.

O fortunatos nimium, sua si bona norint

may most truly be applied to these people; benevolent nature has not only provided them with necessaries, but with an abundance of superfluities. The sea, in the neighbourhood of which they always live, supplies them with vast variety of fish, better than is generally met with between the tropics, but these they get not without some trouble. Every one desires to have them, and there is not enough for all, though while we remained in these seas we saw more species perhaps than our island can boast of. I speak now only of what is more properly called fish, but almost everything which comes out of the sea is eaten and esteemed by these people. Shell-fish, lobsters, crabs, even sea insects, and what the seamen call blubbers of many kinds, conduce to their support; some of the latter, indeed, which are of a tough nature, are prepared by suffering them to stink. Custom will make almost any meat palatable, and the women, especially, are fond of this, though after they had eaten it, I confess I was not extremely fond of their company.

Besides the bread-fruit the earth almost spontaneously produces cocoanuts; bananas of thirteen sorts, the best I have ever eaten; plantains, but indifferent; a fruit not unlike an apple, which, when ripe, is very pleasant; sweet potatoes;

yams; cocos, a kind of arum, known in the East Indies by the name of *Habava*;[1] a fruit known there by the name of *eng. mallow*,[2] and considered most delicious; sugar-cane, which the inhabitants eat raw; a root of the salop kind, called by the inhabitants pea;[3] the root also of a plant called *ethee;* and a fruit in a pod like a large hull of a kidney bean,[4] which, when roasted, eats much like a chestnut, and is called *ahee.* Besides these there is the fruit of a tree called *wharra*,[5] in appearance like a pine-apple; the fruit of a tree called *nono;* the roots, and perhaps leaves of a fern; and the roots of a plant called *theve:* which four are eaten only by the poorer sort of people in times of scarcity.

Of tame animals they have hogs, fowls, and dogs, which latter we learned to eat from them; and few were there of the nicest of us but allowed that a South Sea dog was next to an English lamb. This indeed must be said in their favour, that they live entirely upon vegetables; probably our dogs in England would not eat half as well. Their pork certainly is most excellent, though sometimes too fat; their fowls are not a bit better, rather worse maybe, than ours at home, and often very tough. Though they seem to esteem flesh very highly, yet in all the islands I have seen, the quantity they have of it is very unequal to the number of their people; it is therefore seldom used among them, even the principal chiefs do not have it every day or even every week, though some of them had pigs that we saw quartered upon different estates, as we send cocks to walk in England. When any of these chiefs kills a hog, it seems to be divided almost equally among all his dependents, he himself taking little more than the rest. Vegetables are their chief food, and of these they eat a large quantity.

Cookery seems to have been but little studied here; they have only two methods of applying fire. Broiling

---

[1] *Colocasia antiquorum*, Schott., better known by its New Zealand name *taro* (see p. 253). [2] *Hibiscus esculentus*, Linn. ?.
[3] *Tacca pinnatifida*, Forst. [4] *Lablab vulgaris*, Savi.
[5] *Pandanus odoratissimus*, Linn. f.

or baking, as we called it, is done thus: a hole is dug, the depth and size varying according to what is to be prepared, but seldom exceeding a foot in depth; in this is made a heap of wood and stones laid alternately, fire is then put to it, which, by the time it has consumed the wood, has heated the stones just sufficiently to discolour anything which touches them. The heap is then divided, half is left in the hole, the bottom being paved with them, and on them any kind of provisions are laid, always neatly wrapped up in leaves. Above these again are laid the remaining hot stones, then leaves again to the thickness of three or four inches, and over them any ashes, rubbish or dirt that is at hand. In this situation the food remains about two hours, in which time I have seen a middling-sized hog very well done; indeed, I am of opinion that victuals dressed in this way are more juicy, if not more equally done, than when cooked by any of our European methods, large fish more especially. Bread-fruit cooked in this manner becomes soft, and something like a boiled potato, though not quite so farinaceous as a good one. Of this two or three dishes are made by beating it with a stone pestle till it becomes a paste, mixing water or cocoanut liquor with it, and adding ripe plantains, bananas, sour paste, etc.

As I have mentioned sour paste, I will proceed to describe what it is. Bread-fruit, by what I can find, remains in season during only nine or ten of their thirteen months, so that a reserve of food must be made for those months when they are without it. For this purpose, the fruit is gathered when just upon the point of ripening, and laid in heaps, where it undergoes a fermentation, and becomes disagreeably sweet. The core is then taken out, which is easily done, as a slight pull at the stalk draws it out entire, and the rest of the fruit is thrown into a hole dug for that purpose, generally in their houses. The sides and bottom of this hole are neatly lined with grass, the whole is covered with leaves, and heavy stones laid upon them. Here it undergoes a second fermentation and becomes sourish, in which condition it will keep, as they told me, many months.

Custom has, I suppose, made this agreeable to their palates, though we disliked it extremely; we seldom saw them make a meal without some of it in some shape or form.

As the whole making of this *mahie*, as they call it, depends upon fermentation, I suppose it does not always succeed; it is always done by the old women, who make a kind of superstitious mystery of it, no one except the people employed by them being allowed to come even into that part of the house where it is. I myself spoiled a large heap of it only by inadvertently touching some leaves that lay upon it as I walked by the outside of the house where it was; the old directress of it told me that from that circumstance it would most certainly fail, and immediately pulled it down before my face, who did less regret the mischief I had done, as it gave me an opportunity of seeing the preparation, which, perhaps, I should not otherwise have been allowed to do.

To this plain diet, prepared with so much simplicity, salt water is the universal sauce; those who live at the greatest distance from the sea are never without it, keeping it in large bamboos set up against the sides of their houses. When they eat, a cocoanut-shell full of it always stands near them, into which they dip every morsel, especially of fish, and often leave the whole soaking in it, drinking at intervals large sups of it out of their hands, so that a man may use half a pint of it at a meal. They have also a sauce made of the kernels of cocoanuts fermented until they dissolve into a buttery paste, and beaten up with salt water; the taste of this is very strong, and at first was to me most abominably nauseous. A very little use, however, reconciled me to it, so much so that I should almost prefer it to our own sauces with fish. It is not common among them, possibly it is thought ill-management among them to use cocoanuts so lavishly, or we were on the islands at a time when they were scarcely ripe enough for this purpose.

Small fish they often eat raw, and sometimes large ones. I myself, by being constantly with them, learnt to do the same, insomuch that I have often made meals of raw fish

and bread-fruit, by which I learnt that with my stomach at
least it agreed as well as if dressed, and, if anything, was
still easier of digestion, however contrary this may appear
to the common opinion of the people at home.

Drink they have none except water and cocoanut juice,
nor do they seem to have any method of intoxication among
them. Some there were who drank pretty freely of our
liquors, and in a few instances became very drunk, but
seemed far from pleased with their intoxication, the individuals afterwards shunning a repetition of it, instead of
greedily desiring it, as most Indians are said to do.

Their tables, or at least their apparatus for eating, are
set out with great neatness, though the small quantity of
their furniture will not admit of much elegance. I will
describe the manner in which that of their principal people
is served. They commonly eat alone, unless some stranger
makes a second in their mess. The man usually sits
under the shade of the nearest tree, or on the shady side
of the house. A large quantity of leaves, either of bread-
fruit or banana, are neatly spread before him, and serve
instead of a table-cloth. A basket containing his provisions
is then set by him, and two cocoanut-shells, one full of
fresh, the other of salt, water. He begins by washing his
hands and mouth thoroughly with the fresh water, a process
which he repeats almost continually throughout the whole
meal. Suppose that his provisions consist (as they often did)
of two or three bread-fruits, one or two small fish about as big
as an English perch, fourteen or fifteen ripe bananas or half
as many apples. He takes half a bread-fruit, peels off the
rind, and picks out the core with his nails; he then crams
his mouth as full with it as it can possibly hold, and while
he chews that, unwraps the fish from the leaves in which
they have remained tied up since they were dressed, and
breaks one of them into the salt water. The rest, as well
as the remains of the bread-fruit, lie before him upon the
leaves. He generally gives a fish, or part of one, to some
one of his dependents, many of whom sit round him, and
then takes up a very small piece of that which he has

broken into the salt water in the ends of all the fingers in one hand, and sucks it into his mouth to get as much salt water as possible, every now and then taking a small sup of it, either out of the palm of his hand or out of the cocoanut-shell.

In the meanwhile one of the attendants has prepared a young cocoanut by peeling off the outer rind with his teeth, an operation which at first appears very surprising to Europeans, but depends so much upon a knack, that before we left the island, many of us were ourselves able to do it, even myself, who can scarce crack a nut. When he chooses to drink, the master takes this from him, and, boring a hole through the shell with his finger, or breaking the nut with a stone, drinks or sucks out the water. When he has eaten his bread-fruit and fish, he begins with his plantains, one of which makes no more than a mouthful, if they are as big as black puddings. If he has apples a shell is necessary to peel them ; one is picked off the ground, where there are always plenty, and tossed to him; with this he scrapes or cuts off the skin, rather awkwardly, as he wastes almost half the apple in doing it. If he has any tough kind of meat instead of fish, he must have a knife, for which purpose a piece of bamboo is tossed to him, of which he in a moment makes one, by splitting it transversely with his nail. With this he can cut tough meat or tendons at least as readily as we can with a common knife. All this time one of his people has been employed in beating bread-fruit with a stone pestle and a block of wood ; by much beating and sprinkling with water, it is reduced to the consistence of soft paste ; he then takes a vessel like a butcher's tray, and in it lays his paste, mixing it with either bananas, sour paste, or making it up alone, according to the taste of his master ; to this he adds water, pouring it on by degrees, and squeezing it often through his hand till it comes to the consistence of a thick custard. A large cocoanut-shell full of this he then sets before his master, who sups it down as we should a custard, if we had not a spoon to eat it with. His dinner is then finished by washing his hands and mouth, cleaning the cocoanut-shells and putting anything that may be left into the basket again.

It may be thought that I have given rather too large a quantity of provision to my eater, when I say that he has eaten three bread-fruits, each bigger than two fists, two or three fish, fourteen or fifteen plantains or bananas, each, if they are large, six or nine inches long and four or five round, and concluded his dinner with about a quart of a food as substantial as the thickest unbaked custard. But this I do affirm, that it is but few of the many I was acquainted with that eat less, while many eat a good deal more. However, I shall not insist that any man who may read this should believe it as an article of faith; I shall be content if politeness makes him think, as Joe Miller's friend said: "Well, sir, as you say so, I believe it, but by God, had I seen it myself, I should have doubted it exceedingly."

I have said that they seldom eat together; the better sort hardly ever do so. Even two brothers or two sisters have each their respective baskets, one of which contains victuals, the other cocoanut-shells, etc., for the furniture of their separate tables. These were brought every day to our tents to those of our friends who, having come from a distance, chose to spend the whole day, or sometimes two or three days in our company. These two relations would go out, and sitting down upon the ground within a few yards of each other, turn their faces different ways, and make their meals without saying a word to each other.

The women carefully abstain from eating with the men, or even any of the victuals that have been prepared for them; all their food is prepared separately by boys, and kept in a shed by itself, where it is looked after by the same boys who attend them at their meals. Notwithstanding this, when we visited them at their houses, the women with whom we had any particular acquaintance or friendship would constantly ask us to partake of their meals, which we often did, eating out of the same basket and drinking out of the same cup. The old women, however, would by no means allow the same liberty, but would esteem their victuals polluted if we touched them; in some instances I have seen them throw them away when we had inadvertently defiled them by handling the vessels which contained them.

What can be the motive for so unsocial a custom I cannot in any shape guess, especially as they are a people in every other instance fond of society, and very much so of their women. I have often asked them the reason, but they have as often evaded the question, or answered merely that they did it because it was right, and expressed much disgust when I told them that in England men and women ate together, and the same victuals. They, however, constantly affirm that it does not proceed from any superstitious motive: *Eatua*, they say, has nothing to do with it. Whatever the motive may be, it certainly affects their outward manners more than their principles; in the tents, for example, we never saw an instance of the women partaking of our victuals at our table, but we have several times seen five or six of them go together into the servants' apartment and there eat very heartily of whatever they could find. Nor were they at all disturbed if we came in while they were doing so, though we had before used all the entreaties we were masters of to invite them to partake with us. When a woman was alone with us, she would often eat even in our company, but always extorted a strong promise that we should not let her country-people know what she had done.

After their meals, and in the heat of the day, they often sleep; middle-aged people especially, the better sort of whom seem to spend most of their time in eating or sleeping. The young boys and girls are uncommonly lively and active, and the old people generally more so than the middle-aged, which perhaps is owing to their excessively dissolute manners.

Diversions they have but few: shooting with the bow is the most usual I have seen at Otahite. It is confined almost entirely to the chiefs; they shoot for distance only, with arrows unfledged, kneeling upon one knee, and dropping the bow from their hands the instant the arrow parts from it. I measured a shot made by Tubourai Tamaide; it was 274 yards, yet he complained that as the bow and arrows were bad he could not shoot as far as he ought to have done. At Ulhietea bows were less common, but the people amused themselves by throwing a kind of javelin eight or nine feet long at a mark, which they did with a good deal of dexterity, often striking the trunk of a plantain tree, their mark, in the very centre. I could never observe that either these or the Otahite people staked anything; they seemed to contend merely for the honour of victory.

Music is very little known to them, and this is the more wonderful as they seem very fond of it. They have only two instruments, the flute and the drum. The former is made of a hollow bamboo, about a foot long, in which are three holes: into one of these they blow with one nostril, stopping the other nostril with the thumb of the left hand; the other two they stop and unstop with the forefinger of the left, and middle finger of the right hand. By this means they produce four notes, and no more, of which they have made one tune that serves them for all occasions. To it they sing a number of songs, *pehay* as they call them, generally consisting of two lines, affecting a coarse metre, and generally in rhyme. Maybe these lines would appear more musical if we well understood the accent of their language, but they are as downright prose as can be written. I give two or three specimens of songs made upon our arrival.

> Te de pahai de parow-a
> Ha maru no mina.
>
> E pahah tayo malama tai ya
> No tabane tonatou whannomi ya.
>
> E turai eattu terara patee whennua toai
> Ino o maio pretane to whennuaia no tute.

At any time of the day when they are lazy they amuse themselves by singing the couplets, but especially after dark;

their candles—made of the kernel of a nut abounding much in oil—are then lighted. Many of these are stuck upon a skewer of wood, one below the other, and give a very tolerable light, which they often keep burning an hour after dark, and if they have any strangers in the house it is sometimes kept up all night.

Their drums they manage rather better: they are made of a hollow block of wood, covered with shark's skin; with these they make out five or six tunes, and accompany the flute not disagreeably. They know also how to tune two drums of different notes into concord, which they do nicely enough. They also tune their flutes; if two persons play upon flutes which are not in unison, the shorter is lengthened by adding a small roll of leaf tied round the end of it, and moved up and down till their ears (which are certainly very nice) are satisfied. The drums are used chiefly in their *heivas*, which are at Otahite no more than a set of musicians, two drums for instance, two flutes and two singers, who go about from house to house and play. They are always received and rewarded by the master of the family, who gives them a piece of cloth or whatever else he can spare; and during their stay of maybe three or four hours, receives all his neighbours, who crowd his house full. This diversion the people are extravagantly fond of, most likely because, like concerts, assemblies, etc., in Europe, they serve to bring the sexes easily together at a time when the very thought of meeting has opened the heart and made way for pleasing ideas. The grand dramatic *heiva* which we saw at Ulhietea is, I believe, occasionally performed in all the islands, but that I have so fully described in the journal (3rd, 7th, and 8th August) that I need say no more about it.

Besides this they dance, especially the young girls, whenever they can collect eight or ten together, and setting their mouths askew in a most extraordinary manner, in the practice of which they are brought up from their earliest childhood. In doing this they keep time to a surprising nicety; I might almost say as truly as any dancers I have seen in Europe, though their time is certainly much more simple. This exercise is, however, left off as they arrive at years of maturity.

The great facility with which these people have always procured the necessaries of life may very reasonably be thought to have originally sunk them into a kind of indolence, which has, as it were, benumbed their inventions, and prevented their producing such a variety of arts as might reasonably be expected from the approaches they have made in their manners to the politeness of the Europeans. To this may also be added a fault which is too frequent even among the most civilised nations, I mean an invincible attachment to the customs which they have learnt from their forefathers. These people are in so far excusable, as they derive their origin, not from creation, but from an inferior divinity, who was herself, with others of equal rank, descended from the god, causer of earthquakes. They therefore look upon it as a kind of sacrilege to attempt to mend customs which they suppose had their origin either among their deities or their ancestors, whom they hold as little inferior to the divinities themselves.

They show their greatest ingenuity in marking and dyeing cloth ; in the description of these operations, especially the latter, I shall be rather diffuse, as I am not without hopes that my countrymen may receive some advantage, either from the articles themselves, or at least by hints derived from them.

The material of which it is made is the internal bark or liber of three sorts of trees, the Chinese paper mulberry (*Morus papyrifera*), the bread-fruit tree (*Sitodium utile*[1]), and a tree much resembling the wild fig-tree of the West Indies (*Ficus prolixa*). Of the first, which they name *aouta*, they make the finest and whitest cloth, which is worn chiefly by the principal people ; it is likewise the most suitable for dyeing, especially with red. Of the second, which they call *ooroo*, is made a cloth inferior to the former in whiteness and softness, worn chiefly by people of inferior degree. Of the

---

[1] *Artocarpus incisa*, Linn. f.

L

third, which is by far the rarest, is made a coarse, harsh cloth of the colour of the deepest brown paper: it is the only one they have that at all resists water, and is much valued; most of it is perfumed and used by the very great people as a morning dress. These three trees are cultivated with much care, especially the former, which covers the largest part of their cultivated land. Young plants of one or two years' growth only are used; their great merit is that they are thin, straight, tall, and without branches; to prevent the growth of these last they pluck off with great care all the lower leaves and their germs, as often as there is any appearance of a tendency to produce branches.

Their method of manufacturing the bark is the same for all the sorts : one description of it will therefore be sufficient. The thin cloth they make thus : when the trees have grown to a sufficient size they are drawn up, and the roots and tops cut off and stripped of their leaves ; the best of the *aouta* are in this state about three or four feet long and as thick as a man's finger, but the *ooroo* are considerably larger. The bark of these rods is then slit up longitudinally, and in this manner drawn off the stick ; when all are stripped, the bark is carried to some brook or running water, into which it is laid to soak with stones upon it, and in this situation it remains some days. When sufficiently soaked the women servants go down to the river, and stripping themselves, sit down in the water and scrape the pieces of bark, holding them against a flat smooth board, with the shell called by the English shell merchants Tiger's tongue (*Tellina gargadia*), dipping it continually in the water until all the outer green bark is rubbed and washed away, and nothing remains but the very fine fibres of the inner bark. This work is generally finished in the afternoon : in the evening the pieces are spread out upon plantain leaves, and in doing this I suppose there is some difficulty, as the mistress of the family generally presides over the operation. All that I could observe was that they laid them in two or three layers, and seemed very careful to make them everywhere of equal thickness, so that if any part of a piece of bark had been scraped too thin, another thin piece was laid over it, in order to render it of the same thickness as the rest. When laid out in this manner, a piece of cloth is eleven or twelve yards long, and not more than a foot broad, for as the longitudinal fibres are all laid lengthwise, they do not expect it to stretch in that direction, though they well know how considerably it will in the other.

In this state they suffer it to remain till morning, by which time a large proportion of the water with which it was thoroughly soaked has either drained off or evaporated, and the fibres begin to adhere together, so that the whole may be lifted from the ground without dropping in pieces. It is then taken away by the women servants, who beat it in the following manner. They lay it upon a long piece of wood, one side of which is very even and flat, this side being put under the cloth: as many women then as they can muster, or as can work at the board together, begin to beat it. Each is furnished with a baton made of the hard wood, *etoa* (*Casuarina equisetifolia*): it is about a foot long and square with a handle ; on each of the four faces of the square are many small furrows, whose width differs on each face, and which cover the whole face.[1] They begin with the coarsest side, keeping time with their strokes in the same manner as smiths, and continue until the cloth, which extends rapidly under these strokes, shows by the too great thinness of the groves which are made in it that a finer side of the beater is requisite. In this manner they proceed to the finest side, with which they finish ; unless the cloth is to be of that very fine sort *hoboo*, which is almost as thin as muslin. In making this last they double the piece several times, and beat it out again and afterwards bleach it in the sun and air, which in these climates produce whiteness in a very

---

[1] The instrument is apparently something like a razor strop, of which the cross section is square, having longitudinal furrows, a varying number on each face. By the "coarsest side" is to be understood the face with the fewest furrows, which are larger and more deeply indented.

short time. But I believe that the finest of their *hoboo* does not attain either its whiteness or softness until it has been worn some time, then washed and beaten over again with the very finest beaters.

Of this thin cloth they have almost as many different sorts as we have of linen, distinguishing it according to its fineness and the material of which it is made. Each piece is from nine to fifteen yards in length, and about two and a half broad. It serves them for clothes in the day and bedding at night. When, by use, it is sufficiently worn and becomes dirty, it is carried to the river and washed, chiefly by letting it soak in a gentle stream, fastened to the bottom by a stone, or, if it is very dirty, by wringing it and squeezing it gently. Several of the pieces of cloth so washed are then laid on each other, and being beaten with the coarsest side of the beater, adhere together, and become a cloth as thick as coarse broad-cloth, than which nothing can be more soft or delicious to the touch. This softness, however, is not produced immediately after the beating : it is at first stiff as if newly starched, and some parts not adhering together as well as others it looks ragged, and also varies in thickness according to any faults in the cloth from which it was made.

To remedy this is the business of the mistress and the principal women of the family, who seem to amuse themselves with this, and with dyeing it, as our English women do with making caps, ruffles, etc. In this way they spend the greater part of their time. Each woman is furnished with a knife made of a piece of bamboo cane, to which they give an edge by splitting it diagonally with their nails. This is sufficient to cut any kind of cloth or soft substance with great ease. A certain quantity of a paste made of the root of a plant which serves them also for food, and is called by them *Pea* (*Chaitœa tacca*[1]), is also required. With the knife they cut off any ragged edges or ends which may not have been sufficiently fixed down by the beating, and with the paste they fasten down others which are less ragged, and

[1] *Tacca pinnatifida*, Forst.

also put patches on any part which may be thinner than the rest, generally finishing their work, if intended to be of the best kind, by pasting a complete covering of the finest thin cloth or *hoboo* over the whole. They sometimes make a thick cloth also of only half-worn cloth, which, having been worn by cleanly people, is not soiled enough to require washing : of this it is sufficient to paste the edges together. The thick cloth made in either of these ways is used either for the garment called *maro*, which is a long piece passed between the legs and round the waist, and which serves instead of breeches, or as the *tebuta*, a garment used equally by both sexes instead of a coat or gown, which exactly resembles that worn by the inhabitants of Peru and Chili, and is called by the Spaniards *poncho*.

The cloth itself, both thick and thin, resembles the finest cottons, in softness especially, in which property it even exceeds them ; its delicacy (for it tears by the smallest accident) makes it impossible that it can ever be used in Europe, indeed it is properly adapted to a hot climate. I used it to sleep in very often in the islands, and always found it far cooler than any English cloth.

Having thus described their manner of making the cloth, I shall proceed to their method of dyeing. They use principally two colours, red and yellow. The first of these is most beautiful, I might venture to say a more delicate colour than any we have in Europe, approaching, however, most nearly to scarlet. The second is a good bright colour, but of no particular excellence. They also on some occasions dye the cloth brown and black, but so seldom that I had no opportunity during my stay of seeing the method, or of learning the materials which they make use of. I shall therefore say no more of these colours than that they were so indifferent in their qualities that they did not much raise my curiosity to inquire concerning them.

To begin then with the red, in favour of which I shall premise that I believe no voyager has passed through these seas but that he has said something in praise of this colour, the brightness and elegance of which is so great that it cannot avoid being taken notice of by the most superficial observer. This colour is made by the admixture of the juices of two vegetables, neither of which in their separate state have the least tendency to the colour of red, nor, so far at least as I have been able to observe, are there any circumstances relating to them from whence any one would be led to conclude that the red colour was at all latent in them. The plants are *Ficus tinctoria*, called by them *matte* (the same name as the colour), and *Cordia Sebestena*, called *etou*: of these, the fruits of the first, and the leaves of the second, are used in the following manner.

The fruit, which is about as large as a rounceval pea, or very small gooseberry, produces, by breaking off the stalk close to it, one drop of a milky liquor resembling the juice of a fig-tree in Europe. Indeed, the tree itself is a kind of wild fig. This liquor the women collect, breaking off the foot-stalk, and shaking the drop which hangs to the little fig into a small quantity of cocoanut water. To sufficiently prepare a gill of cocoanut water will require three or four quarts of the little figs, though I never could observe that they had any rule in deciding the proportion, except by observing the cocoanut water, which should be of the colour of whey, when a sufficient quantity of the juice of the little figs was mixed with it. When this liquor is ready, the leaves of the *etou* are brought and well wetted in it; they are then laid upon a plantain leaf, and the women begin, at first gently, to turn and shake them about; afterwards, as they grow more and more flaccid by this operation, to squeeze them a little, increasing the pressure gradually. All this is done merely to prevent the leaves from breaking. As they become more flaccid and spongy, they supply them with more of the juice, and in about five minutes the colour begins to appear on the veins of the *etou* leaves, and in ten, or a little more, all is finished and ready for straining, when they press and squeeze the leaves as hard as they possibly can. For straining they have a large quantity of the fibres of a kind of *Cyperus* grass (*Cyperus stupeus*) called by them *mooo*, which the boys prepare very nimbly by drawing the stalks of it through their teeth, or between two little sticks until all the green bark and the bran-like substance which lies between them is gone. In a covering of these fibres, then, they envelop the leaves, and squeezing or wringing them strongly, express the dye, which turns out very little more in quantity than the liquor employed; this operation they repeat several times, as often soaking the leaves in the dye and squeezing them dry again, until they have sufficiently extracted all their virtue. They throw away the remaining leaves, keeping however the *mooo*, which serves them instead of a brush to lay the colour on the cloth. The receptacle used for the liquid dye is always a plantain leaf, whether from any property it may have suitable to the colour, or the great ease with which it is always obtained, and the facility of dividing it, and making of it many small cups, in which the dye may be distributed to every one in the company, I do not know. In laying the dye upon the cloth, they take it up in the fibres of the *mooo*, and rubbing it gently over the cloth, spread the outside of it with a thin coat of dye. This applies to the thick cloth : of the thin they very seldom dye more than the edges ; some indeed I have seen dyed through, as if it had been soaked in the dye, but it had not nearly so elegant a colour as that on which a thin coat only was laid on the outside.

Though the *etou* leaf is the most generally used, and I believe produces the finest colour, yet there are several more, which by being mixed with the juice of the little figs produce a red colour. Such are *Tournefortia sericea* (which they call *taheino*), *Convolvulus brasiliensis, Solanum latifolium (ebooa)*. By the use of these different plants or of different proportions of the materials many varieties of the colour are observable among their cloths, some of which are very conspicuously superior to others.

When the women have been employed in dyeing cloth, they industriously preserve the colour upon their fingers and nails, upon which it shows with its greatest beauty ; they look upon this as no small ornament, and I have been sometimes inclined to believe that they even borrow the dye of each other, merely for the purpose of colouring their fingers. Whether it is esteemed as a beauty, or a mark of their housewifery in being able to dye, or of their riches in having cloth to dye, I know not.

Of what use this preparation may be to my country-men, either in itself, or in any tints which may be drawn from an admixture of vegetable substances so totally different from anything of the kind that is practised in Europe, I am not enough versed in chemistry to be able to guess. I must, however, hope that it will be of some value. The latent qualities of vegetables have already furnished our most valuable dyes. No one from an inspection of the plants could guess that any colour was hidden in the herbs of indigo, woad, dyer's weed, or indeed most of the plants whose leaves are used in dyeing: and yet those latent qualities have, when discovered, produced colours without which our dyers could hardly maintain their trade.

The painter whom I have with me tells me that the nearest imitation of the colour that he could make would be by mixing together vermilion and carmine, but even thus he could not equal the delicacy, though his would be a body colour, and the Indian's only a stain. In the way that the Indians use it, I cannot say much for its lasting; they commonly keep their cloth white up to the very time it is to be used, and then dye it, as if conscious that it would soon fade. I have, however, used cloth dyed with it myself for a fortnight or three weeks, in which time it has very little altered, and by that time the cloth itself was pretty well worn out. I have now some also in chests, which a month ago when I looked into them had very little changed their colour: the admixture of fixing drugs would, however, certainly not a little conduce to its keeping.

Their yellow, though a good colour, has certainly no particular excellence to recommend it in which it is superior to our known yellows. It is made of the bark of a root of a shrub called *nono* (*Morinda umbellata*). This they scrape into water, and after it has soaked a sufficient time, strain the water, and dip the cloth into it. The wood of the root is no doubt furnished in some degree with the same property as the bark, but not having any vessels in which they can boil it, it is useless to the inhabitants. The genus of *Morinda* seems worthy of being examined as to its properties for dyeing. Browne, in his *History of Jamaica*, mentions three species whose roots, he says, are used to dye a brown colour; and Rumphius says of his *Bancudus angustifolia*,[1] which is very nearly allied to our *nono*, that it is used by the inhabitants of the East Indian Islands as a fixing drug for the colour of red, with which he says it particularly agrees.

They also dye yellow with the fruit of a tree called *tamanu* (*Calophyllum inophyllum*), but their method I never had the fortune to see. It seems, however, to be chiefly esteemed by them for the smell, more agreeable to an Indian than an European nose, which it gives to the cloth.

Besides their cloth, the women make several kinds of matting, which serves them to sleep upon, the finest being also used for clothes. With this last they take great pains, especially with that sort which is made of the bark of the *poorou* (*Hibiscus tiliaceus*), of which I have seen matting almost as fine as coarse cloth. But the most beautiful sort, *vanne*, which is white and extremely glossy and shining, is made of the leaves of the *wharra*, a sort of *Pandanus*, of which we had not an opportunity of seeing either flowers or fruit. The rest of their *moeas*, which are used to sit down or sleep upon, are made of a variety of sorts of rushes, grasses, etc.; these they are extremely nimble in making, as indeed they are of everything which is plaited, including baskets of a thousand different patterns, some being very neat. As for occasional baskets or panniers made of a cocoanut leaf, or the little bonnets of the same material which they wear to shade their eyes from the sun, every one knows how to make them at once. As soon as the sun was pretty high, the women who had been with us since morning, generally sent out for cocoanut leaves, of which they made such

---

[1] *Bancudus angustifolia*, Rumph. = *Morinda angustifolia*, Roxb.

bonnets in a few minutes, and threw away as soon as the sun became again low in the afternoon. These, however, serve merely for a shade: coverings for their heads they have none except their hair, for these bonnets or shades only fit round their heads, not upon them.

Besides these things, they are very neat in making fishing-nets in the same manner as we do, ropes of about an inch thick, and lines from the *poorou*, threads with which they sew together their canoes, and also belts from the fibres of the cocoanut, plaited either round or flat. All their twisting work they do upon their thighs in a manner very difficult to describe, and, indeed, unnecessary, as no European can want to learn how to perform an operation which his instruments will do for him so much faster than it can possibly be done by hand. But of all the strings that they make none are so excellent as the fishing-lines, etc., made of the bark of the *erowa*, a kind of frutescent nettle (*Urtica argentea*) which grows in the mountains, and is consequently rather scarce. Of this they make the lines which are employed to take the briskest and most active fish, bonitos, albecores, etc. As I never made experiments with it, I can only describe its strength by saying that it was infinitely stronger than the silk lines which I had on board made in the best fishing shops in London, though scarcely more than half as thick.

In every expedient for taking fish they are vastly ingenious; their seine nets for fish to mesh themselves in, etc., are exactly like ours. They strike fish with harpoons made of cane and pointed with hard wood more dexterously than we can do with ours that are headed with iron, for we who fasten lines to ours need only lodge them in the fish to secure it, while they, on the other hand, throwing theirs quite from them, must either mortally wound the fish or lose him. Their hooks, indeed, as they are not made of iron, are necessarily very different from ours in construction. They are of two sorts; the first, *witte-witte*, is used for towing. Fig. 1 represents this in profile, and Fig. 2 the view of the bottom part. The shank (*a*) is made of mother-of-pearl, the most glossy that can be got, the inner or naturally bright side being put undermost. In Fig. 2, *b* is a tuft of white dog's or hog's hair, which serves, maybe, to imitate the tail of a fish. These hooks require no bait: they are used with a fishing-rod of bamboo. The people having found by the flight of birds, which constantly attend shoals

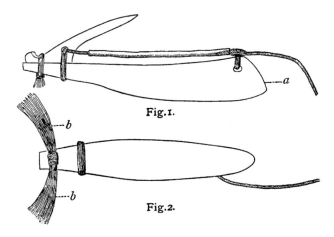

Fig.1.

Fig.2.

of bonitos, where the fish are, paddle their canoes as swiftly as they can across them, and seldom fail to take some. This Indian invention seems far to exceed anything of the kind that I have seen among Europeans, and is certainly more successful than any artificial flying fish or other thing which is generally used for taking bonitos. So far, it deserves imitation at any time when taking bonitos is at all desirable.

The other sort of hook which they have is made likewise of mother-of-pearl, or some hard shell, and as they cannot make them bearded as our own, they supply that fault by making the points turn much inwards, as in the annexed figure. They have them of all sizes, and catch with them all kinds of fish  very successfully, I believe. The manner of making them is very simple; every fisherman makes them for himself.

The shell is first cut by the edge of another shell into square pieces. These are shaped with files of coral, with which they work in a manner surprising to any one who does not know how sharp corals are. A hole is then bored in the middle by a drill, which is simply any stone that may chance to have a sharp corner in it tied to the handle of a cane. This is turned in the hand like a chocolate mill until the hole is made; the file then comes into the hole and completes the hook. This is made, in such a one as the figure shows, in less than a quarter of an hour.

In their carpentry, joinery, and stone-cutting, etc., they are scarcely more indebted to the use of tools than in making these hooks. A stone axe in the shape of an adze, a chisel or gouge made of a human bone, a file or rasp of coral, the skin of sting-rays and coral sand to polish with, are a sufficient set of tools for building a house and furnishing it with boats, as well as for quarrying and squaring stones for the pavement of anything which may require it in the neighbourhood. Their axes are made of a black stone, not very hard, but tolerably tough: they are of different sizes, some, intended for felling, weigh three or four pounds; others, which are used only for carving, not as many ounces. Whatever quality is lacking in these tools, is made up by the industry of the people who use them. Felling a tree is their greatest labour; a large one requires many hands to assist, and some days before it can be finished, but when once it is down they manage it with far greater dexterity than is credible to a European. If it is to be made into boards they put wedges into it, and drive them with such dexterity (as they have told me, for I never saw it) that they divide it into slabs of three or four inches in thickness, seldom meeting with an accident if the tree is good. These slabs they very soon dubb down with their axes to any given thinness, and in this work they certainly excel; indeed, their tools are better adapted for this than for any other labour. I have seen them dubb off the first rough coat of a plank at least as fast as one of our carpenters could have done it; and in hollowing, where they are able to raise large slabs of the wood, they certainly work more quickly, owing to the weight of their tools. Those who are masters of this business will take off a surprisingly thin coat from a whole plank without missing a stroke. They can also work upon wood of any shape as well as upon a flat piece, for in making a canoe every piece, bulging or flat, is properly shaped at once, as they never bend a plank; all the bulging pieces must be shaped by hand, and this is done entirely with axes. They have also small axes for carving; but all this latter kind of work was so bad, and in so very mean a taste, that it scarcely deserved that name. Yet they are very fond of having carvings and figures stuck about their canoes, the great ones especially, which generally have a figure of a man at the head and another at the stern. Their *marais* also are ornamented with different kinds of figures, one device representing many men standing on each other's heads. They have also figures of animals, and planks of which the faces are carved in patterns of squares and circles, etc. All their work, however, in spite of its bad taste, acquires a certain neatness in finish, for they polish everything, even the side of a canoe or the post of a house, with coral-sand rubbed on in the outer husk of a cocoanut and ray's skin, which makes it very smooth and neat.

Their boats, all at least that I have seen of them, may be divided into two general classes. The first, or *ivahah*, are the only sort used at Otahite; they serve for fishing and for short trips to sea, but do not seem at all calculated for long voyages; the others, or *pahie*, are used by the inhabitants of the Society Isles, viz. Ulhietea, Bola Bola, Huahine, etc., and are rather too clumsy for fishing, for which reason the inhabitants of those islands have also *ivahahs*. The *pahie* are much better adapted for long voyages. The figures below (p. 158) give a section of both kinds: Fig. 1 is the *ivahah* and Fig. 2 the *pahie*.

To begin, then, with the *ivahah*. These differ very much in length: I have measured them from 10 feet to 72 feet, but by no means proportional in breadth, for while that of 10 feet was about 1 foot in breadth, that of 72 feet was scarce 2 feet, nor is their height increased in much greater proportion. They may be subdivided into three sorts, the fighting *ivahah*, the common sailing or fishing *ivahah*, and the travelling *ivahah*. The fighting *ivahah* is by far the longest; the head and stern of these are considerably raised above the body in a semicircular form, 17 or 18 feet in height when the centre is scarcely 3 feet. These boats never go to sea singly; two are always fastened together side by side at the distance of about two feet by strong poles of wood extending across both, and upon them is built a stage in the fore-part about ten or twelve feet long, and a little broader than the two boats: this is supported by pillars about six feet high, and

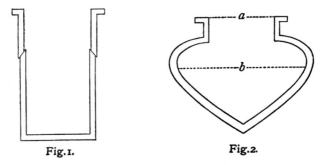

Fig. 1.   Fig. 2.

upon it stand the people who fight with slings, spears, etc. Below are the rowers, who are much less engaged in the battle on account of their confined situation, but who receive the wounded from the stage, and furnish fresh men to ascend in their room. (This much from description, for I never saw any of their battles.)

The sailing and fishing *ivahahs* vary in size from about 40 feet in length to the smallest I have mentioned, but those which are under 25 feet in length seldom or never carry sail: their sterns only are raised, and those not above four or five feet: their prows are quite flat, and have a flat board projecting forwards about four feet beyond them.

Those which I have called travelling *ivahahs* differ from these in nothing except that two are constantly joined together in the same manner as the war-boats, and that they have a small neat house five or six feet broad by seven or eight long fastened upon the fore-part of them, in which the principal people, who use them very much, sit while they are carried from place to place. The sailing *ivahahs* have also this house upon them when two are joined together, which is, however, but seldom. Indeed, the difference between these two consists almost entirely in the rigging, and I have divided them into two more because they are generally seen employed in very different occupations than from any real difference in their build.

All *ivahahs* agree in the sides built like walls and the bottoms flat. In this they differ from the *pahie* (Fig. 2), of which the sides bulge out and the bottom is sharp, answering, in some measure, instead of a keel.

These *pahies* differ very much in size: I have seen them from 30 to 60 feet in length, but, like the *ivahahs*, they are very narrow in proportion to their length. One that I measured was 51 feet in length, but only $1\frac{1}{2}$ feet in breadth at the top (*a*) and 3 feet in the bilge (*b*, see Fig. 2). This is about the general proportion. Their round sides, however, make them capable of carrying much greater burthens and being much safer sea-boats, in consequence of which they are used merely for fighting and making long voyages. For purposes of fishing and travelling along shore the natives of the islands where they are chiefly used have *ivahahs*. The fighting *pahies*, which are the longest, are fitted in the same manner as the fighting *ivahahs*, only as they carry far greater burthens, the stages are proportionately larger. Two sailing boats are most generally fastened together for this purpose; those of a middling size are said to be best, and least liable to accident in stormy weather. In these, if we may credit the reports of the inhabitants, they make very long voyages, often remaining several months from home, visiting in that time many different islands, of which they reported to us the names of nearly a hundred; they cannot, however, remain at sea above a fortnight or twenty days, although they live as sparingly as possible, for want of proper provisions and place to store them in, as well as water, of which they carry a tolerable stock in bamboos.

All the boats are disproportionately narrow in respect to their length, which causes them to be very easily overset, so that not even the Indians dare venture in them till they are fitted with a contrivance to prevent this inconvenience, which is done, either by fastening two together side by side, as has been before described, in which case one supports the other and they become as steady a vehicle as can be imagined; or, if one of them is going out alone, by fastening a log of wood to two poles laid across the boat: this serves to balance it tolerably, though not so securely, but that I have seen the Indians overturn them very often. This is the same principle as that adopted in the flying *proa* of the Ladrone Islands described in Lord Anson's voyage, where it is called an outrigger; indeed, the vessels themselves as much resemble the flying *proa* as to make appear at least possible that either the latter is a very artful improvement of these, or these a very awkward imitation of the *proa*.

These boats are propelled with large paddles, which have a long handle and a flat blade resembling, more than anything I can recollect, a baker's peel; of these every person in the boat generally has one, except those who sit under the houses; and with these they push themselves on fairly fast through the water. The boats are so leaky, however, that one person at least is employed almost constantly in throwing out the water. The only thing in which they excel is landing in a surf, for by reason of their great length and high sterns they land dry when our boats could scarcely land at all, and in the same manner they put off from the shore, as I have often experienced.

When sailing, they have either one or two masts fitted to a frame which is above the canoe: they are made of a single stick; in one that I measured of 32 feet in length, the mast was 25 feet high, which seems to be about the common proportion. To this is fastened a sail about one-third longer, but narrow and of a triangular shape, pointed at the top, and the outside curved; it is bordered all round with a frame of wood, and has no contrivance either for reefing or furling, so that in case of bad weather it must be entirely cut away; but I fancy that in these moderate climates they are seldom brought to this necessity. The material of which it is made is universally matting. With these sails their canoes go at a very good rate, and lie very near the wind, probably on account of their sail being bordered with wood, which makes them stand better than any bow-lines could possibly do. On the top of this sail they carry an ornament which, in taste, resembles much our pennants; it is made of feathers, and reaches down to the very water, so that when blown out by the wind it makes no inconsiderable show. They are fond of ornaments in all parts of their boats; in the good ones they commonly have a figure at the stern, and in the *pahies* they have a figure at both ends, and the smaller *ivahahs* have usually a small carved pillar upon the stern.

Considering that these people are so entirely destitute of iron, they build these canoes very well. Of the *ivahahs* the foundation is always the trunks of one or more trees hollowed out: the ends of these are sloped off, and sewed together with the fibres of the husk of the cocoanut; the sides are then raised with planks sewed together in the same manner.

The *pahies*, as they are much better embarkations, so they are built in a more ingenious manner. Like the others they are laid upon a long keel, which, however, is not more than four or five inches deep. Upon this they raise two ranges of planks, each of which is about eighteen inches high, and about four or five feet in length: such a number of pieces must necessarily be framed and fitted together before they are sewed; and this they do very dexterously, supporting the keel by ropes made fast to the top of the house under which they work, and each plank by a stanchion; so that the canoe is completely put together before any one part is fastened to the next, and in this manner it is supported till the sewing is completed. This, however, soon rots in the salt water; it must be renewed

M

once a year at least; in doing so the canoe is entirely taken to pieces and every plank examined. By this means they are always in good repair; the best of them are, however, very leaky, for as they use no caulking the water must run in at every hole made by the sewing. This is no great inconvenience to them, who live in a climate where the water is always warm, and who go barefoot.

For the convenience of keeping these *pahies* dry, we saw in the islands where they are used a peculiar sort of house built for their reception and put to no other use. It was built of poles stuck upright in the ground and tied together at the top, so that they make a kind of Gothic arch: the sides of these are completely covered with thatch down to the ground, but the ends are left open. One of these I measured was fifty paces in length, ten in breadth, and twenty-four feet in height, and this was of an average size.

The people excel much in predicting the weather, a circumstance of great use to them in their short voyages from island to island. They have various ways of doing this, but one only that I know of which I never heard of being practised by Europeans, and that is foretelling the quarter of the heavens from whence the wind will blow by observing the Milky Way, which is generally bent in an arch either one way or the other : this arch they conceive as already acted upon by the wind, which is the cause of its curving, and say that if the same curve continues a whole night the wind predicted by it seldom fails to come some time in the next day, and in this as well as their other predictions we found them indeed not infallible, but far more clever than Europeans.

In their longer voyages they steer in the day by the sun, and in the night by the stars : of these they know a very large number by name, and the cleverest among them will tell in what part of the heavens they are to be seen in any month when they are above their horizon : they know also the time of their annual appearance and disappearance to a great nicety, far greater than would be easily believed by an European astronomer.

I was not able to get a complete idea of their method of dividing time. I shall, however, set down what little I know. In speaking of time either past or to come, they never use any term but moons, of which they count thirteen, and then begin again: this of itself sufficiently shows that they have some idea of the solar year, but how they manage to make their thirteen months agree with it I never could find out. That they do, however, I believe, because in mentioning the names of months they very frequently told us the fruits that would be in season in each of them, etc. They also have a name for the thirteen months collectively, but they never use it in speaking of time; it is employed only in explaining the mysteries of their religion. In their metaphorical year they say that the year *Tettowma ta tayo* was the daughter of the chief divinity *Taroataihetoomoo*, and that she in time brought forth the months, who in their turn produced the days, of which they count twenty-nine in every month, including one in which the moon is invisible. Every one of these has its respective name, and is again subdivided into twelve parts, containing about two hours each, six for the day and six for the night, each of which has likewise its respective name. In the day-time they guess the divisions of these parts very well, but in the night, though they have the same number of divisions as in the day, seem very little able to tell at any time which hour it is, except the cleverest among them who know the stars.

In counting they proceed from one to ten, having a different name for each number; from thence they say one more, two more, etc., up to twenty, which after being called in the general count ten more, acquires a new name as we say a score: by these scores they count till they have got ten of them, which again acquires a new name, 200; these again are counted till they get ten of them, 2000; which is the largest denomination I have ever heard them make use of, and I suppose is as large as they can ever have occasion for, as they can count ten of these (*i.e.* up to 20,000) without any new term.

In measures of space they are very poor indeed: one

fathom and ten fathoms are the only terms I have heard among them. By these they convey the size of anything, as a house, a boat, depth of the sea, etc., but when they speak of distances from one place to another they have no way of making themselves understood but by the number of days it takes them in their canoes to go the distance.

Their language appeared to me to be very soft and tuneful; it abounds in vowels, and was easily pronounced by us, while ours was to them absolutely impracticable. I instance particularly my own name, which I took much pains to teach them and they to learn; after three days' fruitless trial I was forced to select from their many attempts *Tapane*, the only one I had been able to get from them that had the least similitude to it. Spanish or Italian words they pronounced with ease, provided they ended with a vowel, for few or none of theirs end with a consonant.

I cannot say that I am sufficiently acquainted with it to pronounce whether it is copious or not; in one respect, however, it is beyond measure inferior to all European languages, and that is in its almost total want of inflection both of nouns and verbs, few or none of the former having more than one case or the latter one tense. Notwithstanding this want, however, we found it very easy to make ourselves understood in matters of common necessaries, however paradoxical it may appear to an European.

They have certain suffixes and make very frequent use of them. This puzzled us at first very much, though they are but few in number. An instance or two may be necessary to make myself understood, as they do not exist in any modern European language. One asks another "Harre nea?" "Where are you going?" The other answers "Ivahinera," "To my wives," on which the first questioning him still further "Ivahinera?" "To your wives?" is answered "Ivahinereiaa," "Yes, I am going to my wives." Here the suffixes *era* and *eiaa* save several words to both parties.

From the vocabularies given in Le Maire's voyage (see *Histoire des Navigations aux Terres Australes*, tom. i. p. 410[1])

---

[1] By C. de Brosse, 1756.

it appears clearly that the languages given there as those of
the Isles of Solomon and the Isle of Cocos[1] are radically the
identical language we met with, most words differing in
little, but the greater number of consonants. The languages
of New Guinea and Moyse Isle[2] have also many words radically the same, particularly their numbers, although they are
so obscured by a multitude of consonants that it is scarcely
possible that they should be detected but by those who are in
some measure acquainted with one of the languages. For
instance the New Guinea *hisson* (fish) is found to be the
same as the Otahite *eia* by the medium of *ica* of the Isle of
Solomon; *talingan* (ears) is in Otahite *terrea; limang* (a
hand) becomes *lima* or *rima; paring* (cheeks) is *paperea;
mattanga* (eyes) *mata;* "they called us," says the author,
"*tata*," which in Otahite signifies men in general.

That the people who inhabit this numerous range of
islands should have originally come from one and the same
place, and brought with them the same numbers and
language, which latter especially have remained not materially altered to this day, is in my opinion not at all beyond
belief; but that the numbers of Madagascar should be the
same as all these is almost if not quite incredible. I shall
give them from a book called a *Collection of Voyages by the
Dutch East Company*, Lond. 1703, p. 116, where, supposing
the author who speaks of ten numbers and gives only nine
to have lost the fifth, their similarity is beyond dispute.

Madagascar.	Otahite.	Cocos Isle.	New Guinea.
1. Issa	Tahie	Taci	Tika
2. Rove	Rua	Loua	Roa
3. Tello	Torou	Tolou	Tola
4. Effat	Hea	Fa	Fatta
6. Enning	Whene	Houno	Wamma
7. Fruto	Hetu	Fitou	Fita
8. Wedo	Waru	Walou	Walla
9. Sidai	Heva	Ywore	Siwa
10. Scula	Ahourou	Ongefoula	Sangafoula

[1] Probably one of the Samoa group, not the Keeling Islands.
[2] An island off the N.E. coast of New Guinea, so named by Le Maire.

It must be remembered, however, that the author of this voyage, during the course of it, touched at Java and several other East Indian Isles, as well as at Madagascar; so that if by any disarrangement of his papers he has given the numerals of some of those islands for those of Madagascar, our wonder will be much diminished; for after having traced them from Otahite to New Guinea it would not seem very wonderful to carry them a little farther to the East Indian Isles, which from their situation seem not unlikely to be the place from whence our islanders originally came. But I shall waive saying any more on this subject till I have had an opportunity of myself seeing the customs, etc. of the Javans, which this voyage will in all probability give me an opportunity of doing.

The language of all the islands I was upon was the same, so far as I could understand it; the people of Ulhietea only changed the *t* of the Otahiteans to *k*, calling *tata*, which signifies a man or woman, *kaka*, a peculiarity which made the language much less soft. The people of Oheteroa, so far as I could understand their words, which were only shouted out to us, seemed to do the same thing, and add many more consonants, which made their language much less musical. I shall give a few of the words, from whence an idea may be got of their language.

Eupo	the head	Oboo	the belly
Ahewh	the nose	Rema	the arm
Roourou	the hair	Aporema	the hand
Outou	the mouth	Manneow	the fingers
Nihëo	the teeth	Mieu	the nails
Arrero	the tongue	Touhe	the buttocks
Meu-Eumi	the beard	Hoouhah	the thighs
Tiarraboa	the throat	Mae	fat
Tuamo	the shoulders	Huru-puru	hair
Tuah	the back	Eraou	a tree
Aoai	the legs	Ama	a branch
Tapoa	the feet	Tiale	a flower
Booa	a hog	Huero	fruit
Moa	a fowl	Etummoo	the stem
Eurèe	a dog	Aāā	the root
Eurè-eure	iron	Eiherre	herbaceous plants
Ooroo	bread-fruit	Oboopa	a pigeon
Hearee	cocoanuts	Avigne	a parroquet
Mia	bananas	Aa	another species
Vaè	wild plantains	Mannu	a bird
Ooma	the breast	Mora	a duck
Eu	the nipples	Mattow	a fish-hook

Toura	a rope	Eno	bad
Mow	a shark	A	yes
Mattera	a fishing-rod	Ima	no
Eupea	a net	Paree	ugly
Mahanna	the sun	Pororee	hungry
Malama	the moon	Pia	full
Whettu	a star	Tuhea	lean
Whettu-euphe	a comet	Timahah	heavy
Erai	the sky	Mama	light
Eatta	a cloud	Poto	short
Mahi mahi	a dolphin	Roa	tall
Poe	beads	Neuenne	sweet
Poe Matawewwe	pearl	Mala	bitter
Ahow	a garment	Whanno	to go far
Avee	a fruit like an apple	Harre	to go
Ahee	another like a chestnut	Arrea	to stay
		Enoho	to remain or tarry
Ewharre	a house	Rohe-rohe	to be tired
Whennua	a high island	Maa	to eat
Motu	a low island	Inoo	to drink
Toto	blood	Ete	to understand
Aeve	bone	Warriddo	to steal
Aeo	flesh	Woridde	to be angry
Miti	good	Teparahie	to beat

Among people whose diet is so simple and plain distempers cannot be expected to be as frequent as among us Europeans ; we observed but few, and those chiefly cutaneous, as erysipelas and scaly eruptions on the skin. This last was almost, if not quite, advanced to leprosy; the people who were in that state were secluded from society, living by themselves each in a small house built in some unfrequented place, where they were daily supplied with provisions. Whether these had any hope of relief, or were doomed in this manner to languish out a life of solitude, we did not learn. Some, but very few, had ulcers on different parts of their bodies, most of which looked very virulent ; the people who were afflicted with them did not, however, seem much to regard them, leaving them entirely without any application, even to keep off the flies. Acute distempers no doubt they have, but while we stayed upon the island they were very uncommon ; possibly in the rainy season they are more frequent. Among the numerous acquaintances I had upon the island only one was taken ill during our stay. I visited her and found her, as is their custom, left by everybody but her three children, who sat by her ; her complaint was colic, which did not appear to me to be at all violent. I asked her what medicine she took, she told me none, and that she depended entirely upon the priest, who had been trying to free her from her distemper by his prayers and ceremonies, which, she said, he would repeat till she was well, showing me at the same time branches of the *Thespesia populnea*, which he had left with her. After this I left her, and whether through the priest's ceremonies or her own constitution, she came down to our tents completely recovered in three days' time.

I never happened to be present when the priests performed their ceremonies for the cure of sick people; but one of our gentlemen who was informed me that they consisted of nothing but the repetition of certain fixed sentences, during which time the priest plaited leaves of the cocoanut tree into different figures, neatly enough; some of which he fastened to the fingers and toes of the sick man, who was at the time uncovered, out of respect to the prayers. The whole ceremony almost exactly resembled their method of praying at the *marais*, which I shall by and by describe. They appear, however, to have some knowledge of medicine, besides these operations of priestcraft. That they have skilful surgeons among them we easily gathered from the dreadful scars of wounds which we frequently saw cured, some of which were far greater than any I have seen anywhere else; and these were made by stones which these people throw with slings with great dexterity and force. One man I particularly recollect whose face was almost entirely destroyed; yet this dreadful wound had healed cleanly without any ulcer remaining. Tupia, who has had several wounds, had one made by a spear headed with the bone of a sting-ray's tail which had pierced right through his body, entering at his back and coming out just under his breast; yet this has been so well cured that the remaining scar is as smooth and as small as any I have seen from the cures by our best European surgeons.

Vulnerary herbs they have many, nor do they seem at all nice in the choice of them. They have plenty of such herbaceous plants as yield mild juices devoid of all acridity, similar to the English chickweed, groundsel, etc.; with these they make fomentations, which they frequently apply to the wound, taking care to cleanse it as often as possible; the patient all the time observing great abstinence. By this method, if they have told me truly, their wounds are cured in a very short time. As for their medicines we learned but little concerning them; they told us, and indeed freely, that such and such plants were good for such and such distempers, but it required a much better knowledge of the language than we were able to obtain during our short stay to understand the method of application.

Their manner of disposing of their dead as well as the ceremonies relating to their mourning are so remarkable that they deserve a very particular description. As soon as any one is dead the house is immediately filled with his relations, who bewail their loss with loud lamentations, especially those who are the farthest removed in blood from, or who profess the least grief for, the deceased. The nearer relations and those who are really affected spend their time in more silent sorrow, while the rest join in a chorus of grief at certain intervals, between which they laugh, talk, and gossip as if totally unconcerned. This lasts till daylight of the next day, when the body, being shrouded in cloth, is laid upon a kind of bier on which it can conveniently be carried on men's shoulders. The priest's office now begins; he prays over the body, repeating his sentences, and orders it to be carried down to the sea-side. Here his prayers are renewed; the corpse is brought down near the water's edge, and he sprinkles water towards but not upon it; it is then removed forty or fifty yards from the sea, and soon after brought back. This ceremony is repeated several times. In the meantime a house has been built and a small space of ground round it railed in; in the centre of this house are posts, upon which the bier, as soon as the ceremonies are finished, is set. On these the corpse is to remain and putrefy in state, to the no small disgust of every one whose business requires him to pass near it.

These houses of corruption, *tu papow*, are of a size proportionate to the rank of the person contained in them. If he is poor it merely covers the bier, and generally has no railing round it. The largest I ever saw was eleven yards in length. These houses are ornamented according to the ability and inclination of the surviving relations, who never fail to lay a profusion of good cloth about the body, and often almost cover the outside of the house; the two ends, which are open, are also hung with garlands of the fruits of the palm-nut (*Pandanus*), cocoanut leaves knotted by the priests, mystic roots, and a plant called by them *ethee nota marai* (*Terminalia*), which is particularly consecrated to funerals. Near the house is also laid fish, fruits, and cocoanuts, or common water, or such provisions as can well be spared; not that they suppose the dead in any way capable of eating this provision, but they think that if any of their gods should descend upon that place, and being hungry find that these preparations had been neglected, he would infallibly satisfy his appetite with the flesh of the corpse.

No sooner is the corpse fixed up within the house, or *ewhatta*, as they call it, than the ceremony of mourning begins again. The women (for the men seem to think lamentations beneath their dignity) assemble, led on by the nearest relative, who, walking up to the door of the house, swimming almost in tears, strikes a shark's tooth several times into the crown of her head; the blood which results from these wounds is carefully caught in their linen, and thrown under the bier. Her example is imitated by the rest of the women; and this ceremony is repeated at intervals of two or three days, as long as the women are willing or able to keep it up; the nearest relation thinking it her duty to continue it longer than any one else. Besides this blood—which they believe to be an acceptable present to the deceased, whose soul they believe to exist, and hover about the place where the body lays, observing the action of the survivors—they throw in cloths wet with tears, of which all that are shed are carefully preserved for that purpose; and the younger people cut off all or a part of their hair, and throw that also under the bier.

When the ceremonies have been performed for two or three days, the men, who till now seemed to be entirely insensible of their loss, begin their part. They have a peculiar dress for this occasion, and patrol the woods early in the morning and late at night, preceded by two or three boys, who have nothing upon them but a small piece of cloth round their waists, and who are smutted all over with charcoal. These sable emissaries run about their principal in all directions, as if in pursuit of people on whom he may vent the rage inspired by his sorrow, which he does most unmercifully if he catches any one, cutting them with his stick, the edge of which is set with shark's teeth. But this rarely or never happens, for no sooner does this figure appear than every one who sees either him or his emissaries, inspired with a sort of religious awe, flies with the utmost speed, hiding wherever he thinks himself safest, but by all means quitting his house if it lies even near the path of this dreadful apparition.

These ceremonies continue for five moons, decreasing, however, in frequency very much towards the latter part of that time. The body is then taken down from the *ewhatta*, the bones washed and scraped very clean, and buried according to the rank of the person, either within or without some one of their *marais* or places of public worship; and if it is one of their *earees*, or chiefs, his skull is preserved, and, wrapped up in fine cloth, is placed in a kind of case made for the purpose, which stands in the *marai*. The mourning then ceases, unless some of the women, who find themselves more than commonly afflicted by their loss, repeat the ceremony of *poopooing*, or bleeding themselves in the head, which they do at any time or in any place they happen to be when the whim takes them.

The ceremonies, however, are far from ceasing at this stage; frequent prayers must be said by the priest, and frequent offerings made for the benefit of the deceased, or more properly for that of the priests, who are well paid for their prayers by the surviving relations. During the ceremony emblematical devices are made use of; a young plantain tree signifies the deceased, and a bundle of feathers the deity invoked. Opposite to this the priest places himself, often attended by relations of the deceased, and always furnished with a small offering of some kind of eatables intended for the god. He begins by addressing the god by a set form of sentences, and during the time he repeats them employs himself in weaving cocoanut leaves into different forms, all which he disposes upon the grave where the bones have been deposited; the deity is then addressed by a shrill screech, used only on that occasion, and the offering presented to his representative (the little tuft of feathers), which after this is removed, and everything else left *in statu quo*, to the no small emolument of the rats, who quietly devour the offering.

Religion has been in all ages, and is still in all countries, clothed in mysteries inexplicable to human understanding. In the South Sea Islands it has still another disadvantage to any one who desires to investigate it: the language in which it is conveyed, or at least many words of it, is different from that of common conversation; so that although Tupia often showed the greatest desire to instruct us in it, he found it almost impossible. It is only necessary to remember how difficult it would be to reconcile the apparent inconsistencies of our own religion to the faith of an infidel, and to recollect how many excellent discourses are daily read to instruct even us in the faith which we profess, to excuse me when I declare that I know less of the religion of these people than of any other part of their policy. What I do know, however, I shall here write down, hoping that inconsistencies may not appear to the eye of the candid reader as absurdities.

This universe and its marvellous parts must strike the most stupid with a desire of knowing from whence they themselves and it were produced; their priests, however, have not ideas sufficiently enlarged to adopt that of creation. That this world should have been originally created from nothing far surpasses their comprehension. They observed, however, that every animal and every plant produced others, and adopted the idea; hence it is necessary to suppose two original beings, one of whom they called *Ettoomoo*, and the other, which they say was a rock, *Tepapa*. These, at some very remote period of time, produced men and women, and from their children is derived all that is seen or known to us. Some things, however, they imagine, increased among themselves, as the stars, the different species of plants, and even the different divisions of time—the year, say they, produced the months, who in their turn produced the days.

Their gods are numerous, and are divided into two classes, the greater and the lesser gods, and in each class some are of both sexes. The chief of all is *Tarroatiettoomoo*, the father of all things, whom they emphatically style the "Causer of Earthquakes"; his son, *Tane*, is, however, much more generally invoked, as he is supposed to be the more active deity. The men worship the male gods, and the women the females; the men, however, supply the office of priest for both sexes.

They believe in a heaven and a hell: the first they call *Tavirua l'orai*, the other *tiahoboo*. Heaven they describe as a place of great happiness, while hell is only a place enjoying less of the luxuries of life: to this, they say, the souls of the inferior people go after death, and those of the chiefs and rich men go to heaven. This is one of the strongest instances to show that their religion is totally independent of morality, no actions regarding their neighbours are supposed to come at all under the cognisance of the diety: a humble regard only is to be shown him, and his assistance asked on all occasions with much ceremony and some sacrifice, from whence are derived the perquisites of the priests.

The *Tahowa*, or priest, is here a hereditary dignity. These priests are numerous: the chief of them is generally the younger brother of some very good family, and ranks next to the king. All priests are commonly more learned than the laity: their learning consists chiefly in knowing well the names and rank of the different *Eatuas,* or divinities, the origin of the universe and all its parts, etc. This knowledge has been handed down to them in set sentences, of which those who are clever can repeat an almost infinite number.

Besides religion, the practice of physic and the knowledge of navigation and astronomy is in the possession of the priests: the name indeed, *Tahowa,* signifies a man of knowledge, so that even here the priests monopolise the greater part of the learning of the country in much the same manner as they formerly did in Europe. From their learning they gain profit as well as respect, each in his particular order; for each order has priests of its own; nor would those of the *manahounis* do anything for a *toutou* who is below them.

Marriage in these islands is no more than an agreement between man and woman, totally independent of the priest; it is in general, I believe, well kept, unless the parties agree to separate, which is done with as little trouble as they came together. Few people, however, enter this state, but rather choose freedom, though bought at the inhuman expense of murdering their children, whose fate is in that case entirely dependent on the father, who if he does not choose to acknowledge both them and the woman, and engage to contribute his part towards their support, orders the child to be strangled, which is instantly put in execution.

If our priests have excelled theirs in persuading us that marriage cannot be lawful without their benediction having been bought, they have done it by intermingling it so far with religion that the fear of punishment from above secures their power over us; but these untaught persons have secured to themselves the profit of two operations without being driven to the necessity of so severe a penalty on the refusal, viz. tattowing and circumcision; neither of these can be performed by any but priests, and as the highest degree of shame attaches to the neglect of either, the people are as much obliged to make use of them as if bound by the highest ties of religion, of which both customs are totally independent. They give no reason for the tattowing but

that their ancestors did the same : for both these operations
the priests are paid by every one according to his ability,
in the same manner as weddings, christenings, etc., etc., are
paid for in Europe. Their places of public worship, or
marais, are square enclosures of very different sizes, from
ten to a hundred yards in length. At one end a heap or
pile of stones is built up, near which the bones of the
principal people are interred, those of their dependents
lying all round on the outside of the wall. Near or in
these enclosures are often placed planks carved into different
figures, and very frequently images of many men standing
on each other's heads ; these, however, are in no degree the
objects of adoration, every prayer and sacrifice being offered
to invisible deities.

Near, or even within the *marai*, are one or more large
altars, raised on high posts ten or twelve feet above the
ground, which are called *ewhattas ;* on these are laid the
offerings, hogs, dogs, fowls, fruits, or whatever else the piety
or superfluity of the owner thinks proper to dedicate to the
gods.

Both these places are reverenced in the highest degree :
no man approaches them without taking his clothes from off
his shoulders, and no woman is on any account permitted
to enter them. The women, however, have *marais* of their
own, where they worship and sacrifice to their goddesses.

Of these *marais* each family of consequence has one,
which serves for himself and his dependents. As each
family values itself on its antiquity, so are the *marais*
esteemed : in the Society Isles, especially Ulhietea, were
some of great antiquity, particularly that of *Tapo de boatea*.
The material of these is rough and coarse, but the stones of
which they are composed are immensely large. At Otahite
again, where from frequent wars or other accidents many
of the most ancient families are extinct, they have tried to
make them as elegant and expensive as possible, of which
sort is that of Oamo (described on pp. 102-4).

Besides their gods, each island has a bird, to which the
title of *Eatua* or god is given : for instance Ulhietea has the

heron, and Bola-Bola a kind of kingfisher : these birds are
held in high respect, and are never killed or molested : they
are thought to be givers of good or bad fortune, but no sort
of worship is offered to them.

Though I dare not assert that these people, to whom the
art of writing, and consequently of recording laws, etc., is
totally unknown, live under a regular form of government,
yet the subordination which takes place among them very
much resembles the early state of the feudal laws, by which
our ancestors were so long governed, a system evidently
formed to secure the licentious liberty of a few, while the
greater part of the society are unalterably immersed in the
most abject slavery.

Their orders are *Earee ra hie*, which answers to king ;
earee, baron ; *manahouni*, vassal ; and *toutou*, villain.   The
earee ra hie is always the head of the best family in the
country : to him great respect is paid by all ranks, but in
power he seemed to be inferior to several of the principal
earees, nor indeed did he once appear in the transaction of
any part of our business.   Next to him in rank are the
earees, each of whom holds one or more of the districts into
which the island is divided : in Otahite there may be about
a hundred such districts, which are by the *earees* parcelled
out to the *manahounis*, each of whom cultivates his part,
and for the use of it owes his chief service and provisions
when called upon, especially when the latter travels, which he
constantly does, accompanied by many of his friends and
their families, often amounting to nearly a hundred principals,
besides their attendants.   Inferior to the *manahounis* are
the *toutous*, who are almost upon the same footing as the
slaves in the East Indian Islands, only that they never
appeared transferable from one to the other.   These do all
kinds of laborious work : till the land, fetch wood and water,
dress the victuals, under the direction, however, of the
mistress of the family, catch fish, etc.   Besides these are
the two classes of *erata* and *towha*, who seem to answer to
yeomen and *gentlemen*, as they came between the *earee* and
manahouni : but as I was not acquainted with the existence

of these classes during our stay in the island, I know little of their real situation.

Each of the *earees* keeps a kind of court, and has a large attendance, chiefly of the younger brothers of his own family and of other *earees*. Among these were different officers of the court, as *Heewa no t' Earee, Whanno no t' Earee*, who were sometimes sent to us on business. Of all these courts Dootahah's was the most splendid, indeed we were almost inclined to believe that he acted as *locum tenens* for Otow, the *Earee ra hie* being his nephew, as he lived upon an estate belonging to him, and we never could hear that he had any other public place of residence.

The *earees*, or rather the districts which they possess, are obliged in time of a general attack to furnish each their quota of soldiers for the public service; those of the principal districts which Tupia recollected, when added together, amounted to 6680 men, to which army it is probable that the small quotas of the rest would not make any great addition.

Besides these public wars, which must be headed by the *Earee ra hie*, any private difference between two *earees* is decided by their own people without in the least disturbing the tranquillity of the public. Their weapons are slings, which they use with great dexterity, pikes headed with the stings of sting-rays, and clubs six or seven feet long, made of a very heavy and hard wood; with these they fight by their own account very obstinately, which appears the more probable as the conquerors give no quarter to any man, woman, or child who is unfortunate enough to fall into their hands during or for some time after the battle, that is, until their passion has subsided.

Otahite at the time of our stay there was divided into two kingdoms, Oporenoo, the larger, and Tiarrebo; each had its separate king, etc. etc., who were at peace with each other; the king of Oporenoo, however, called himself king of both, in just the same manner as European monarchs usurp the title of king over kingdoms in which they have not the least influence.

It is not to be expected that in a government of this kind justice can be properly administered, we saw indeed no signs of punishment during our stay. Tupia, however, always insisted upon it that theft was punished with death, and smaller crimes in proportion. All punishments, however, were the business of the injured party, who, if superior to him who committed the crime, easily executed them by means of his more numerous attendants; equals seldom chose to molest each other, unless countenanced by their superiors, who assisted them to defend their unjust acquisitions. The chiefs, however, to whom in reality all kinds of property belong, punish their dependents for crimes committed against each other, and the dependents of others, if caught doing wrong within their districts.

CHAPTER VIII

16*th August* 1769.   Early this morning we were told that
land was in sight.   It proved to be a cloud, but at first sight
was so like land that it deceived every man in the ship ; even
Tupia gave it a name.

17*th.*   A heavy swell from the south-west all day, so we
are not yet under the lee of the continent.   Our *taros*
(roots like a yam, called in the West Indies *cocos*) failed us
to-day ; many of them were rotten.   They would probably
have kept longer had we had either time or opportunity of
drying them well, but I believe that at the best they are
very much inferior to either yams or potatoes for keeping.

24*th.* The morning was calm.   About nine it began
to blow fresh with rain, which came on without the least
warning ; at the same time a waterspout was seen to leeward.   It appeared to me so inconsiderable, that had it not
been pointed out to me, I should not have particularly
noticed the appearance.   It resembled a line of thick mist,
as thick as a middling-sized tree, which reached, not in a

straight line, almost to the water's edge, and in a few minutes totally disappeared. Its distance, I suppose, made it appear so trifling, as the seamen judged it to be not less than two or three miles from us.

29th. In the course of last night a phenomenon was seen in the heavens which Mr. Green says is either a comet or a nebula; he does not know which; the seamen have observed it these three nights.

30th. Our comet is this morning acknowledged, and proves a very large one, but very faint.   Tupia, as soon as he saw it, declared that the people of Bola-Bola would, upon the sight of it, kill the people of Ulhietea, of whom as many as were able would fly into the mountains.   Several birds were seen : pintados, albatrosses of both kinds, the little silver-backed bird which we saw off the Falkland Isles and Cape Horn (*Procellaria velox*), and a gray shearwater. Peter saw a green bird about the size of a dove : the colour makes us hope that it is a land bird; it took, however, not the least notice of the ship.   Some seaweed was also seen to pass by the ship, but as it was a very small piece, our hopes are not very sanguine on that head.

31st. Many millions, I may safely say, of the *Procellaria velox* mentioned yesterday were about the ship to-day; they were grayish on the back, and some had a dark-coloured mark going in a crooked direction over the back and wings. I tried to-day to catch some of these numerous attendants with a hook; but after the whole morning spent in the attempt caught only one pintado, which proved to be *Procellaria capensis,* Linn.

19th September.   Shot *Procellaria velox* (the dove of the 31st), *P. vagabunda* (a gray-backed shearwater) and a *Passerina.*   Took with the dipping-net *Medusa vitrea, Phyllodoce velella* (to one species of which adhered *Lepas anatifera*), *Doris complanata, Helix violacea,*[1] and a *Cancer.*

23rd. Dr. Solander has been unwell for some days, so to-day I opened Dr. Hulme's essence of lemon juice, Mr. Monkhouse having prescribed it for him; it proved perfectly

---

[1] A species of *Ianthina.*

good, little, if at all, inferior in taste to fresh lemon juice. We also to-day made a pie of the North American apples which Dr. Fothergill had given me, and which proved very good; if not quite equal to the apple pies which our friends in England are now eating, good enough to please us who have been so long deprived of the fruits of our native country. In the main, however, we are very well off for refreshments and provisions of most sorts. Our ship's beef and pork are excellent; peas, flour, and oatmeal are at present, and have been in general, very good; our water is as sweet and has rather more spirit than it had when drank out of the river at Otahite; our bread, indeed, is but indifferent, occasioned by the quantity of vermin that are in it. I have often seen hundreds, nay, thousands, shaken out of a single biscuit. We in the cabin have, however, an easy remedy for this, by baking it in an oven, not too hot, which makes them all walk off; but this cannot be allowed to the ship's people, who must find the taste of these animals very disagreeable, as they every one taste as strong as mustard, or rather spirits of hartshorn. They are of five kinds, three *Tenebrio*, one *Ptinus*, and the *Phalangium canchroides*; this last, however, is scarce in the common bread, but vastly plentiful in white meal biscuits, as long as we had any left.

Wheat has been boiled for the breakfasts of the ship's company two or three times a week, in the same manner as frumenty is made. This has, I believe, been a very useful refreshment to them, as well as an agreeable food, which I myself and most of the officers in the ship have constantly breakfasted upon in the cold weather. The grain was originally of a good quality, and has kept without the least damage. This, however, cannot be said of the malt, of which we have plainly had two kinds, one very good, which was used up some time ago. What we are at present using is good for nothing at all; it was originally of a bad light grain, and so little care has been taken in making it that the tails are left in with innumerable other kinds of dirt; add to all this that it has been damped on board ship; so that, with all the care that can be used, it will scarce give a tincture to

water.   Portable soup is very good; it has now and then
required an airing to prevent it from moulding.   Sour crout
is as good as ever.

So much for the ship's company : we ourselves are hardly
as well off as they.   Our live stock consists of seventeen
sheep, four or five fowls, as many South Sea hogs, four or five
Muscovy ducks, and an English boar and sow with a litter
of pigs.   In the use of these we are rather sparing, as the
time of our getting a fresh supply is rather precarious.
Salt stock we have nothing worth mentioning, except a kind
of salt beef and salted cabbage.   Our malt liquors have
answered extremely well; we have now both small beer and
porter upon tap, as good as I ever drank them, especially
the latter.   The small beer had some art used to make it
keep.   Our wine I cannot say much for, though I believe it
to be good in its nature ; we have not had a glass full these
many months, I believe chiefly owing to the carelessness or
ignorance of the steward.

2nd October.   Took *Dagysa rostrata, serena,* and *polyedra ;
Beroe incrassata* and *coarctata ; Medusa vitrea ; Phyllodoce
velella,* with several other things which are all put in spirits ;
Diomedea exulans ; Procellaria velox, palmipes, latirostris, and
longipes ; and *Nectris fuliginosa.*

3rd. In the course of the day several pieces of a new
species of seaweed were taken, and one piece of wood covered
with striated barnacles (*Lepas anserina*).

5th. Two seals passed the ship asleep, and three birds
which Mr. Gore calls Port Egmont hens (*Larus catarrhactes*).
He says they are a sure sign of our being near land.   They
are something larger than a crow ; in flight much like one,
flapping their wings often with a slow motion.   Their
bodies and wings are of a dark chocolate or soot colour ;
under each wing is a small broadish bar of a dirty white,
which makes them so remarkable that it is hardly possible
to mistake them.   They are seen, as he says, all along the
coast of South America and the Falkland Isles.   I myself
remember to have seen them at Terra del Fuego, but by
some accident did not note them down.

7th. This morning the land was plainly seen from the deck; it appears to be very large. About eleven a large smoke was seen, and soon after several more sure signs of inhabitants. I shot *Nectris munda* and *Procellaria velox,* and took with the dipping-net *Dagysa gemma,* and a good deal of *Fucus sertularia,* etc., the examination of which is postponed till we shall have more time than we are likely to have at present.

8th. This morning we are very near the land, which forms many white cliffs like chalk. The hills are in general clothed with trees; in the valleys some appear to be very large. The whole appearance is not so fruitful as we could wish. We stood in for a large bay in hopes of finding a harbour, and before we were well within the heads we saw several canoes standing across the bay, which after a little time returned to the place they came from without appearing to take the least notice of us. Some houses were also seen, which appeared low but neat; near one of them there were a good many people collected, who sat down upon the beach, seemingly observing us. On a small peninsular at the north-east head we could plainly see a regular paling, pretty high, inclosing the top of a hill, for what purpose many conjectures were made; most are of opinion, or say at least, that it must be either a park of deer or a field of oxen and sheep. By four o'clock we came to an anchor nearly two miles from the shore. The bay appears to be quite open, without the least shelter; the two sides of it make in high white cliffs; the middle is lowland, with hills gradually rising behind one another to a chain of high mountains inland. Here we saw many great smokes, some near the beach, others between the hills, some very far within land, which we looked upon as great indications of a populous country.

In the evening I went ashore with the marines. We marched from the boats in hopes of finding water, etc., and saw a few of the natives, who ran away immediately on seeing us. While we were absent four of them attacked our small boat, in which were only four boys. They got off

from the shore in a river; the people followed them and
threatened with long lances; the pinnace soon came to their
assistance, fired upon the natives, and killed the chief. The
other three dragged the body about a hundred yards and
then left it. At the report of the muskets we drew
together and went to the place where the body was left; it
was shot through the heart. He was a middle-sized man,
tattowed on the face on one cheek only, in spiral lines very
regularly formed. He was covered with a fine cloth of a
manufacture totally new to us; it was tied on exactly as
represented in Mr. Dalrymple's book,[1] p. 63; his hair was
also tied in a knot on the top of his head, but there was no
feather stuck in it; his complexion brown but not very dark.

Soon after we came on board we very distinctly heard
the people ashore talking very loud, although they were not
less than two miles distant from us.

9th. On attempting to land this morning the Indians
received us with threatening demonstrations, but a musket
fired wide of them intimidated them, and they allowed us
to approach near enough to parley. Tupia found their
language so near his own that he could tolerably well
understand them. He induced them to lay down their
arms, and we gave them some beads and iron, neither of
which they seemed to value; indeed, they seemed totally
ignorant of the use of the latter. They constantly
attempted to seize our arms, or anything they could get, so
that we were obliged to fire on them and disperse them;
none were, we hope, killed. Soon after we intercepted a
native canoe; but when we came up with it, the owners
made so desperate a resistance that we were compelled to
fire upon them, killing four; the other three (boys)
attempted to swim to shore, but were captured and taken
on board the ship. On finding that they were not to be
killed, they at once recovered their spirits, and soon
appeared to have forgotten everything that had happened.
At supper they ate an enormous quantity of bread, and

---

[1] *An Account of the Discoveries made in the South Pacifick Ocean, previous to*
1764. By Alexander Dalrymple. London, 1767.

drank over a quart of water apiece. Thus ended the most disagreeable day my life has yet seen; black be the mark for it, and heaven send that such may never return to embitter future reflection.

10*th.* The native boys, after being loaded with presents, were put in the boats and rowed ashore by our men. They at first begged hard not to be set ashore at the place where we had landed yesterday, and to which we first rowed to-day, but afterwards voluntarily landed there. The natives again appeared threatening, but it was presently discovered that they were friends of the boys we had captured, and a peace was presently concluded by our acceptance of green boughs which they presented to us; a not unimportant ratification apparently being the removal by them of the body of the man killed yesterday, which had remained till now on the same spot.

11*th.* This morning we took leave of Poverty Bay, as we named it, with not above forty species of plants in our boxes, which is not to be wondered at, as we were so little ashore, and always upon the same spot. The only time when we wandered about a mile from the boats was upon a swamp where not more than three species of plants were found.

Several canoes put off from the shore, and came towards us within less than a quarter of a mile, but could not at first be persuaded to come nearer. At last one was seen coming from Poverty Bay, or near it. She had only four people in her, one of whom I well remembered to have seen at our first interview on the rock. These never stopped to look at anything, but came at once alongside of the ship, and with very little persuasion came on board. Their example was quickly followed by the rest, seven canoes in all, and fifty men. Many presents were given to them, notwithstanding which they very quickly sold almost everything that they had with them, even their clothes from their backs, and the paddles out of their boats. Arms they had none, except two men, one of whom sold his *patoo patoo*, as he called it, a short weapon of green talc of this shape, intended, doubtless, for fighting hand-to-hand, and certainly well contrived for splitting skulls, as it weighs not less than four or five pounds, and has sharp edges excellently polished.

The people were, in general, of a middling size, though there was no one who measured more than six feet. Their colour was a dark brown. Their lips were stained with something put under the skin (as in the Otahite tattow), and their faces marked with deeply-engraved furrows, also coloured black, and formed in regular spirals. Of these, the oldest people had much the greatest quantity, and most deeply channelled, in some not less than $\frac{1}{16}$ part of an inch. Their hair was black, and tied up on the tops of their heads in a little knot, in which were stuck feathers of various birds in different tastes, according to the humour of the wearer. Sometimes they had one knot on each side, and pointing forwards, which made a most disagreeable appearance. In their ears they generally wore a large bunch of the milk-white down of some bird. The faces of some were painted with a red colour in oil, some all over, others in parts only. In their hair was much oil, which had very little smell, but more lice than ever I saw before. Most of them had a small comb, neatly enough made, sometimes of wood, sometimes of bone, which they seem to prize much. A few had on their faces or arms regular scars, as if made with a sharp instrument, such as I have seen on the faces of negroes. The inferior sort were clothed in something that very much resembled hemp: the loose strings of this were fastened together at the top, and it hung down about two feet like a petticoat. Of these garments they wore two, one round their shoulders, and the other about their waists. The richer had garments probably of a finer sort of the same stuff, most beautifully made, and exactly like that of the South American Indians at this day, and as fine, or finer, than a piece which I bought at Rio de Janeiro for thirty-six shillings, and which was esteemed uncommonly cheap at that price. Their boats were not large, but well made, something like our whale boats, not longer. The bottom was the trunk of a tree hollowed out, and very thin. This was raised by a board on each side, with a strip of wood sewed over the seam to make it tight. On the prow of every one was carved the head of a man with an enormous tongue reaching out of his mouth. These grotesque figures were generally very well executed; some had eyes inlaid with something that shone very much. The whole served to give us an idea of their taste, as well as ingenuity in execution. It was certainly much superior to anything we have yet seen.

Their behaviour while on board showed every sign of friendship. They invited us very cordially to come back to our old bay, or to a small cove near it. I could not help wishing that we had done so, but the captain chose rather to stand on in search of a better harbour. God send that we may not have the same tragedy to act over again as we so lately perpetrated. The country is certainly divided into many small principalities, so we cannot hope that an account of our weapons and management of them can be conveyed as far as we must in all probability go; and of this I am well convinced, that till these warlike people have severely felt our superiority they will never behave to us in a friendly manner.

About an hour before sunset the canoes left us, and with us three of their people, who were very desirous to have gone with them, but were not permitted to return. What their reason for so doing is we can only guess; possibly they may think that their being on board may induce us to remain here till to-morrow, when they will return and renew the traffic by which they find themselves so great gainers. The three people were tolerably cheerful; entertained us with dancing and singing after their custom; ate their suppers and went to bed very quietly.

12th. During last night the ship sailed some leagues, which, as soon as the three men saw, they began to lament and weep very much, and Tupia could with difficulty comfort them. About seven o'clock two canoes appeared, one of which contained an old man who seemed to be a chief, from the fineness of his garment and *patoo patoo*, which was made of bone (he said of a whale). He stayed but a short time, and when he went he took with him our three guests, much to our, as well as their, satisfaction.

In sailing along shore, we could clearly see several cultivated spots of land, some freshly turned up, and lying in furrows, as if ploughed; others with plants growing upon them, some younger and some older. We also saw in two places high rails upon the ridges of hills, but could only guess that they are a part of some superstition, as they were in lines not inclosing anything.

15th. Snow was still to be seen upon the mountains inland. In the morning we were abreast of the southernmost cape of a large bay, the northernmost of which was named Portland Isle. The bay itself was called Hawke's Bay. The southern point was called Cape Kidnappers, on account of an attempt made by the natives to steal Tayeto, Tupia's boy. He was employed in handing up the articles which the natives were selling, when one of the men in a canoe seized him and pushed off. A shot was fired into the canoe, whereupon they loosed the boy, who immediately leaped into the water and swam to the ship. When he had a little recovered from his fright, Tayeto brought a fish to Tupia, and told him that he intended it as an offering to his *eatua*, in gratitude for his escape. Tupia approved it, and ordered him to throw it in the water, which he did.

16th. Mountains covered with snow were in sight again this morning, so that a chain of them probably runs within the country. Vast shoals of fish were about the ship, pursued by large flocks of brownish birds a little bigger than a pigeon (*Nectris munda*). Their method of fishing was amusing enough: a whole flock of birds would follow the fish, which swam fast; they continually plunged under water, and soon after rose again in another place, so that the whole flock sometimes vanished altogether, and rose again, often where you did not expect them; in less than a minute's time they were down again, and so alternately as long as we saw them. Before dinner we were abreast of another cape, which made in a bluff rock, the upper part of a reddish-coloured stone or clay, the lower white. Beyond this the country appeared pleasant, with low smooth hills like downs. The captain thought it not necessary to proceed any farther on this side of the coast, so the ship's head was turned to the northward, and the cape thence called Cape Turnagain. At night we were off Hawke's Bay and saw two monstrous fires inland on the hills. We are now inclined to think that these, and most if not all the great fires that we have seen, are made for the convenience of clearing the land for tillage, but for whatever purpose they are a certain indication that where they are the country is inhabited.

20*th.* Several canoes followed us, and seemed very peaceably inclined, inviting us to go into a bay they pointed out, where they said was plenty of fresh water. We followed them in, and by eleven came to an anchor. We then invited two, who seemed by their dress to be chiefs, to come on board; they immediately accepted our invitation. In the meantime those who remained in the canoes traded with our people very fairly for whatever they had in their boats. The chiefs, who were two old men, the one dressed in a jacket ornamented after their fashion with dog skin, the other in one covered almost entirely with some tufts of red feathers, received our presents, and stayed with us till we had dined.

21*st.* At daybreak the waterers went ashore, and soon after Dr. Solander and myself did the same. There was a good deal of surf upon the beach, but we landed without much difficulty. The natives sat by our people, but did not intermix with them. They traded, however, for cloth chiefly, giving whatever they had, though they seemed pleased with observing our people, as well as with the gain they got by trading with them; yet they did not neglect their ordinary occupations. In the morning several of their boats went out fishing, and at dinner-time all went to their respective homes, returning after a certain time. Such fair appearances made Dr. Solander and myself almost trust them; we ranged all about the bay and were well repaid by finding many plants, and shooting some most beautiful birds. In doing this we visited several houses, and saw a little of their customs, for they were not at all shy of showing us anything we desired to see, nor did they on our account interrupt their meals, the only employment we saw them engaged in.

Their food at this time of the year consisted of fish, with which, instead of bread, they eat the roots of a kind of fern, *Pteris crenulata*,[1] very like that which grows upon our commons in England. These were slightly roasted on the fire and then beaten with a stick, which took off the bark and dry outside; what remained had a sweetish, clammy, but not disagreeable taste. It might be esteemed a tolerable food, were it not for the quantity of strings and fibres in it, which in quantity three or four times exceed the soft part. These were swallowed by some, but the greater number spit them out, for which purpose they had a basket standing under them to receive their chewed morsels, in shape and colour not unlike chaws of tobacco. Though at this time of the year this most homely fare was their principal diet, yet in the proper seasons they certainly have plenty of excellent vegetables. We have seen no sign of tame animals among them, except very small and ugly dogs. Their plantations were now hardly finished, but so well was the ground tilled that I have seldom seen land better broken up. In them were planted sweet potatoes, cocos, and a plant of the cucumber kind, as we judged from the seed leaves which just appeared above ground.

The first of these were planted in small hills, some in rows, others in quincunx, all laid most regularly in line. The cocos were planted on flat land, and had not yet appeared above ground. The cucumbers were set in small hollows or ditches, much as in England. These plantations varied in size from 1 to 10 acres each. In the bay there might be 150 or 200 acres in cultivation, though we did not see 100 people in all. Each distinct patch was fenced in, generally with reeds placed close one by another, so that a mouse could scarcely creep through.

When we went to their houses, men, women and children

---

[1] The same plant as the British bracken, *Pteris aquilina*.

received us; no one showed the least signs of fear. The women were plain, and made themselves more so by painting their faces with red ochre and oil, which was generally fresh and wet upon their cheeks and foreheads, easily transferable to the noses of any one who should attempt to kiss them, not that they seemed to have any objection to such familiarities, as the noses of several of our people evidently showed. But they were as coquettish as any Europeans could be, and the young ones as skittish as unbroken fillies. One part of their dress I cannot omit to mention: besides their cloth, each one wore round the waist a string made of the leaves of a highly-perfumed grass,[1] to which was fastened a small bunch of the leaves of some fragrant plant. Though the men did not so frequently paint their faces, yet they often did so; one especially I observed, whose whole body and garments were rubbed over with dry ochre; of this he constantly kept a piece in his hand, and generally rubbed it on some part or other.

In the evening, all the boats being employed in carrying on board water, we were likely to be left ashore till after dark. We did not like to lose so much of our time for sorting our specimens and putting them in order, so we applied to our friends the Indians for a passage in one of their canoes. They readily launched one for us; but we, in number eight, not being used to so ticklish a conveyance, overset her in the surf, and were very well soused. Four of us were obliged to remain, and Dr. Solander, Tupia, Tayeto and myself embarked again, and came without accident to the ship, well pleased with the behaviour of our Indian friends, who would a second time undertake to carry off such clumsy fellows.

24th. Dr. Solander and I went ashore botanising, and found many new plants. The people behaved perfectly well, not mixing with or at all interrupting our people in what they were about, but on the contrary selling them whatever they had for Otahite cloth and glass bottles, of which they were uncommonly fond.

[1] *Hierochloe redolens*, Br.

In our walks we met with many houses in the valleys that seemed to be quite deserted. The people lived on the ridges of hills in very slightly-built houses, or rather sheds. For what reason they have left the valleys we can only guess, maybe for air, but if so they purchase that convenience at a dear rate, as all their fishing tackle and lobster pots, of which they have many, must be brought up with no small labour.

We saw also an extraordinary natural curiosity. In pursuing a valley bounded on each side by steep hills, we suddenly saw a most noble arch or cavern through the face of a rock leading directly to the sea, so that through it we had not only a view of the bay and hills on the other side, but an opportunity of imagining a ship or any other grand object opposite to it. It was certainly the most magnificent surprise I have ever met with; so much is pure nature superior to art in these cases. I have seen such places made by art, where from an inland view you were led through an arch 6 feet wide, and 7 feet high, to a prospect of the sea; but here was an arch 25 yards in length, 9 in breadth, and at least 15 in height.

In the evening we returned to the watering-place, in order to go on board with our treasure of plants, birds, etc., but were prevented by an old man who detained us some time in showing us their exercises with arms, lances, and *patoo patoos*. The lance is made of a hard wood, from 10 to 14 feet long, and very sharp at the ends. A stick was set up as an enemy; to this he advanced with a most furious aspect, brandishing his lance, which he held with great firmness; after some time he ran at the stick, and, supposing it a man run through the body, immediately fell upon the upper end of it, dealing it most merciless blows with his *patoo patoo*, any one of which would have probably split most skulls. From this I should conclude that they give no quarter.

25*th*. Went ashore this morning and renewed our search for plants, etc., with great success. In the meantime Tupia, who stayed with the waterers, had much conver-

sation with one of their priests; they seemed to agree very
well in their notions of religion, only Tupia was much
more learned than the other, and all his discourse was
received with much attention. He asked them in the course
of his conversation many questions, among the rest whether
or no they really ate men, which he was very loth to
believe; they answered in the affirmative, saying that they
ate the bodies only of those of their enemies who were killed
in war.

Among other knicknacks, Dr. Solander bought a boy's
top, which resembled those our boys play with in England,
and which they made signs was to be whipped in the same
manner.

28*th.* On an island called Jubolai we saw the largest
canoe which we had met with; her length was 68½ feet,
her breadth 5 feet, and her height 3 feet 6 inches. She
was built with a sharp bottom, made in three pieces of
trunks of trees hollowed out, the middlemost of which was
much longer than either of the other two; their gunnel
planks were in one piece 62 feet 2 inches in length, carved
prettily enough in bas-relief; the head also was richly
carved in their fashion. We saw also a house larger than
any we had seen, though not more than 30 feet long; it
seemed as if it had never been finished, being full of chips;
the woodwork was squared so evenly and smoothly that we
could not doubt of their having very sharp tools. All the
side-posts were carved in a masterly style of their whimsical
taste, which seems confined to making spirals and distorted
human faces; all these had clearly been moved from some
other place, so that such work probably bears a value among
them.

While Mr. Sporing was drawing on the island he saw a
most strange bird fly over his head. He described it as
being about as large as a kite, and brown like one; his tail,
however, was of so enormous a length that he at first took
it for a flock of small birds flying after him: he who is a
grave thinking man, and is not at all given to telling
wonderful stories, says he judged it to be yards in length.

29*th.* Our water having been got on board the day before yesterday, and nothing done yesterday but getting a small quantity of wood and a large supply of excellent celery, with which this country abounds, we this morning sailed.

30*th.* Before noon we passed by a cape which the captain judged to be the easternmost point of the country, and therefore called it East Cape, at least till another is found which better deserves that name.

1*st November.* Just at nightfall we were under a small island, from whence came off a large double canoe, or rather two canoes lashed together at a distance of about a foot, and covered with boards so as to make a kind of deck. She came pretty near the ship, and the people in her talked with Tupia with much seeming friendship ; but when it was just dark they ran the canoe close to the ship and threw in three or four stones, after which they paddled ashore.

2*nd.* Passed this morning between an island and the main, which appeared low and sandy, with a remarkable hill inland : flat and smooth as a molehill, though very high and large. Many canoes and people were seen along shore. Some followed us, but could not overtake us. A sailing canoe that had chased us ever since daybreak then came up with us, and proved the same double canoe which had pelted us last night, so that we prepared for another volley of their ammunition, dangerous to nothing on board but our windows. The event proved as we expected, for after having sailed with us an hour they threw their stones again. A musket was fired over them and they dropped astern, not, I believe, at all frightened by the musket, but content with having showed their courage by twice insulting us. We now begin to know these people, and are much less afraid of any daring attempt from them than we were.

The country appeared low, with small cliffs near the shore, but seemingly very fertile inland ; we saw plainly with our glasses villages larger than any we had before seen, situated on the tops of cliffs in places almost inaccessible, besides which they were guarded by a deep fosse and a high paling within it, so that probably these people are much given to war. In the evening many towns were in sight, larger than those seen at noon, and always situated like them on the tops of cliffs and fenced in the same manner : under them, upon the beach, were many very large canoes, some hundreds I may safely say, some of which either had or appeared to have awnings, but not one of them put off. From all these circumstances we judged the country to be much better peopled hereabouts, and inhabited by richer people than we had before seen ; maybe it was the residence of some of their princes. As far as we have yet gone along the coast from Cape Turnagain to this place, the people have acknowledged only one chief, Teratu. If his dominion is really so large, he may have princes or governors under him capable of drawing together a vast number of people, for he himself is always said to live far inland.

3rd. The continent appeared this morning barren and rocky, but many islands were in sight, chiefly with such towns upon them as we saw yesterday. Two canoes put off from one, but could not overtake us. At breakfast a cluster of islands and rocks was in sight, which made an uncommon appearance from the number of perpendicular rocks or needles (as the seamen call them) which were in sight at once. These we called the Court of Aldermen, in respect to that worthy body, and entertained ourselves some time with giving names to each of them from their resemblance, thick and squab or lank and tall, to some one or other of those respectable citizens. Soon after this we passed an island, on which were houses built on the steep sides of rocks, inaccessible, I had almost said, to birds. How their inhabitants could ever have got to them surpassed my comprehension. At present, however, we saw none, so that these situations are probably no more than places to retire to in case of danger, which are totally evacuated in peaceable times.

5th. Two Indians were seen fighting about some quarrel

of their own ; they began with lances, which were soon taken
from them by an old man, apparently a chief, but they were
allowed to continue their battle, which they did like
Englishmen with their fists for some time, after which all
of them retired behind a little hill, so that our people did
not see the event of the combat.

6th. The Indians, as yesterday, were tame. Their
habitations were certainly at a distance, as they had no
houses, but slept under the bushes. The bay where we now
are may be a place to which parties of them often resort for
the sake of shell-fish, which are here very plentiful ; indeed,
wherever we went, on hills or in valleys, in woods or plains,
we continually met with vast heaps of shells, often many
waggon-loads together, some appearing to be very old.
Wherever these were it is more than probable that parties of
Indians had at some time or other taken up their residence,
as our Indians had made such a pile about them. The
country in general was very barren, but the tops of the hills
were covered with a very large fern, the roots of which they
had got together in large quantities, as they said, to carry
away with them. We did not see any kind of cultivation.

8th. We botanised with our usual good success, which
could not be doubted in a country so totally new. In the
evening we went to our friends the Indians that we might
see the method in which they slept : it was, as they had
told us, on the bare ground, without more shelter than a
few trees over their heads. The women and children were
placed innermost, or farthest from the sea ; the men lay in a
kind of semicircle round them, and on the trees close by
were ranged their arms, in order, so no doubt they were
afraid of an attack from some enemy not far off. They do
not acknowledge any superior king, as did all those whom
we had before seen, so possibly these are a set of outlaws
from Teratu's kingdom. Their having no cultivation or
houses makes it clear at least either that it is so or that this
is not their real habitation ; they say, however, that they
have houses and a fort somewhere at a distance, but do not
say that even there there is any cultivation.

9th. At daybreak this morning a vast number of boats came on board, almost loaded with mackerel of two sorts, one exactly the same as is caught in England. We concluded that they had caught a large shoal and sold us the surplus, as they set very little value upon them. It was, however, a fortunate circumstance for us, as we soon had more fish on board than all hands could eat in two or three days, and before night so many that every mess who could raise any salt corned as many as will last them this month or more.

After an early breakfast, the astronomer went on shore to observe the transit of Mercury, which he did without the smallest cloud intervening, a fortunate circumstance, as except yesterday and to-day we have not had a clear day for some time.

10th. This day was employed in an excursion to view a large river at the bottom of a bay. Its mouth proved to be a good harbour, with sufficient water for our ship, but scarcely enough for a larger. The stream was in many places very wide, with large flats of mangroves, which at high water are covered. We went up about a league, where it was still wider than at the mouth, and divided itself into innumerable channels separated by mangrove flats, the whole several miles in breadth. The water was shoal, so we agreed to stop our disquisition here, and go ashore to dine. A tree in the neighbourhood, on which were many shags' nests, and old shags sitting by them, confirmed our resolution. An attack was consequently made on the shags, and about twenty were soon killed, and as soon broiled and eaten; every one declaring that they were excellent food, as indeed I think they were. Hunger is certainly most excellent sauce; but since we have no fowls and ducks left, we find ourselves able to eat any kind of bird (for indeed we throw away none) without even that kind of seasoning. Fresh provision to a seaman must always be most acceptable, if he can get over the small prejudices which once affected several in this ship, most or all of whom are now by virtue of good example

completely cured. Our repast ended, we proceeded down
the river again. At the mouth of it was a small Indian
village, where we landed, and were most civilly received
by the inhabitants, who treated us with hot cockles, or
at least a small flat shell-fish (*Tellina*), which was most
delicious food.

11*th*. An oyster bank was found in the river, about half
a mile up, just above a small island which is covered at high
water; here the long-boat was sent and soon returned
deeply loaded with as good oysters as ever came from Col-
chester, and of about the same size. They were laid down
under the booms, and employed the ship's company very
well, who, I sincerely believe, did nothing but eat from the
time they came on board till night, by which time a large
part were expended. But this gave us no kind of uneasi-
ness, since we well knew that not the boat only but the
ship might be loaded in one tide almost, as they are dry
at half ebb.

12*th*. We all went ashore to see an Indian fort, or *heppah*,
in the neighbourhood, uncertain, however, what kind of a reception we should meet with, as they might be jealous about
letting us into a place where all their valuable effects were
probably lodged. We went to a bay where were two *heppahs*,
and landed first near a small one, the most beautiful romantic
thing I ever saw. It was built on a small rock detached
from the main, and surrounded at high water; the top of
this was fenced round with rails after their manner, but was
not large enough to contain above five or six houses; the
whole appeared totally inaccessible to any animal who was
not furnished with wings, indeed, it was only approachable
by one very narrow and steep path, but what made it most
truly romantic was that much the greater part of it was
hollowed out into an arch, which penetrated quite through
it, the top being not less than twenty perpendicular yards
above the water, which ran through it.

The inhabitants on our approach came down, and invited
us to go in; but we refused, intending to visit a much larger
and more perfect one about a mile off: we spent, however,

some little time in making presents to their women.   In
the meanwhile we saw the inhabitants of the other come
down from it, men, women and children, about one hundred
in number, and march towards us; as soon as they came
near enough they waved, and called *haromai*, and sat down
in the bushes near the beach (a sure mark of their good
intentions).

We went to them, made a few presents, and asked leave
to go up to their *heppah*, which they with joy invited us to
do, and immediately accompanied us to it.   It was called
Wharretoueva, and was situated at the end of a hill where
it jutted out into the sea, which washed its two sides : these
were sufficiently steep, but not absolutely inaccessible.   Up
one of the land sides, which was also steep, went the road ;
the other side was flat and open.   The whole was enclosed
by a palisade about ten feet high, made of strong poles
bound together with withies : the weak side next the hill
had also a ditch, twenty feet in depth nearest the palisade.
Besides this, beyond the palisade was built a fighting stage,
which they call *porāvā*.   It is a flat stage covered with
branches of trees upon which they stand to throw darts or
stones at their assailants, they themselves being out of
danger.   Its dimensions were as follows : its height above
the ground $20\frac{1}{2}$ feet, breadth 6 feet 6 inches, length 43 feet ;
upon it were laid bundles of darts, and heaps of stones, ready
in case of an attack.   One of the young men at our desire
went up to show their method of fighting, and another went
to the outside of the ditch to act as assailant ; they both
sang their war-song, and danced with the same frightful
gesticulations as we have often seen, threatening each other
with their weapons.   This, I suppose, they do in their attacks,
to work themselves into a sufficient fury of courage, for
what we call calm resolution is, I believe, found in few uncivilised people.   The side next the road was also defended
by a similar stage, but much longer ; the other two were by
their steepness thought to be sufficiently secure with the
palisade.   The inside was divided into, I believe, twenty
larger and smaller divisions, some of which contained not

more than one or two houses, others twelve or fourteen. Every one of these was enclosed by its own palisade, though not so high and strong as the general one; in these were vast heaps of dried fish and fern roots piled up, so much so that if they had had water, I should have thought them well prepared for a siege, but that had to be fetched from a brook below; so that they probably do not besiege a town as we do in Europe. Without the fence were many houses and large nets, the latter, I suppose, being brought in upon any alarm; there was also about half an acre planted with gourds and sweet potatoes, the only cultivation we have seen in this bay.

14*th.* As we were resolved to stay no longer here, we all went ashore, the boats to get as much celery and oysters as possible, Dr. Solander and myself to get as many green plants as possible, in order to finish the sketches, etc., while at sea; so an enormous number of all these articles came on board.

Dr. Solander, who was to-day in a cove different from that I was in, saw the natives catch many lobsters in a very simple manner; they walked among the rocks at low water, about waist-deep in water, and moved their feet about till they felt one, on which they dived down, and constantly brought him up. I do not know whether I have before mentioned these lobsters, but we have had them in tolerable plenty in almost every place we have been in, and they are certainly the largest and best I have ever eaten.

20*th.* We had yesterday resolved to employ this day in examining a bay we saw, so at daybreak we set out in the boats. A fresh breeze of wind soon carried us to the bottom of the bay, where we found a very fine river, broad as the Thames at Greenwich, though not quite so deep; there was, however, water enough for vessels of more than a middling size, and a bottom of mud so soft that nothing could possibly take damage by running ashore.

About a mile up this was an Indian town built upon a small bank of dry sand, but totally surrounded by deep mud, so much so that I believe they had purposely built it there as a defence. The people came out in flocks upon the banks, inviting us in ; they had heard of us from our last friends. We landed, and while we stayed they were most perfectly civil, as indeed they have always been where we were known, but never where we were not. We proceeded up the river and soon met with another town with but few inhabitants. Above this the banks were completely clothed with the finest timber [1] my eyes ever beheld, of a tree we had before seen, but only at a distance, in Poverty Bay and Hawke's Bay. Thick woods of it were everywhere upon the banks, every tree as straight as a pine, and of immense size, and the higher we went the more numerous they were. About two leagues from the mouth we stopped and went ashore. Our first business was to measure one of these trees. The woods were swampy, so we could not range far; we found one, however, by no means the largest we had seen, which was 19 feet 8 inches [2] in circumference, and 89 feet in height without a branch. But what was most remarkable was that it, as well as many more that we saw, carried its thickness so truly up to the very top, that I dare venture to affirm that the top, where the lowest branch took its rise, was not a foot less in diameter than where we measured it, which was about 8 feet from the ground. We cut down a young one of these trees ; the wood proved heavy and solid, too much so for masts, but it would make the finest plank in the world, and might possibly by some art be made light enough for masts, as the pitch-pine in America (to which our carpenter likened this timber) is said to be lightened by tapping.

Up to this point the river has kept its depth and very little decreased in breadth ; the captain was so much pleased with it that he resolved to call it the Thames. It was now time for us to return ; the tide turning downwards gave us warning, so away we went, and got out of the river into the bay before it was dark. We rowed for the ship as fast as we

---

[1] *Podocarpus dacrydioides*, A. Cunn.

[2] The dimensions were left blank in Banks's Journal. In Wharton's *Cook*, p. 159, it is stated to be 19 feet 8 inches at 6 feet above the ground, and its length from the root to the first branch 89 feet; and it tapered so little that Cook judged it to contain 356 feet of solid timber, clear of the branches.

could, but night overtook us before we could get within some miles of her.   It blew fresh with showers of rain. In this situation we rowed until nearly twelve, and then gave over, and running under the land came to a grappling, and all went to sleep as well as we could.

21*st.* Before daybreak we set out again.   It still blew fresh with mizzling rain and fog, so that it was an hour after day before we got a sight of the ship.   However, we made shift to get on board by seven, tired enough ; and lucky for us it was we did, for before nine it blew a fresh gale, so that our boat could not have rowed ahead, and, had we been out, we must have either gone ashore or sheltered ourselves.   Before evening, however, it moderated, so that we got under way with the ebb, but did little or nothing.

CHAPTER IX

CIRCUMNAVIGATION OF NEW ZEALAND

Nov. 22, 1769—March 30, 1770

Tattowing—Thieving of the natives—Cannibalism—Rapid healing of shot-
wounds — Native seines — Paper mulberry—Native accounts of their
ancestors' expedition to other countries—Three Kings Islands—Christmas
Day—Albatross swimming—Mount Egmont—Murderers' Bay—Queen
Charlotte's Sound—Threats of natives—Corpses thrown into the sea—
Cannibalism—Singing-birds—Fishing-nets—Human head preserved—
Discovery of Cook's Straits—Native names for New Zealand, and tradi-
tions—Courteous native family—Leave Queen Charlotte's Sound—Tides
—Cape Turnagain—Coast along the southern island—Banks' Peninsula
—Appearance of minerals—Mountains along the west coast—Anchor in
Admiralty Bay.

26th. Two large canoes came from a distance; the people
in them were numerous and appeared rich; the canoes were
well carved and ornamented, and they had with them many
patoo-patoos of stone and whale-bone which they value very
much. They had also ribs of whales, of which we had often
seen imitations in wood carved and ornamented with tufts
of dog's hair. The people themselves were browner than
those to the southward, as indeed they have been ever since
we came to Opoorage, as this part is called, and they had a
much larger quantity of *amoca* or black stains upon their
bodies and faces. They had almost universally a broad
spiral on each buttock, and many had their thighs almost
entirely black, small lines only being left untouched, so that
they looked like striped breeches. In this particular, I
mean the use of *amoca*, almost every tribe seems to have a
different custom; we have on some days seen canoes where

every man was almost covered with it, and at the same time others where scarcely a man had a spot, except on his lips, which seems to be always essential.

These people would not part with any of their arms, etc., for any price we could offer. At last, however, one produced an axe of talc and offered it for cloth; it was given, and the canoe immediately put off with it; a musket ball was fired over their heads, on which they immediately came back and returned the cloth, but soon after put off and went ashore.

In the afternoon other canoes came off, and through some inattention of the officers were suffered to cheat, unpunished and unfrightened; this put one of the midshipmen who had suffered upon a droll, though rather mischievous, revenge. He got a fishing-line, and when the canoe was close to the ship hove the lead at the man who had cheated him with such good success that he fastened the hook into his back, on which he pulled with all his might; the Indian kept back, so that the hook soon broke in the shank, leaving its beard in the man, no very agreeable legacy.

30th. Several canoes came off to the ship very early, but sold little or nothing; indeed, no merchandise that we can show them seems to take with them. Our island cloth, which used to be so much esteemed, has now entirely lost its value. The natives have for some days past told us that they have some of it ashore, and showed us small pieces in their ears, which they said was of their own manufacture. This accounts for their having been once so fond of it, and now setting so little value upon it. Towards noon, however, they sold us a little dried fish for paper, chiefly, or very white Indian cloth.

In the evening we went ashore upon the continent. The people received us very civilly, and were as tame as we could wish. One general observation I here set down : they always, after one night's consideration, have acknowledged our superiority, but hardly ever before. I have often seen a man, when his nearest companion was wounded or killed by our shot, not give himself the trouble to inquire how or by what means he was hurt. When they attack they work themselves up into a kind of artificial courage, which does not allow them time to think much.

1st December. It is now some time since I mentioned their custom of eating human flesh, as I had been for a long time loth to believe that any human beings could have among them so brutal a custom. I am now, however, convinced, and shall here give a short account of what we have heard from the Indians concerning it.

At Taoneroa, where we first landed, the boys whom we had on board mentioned it of their own accord, asking whether the meat they ate was not human flesh, as they had no idea of any animal so large, except a man, till they saw our sheep. They, however, seemed ashamed of the custom, saying that the tribe to which they belonged did not use it, but that another living very near them did. Since then we have never failed to ask the question, and we have without one exception been answered in the affirmative. Several times, as at Tolago and here, the people have put themselves into a heat by defending the custom, which Tupia, who had never before heard of such a thing, takes every occasion to speak ill of, exhorting them often to leave it off. They, however, universally agree that they eat none but the bodies of those of their enemies who are killed in war; all others are buried.

3rd. Many canoes visited us in the morning; one very large carrying eighty-two people. Dr. Solander and myself went ashore; we found few plants, and saw but few people, but they were perfectly civil. We went on their invitation to their little town, which was situated at the bottom of a cove, without the least defence. One of the old men here showed us the instrument with which they stain their bodies; it was exactly like that used at Otahite. We saw also here a man who had been shot on the 29th while attempting to steal our buoy. The ball had gone through the fleshy part of his arm and grazed his breast. The wound was open to the air, without the smallest application upon it, yet it had as good an appearance, and seemed to give him as little pain as if it had had the very best dressing possible. We gave him a musket ball, and with a little talking he seemed to be fully sensible of the escape he had had.

In the evening we went ashore on another island where were many more people, who lived in the same peaceable style, and had very large plantations of sweet potatoes, yams, etc., about their village. They received us much as our friends in the morning had done, and, like them, showed much satisfaction at the little presents of necklaces, etc., which were given to them.

4*th*. We went ashore at a large Indian fort or *heppah*. A great number of people immediately crowded about us, and sold almost a boat-load of fish in a very short time. They then showed us their plantations, which were very large, of yams, cocos, and sweet potatoes : and after having a little laugh at our seine, a common king's seine, showed us one of theirs, which was five fathoms deep. Its length we could only guess, as it was not stretched out, but it could not from its bulk be less than four or five hundred fathoms. Fishing seems to be the chief business of this part of the country. About all their towns are abundance of nets laid upon small heaps like haycocks, and thatched over, and almost every house you go into has nets in process of making.

After this they showed us a great rarity, six plants of what they called *aouta*, from whence they make cloth like that of Otahite. The plant proved exactly the same, as the name is the same, *Morus papyrifera*, Linn. (the Paper Mulberry). The same plant is used by the Chinese to make paper. Whether the climate does not well agree with it I do not know, but they seemed to value it very much ; that it was very scarce among them I am inclined to believe, as we have not yet seen among them pieces large enough for any use, but only bits sticking into the holes of their ears.

9*th*. Many canoes came off, and Tupia inquired about the country : they told him that at the distance of three days' rowing in their canoes, at a place called Moorewhennua, the land would turn to the southward, and from thence extend no more to the west. This place we concluded must be Cape Maria Van Diemen; and finding these people so intelligent, desired Tupia to inquire if they knew of any countries besides this, or ever went to any. They said no, but that their ancestors had told them that to the N.W. by N. or N.N.W. was a large country to which some people had sailed in a very large canoe, which passage took them a month. From the expedition a part only returned, who told their countrymen that they had seen a country where the people eat hogs, for which animal they used the same name (*Booah*) as is used in the islands. " And have you no hogs among you ? " said Tupia.—" No." —" And did your ancestors bring none back with them ? " —" No."—" You must be a parcel of liars then," said he, " and your story a great lie, for your ancestors would never have been such fools as to come back without them." Thus much as a specimen of Indian reasoning.

10*th*. This morning we were near the land, which was quite barren, hills beyond hills, and ridges even far inland were covered with white sand on which no kind of vegetable was to be seen. It was conjectured by some that the land here might be very narrow, and that the westerly wind blew the sand right across it. Some Indian forts or *heppahs* were seen.

18*th*. On a rock pretty near us we saw through our glasses an Indian fort, which we all thought was encircled with a mud wall; if so, it is the only one of the kind we have seen.

24*th*. Land in sight: an island, or rather several small ones, most probably the Three Kings, so that it was conjectured that we had passed the cape, which had so long troubled us. From a boat I killed several gannets or solan geese, so like European ones that they are hardly distinguishable from them. As it was the humour of the ship to keep Christmas in the old-fashioned way, it was resolved to make a goose-pie for to-morrow's dinner.

25*th*. Christmas Day: our goose-pie was eaten with

great approbation ; and in the evening all hands were as drunk as our forefathers used to be upon like occasions.

1st January 1770.—The new year began with more moderate weather than the old one ended with, but wind as foul as ever : we ventured to go a little nearer the land, which appeared on this side the cape much as it had done on the other, almost entirely occupied by vast sands. Our surveyors suppose the cape to be shaped like a shoulder of mutton with the knuckle placed inwards, where they say that the land cannot be above two or three miles across, and that most probably in high winds the sea washes quite over the sands, which here are low.

6th. Calm to day. Shot *Procellaria longipes, P. velox,* and *Diomedea exulans* (the albatross). I had an opportunity of seeing this last sit upon the water ; and as it is commonly said by seamen that they cannot in a calm rise upon the wing, I tried the experiment. There were two of them. One I shot dead : the other, which was near it, swam off nearly as fast as my small boat could row. We gave chase and gained a little ; the bird attempted to fly by trying to take off from a falling wave, but did not succeed : I who was so far off that I knew I could not hurt him, fired at him to make his attempts more vigorous, this had the desired result, for at the third effort he got upon the wing, though I believe that had it not been for a little swell upon the water he could not have done it.

10th. The country we passed by appeared fertile, more so, I think, than any part of this country that I have seen ; rising in gentle slopes not over well wooded, but what trees there were, were well grown. Few signs of inhabitants were seen : one fire and a very few houses.

About noon we passed between the main and a small island or rock, which seemed almost totally covered with birds, probably gannets. Towards evening a very high hill was in sight, but very distant.

12th. This morning we were abreast of the great hill,[1] but it was wrapped in clouds, and remained so the whole

---

[1] Mount Egmont.

day; it is probably very high, as a part of its side, which was for a moment seen, was covered with snow. The country beyond it appeared very pleasant and fertile, the sides of the hills sloping gradually. With our glasses we could distinguish many white lumps in companies, fifty or sixty together, which were probably stones or tufts of grass, but bore much resemblance to flocks of sheep:[1] at night a small fire, which burned about half an hour, made us sure that there were inhabitants, of whom we had seen no signs since the 10th.

13th. This morning, soon after daybreak, we had a momentary view of our great hill, the top of which was thickly covered with snow, though this month answers to July in England. How high it may be I do not take upon me to judge, but it is certainly the noblest hill I have ever seen, and it appears to the utmost advantage, rising from the sea without another hill in its neighbourhood one-fourth of its height.

14th. In a large bay, called in the draughts Murderers' Bay; the appearance of a harbour just ahead made us resolve to anchor in the morning.

15th. In the course of last night we were driven to the eastward more than we had any reason to expect, so much that we found ourselves in the morning past the harbour we intended to go into. Another, however, was in sight, into which we went.[2] The land on both sides appeared most miserably barren, till we got some way up the harbour, when it began to mend gradually. Here we saw some canoes, which, instead of coming towards us, went to an Indian town or fort built upon an island nearly in the middle of the passage, which appeared crowded with people, as if they had flocked to it from all parts. As the ship approached it they waved to us as if inviting us to come to them, but the moment we had passed, they set up a loud shout, and every man brandished his weapons.

---

[1] Clumps of the remarkable Composite plant *Raoulia mammillaris*, Hook. f., or an allied species, called "vegetable sheep" in New Zealand.

[2] Ship's Cove, Queen Charlotte's Sound.

The country about us now was very fertile to appearance, and well wooded, so we came to anchor about a long cannon shot from the fort, from whence four canoes were immediately despatched to reconnoitre, I suppose, and, if might be, to take us, as they were all well armed. The men in these boats were dressed much as they are represented in Tasman's figure, that is, two corners of the cloth they wore were passed over their shoulders and fastened to the rest of it just below their breasts; but few or none had feathers in their hair. They rowed round and round the ship, defying and threatening us as usual, and at last hove some stones aboard, which we all expected to be a prelude of some behaviour which would oblige us to fire upon them; but just at this time a very old man in one of the boats expressed a desire of coming on board, which we immediately encouraged him to do, and threw a rope into his canoe, by which he was immediately hauled up alongside, contrary to the desire of all the other Indians, who went so far as to hold him fast for some time. We received him in as friendly a manner as possible, and gave him many presents, with which he returned to the canoes, who immediately joined in a war dance, whether to show their enmity or friendship it is impossible to say. We have so often seen them do it upon both occasions.

After this they retired to their town, and we went ashore abreast of the ship, where we found good wood and water, and caught more fish in the seine than all our people could possibly consume, besides shooting a multitude of shags. The country, however, did not answer so well to Dr. Solander and myself as to the ship, as we found only two new plants in the whole evening.

16th. The women and some of the men wore an article of dress which we had not before seen, a round bunch of black feathers tied upon the tops of their heads, which it entirely covered, making them look twice as large as they really were. On seeing this, my judgment paid an involuntary compliment to my fair English countrywomen, for, led astray by the head-dress, which in some measure resembles the high foretops in England, I was forward to declare it as my opinion that these were much the handsomest women we had seen upon the coast; but upon their near approach I was convinced that nothing but the head-dress had misled me, as I saw not one who was even tolerably handsome.

After dinner we went in the boat towards a cove about two miles from the ship. As we rowed along, something was seen floating upon the water, which we took to be a dead seal. It proved, to our great surprise, to be the body of a woman, who seemed to have been dead some time. We left it, and proceeded to our cove, where we found a small family of Indians, who were a little afraid of us, as they all ran away but one. They soon, however, returned except an old man and a child, who stayed in the woods, but not out of sight of us. Of these people we inquired about the body we had seen. They told Tupia that the woman was a relation of theirs, and that instead of burying their dead, their custom was to tie a stone to them, and throw them into the sea, which stone they suppose to have been unloosened by some accident.

The family were employed, when we came ashore, in dressing their provisions, which were a dog, at that time buried in their oven. Near by were many provision baskets. Looking carelessly upon one of these, we by accident observed two bones pretty cleanly picked, which, as appeared upon examination, were undoubtedly human bones.

Though we had from the beginning constantly heard the Indians acknowledge the custom of eating their enemies, we had never before had a proof of it, but this amounted almost to demonstration. The bones were clearly human; upon them were evident marks of their having been dressed on the fire; the meat was not entirely picked off them, and on the gristly ends, which were gnawed, were evident marks of teeth; and they were accidentally found in a provision basket. On asking the people what bones they were, they answered: "The bones of a man."—"And have you eaten the flesh?"—"Yes."—"Have you none of it left?"—"No." —"Why did you not eat the woman whom we saw to-day in

the water?"—"She was our relation."—"Whom, then, do
you eat?"—"Those who are killed in war."—"And who
was the man whose bones these are?"—"Five days ago a
boat of our enemies came into this bay, and of them we
killed seven, of whom the owner of these bones was one."
The horror that appeared in the countenances of the seamen
on hearing this discourse, which was immediately trans-
lated for the good of the company, is better conceived than
described.   For ourselves, and myself in particular, we were
too well convinced of the existence of such a custom to be
surprised, though we were pleased at having so strong a
proof of a custom which human nature holds in too great
abhorrence to give easy credit to.

17*th*. I was awakened by the singing of the birds ashore,
from whence we are distant not a quarter of a mile.   Their
numbers were certainly very great.   They seemed to strain
their throats with emulation, and made, perhaps, the most
melodious wild music I have ever heard, almost imitating
small bells, but with the most tunable silver sound imaginable, to which, maybe, the distance was no small addition.
On inquiring of our people, I was told that they had
observed them ever since we had been here, and that they
begin to sing about one or two in the morning, and continue
till sunrise, after which they are silent all day, like our
nightingales.

18*th*. Among other things that the Indians told us
yesterday, one was that they expected their enemies to come
and revenge the death of the seven men, and some of our
people thought that they had intelligence of their coming
to-day, which made us observe the Indian town, where the
people seemed more quiet than usual, not attending to their
usual occupations of fishing, etc.   No canoe attempted to
come near the ship.

After breakfast we went in the pinnace to explore some
parts of the bay, which we had not seen, as it was immensely
large, or, rather, consisted of numberless small harbours,
coves, etc.   We found the country on our side of the bay
very well wooded everywhere, but on the opposite side very

bare. In turning a point, we saw a man in a small canoe
fishing, who, to our surprise, showed not the least fear of us.
We went to him, and at our request he took up his nets,
and showed us his implement, which was a circular net
about seven or eight feet in diameter, extended by two
hoops. The top of this was open, and to the bottom were
tied sea-ears, etc., as bait : this he let down upon the
ground, and when he thought that fish enough were assembled
over it, he lifted it up by a very gentle and even motion,
so that the fish were hardly sensible of being lifted till they
were almost out of the water. By this simple method he
had caught abundance of fish, and I believe it is the general
way of fishing all over this coast, as many such nets have
been seen at almost every place we have been in. In this
bay, indeed, fish were so plentiful that it is hardly possible
not to catch abundance by whatever method is adopted.

20th. Our old man came this morning with the heads
of four people, which were preserved with the flesh and hair
on, and kept I suppose as trophies, as possibly scalps were
by the North Americans before the Europeans came among
them. The brains were, however, taken out ; maybe they
are a delicacy here. The flesh and skin upon these heads
were soft ; but they were somehow preserved so as not to
stink at all.

The bay, wherever we have yet been, is very hilly ;
we have hardly seen a flat large enough for a potato
garden. Our friends here do not seem to feel the want of
such places ; as we have not seen the least appearance of
cultivation, I suppose they live entirely upon fish, dogs, and
enemies.

22nd. Made an excursion to-day in the pinnace, in order
to see more of the bay. While Dr. Solander and I were
botanising, the captain went to the top of a hill, and in
about an hour returned in high spirits, having seen the
eastern sea, and satisfied himself of the existence of a strait
communicating with it, the idea of which has occurred to us
all, from Tasman's as well as our own observations.

23rd. Mr. Monkhouse told me that on the 21st he had

been ashore at a spot where were many deserted Indian houses : here he had seen several things tied up to the branches of trees, particularly human hair, which he brought away with him, enough to have made a sizable wig. This induced him to think that the place was consecrated to religious purposes ; possibly it was, as they certainly have such places among them, though I have not yet been lucky enough to meet with them.

24th. Went to-day to the *heppah* or town, to see our friends the Indians, who received us with much confidence and civility, and showed us every part of their habitations, which were neat enough. The town was situated upon a small island or rock separated from the main by a breach in the rock, so small that a man might almost jump over it ; the sides were everywhere so steep as to render fortifications, even in their fashion, almost totally unnecessary ; accordingly there was nothing but a slight palisade, and one small fighting stage at one end where the rock was most accessible. The people brought us several bones of men, the flesh of which they had eaten. These are now become a kind of article of trade among our people, who constantly ask for and purchase them for whatever trifles they have. In one part we observed a kind of wooden cross ornamented with feathers, made exactly in the form of a crucifix. This engaged our attention, and we were told that it was a monument to a dead man ; maybe a cenotaph, as the body was not there. This much they told us, but would not let us know where the body was.

25th. Dr. Solander and I (who have now nearly exhausted all the plants in our neighbourhood) went to-day to search for mosses and small things, in which we had great success, gathering several very remarkable ones. In the evening we went out in the pinnace, and fell in with a large family of Indians, who have now begun to disperse themselves, as is, I believe, their custom, into the different creeks and coves where fish are most plentiful. A few only remain in the *heppah*, to which they all fly in times of danger. These people came a good way to meet us at a place where we were shooting shags, and invited us to join the rest of them, twenty or thirty in number, men, women, and children, dogs, etc. We went, and were received with all possible demonstrations of friendship, if the numberless hugs and kisses we got from both sexes, old and young, in return for our ribbons and beads may be accounted such.

26th. Went to-day to take another view of our new straits,[1] as the captain was not quite sure of the westernmost end. We found a hill in a tolerably convenient situation, and climbing it, saw the strait quite open, and four or five leagues wide. We then erected a small monument of stone, such as five stout men could do in half an hour, and laid in it musket balls, beads, shot, etc., so that if perchance any Europeans should find and pull it down, they will be sure it is not of Indian workmanship.

5th February. Our old man, *Topaa*, was on board, and Tupia asked him many questions concerning the land, etc. His answers were nearly as follows: "That the straits we had seen from the hills were a passage into the eastern sea; that the land to the south consisted of two or several islands round which their canoes might sail in three or four days; that he knew of no other great land than that we had been upon (Aehie no Mauwe), of which Tera Whitte was the southern part; that he believed his ancestors were not born there, but came originally from Heawije"[1] (from whence Tupia and the islanders also derive their origin), "which lay to the northwards where were many lands; that neither himself, his father, nor his grandfather had ever heard of ships as large as this being here before, but that they have a tradition of two large vessels, much larger than theirs, which some time or other came here, and were totally destroyed by the inhabitants, and all the people belonging to them killed."

This last Tupia says is a very old tradition, much older

---

[1] Cook's Straits.

[2] The Maoris are by some authorities supposed to have originally come from Hawaii, the direction of which agrees very fairly with that given by the natives to Banks. The Sandwich Islands really lie N.N.E. from New Zealand.

than his great-grandfather, and relates to two large canoes which came from Olimaroa, one of the islands he has mentioned. Whether he is right, or whether this is a tradition of Tasman's ships (which they could not well compare with their own by tradition, and which their warlike ancestors had told them they had destroyed), is difficult to say. Tupia has all along warned us not to put too much faith in anything these people tell us, " for," says he, " they are given to lying; they told you that one of their people was killed by a musket and buried, which was absolutely false."

The doctor and I went ashore to-day, and fell in by accident with the most agreeable Indian family we had seen upon the coast, indeed the only one in which we have observed any order or subordination. It consisted of seventeen people; the head of it was a pretty boy of about ten years old, who, they told us, was the owner of the land about where we wooded. This is the only instance of property we have met with among these people. He and his mother (who mourned for her husband with tears of blood, according to their custom) sat upon mats, the rest sat round them: houses they had none, nor did they attempt to make for themselves any shelter against the inclemencies of the weather, which I suppose they by custom very easily endure. Their whole behaviour was so affable, obliging, and unsuspicious, that I should certainly have accepted their invitation to stay the night with them, were not the ship to sail in the morning. Most unlucky shall I always esteem it that we did not sooner make acquaintance with these people, from whom we might have learnt more in a day of their manners and dispositions than from all we have yet seen.

6th. Foul wind continued, but we contrived to get into the straits, which are to be called Cook's Straits. Here we were becalmed, and almost imperceptibly drawn by the tide near the land. The lead was dropped, and gave seventy fathoms; soon after we saw an appearance like breakers, towards which we drove fast. It was now sunset, and night came on apace; the ship drove into the rough water, which proved to be a strong tide, and which set her directly upon a rock. We had approached very near to this when the anchor was dropped, and she was brought up about a cable's length from it. We were now sensible of the force of the tide, which roared like a mill-stream, and ran at four knots at least when it flowed the fastest, for the rate varied much. It ran in this manner till twelve o'clock, when, with the slack water, we got up the anchor with great difficulty, and a light breeze from the northward soon cleared us from our dangers.

8th. As some of the officers declared last night that they thought it probable that the land we have been round might communicate by an isthmus situated somewhere between where we now are and Cape Turnagain (though the whole distance is estimated at no more than ninety miles), the captain resolved to stand to the northward till he should see that cape, which was accordingly done.

Three canoes put off from the shore, and with very little invitation came on board. The people appeared richer and more cleanly than any we have seen since we were in the Bay of Islands; their canoes also were ornamented in the same manner as those we had formerly seen in the north of the island. They were always more civil in their behaviour, and on having presents made them, immediately made presents to us in return (an instance we have not before met with in this island). All these things inclined me to believe that we were again come to the dominions of Teratu, but on asking they said that he was not their king.

9th. By eleven o'clock Cape Turnagain was in sight, which convinced everybody that the land was really an island, on which we once more turned the ship's head to the southward.

14th. I had two or three opportunities this evening of seeing albatrosses rise from the water, which they did with great ease; maybe they are not able to do so (as I have seen) when they are gorged with food.

17th. This morning we were close to a new island [1] which

---

[1] Banks' Peninsula : it is not an island.

made in ridges not unlike the South Sea Islands (between the tropics); the tops of these were bare, but in the valleys was plenty of wood.

23rd. As we have now been four days upon nearly the same part of the coast without seeing any signs of inhabitants, I think there is no doubt that this part at least is without inhabitants.

In the evening the land [1] inclined a good deal to the west. We on board were now of two parties, one who wished that the land in sight might, the other that it might not, be a continent. I myself have always been most firm in the former wish, though sorry I am to say that my party is so small, that I firmly believe that there are none more heartily of it than myself and one poor midshipman : the rest begin to sigh for roast beef.

4th March. A large smoke was seen, and proved to be an immense fire on the side of a hill which we supposed to have been set on fire by the natives, for though this is the only sign of people we have seen, yet I think it must be an indisputable proof that there are inhabitants, though probably very thinly scattered over the face of this very large country.

9th. The land [2] appeared barren, and seemed to end in a point to which the hills gradually declined, much to the regret of us continent-mongers, who could not help thinking that the great swell from the south-west and the broken ground without it were a pretty sure mark of some remarkable cape being here. By noon we were near the land, which was uncommonly barren ; the few flat places we saw seemingly produced little or nothing, and the rest was all bare rocks which were amazingly full of large veins, and patches of some mineral that shone as if it had been polished, or rather looked as if the rocks were really paved with glass ; what it was I could not at all guess, but it was certainly some mineral, and seemed to argue by its immense abundance a country abounding in minerals, where, if one may judge

---

[1] Near Otago Harbour.

[2] Stewart Island, which was supposed to be a peninsula.

from the corresponding latitudes of South America, in all human probability something very valuable might be found.

10th. Blew fresh all day: we were carried round the point, to the total destruction of our aerial fabric called continent.

13th. The rocks were very large, and had veins in them filled with a whitish appearance different from what we saw on the 9th. The sides of the hills appeared well wooded, and the country in general as fertile as in so hilly a country could be expected, but without the least signs of inhabitants.

14th. Stood along shore with a fine breeze, and passed three or four places which had much the appearance of harbours, much to my regret, as I wished to examine the mineral appearance from which I had formed great hopes.[1] The country rose immediately from the sea-side in steep hills, tolerably covered with wood; behind these was another ridge covered in many places with snow, which, from its pure whiteness and smoothness in the morning, and the many cracks and intervals that appeared among it at night, we conjectured to be newly fallen.

15th. The country to-day appeared covered with steep hills, whose sides were but ill wooded, but on their tops were large quantities of snow, especially on the sides looking towards the south. We imagined that about noon we passed by some considerable river; the sea was almost covered with leaves, small twigs, and blades of grass.

16th. Much snow on the ridges of the high hills; two were, however, seen on which was little or none, whatever the cause of it might be I could not guess. They were quite bare of trees or any kind of vegetables, and seemed to consist of a mouldering soft stone of the colour of brick or light red ochre. About noon the country near the sea changed much for the better, appearing in broad valleys clothed with prodigious fine woods, out of which came many fine streams of water; but, notwithstanding the beauty of the country, there was not the smallest sign of inhabitants, nor, indeed,

---

[1] Tin abounds in Stewart Island, but Banks's observations are no evidence of its presence.

have we seen any since we made this land, except the fire on the 4th.

18*th*. Immense quantities of snow newly fallen on the hills were by noon plainly seen to begin to melt.

21*st*. At night saw a phenomenon which I have but seldom seen ; at sunset the flying clouds were of almost all colours, among which green was very conspicuous, though rather faint.

24*th*. Just turned the most westerly point,[1] and stood into the mouth of the straits.

26*th*. At night came to an anchor in a bay,[2] in some part of which it is probable that Tasman anchored.

30*th*. I examined the stones which lay on the beach : they showed evident signs of mineral tendency, being full of veins, but I had not the fortune to discover any ore of metal (at least that I know to be so) in them. As the place we lay in had no bare rocks in its neighbourhood, this was the only method I had of even conjecturing.

---

[1] Cape Farewell.

[2] Admiralty Bay : Tasman anchored in Blind or Tasman's Bay, and the massacre of three of his crew is supposed to have taken place in a small bay on its north-west side.—Wharton's *Cook*, p. 214, note.

CHAPTER X

GENERAL ACCOUNT OF NEW ZEALAND

As we intend to leave this place to-morrow, I shall spend
a few sheets in drawing together what I have observed of
the country and of its inhabitants, premising that in this,
and in all other descriptions of the same kind which may
occur in this journal, I shall give myself liberty to conjecture,
and draw conclusions from what I have observed.   In these
I may doubtless be mistaken ; in the daily Journal, however,
the observations may be seen, and any one who refers to
that may draw his own conclusions from them, attending as
little as he pleases to any of mine.

This country was first discovered by Abel Jansen Tasman
on the 13th of December 1642, and called by him New
Zealand.   He, however, never went ashore on it, probably
from fear of the natives, who, when he had come to an
anchor, set upon one of his boats and killed three or four
out of the seven people in her.

Tasman certainly was an able navigator ; he sailed into
the mouth of Cook's Straits, and finding himself surrounded, to
all appearance, by land, observed the flood tide to come from

the south-east; from thence he conjectured that there was in that place a passage through the land, which conjecture we proved to be true, as he himself had certainly done, had not the wind changed as he thought in his favour, giving him an opportunity of returning the way he came in, which he preferred to standing into a bay with an on-shore wind, upon the strength of conjecture only.   Again, when he came the length of Cape Maria Van Diemen he observed hollow waves to come from the north-east, from whence he concluded it to be the northernmost part of the land, which we really found it to be.   Lastly, to his eternal credit be it spoken, although he had been four months absent from Batavia when he made this land, and had sailed both west and east, his longitude (allowing for an error in that of Batavia, as he has himself stated it) differs no more than [1]   from ours, which is corrected by an innumerable number of observations of the moon and sun, etc., as well as of a transit of Mercury over the sun, all calculated and observed by Mr. Green, a mathematician of well-known abilities, who was sent out in this ship by the Royal Society to observe the transit of Venus.   Thus much for Tasman; it were too much to be wished, however, that we had a fuller account of his voyage than that published by Dirk Rembrantz, which seems to be no more than a short extract, and that other navigators would imitate him in mentioning the supposed latitudes and longitudes of the places from whence they take their departures; which precaution, useful as it is, may almost be said to have been used by Tasman alone.

The face of the country is in general mountainous, especially inland, where probably runs a chain of very high hills, parts of which we saw at several times.   They were generally covered with snow, and certainly very high; some of our officers, men of experience, did not scruple to say as

---

[1] Left blank in Banks's Journal. The following note was appended by Banks at the end of the chapter :—

Though Tasman's longitude of Cape Maria Van Diemen comes near the truth, our seamen affirm, and seem to make it appear, that he erred no less than 4° 49′ in running from the first land he made to Cape Maria Van Diemen ; if so, his exactness must be attributed more to chance than skill.

much as the Peak of Teneriffe : in that particular, however, I cannot quite agree with them, though that they must be very high is proved by the hill to the northward of Cook's Straits, which was seen, and made no inconsiderable figure, at the distance of many leagues.

The sea coast, should it ever be examined, will probably be found to abound in good harbours. We saw several, of which the Bay of Islands, or Motuaro, and Queen Charlotte's Sound, or Totarra-nue, are as good as any which seamen need desire to come into, either for good anchorage or for convenience of wooding and watering. The outer ridge of land which is open to the sea is (as I believe is the case of most countries) generally barren, especially to the southward, but within that the hills are covered with thick woods quite to the top, and every valley produces a rivulet of water.

The soil is in general light, and consequently admirably adapted to the uses for which the natives cultivate it, their crops consisting entirely of roots. On the southern and western sides it is the most barren, the sea being generally bounded either by steep hills or vast tracts of sand, which is probably the reason why the people in these parts were so much less numerous, and lived almost entirely upon fish. The northern and eastern shores make, however, some amends for the barrenness of the others; on them we often saw very large tracts of ground, which either actually were, or very lately had been, cultivated, and immense areas of woodland which were yet uncleared, but promised great returns to the people who would take the trouble of clearing them. Taoneroa, or Poverty Bay, and Tolago especially, besides swamps which might doubtless easily be drained, sufficiently evinced the richness of their soil by the great size of all the plants that grew upon them, and more especially of the timber trees, which were the straightest, cleanest, and I may say the largest I have ever seen, at least speaking of them in the gross. I may have seen several times single trees larger than any I observed among these; but it was not one, but all these trees, which were enormous, and doubtless had we had time and opportunity to search, we might have found larger ones than any we saw, as we were never but once ashore among them, and that only for a short time on the banks of the river Thames, where we rowed for many miles between woods of these trees, to which we could see no bounds. The river Thames is indeed, in every respect, the most proper place we have yet seen for establishing a colony.[1] A ship as large as ours might be carried several miles up the river, where she could be moored to the trees as safely as alongside a wharf in London river, a safe and sure retreat in case of an attack from the natives. Or she might even be laid on the mud and a bridge built to her. The noble timber of which there is such abundance would furnish plenty of materials for building either defences, houses, or vessels; the river would furnish plenty of fish, and the soil make ample returns for any European vegetables, etc., sown in it.

I have some reason to think from observations made upon the vegetables that the winters here are extremely mild, much more so than in England; the summers we have found to be scarcely at all hotter, though more equally warm.

The southern part, which is much more hilly and barren than the northern, I firmly believe to abound with minerals in a very high degree : this, however, is only conjecture. I had not to my great regret an opportunity of landing in any place where the signs of them were promising, except the last; nor indeed in any one, where from the ship the country appeared likely to produce them, which it did to the southward in a very high degree, as I have mentioned in my daily Journal.

On every occasion when we landed in this country, we have seen, I had almost said, no quadrupeds originally natives of it. Dogs and rats, indeed, there are, the former

---

[1] A commencement of colonisation was made by Samuel Marsden, a missionary, in 1814, in the Bay of Islands. The first definite attempt to colonise was by the New Zealand Company in 1840, whose settlement was at Wellington. In the same year Captain Hobson, R.N., was sent as Lieut.-Governor : he landed in the Bay of Islands, and transferred his headquarters to the Hauraki Gulf in September, where he founded Auckland (Wharton's *Cook*, p. 231).

as in other countries companions of the men, and the latter probably brought hither by the men; especially as they are so scarce, that I myself have not had opportunity of seeing even one. Of seals, indeed, we have seen a few, and one sea-lion; but these were in the sea, and are certainly very scarce, as there were no signs of them among the natives, except a few teeth of the latter, which they make into a kind of bodkin and value much. It appears not improbable that there really are no other species of quadrupeds in the country, for the natives, whose chief luxury in dress consists in the skins and hair of dogs and the skins of divers birds, and who wear for ornaments the bones and beaks of birds and teeth of dogs, would probably have made use of some part of any other animal they were acquainted with, a circumstance which, though carefully sought after, we never saw the least signs of.

Of birds there are not many species, and none, except perhaps the gannet, are the same as those of Europe. There are ducks and shags of several kinds, sufficiently like the European ones to be called the same by the seamen, both which we eat and accounted good food, especially the former, which are not at all inferior to those of Europe.

Besides these there are hawks, owls, and quails, differing but little at first sight from those of Europe, and several small birds that sing much more melodiously than any I have heard. The sea coast is also frequently visited by many oceanic birds, as albatrosses, shearwaters, pintados, etc., and has also a few of the birds called by Sir John Narbrough penguins, which are truly what the French call a *nuance* between birds and fishes, as their feathers, especially on their wings, differ but little from scales; and their wings themselves, which they use only in diving, by no means attempting to fly or even accelerate their motion on the surface of the water (as young birds are observed to do), might thence almost as properly be called fins.

Neither are insects in greater plenty than birds; a few butterflies and beetles, flesh-flies very like those in Europe, mosquitos and sand-flies, perhaps exactly the same as those

Q

of North America, make up the whole list. Of these last, however, which are most justly accounted the curse of any country where they abound, we never met with any great abundance; a few indeed there were in almost every place we went into, but never enough to make any occupations ashore troublesome, or to give occasion for using shades for the face, which we had brought out to protect us from such insects.

For this scarcity of animals on the land the sea, however, makes abundant recompense; every creek and corner produces abundance of fish, not only wholesome, but at least as well-tasted as our fish in Europe. The ship seldom anchored in, or indeed passed over (in light winds), any place whose bottom was such as fish generally resort to, without our catching as many with hooks and line as the people could eat. This was especially the case to the southward, where, when we lay at anchor, the boats could take any quantity near the rocks; besides which the seine seldom failed of success, insomuch that on the two occasions when we anchored to the southward of Cook's Straits, every mess in the ship that had prudence enough salted as much fish as lasted them many weeks after they went to sea.

For the sorts, there are mackerel of several kinds, one precisely the same as our English, and another much like our horse-mackerel, besides several more. These come in immense shoals and are taken in large seines by the natives, from whom we bought them at very easy rates. Besides these there were many species which, though they did not at all resemble any fish that I at least have before seen, our seamen contrived to give names to, so that hake, bream, cole-fish, etc., were appellations familiar with us, and I must say that those which bear these names in England need not be ashamed of their namesakes in this country. But above all the luxuries we met with, the lobsters, or sea-crawfish, must not be forgotten. They are possibly the same as are mentioned in Lord Anson's voyage as being found at the island of Juan Fernandez, and differ from ours in England in having many more prickles on their backs and being red when taken out of the water. Of them we bought great quantities everywhere to the northward from the natives, who catch them by diving near the shore, feeling first with their feet till they find out where they lie. We had also that fish described by Frézier in his voyage to Spanish South America by the name of *elefant, pejegallo,* or *poisson coq,* which, though coarse, we made shift to eat, and several species of skate or sting-rays, which were abominably coarse. But to make amends for that, we had among several sorts of dog-fish one that was spotted with a few white spots, whose flavour was similar to, but much more delicate than, our skate. We had flat fish also like soles and flounders, eels and congers of several sorts, and many others, which any European who may come here after us will not fail to find the advantage of, besides excellent oysters, cockles, clams, and many other sorts of shell-fish, etc.

Though the country generally is covered with an abundant verdure of grass and trees, yet I cannot say that it is productive of such great variety as many countries I have seen: the entire novelty, however, of the greater part of what we found recompensed us as natural historians for the want of variety. Sow-thistle, garden-nightshade, and perhaps one or two kinds of grasses, were exactly the same as in England, three or four kinds of fern were the same as those of the West Indies: these with a plant or two common to all the world, were all that had been described by any botanist out of about four hundred species, except five or six which we ourselves had before seen in Terra del Fuego.

Of eatable vegetables there are very few; we, indeed, as people who had been long at sea, found great benefit in the article of health by eating plentifully of wild celery and a kind of cress which grows everywhere abundantly near the sea-side. We also once or twice met with a herb[1] like that which the country people in England call "lamb's-quarters" or "fat-hen," which we boiled instead of greens; and once only a cabbage-tree,[2] the cabbage of which made us

---

[1] *Atriplex patula,* Linn. ; it is identical with the English "fat-hen."
[2] The most southern of all palms, *Areca sapida,* Soland.

one delicious meal. These, with the fern roots and one vegetable (*Pandanus*)[1] totally unknown in Europe, which, though eaten by the natives, no European will probably ever relish, are the whole of the vegetables which I know to be eatable, except those which they cultivate and have probably brought with them from the country from whence they themselves originally come.

Nor does their cultivated ground produce many species of esculent plants; three only have I seen, yams, sweet potatoes, and cocos, all three well known and much esteemed in both the East and West Indies. Of these, especially the two former, they cultivate often patches of many acres, and I believe that any ship that found itself to the northward, in the autumn, about the time of digging them up, might purchase any quantity. They also cultivate gourds, the fruits of which serve to make bottles, jugs, etc., and a very small quantity of the Chinese paper mulberry tree.

Fruits they have none, except I should reckon a few kinds of insipid berries which had neither sweetness nor flavour to recommend them, and which none but the boys took the pains to gather.

The woods, however, abound in excellent timber, fit for any kind of building in size, grain, and apparent durability. One, which bears a very conspicuous scarlet flower[2] made up of many threads, and which is as big as an oak in England, has a very heavy hard wood which seems well adapted for the cogs of mill-wheels, etc., or any purpose for which very hard wood is used. That which I have before mentioned to grow in the swamps,[3] which has a leaf not unlike a yew and bears small bunches of berries, is tall, straight, and thick enough to make masts for vessels of any size, and seems likewise by the straight direction of the fibres to be tough, but it is too heavy. This, however, I have been told, is the case with the pitch-pine in North America, the timber of which this much resembles, and which the North Americans lighten by tapping, and actually use for masts.

[1] *Freycinetia Banksii*, A. Cunn.   [2] *Metrosideros robusta*, A. Cunn.
[3] *Podocarpus dacrydioides*, A. Cunn.

But of all the plants we have seen among these people, that which is the most excellent in its kind, and which really excels most if not all that are put to the same uses in other countries, is the plant which serves them instead of hemp or flax.[1] Of this there are two sorts. The leaves of both much resemble those of flags; the flowers are smaller and grow many more together. In one sort they are yellowish, in the other of a deep red. Of the leaves of these plants all their common wearing apparel is made with very little preparation, and all strings, lines, and cordage for every purpose, and that of a strength so much superior to hemp as scarce to bear comparison with it. From these leaves also by another preparation a kind of snow-white fibre is drawn, shining almost as silk, and likewise surprisingly strong; of this all their finer cloths are made: their fishing-nets are also made of these leaves, without any other preparation than splitting them into proper breadths and tying the strips together. So useful a plant would doubtless be a great acquisition to England, especially as one might hope it would thrive there with little trouble, as it seems hardy and affects no particular soil, being found equally on hills and in valleys, in dry soil and the deepest bogs, which last land it seems, however, rather to prefer, as I have always seen it in such places of a larger size than anywhere else.

When first we came ashore we imagined the country to be much better peopled than we afterwards found it; concluding from the smokes that we saw that there were inhabitants very far inland, which indeed in Poverty Bay and the Bay of Plenty (much the best peopled part of the country that we have seen) may be the case. In all the other parts we have been in we have, however, found the sea coast only inhabited, and that but sparingly, insomuch that the number of inhabitants seems to bear no kind of proportion to the size of the country. This is probably owing to their frequent wars. Besides this the whole coast from Cape Maria Van Diemen to Mount Egmont, and seven-eighths of the Southern Island, seem totally without people.

[1] *Phormium tenax*, Forst, the New Zealand Flax.

The men are of the size of the larger Europeans, stout, clean-limbed, and active, fleshy, but never fat, as the lazy inhabitants of the South Sea Isles, vigorous, nimble, and at the same time clever in all their exercises. I have seen fifteen paddles of a side in one of their canoes move with immensely quick strokes, and at the same time as much justness as if the rowers were animated by one soul, not the fraction of a second could be observed between the dipping and raising any two of them, the canoe all the while moving with incredible swiftness. To see them dance their war dance was an amusement which never failed to please every spectator. So much strength, firmness, and agility did they show in their motions, and at the same time such excellent time did they keep, that I have often heard above a hundred paddles struck against the sides of their boats, as directed by their singing, without a mistake being ever made. In colour they vary a little, some being browner than others ; but few are browner than a Spaniard a little sunburnt might be supposed to be. The women, without being at all delicate in their outward appearance, are rather smaller than European women, but have a peculiar softness of voice which never fails to distinguish them from the men. Both are dressed exactly alike. The women are like those of the sex that I have seen in other countries, more lively, airy, and laughter-loving than the men, and with more volatile spirits. Formed by nature to soften the cares of more serious man, who takes upon himself the laborious and toil-some part, as war, tilling the ground, etc., that disposition appears even in this uncultivated state of nature, showing in a high degree that, in uncivilised as well as in the most polished nations, man's ultimate happiness must at last be placed in woman. The dispositions of both sexes seem mild, gentle, and very affectionate to each other, but im-placable towards their enemies, whom after having killed they eat, probably from a principle of revenge. I believe they never give quarter or take prisoners. They seem inured to war, and in their attacks work themselves up by their own war dance to a kind of artificial courage, which will not let them think in the least. Whenever they met with us and thought themselves superior they always attacked us, though seldom seeming to intend more than to provoke us to show them what we were able to do in this case. By many trials we found that good usage and fair words would not avail the least with them, nor would they be convinced by the noise of our firearms alone that we were superior to them; but as soon as they had felt the smart of even a load of small shot, and had time to recollect themselves from the effects of their artificial courage, which commonly took a day, they were sensible of our superiority and became at once our good friends, upon all occasions placing the most unbounded confidence in us. They are not, like the islanders,[1] addicted to stealing; but (if they could) would sometimes, before peace was concluded, by offering anything they had to sell, entice us to trust something of ours into their hands, and refuse to return it with all the coolness in the world, seeming to look upon it as the plunder of an enemy.

Neither of the sexes are quite so cleanly in their persons as the islanders; not having the advantage of so warm a climate, they do not wash so often. But the disgustful thing about them is the oil with which they daub their hair, smelling something like a Greenland dock when they are " trying " whale blubber. This is melted from the fat either of fish or birds. The better sort indeed have it fresh, and then it is entirely void of smell.

Both sexes stain themselves in the same manner with the colour of black, and somewhat in the same way as the South Sea Islanders, introducing it under the skin by a sharp instrument furnished with many teeth. The men carry this custom to much greater lengths; the women are generally content with having their lips blacked, but sometimes have little patches of black on different parts of the body. The man on the contrary seems to add to the

---

[1] Throughout the remainder of the Journal Banks constantly speaks of the South Sea Islands simply as "the islands," and their inhabitants as "the islanders."

quantity every year of his life, so that some of the elders were almost covered with it. Their faces are the most remarkable; on them, by some art unknown to me, they dig furrows a line deep at least, and as broad, the edges of which are often again indented, and absolutely black. This may be done to make them look frightful in war, indeed it has the effect of making them most enormously ugly; the old ones especially, whose faces are entirely covered with it. The young, again, often have a small patch on one cheek or over one eye, and those under a certain age (maybe twenty-five or twenty-six) have no more than their lips black. Yet ugly as this certainly looks, it is impossible to avoid admiring the extreme elegance and justness of the figures traced, which on the face are always different spirals, and upon the body generally different figures, resembling somewhat the foliages of old chasing upon gold or silver. All these are finished with a masterly taste and execution, for of a hundred which at first sight would be judged to be exactly the same, no two on close examination prove alike, nor do I remember ever to have seen any two alike. Their wild imagination scorns to copy, as appears in almost all their works. In different parts of the coast they varied very much in the quantity and parts of the body on which this *amoca*, as they call it, was placed; but they generally agreed in having the spirals upon the face. I have generally observed that the more populous a country the greater was the quantity of *amoca* used; possibly in populous countries the emulation of bearing pain with fortitude may be carried to greater lengths than where there are fewer people, and consequently fewer examples to encourage. The buttocks, which in the islands were the principal seat of this ornament, in general here escape untouched; in one place only we saw the contrary.

Besides this dyeing in grain, as it may be called, they are very fond of painting themselves with red ochre, which they do in two ways, either rubbing it dry upon their skins, as some few do, or daubing their faces with large patches of it mixed with oil, which consequently never dries. This latter is generally practised by the women, and was not universally condemned by us, for if any of us had unthinkingly ravished a kiss from one of these fair savages, our transgressions were written in most legible characters on our noses, which our companions could not fail to see on our first interview.

The common dress of these people is certainly to a stranger one of the most uncouth and extraordinary sights that can be imagined. It is made of the leaves of the flag described before, each being split into three or four slips; and these, as soon as they are dry, are woven into a kind of stuff between netting and cloth, out of the upper side of which all the ends, of eight or nine inches, are suffered to hang in the same manner as thrums out of a thrum mat. Of these pieces of cloth two serve for a complete dress: one is tied over the shoulders, and reaches to about their knees; the other is tied about the waist, and reaches to near the ground. But they seldom wear more than one of these, and when they have it on resemble not a little a thatched house. These dresses, however, ugly as they are, are well adapted for their convenience, as they often sleep in the open air, and live some time without the least shelter, even from rain, so that they must trust entirely to their clothes as the only chance they have of keeping themselves dry. For this they are certainly not ill adapted, as every strip of leaf becomes in that case a kind of gutter which serves to conduct the rain down, and hinder it from soaking through the cloth beneath.

Besides this they have several kinds of cloth which are smooth, and ingeniously worked; these are chiefly of two sorts, one coarse as our coarsest canvas, and ten times stronger, but much like it in the lying of the threads; the other is formed by many threads running lengthwise, and a few only crossing them to tie them together. This last sort is sometimes striped, and always very pretty; for the threads that compose it are prepared so as to shine almost as much as silk. To both these they work borders of different colours in fine stitches, something like carpeting or girls' samplers in various patterns, with an ingenuity truly surprising to any one who will reflect that they are without needles. They have also mats with which they sometimes cover themselves; but the great pride of their dress seems to consist in dogs' fur, which they use so sparingly that to avoid waste they cut it into long strips, and sew them at a distance from each other upon their cloth, often varying the colours prettily enough. When first we saw these dresses we took them for the skins of bears or some animal of that kind, but we were soon undeceived, and found upon inquiry that they were acquainted with no animal that had fur or long hair but their own dogs. Some there were who had their dresses ornamented with feathers, and one who had an entire dress of the red feathers of parrots ; but these were not common.

The first man we saw when we went ashore at Poverty Bay, and who was killed by one of our people, had his dress tied exactly in the same manner as is represented in Mr. Dalrymple's account of Tasman's voyage, in a plate which I believe is copied from Valentijn's *History of the East Indies ;* it was tied over his shoulders, across his breast, under his armpits, again across his breast, and round his loins. Of this dress we saw, however, but one more instance during our whole stay on the coast, though it seems convenient, as it leaves the arms quite at liberty, while the body is covered. In general, indeed, when they choose to set their arms at liberty, they at the same time free all their limbs by casting off their clothes entirely.

The men always wear short beards, and tie their hair in a small knot on the top of their heads, sticking into it a kind of comb, and at the top two or three white feathers. The women, contrary to the custom of the sex in general, seem to affect rather less dress than the men. Their hair, which they wear short, is seldom tied, and when it is, it is behind their heads, and never ornamented with feathers. Their cloths are of the same stuff, and in the same form, as those of the men.

Both sexes bore their ears, and wear in them a great variety of ornaments; the holes are generally (as if to keep them upon the stretch) filled up with a plug of some sort or other, either cloth, feathers, bones of large birds, or sometimes only a stick of wood: into this hole they often also put nails or anything we gave them which could go there. The women also often wear bunches, nearly as large as a fist, of the down of the albatross, which is snow-white. This, though very odd, makes by no means an inelegant appearance. They hang from them by strings many very different things, often a chisel and bodkins made of a kind of green talc, which they value much; the nails and teeth also of their deceased relations, dogs' teeth, and, in short, anything which is either valuable or ornamental. Besides these the women sometimes wear bracelets and anklets made of the bones of birds, shells, etc., and the men often carry the figure of a distorted man made of the beforementioned green talc, or the tooth of a whale cut slantwise, so as to resemble somewhat a tongue, and furnished with two eyes. These they wear about their necks and seem to value almost above everything else. I saw one instance also of a very extraordinary ornament, which was a feather stuck through the bridge of the nose, and projecting on each side of it over the cheeks; but this I only mention as a singular thing, having met with it only once among the many people I have seen, and never observed in any other even the marks of a hole which might occasionally serve for such a purpose.

Their houses are certainly the most unartificially made of anything among them, scarcely equal to a European dog's kennel, and resembling it, in the door at least, which is barely high or wide enough to admit a man crawling upon all fours. They are seldom more than sixteen or eighteen feet long, eight or ten broad, and five or six high from the ridge pole to the ground: they are built with a sloping roof like our European houses. The material of both walls and roof is dry grass or hay, and very tightly it is put together, so that they must necessarily be very warm; some are lined with the bark of trees on the inside, and many have either over the door or somewhere in the house a plank covered with their carving, which they seem to value much as we do a picture, placing it always as conspicuously as possible. All these houses have the door at one end; and near it is a square hole which serves as a window or probably in winter time more as a chimney; for then they light a fire at the end where this door and window are placed. The side walls and roof project generally eighteen inches or two feet beyond the end wall, making a kind of porch, where are benches on which the people of the house often sit. Within is a square place fenced off with either boards or stones from the rest, in the middle of which they can make a fire; the sides of the house are thickly laid with straw, on which they sleep. As for furniture, they are not much troubled with it; one chest commonly contains all their riches, consisting of tools, cloths, arms, and a few feathers to stick into their hair; their gourds or baskets made of bark, which serve them to keep fresh water, their provision baskets, and the hammers with which they beat their fern roots, are generally left without the door.

Mean and low as these houses are, they most perfectly resist all inclemencies of the weather, and answer consequently the purposes of mere shelter as well as larger ones would do. The people, I believe, spend little of the day in them (except maybe in winter); the porch seems to be the place for work, and those who have not room there must sit upon a stone, or on the ground in the neighbourhood.

Some few families of the better sort have a kind of courtyard, the walls of which are made of poles and hay, ten or twelve feet high, and which, as their families are large, encloses three or four houses. But I must not forget the ruins, or rather frame of a house (for it had never been finished), which I saw at Tolaga, as it was so much superior in size to anything of the kind we have met with in any other part of the land. It was 30 feet in length, 15 in breadth, and 12 high; the sides of it were ornamented with many broad carved planks of a workmanship superior to any other we saw on the land. For what purpose this was built or why deserted we could not find out.

Though these people when at home defend themselves so well from the inclemencies of the weather, yet when they are abroad upon their excursions, which they often make in search of fern roots, fish, etc., they seem totally indifferent to shelter. Sometimes they make a small shade to windward of them, but more often omit that precaution. During our stay at Opoorage, or Mercury Bay, a party of Indians were there, consisting of forty or fifty, who during all that time never erected the least covering, though it twice rained almost without ceasing for twenty-four hours together.

Their food, in the use of which they seem to be moderate, consists of dogs, birds (especially sea fowl, as penguins, albatrosses, etc.), fish, sweet potatoes, yams, cocos, some few wild plants, as sow-thistles [1] and palm-cabbage, but above all, the root of a species of fern which seems to be to them what bread is to us. This fern is very common upon the hills, and very nearly resembles that which grows upon our hilly commons in England, and is called indifferently fern, bracken, or brakes. As for the flesh of man, although they certainly do eat it, I cannot in my own opinion debase human nature so much as to imagine that they relish it as a dainty, or even look upon it as common food. Thirst for revenge may drive men to great lengths when their passions are allowed to take their full swing, yet nature, through all the superior part of the creation, shows how much she recoils at the thought of any species preying upon itself. Dogs and cats show visible signs of disgust at the very sight of a dead carcass of their own species; even wolves or bears are said never to eat one another except in cases of absolute necessity, when the stings of hunger have overcome the precepts of nature, in which case the same has been done by the inhabitants of the most civilised nations. Among fish and insects, indeed, there are many instances which prove that

---

[1] The New Zealand bracken and sow-thistle are identical with the English (*Pteris aquilina*, Linn., and *Sonchus asper*, Vill.).

those that live by prey regard little whether what they take is of their own or any other species. But any one who considers the admirable chain of nature, in which man, alone endowed with reason, justly claims the highest rank, and in which the half-reasoning elephant, the sagacious dog, the architect beaver, etc., in whom instinct so nearly resembles reason as to have been mistaken for it by men of no mean capacities, are placed next; from these descending through the less informed quadrupeds and birds to the fish and insects, who seem, besides the instinct of fear which is given them for self-preservation, to be moved only by the stings of hunger to eat, and those of lust to propagate their species, which, when born, are left entirely to their own care; and at last by the medium of the oysters, etc., which not being able to move, but as tossed about by the waves, must in themselves be furnished with both sexes, that the species may be continued; shading itself away into the vegetable kingdom, for the preservation of whom neither sensation nor instinct is wanted; whoever considers this, I say, will easily see that no conclusion in favour of such a practice can be drawn from the actions of a race of beings placed so infinitely below us in the order of nature.

But to return to my subject. Simple as their food is, their cookery so far as I saw is as simple: a few stones heated and laid in a hole, with the meat laid upon them and covered with hay, seems to be the most difficult part of it. Fish and birds they generally broil, or rather toast, spiking them upon a long skewer, the bottom of which is fixed under a stone, another stone being put under the fore part of the skewer, which is raised or lowered by moving the second stone as circumstances may require. The fern roots are laid upon the open fire until they are thoroughly hot and their bark burnt to a coal; they are then beaten with a wooden hammer over a stone, which causes all the bark to fly off, and leaves the inside, consisting of a small proportion of a glutinous pulp mixed with many fibres, which they generally spit out, after having sucked each mouthful a long time. Strange and unheard of as it must appear to a European, to draw nourishment from a class of plant which in Europe no animal, hardly even insects, will taste, I am much inclined to think that it affords a nourishing and wholesome diet. These people eat but little, and this is the foundation of their meals all summer, at least from the time that their roots are planted, till the season for digging them up. Among them I have seen several very healthy old men, and in general the whole of them are as vigorous a race as can be imagined.

To the southward, where little or nothing is planted, fern roots and fish must serve them all the year. Accordingly, we saw that they had made vast piles of both, especially the latter, which were dried in the sun very well, and I suppose meant for winter stock, when possibly fish is not so plentiful or the trouble of catching it is greater than in summer.

Water is their universal drink, nor did I see any signs of any other liquor being at all known to them, or any method of intoxication. If they really have not, happy they must be allowed to be above all other nations that I have heard of.

So simple a diet, accompanied with moderation, must be productive of sound health, which indeed these people are blessed with in a very high degree. Though we were in several of their towns, where young and old crowded to see us, actuated by the same curiosity as made us desirous of seeing them, I do not remember a single instance of a person distempered in any degree that came under my inspection, and among the numbers of them that I have seen naked, I have never seen an eruption on the skin or any signs of one, scars or otherwise. Their skins, when they came off to us in their canoes, were often marked in patches with a little floury appearance, which at first deceived us, but we afterwards found that it was owing to their having been in their passage wetted with the spray of the sea, which, when it was dry, left the salt behind it in a fine white powder.

Such health drawn from so sound principles must make

physicians almost useless; indeed I am inclined to think
that their knowledge of physic is but small, judging from the
state of their surgery which more than once came under my
inspection. Of this art they seemed totally ignorant. I saw
several wounded by our shot, without the smallest application on their wounds; one in particular who had a musket
ball shot right through the fleshy part of his arm, came out
of his house and showed himself to us, making a little use
of the wounded arm. The wound, which was then of several
days' standing, was totally void of inflammation, and in
short appeared to be in so good a state, that had any
application been made use of, I should not have failed to
inquire carefully what it had been which had produced so
good an effect.

A further proof, and not a weak one, of the sound
health that these people enjoy, may be taken from the
number of old people we saw. Hardly a canoe came off to
us without bringing one or more; and every town had
several, who, if we may judge by grey hairs and worn-out
teeth, were of a very advanced age. Of these few or none
were decrepit; the greater number seemed in vivacity and
cheerfulness to equal the young, and indeed to be inferior
to them in nothing but the want of equal strength and
agility.

That the people have a larger share of ingenuity than
usually falls to the lot of nations who have had so little or
no commerce with any others appears at first sight: their
boats, the better sort at least, show it most evidently.
These are built of very thin planks sewn together, their
sides rounding up like ours, but very narrow for their
length. Some are immensely long. One I saw which the
people laid alongside the ship, as if to measure how
much longer she was than the canoe, fairly reached from
the anchor that hung at the bows quite aft, but indeed
we saw few so large as that. All, except a few we saw at
Opoorage or Mercury Bay, which were merely trunks of trees
hollowed out by fire, were more or less ornamented by
carving. The common fishing canoe had no ornament but

the face of a man with a monstrous tongue, whose eyes were generally inlaid with a kind of shell like mother-of-pearl; but the larger sort, which seemed to be intended for war, were really magnificently adorned. The head was formed by a plank projecting about three feet before the canoe, and on the stern stood another, proportioned to the size of the canoe, from ten to eighteen feet high. Both these were richly carved with open work, and covered with loose fringes of black feathers that had a most graceful effect. The gunnel boards were often also carved in grotesque taste, and ornamented with white feathers in bunches placed upon a black ground at certain intervals. They sometimes joined two small canoes together, and now and then made use of an outrigger, as is practised in the islands, but this was more common to the southward.

In managing these canoes, at least in paddling them, they are very expert. In one I counted sixteen paddlers on a side, and never did men, I believe, keep better time with their strokes, driving on the boat with immense velocity. Their paddles are often ornamented with carving, the blade is of an oval shape pointed towards the bottom, broadest in the middle, and again sloping towards the handle, which is about four feet long, the whole being generally about six feet in length, more or less. In sailing they are not so expert; we very seldom saw them make use of sails, and indeed never, unless they were to go right before the wind. They were made of mat, and instead of a mast were hoisted upon two sticks, which were fastened one to each side, so that they required two ropes which answered the purpose of sheets, and were fastened to the tops of these sticks. In this clumsy manner they sailed with a good deal of swiftness, and were steered by two men who sat in the stern, each with a paddle in his hand. I shall set down the dimensions of one which we measured, that was of the largest size. It was in length $68\frac{1}{2}$ feet, breadth 5 feet, depth $3\frac{1}{2}$ feet. This was the only one we measured, or indeed had an opportunity of measuring.

Of the beauty of their carving in general I would fain

say more, but find myself much inferior to the task. I shall therefore content myself with saying that their taste led them into two materially different styles, as I will call them. One was entirely formed of a number of spirals differently connected, the other was in a much more wild taste, and I may truly say was like nothing but itself. The truth with which the lines were drawn was surprising; but even more so was their method of connecting several spirals into one piece, inimitably well, intermingling the ends in so dexterous a manner that it was next to impossible for the eye to trace the connections. The beauty of all their carvings, however, depended entirely on the design, for the execution was so rough that when you came near it was difficult to see any beauty in the things which struck you most at a distance.

After having said so much of their workmanship, it will be necessary to say something of their tools. As they have no metals these are made of stone of different kinds, their hatchets especially of any hard stone they can get, but chiefly of a kind of green talc, which is very hard and at the same time tough. With axes of this stone they cut so clean that it would often puzzle a man to say whether the wood they have shaped was or was not cut with an iron hatchet. These axes they value above all their riches, and would seldom part with them for anything we could offer. Their nicer work, which requires nicer-edged tools, they do with fragments of jasper, which they break and use the sharp edges till they become blunt, after which they throw them away as useless, for it is impossible ever again to sharpen them. I suppose it was with these fragments of jasper that at Tolaga they bored a hole through a piece of glass that we had given them, just large enough to admit a thread in order to convert it into an ornament. I must confess I am quite ignorant of what method they use to cut and polish their weapons, which are made of very hard stone.

Their cloths are made exactly in the same manner as by the inhabitants of South America, some of whose workmanship, procured at Rio de Janeiro, I have on board. The warp or long threads are laid very close together, and each crossing of the woof is distant at least an inch from another. They have besides this several other kinds of cloth, and work borders to them all, but as to their manner of doing so I must confess myself totally ignorant. I never but once saw any of this work going forward; it was done in a kind of frame of the breadth of the cloth, across which it was spread, and the cross threads worked in by hand, which must be very tedious; however, the workmanship sufficiently proves the workmen to be dexterous in their way. One notable point I must not forget, which is that to every garment of the better kind is fixed a bodkin, as if to remind the wearer that if it should be torn by any accident, no time should be lost before it is mended.

Nets for fishing they make in the same manner as ours, of an amazing size; a seine seems to be the joint work of a whole town, and I suppose the joint property. Of these I think I have seen as large as ever I saw in Europe. Besides this they have fish pots and baskets worked with twigs, and another kind of net which they most generally make use of that I have never seen in any country but this. It is circular, seven or eight feet in diameter, and two or three deep; it is stretched by two or three hoops and open at the top for nearly, but not quite, its whole extent. On the bottom is fastened the bait, a little basket containing the guts, etc., of fish and sea ears, which are tied to different parts of the net. This is let down to the bottom where the fish are, and when enough are supposed to be gathered together, it is drawn up with a very gentle motion, by which means the fish are insensibly lifted from the bottom. In this manner I have seen them take vast numbers of fish, and indeed it is a most general way of fishing all over the coast. Their hooks are ill made, generally of bone or shell fastened to a piece of wood; indeed, they seem to have little occasion for them, for with their nets they take fish much easier than they could with hooks.

In tilling they excel, as people who are themselves to eat the fruit of their industry, and have little else to do but cultivate, necessarily must.   When we first came to Tegadu the crops were just covered, and had not yet begun to sprout; the mould was as smooth as in a garden, and every root had its small hillock, all ranged in a regular quincunx by lines, which with the pegs still remained in the field.

We had not an opportunity of seeing them work, but once saw their tool, which is a long and narrow stake, flattened a little and sharpened; across this is fixed a piece of stick for the convenience of pressing it down with the foot.   With this simple tool, industry teaches them to turn pieces of ground of six or seven acres in extent.   The soil is generally sandy, and is therefore easily turned up, while the narrowness of the tool, the blade of which is not more than three inches broad, makes it meet with the less resistance.

Tillage, weaving, and the rest of the arts of peace are best known and most practised in the north-eastern parts; indeed, in the southern there is little to be seen of any of them; but war seems to be equally known to all, though most practised in the south-west.   The mind of man, ever ingenious in inventing instruments of destruction, has not been idle here.   Their weapons, though few, are well calculated for bloody fights, and the destruction of numbers. Defensive weapons they have none, and no missiles except stones and darts, which are chiefly used in defending their forts; so that if two bodies should meet either in boats or upon the plain ground, they must fight hand to hand and the slaughter be consequently immense.

Of their weapons, the spears are made of hard wood pointed at both ends, sometimes headed with human bones; some are fourteen or fifteen feet long.   They are grasped by the middle, so that the end which hangs behind, serving as a balance to keep the front steady, makes it much more difficult to parry a push from one of them than it would from one of a spear only half as long which was held by the end.   Their battle-axes, likewise made of a very hard wood, are about six feet long, the bottom of the handle pointed, and the blade, which is exactly like that of an axe but broader, made very sharp : with these they chop at the heads of their antagonists when an opportunity offers.

The *patoo-patoos*, as they called them, are a kind of small hand bludgeon of stone, bone, or hard wood, most admirably adapted for the cracking of skulls ; they are of different shapes, some like an old-fashioned chopping-knife, others like this, or ; always however, having sharp edges, and sufficient weight to make a second blow unnecessary if the first takes effect. In these they seemed to put their chief dependence, fastening them by a long strap to their wrists, lest they should be wrenched from them. The principal people seldom stirred out without one of them sticking in their girdle, generally made of bone (of whales as they told us) or of coarse, black, and very hard jasper, insomuch that we were almost led to conclude that in peace as well as war they wore them as a warlike ornament, in the same manner as we Europeans wear swords. The darts are about eight feet long, made of wood, bearded and sharpened, but intended chiefly for the defence of their forts, when they have the advantage of throwing them down from a height upon their enemy. They often brought them out in their boats when they meant to attack us, but so little were they able to make use of them against us, who were by reason of the height of the ship above them, that they never but once attempted it ; and then the dart, though thrown with the utmost strength of the man who held it, barely fell on board. Sometimes I have seen them pointed with the stings of sting-rays, but very seldom ; why they do not oftener use them I do not know. Nothing is more terrible to a European than the sharp-jagged beards of those bones ; but I believe that they seldom cause death, though the wounds made by them must be most troublesome and painful. Stones, however, they use much more dexterously, though ignorant of the use of slings. They throw by hand a considerable distance ; when they have pelted us with them on board the ship, I have seen our people attempt to throw them back, and not be able to reach the canoes, although they had so manifest an advantage in the height of their situation.

These are all that can be properly called arms, but besides these the chiefs when they came to attack us carried in their hands a kind of ensign of distinction in the same manner as ours do spontoons : these were either the rib of a whale, as white as snow, carved very much, and ornamented with dogs' hair and feathers, or a stick about six feet long, carved and ornamented in the same manner, and generally inlaid with shell like mother-of-pearl. Of these chiefs there were in their war canoes one, two, or three, according to the size of the canoes. When within about a cable's length of the ship, they generally rose up, dressed themselves in a distinguishing dress (often of dog's skin), and holding in their hands either one of their spontoons or a weapon, directed the rest of the people how to proceed. They were always old, or at least past the middle age, and had upon them a larger quantity of *amoca* than usual. These canoes commonly paddled with great vigour till they came within about a stone's throw of the ship (having no idea that any missive could reach them farther), and then began to threaten us ; this, indeed, the smaller canoes did, as soon as they were within hearing. Their words were almost universally the same, " Haromai haromai, harre uta a patoo-patoo oge," " Come to us, come to us, come but ashore with us, and we will kill you with our patoo-patoos."

In this manner they continued to threaten us, venturing by degrees nearer and nearer till they were close alongside : at intervals talking very civilly, and answering any questions we asked them, but quickly renewing their threats till they had by our non-resistance gained courage enough to begin their war-song and dance ; after which they either became so insolent that we found it necessary to chastise them by firing small shot at them, or else threw three or four stones on board, and, as if content with having offered such an insult unavenged, left us.

The war-song and dance consists of various contortions of the limbs, during which the tongue was frequently thrust out incredibly far, and the orbits of their eyes enlarged so much that a circle of white was distinctly seen round the iris; in short, nothing is omitted which could render a human shape frightful and deformed, which I suppose they think terrible. During this time they brandish their spears, hack the air with their patoo-patoos, and shake their darts as if they meant every moment to begin the attack, singing all the while in a wild but not disagreeable manner, ending every strain with a loud and deep-drawn sigh, in which they all join in concert. The whole is accompanied by strokes struck against the sides of the boats with their feet, paddles, and arms; the whole in such excellent time, that though the crews of several canoes join in concert, you rarely or never heard a single stroke wrongly placed.

This we called the war-song; for though they seemed fond of using it upon all occasions, whether in war or peace, they, I believe, never omit it in their attacks. They have several other songs which their women sing prettily enough in parts. They were all in a slow melancholy style, but certainly have more taste in them than could be expected from untaught savages. Instrumental music they have none, unless a kind of wooden pipe, or the shell called *Triton's Trumpet*, with which they make a noise not very unlike that made by boys with a cow's horn, may be called such. They have, indeed, also a kind of small pipe of wood, crooked and shaped almost like a large tobacco pipe, but it has hardly more music in it than a whistle with a pea. But on none of these did I ever hear them attempt to play a tune or sing to their music.

That they eat the bodies of such of their enemies as are killed in war, is a fact which they universally acknowledged from our first landing at every place we came to. It was confirmed by an old man, whom we supposed to be the chief of an Indian town very near us, bringing at our desire six or seven heads of men, preserved with the flesh on. These it seems the people keep, after having eaten the brains, as trophies of their victories, in the same manner as the Indians of North America do scalps; they had their ornaments in their ears as when alive, and some seemed to have false eyes. The old man was very jealous of showing them;

one I bought, but much against the inclination of its owner,
for though he liked the price I offered, he hesitated much to
send it up; yet, having taken the price, I insisted either on
having that returned or the head given, but could not
prevail until I enforced my threats by showing him a
musket, on which he chose to part with the head rather
than the price he had, which was a pair of old drawers of
my white linen.   The head appeared to have belonged to a
person of about fourteen or fifteen years of age, and evidently
showed, by the contusions on one side, that it had received
many violent blows which had chipped off a part of the
skull near the eye.   From this, and many other circumstances, I am inclined to believe that these Indians give no
quarter, or even take prisoners to eat upon a future
occasion, as is said to have been practised by the Floridan
Indians; for had they done so, this young creature, who
could not make much resistance, would have been a very
proper subject.

The state of war in which they live, constantly in danger
of being surprised when least upon their guard, has taught
them, not only to live together in towns, but to fortify
those towns, which they do by a broad ditch, and a
palisade within it of no despicable construction.

For these towns or forts, which they call *Heppahs*, they
choose situations naturally strong, commonly islands or
peninsulas, where the sea or steep cliffs defend the greater
part of their works; and if there is any part weaker than
the rest, a stage is erected over it of considerable height—
eighteen or twenty feet—on the top of which the defenders
range themselves, and fight with a great advantage, as
they can throw down their darts and stones with much
greater force than the assailants can throw them up.
Within these forts the greater part of the tribe to whom
they belong reside, and have large stocks of provisions:
fern roots and dried fish, but no water; for that article, in
all that I have seen, was only to be had from some distance
without the lines.   From this we concluded that sieges are
not usual among them.   Some, however, are generally out

in small parties in the neighbouring creeks and coves, employed either in taking fish or collecting fern roots, etc., a large quantity of which they bring back with them, a reserve, I suppose, for times when the neighbourhood of an enemy or other circumstances make the procuring of fresh provision difficult or dangerous.

Of these forts or towns we saw many; indeed, the inhabitants constantly lived in such, from the westernmost part of the Bay of Plenty to Queen Charlotte's Sound; but about Hawke's Bay, Poverty Bay, Tegadu and Tolaga, there were none, and the houses were scattered about. There were, indeed, stages built upon the sides of hills, sometimes of great length, which might serve as a retreat to save their lives at the last extremity and nothing else, but these were mostly in ruins. Throughout all this district the people seemed free from apprehension, and as in a state of profound peace; their cultivations were far more numerous and larger than those we saw anywhere else, and they had a far greater quantity of fine boats, fine clothes, fine carved work; in short, the people were far more numerous, and lived in much greater affluence, than any others we saw. This seemed to be owing to their being joined together under one chief or king, as they always called *Teratu*, who lives far up in the country.[1]

It is much to be lamented that we could get no further knowledge of this chief or king than his name only; his dominions are for an Indian monarch certainly most extensive. He was acknowledged for a length of coasts of upwards of eighty leagues, and yet we do not know the western limits of his dominions; we are sure, however, that they contain the greatest share of the rich part of the northernmost island, and that far the greatest number of people upon it are his subjects. Subordinate to him are lesser chiefs, who seem to have obedience and respect paid them

[1] The people who mentioned Teratu to us pointed, as we thought, always inland; but since the country has been laid down upon paper, it appears that over the land in that direction lies the Bay of Plenty; from hence it appears probable that this is the residence of Teratu, and, if so, the country inland will probably be found to be quite void of inhabitants. [Note by Banks.]

by the tribe to whom they belong, and who probably
administer justice to them, though we never saw an instance
of it, except in the case of theft on board the ship, when
upon our complaint the offender received kicks and blows
from the chief with whom he came on board.

These chiefs were generally old men : whether they had
the office of chief by birth or on account of their age, we
never learnt; but in the other parts, where Teratu was not
acknowledged, we plainly learnt that the chiefs whom they
obeyed, of which every tribe had some, received their dignity
by inheritance.   In the northern parts their societies seemed
to have many things in common, particularly their fine
clothes and nets ; of the former they had but few, and we
never saw anybody employed in making them.   It might be
that what they had were the spoils of war.   They were
kept in a small hut erected for that purpose in the middle
of the town.   The latter seemed to be the joint work of
the whole society.   Every house had in it pieces of netting
upon which they were engaged ; by joining these together it
is probable that they made the large seines which we saw.

The women are less regarded here than in the South
Sea Islands, so, at least, thought Tupia, who complained of
it as an insult upon the sex.   They eat with the men, however.   How the sexes divide labour I do not know, but I
am inclined to believe that the men till the ground, fish in
boats, make nets, and take birds, while the women dig up
fern roots, collect shell-fish and lobsters near the beach,
dress the victuals, and weave cloth.   Thus, at least, have
these employments been distributed, when I had an opportunity of observing them, which was very seldom ; for our
approach generally made a holiday wherever we went, men,
women, and children flocking to us either to satisfy their
curiosity or trade with us for whatever they might have.
They took in exchange cloth of any kind, especially linen
or the Indian cloth we had brought from the islands, paper,
glass bottles, sometimes pieces of broken glass, nails, etc.

We saw few or no signs of religion among these people ;
they had no public places of worship, as the inhabitants of

the South Sea Islands, and only one private one came under my notice, which was in the neighbourhood of a plantation of their sweet potatoes. It was a small square bordered round with stones; in the middle was a spade, and on it hung a basket of fern roots—an offering (I suppose) to the gods for the success of the crops—so, at least, one of the natives explained it. They, however, acknowledged the influence of superior beings. Tupia, however, seemed to be much better versed in legends than any of them, for whenever he began to preach, as we called it, he was sure of a numerous audience, who attended with most profound silence to his doctrines.

The burial of the dead, instead of being a pompous ceremony as in the islands, is here kept secret; we never so much as saw a grave where any one had been interred; nor did they always agree in the accounts they gave of the manner of disposing of dead bodies. In the northern parts they told us that they buried them in the ground; and in the southern, said that they threw them into the sea, having first tied to them a sufficient weight to cause their sinking. However they disposed of the dead, their regret for the loss of them was sufficiently visible; few or none were without scars, and some had them hideously large on their cheeks, arms, legs, etc., from the cuts they had given themselves during their mourning. I have seen several with such wounds of which the blood was not yet stanched, and one only, a woman, while she was cutting herself and lamenting; she wept much, repeating many sentences in a plaintive tone of voice, at every one of which she with a shell cut a gash in some part of her body. She, however, contrived her cuts in such a manner that few of them drew blood, and those that did, penetrated a small depth only. She was old, and had probably outlived those violent impressions that grief, as well as other passions of the mind, make upon young people; her grief also was probably of long standing. The scars upon the bodies of the greater part of these people evinced, however, that they had felt sorrows more severely than she did.

Thus much for the manners and customs of these people, as far as they have come to my knowledge in the few opportunities I had of seeing them. They differ in many things, but agree in more, with those of the inhabitants of the South Sea Islands. Their language I shall next give a short specimen of; it is almost precisely the same, at least fundamentally. It is true that they have generally added several letters to the words as used by the inhabitants of Otahite, etc., but the original plainly appears in the composition. The language of the northern and southern parts differs chiefly in this, that the one has added more letters than the other; the original words are, however, not less visible to the most superficial observer. I shall give a short table of each compared with the Otahite, taking care to mention as many words as possible as are either of a doubtful or different origin; premising, however, two things—first, that the words were so much disguised by their manner of pronouncing them that I found it very difficult to understand them until I had written them down; secondly, that Tupia, from the very first, understood and conversed with them with great facility.

I must remark that most of the southern language was not taken down by myself, and I am inclined to believe that the person who did it for me made use of more letters in spelling the words than were absolutely necessary. The genius of the language, especially in the southern parts, is to add some particle—*the* or *a*—before a noun as we do; *the* was generally *ke* or *ko*. They also often add to the end of any word, especially if it is in answer to a question, the word *oeia*, which signifies yes, really, or certainly. This sometimes led our gentlemen into the most long-winded words, one of which I shall mention as an example. In the Bay of Islands a very remarkable island was called by the natives *Motu aro;* some of our gentlemen asked the name of this from one of the natives, who answered, I suppose, as usual *Komotu aro;* the gentleman not hearing well the word, repeated his question, on which the Indian repeated his answer, adding *oeia* to the end of the name, which made it

Kemotuaroeia. In this way at least, and no other, can I account for that island being called in the log-book *Cumettiwarroweia.* The same is practised by the inhabitants of the South Sea Islands, only their particle, instead of *ke* or *ko*, is *to* or *ta*; their *oeia* is exactly the same, and, when I first began to learn the language, produced many difficulties and mistakes.

	Northern.	Southern.	Otahite.
A chief	Eareete	Eareete	Earee
A man	Taata	Taata	Taata
A woman	Ivahine	Ivahine	Ivahine
The head	Eupo	Heaowpoho	Eupo
The hair	Macauwe	Heooo	Roourou
The ear	Terringa	Hetahezei	Terrea
The forehead	Erai	Heai	Erai
The eyes	Mata	Hemata	Mata
The cheeks	Paparinga	Hepapach	Paparea
The nose	Ahewh	Heeih	Ahewh
The mouth	Hangoutou	Hegowai	Outou
The chin	Ecouwai	Hekasewai	...
The arm	Haringaringa	...	Rema
The finger	Maticara	Hemaigawh	Manneow
The belly	Ateraboo	...	Oboo
The navel	Apeto	Hecapeeto	Peto
Come here	Haromai	Horomai	Harromai
Fish	Heica	Heica	Eyea
A lobster	Koura	Kooura	Tooura
Cocos	Taro	Taro	Taro
Sweet potatoes	Cumalo	Cumala	Cumula
Yams	Tuphwhe	Tuphwhe	Tuphwhe
Birds	Mannu	Mannu	Mannu
No	Kaoure	Kaoure	Ima
The teeth	Hennihu	Heneaho	Niheo
The wind	Mehow	...	Mattai
A thief	Amooto	...	Teto
To examine	Mataketaki	...	Mataitai
To sing	Eheara	...	Heiva
Bad	Keno	Keno	Eno
Trees	Cratou	Eratou	Eratou
Grandfather	Toubouna	Toubouna	Toubouna
1.	Tahai	...	Tahie
2.	Rua	...	Rua
3.	Torou	...	Torou
4.	Ha	...	Hea
5.	Rema	...	Rema
6.	Ono	...	Ono
7.	Etu	...	Hetu
8.	Warou	...	Waru
9.	Iva	...	Heva
10.	Augahourou	...	Ahourou

CHAPTER XI

NEW ZEALAND TO AUSTRALIA (ENDEAVOUR RIVER)

MARCH 31—JUNE 18, 1770

Choice of routes—Reasons in favour of and against the existence of a southern continent—Suggestions for a proposed expedition in search of it—Leave New Zealand—Malt wort—Portuguese man-of-war and its sting—Hot weather—Land seen—Waterspouts—Variation of the compass—Natives—Their indifference to the ship—Opposition to landing—Excursion into the country—Vegetation and animals seen—Botanising—Timidity of the natives—Enormous sting-rays—Treachery of natives—Leave Botany Bay—Ants—Stinging caterpillars—Gum trees—Oysters—Crabs—Figs impregnated by *Cynips*—East Indian plants—Ants' nests—Butterflies—Amphibious fish—Ship strikes on a coral rock—Critical position—Fothering the ship—Steadiness of the crew—The ship taken into the Endeavour River—Scurvy.

HAVING now entirely circumnavigated New Zealand, and found it, not as generally supposed, part of a continent, but two islands, and having not the least reason to imagine that any country larger than itself lay in its neighbourhood, it was resolved to leave it and proceed upon further discoveries on our return to England, as we were determined to do as much as the state of the ship and provisions would allow. In consequence of this resolution a consultation was held and three schemes proposed. One, much the most eligible, was to return by Cape Horn, keeping all the way in the high latitudes, by which means we might with certainty determine whether or not a southern continent existed. This was unanimously agreed to be more than the condition of the ship would allow. Our provisions indeed might be equal to it; we had six months' at two-thirds allowance, but our sails and rigging, with which, the former especially, we were at first but ill provided, were rendered so bad by the blowing weather that we had met with off New Zealand that we were by no means in a condition to weather the hard gales which must be expected in a winter passage through high latitudes. The second was to steer to the southward of Van Diemen's Land and stand away directly for the Cape of Good Hope, but this was likewise immediately rejected. If we were in too bad a condition for the former, we were in too good a one for this; six months' provision was much more than enough to carry us to any port in the East Indies, and the overplus was not to be thrown away in a sea where so few navigators had been before us. The third, therefore, was unanimously agreed to, which was to stand immediately to the westward, fall in with the coast of New Holland as soon as possible, and after following that to the northward as far as seemed proper, to attempt to fall in with the lands seen by Quiros in 1606. In doing this we hoped to make discoveries more interesting to trade at least than any we had yet made. We were obliged certainly to give up our first grand object, the southern continent; this for my own part I confess I could not do without much regret.

That a southern continent really exists I firmly believe; but if asked why I believe so, I confess my reasons are weak: yet I have a prepossession in favour of the fact which I find it difficult to account for. Ice in large bodies has been seen off Cape Horn now and then. Sharp saw it, as did Frézier on his return from the coast of Chili in the month of March 1714: he also mentions that it has been seen by other French ships in the same place. If this ice (as is generally believed) is formed by fresh water only, there must be land to the southward, for the coast of Terra del Fuego is by no means cold enough to produce such an effect. I should be inclined to think also that it lies away to the westward, as the west and south-west winds so generally prevail, that the ice must be supposed to have followed the direction of these winds, and consequently have come from these points. When we sailed to the southward, in August

and September 1769, we met with signs of land, seaweed
and a seal, which, though both of them are often seen at
great distances from land, yet are not met with in open
oceans, and we were at that time too far from the coast of
New Zealand, and much too far from that of South America,
to have supposed them to have come from either of these.
The body of this land must, however, be situated in very
high latitudes; a part of it may indeed come to the northward, within our track; but as we never saw any signs of
land except at the time mentioned above, although I made
it my particular business (as well as I believe did most of
us) to look out for such, it must be prodigiously smaller in
extent than the theoretical continent-makers have supposed
it to be.   We have by our track proved the absolute falsity
of over three-fourths of their positions; and the remaining
part cannot be much relied upon, but above all we have
taken from them their finest groundwork, in proving New
Zealand to be an island, which I believe was looked upon,
even by the most thoughtful people, to be in all probability
at least a part of some vast country.   All this we have
taken from them: the land seen by Juan Fernandez, the
land seen by the Dutch squadron under L'Hermite, signs of a
continent seen by Quiros, and the same by Roggeween, etc.
etc., have by us been proved not to be at all related to a
continent.   As for their reasoning about the balancing of
the two poles, which always appeared to me to be a most
childish argument, we have already shorn off so much of
their supposed counterbalancing land, that by their own
account the south pole would already be too light, unless
what we have left should be made of very ponderous
materials.   As much fault as I find with these gentlemen
will, however, probably recoil on myself, when I, on so light
grounds as those I have mentioned, again declare it to be
my opinion that a southern continent exists, an opinion in
favour of which I am strongly prepossessed.   But foolish
and weak as all prepossessions must be thought, I would not
but declare myself so, lest I might be supposed to have
stronger reasons which I concealed.

To search for this continent, then, the best and readiest way by which at once its existence or non-existence might be proved, appears to me to be this: let the ship or ships destined for this service leave England in the spring and proceed directly to the Cape of Good Hope, where they might refresh their people and take in fresh provisions, and thence proceed round Van Diemen's Land to the coast of New Zealand, where they might again refresh in any of the numerous harbours at the mouth of Cook's Straits, where they would be sure to meet with plenty of water, wood, and fish. Here they should arrive by the month of October, so as to have the good season before them to run across to the South Sea, which by reason of the prevailing westerly winds they would easily be able to do in any latitude. If in doing this they should not fall in with a continent, they might still be of service in exploring the islands in the Pacific Ocean, where they might refresh themselves and proceed home by the East Indies. Such a voyage, as a voyage of mere curiosity, should be promoted by the Royal Society, to whom I doubt not that his Majesty upon proper application would grant a ship, as the subject of such a voyage seems at least as interesting to science in general and the increase of knowledge as the observation which gave rise to the present one. The small expense of such an equipment to Government is easily shown. I will venture roundly to affirm that the smallest station sloop in his Majesty's service is every year more expensive than such a ship, where every rope, every sail, every rope-yarn even is obliged to do its duty most thoroughly before it can be dismissed. How trifling then must this expense appear, when in return for it the nation acquires experienced seamen in those who execute it, and the praise which is never denied to countries who in this public-spirited manner promote the increase of knowledge.

At the Cape of Good Hope might be procured beef, bread, flour, peas, spirits, or indeed any kind of provision at reasonable rates. The beef must be bought alive and salted, for which purpose it would be proper to take out salt from

Europe : the general price, which indeed never varies, is two-pence a pound.   It is tolerable meat, but not so fat as ours in England.   Pork is scarce and dear, of that therefore a larger proportion might be taken out.   Bread, which varies in price, is of the rusk kind, very good but rather brown. Spirit is arrack from Batavia, the price of which, after having paid the duties of import and export, is 60 rixdollars (£12 sterling) a legger of 150 gallons.   Wine is in great plenty and very cheap, and while I was there [1] they began to distil a kind of brandy, which, however, at that time was as dear as arrack, and much inferior to it both in strength and goodness.

Should a ship upon this expedition be obliged to go into False Bay, into which the Dutch remove on the 12th of May, most of these articles might be got there at a small advance occasioned by the carriage, which is very cheap, and if anything were wanted it might be bought from Cape Town either by Dutch scouts, of which there are several belonging to the company in the harbour, or by waggons over-land, as the road is good and much frequented at that season of the year.

31st March. Our route being settled in the manner above mentioned, we this morning weighed, and sailed with a fair breeze of wind, inclined to fall in with Van Diemen's Land, as near as possible at the place where Tasman left it.

2nd April. Our malt having turned out so indifferent that the surgeon made little use of it, a method was thought of some weeks ago to bring it into use, which was, to make as strong a wort with it as possible, and in this boil the wheat, which is served to the people for breakfast : it made a mess far from unpleasant, which the people soon grew very fond of.   I myself who have for many months con-stantly breakfasted upon the same wheat as the people, either received, or thought I received, great benefit from the use of

---

[1] This paragraph, if not the whole of this discussion, has evidently been introduced (by Banks himself) *after* having visited the Cape.

this mess.   It totally banished that troublesome costiveness which I believe most people are subject to when at sea. Whether or no this is a more beneficial method of administering wort as a preventative than the common, must be left to the faculty, especially that excellent surgeon Mr. M'Bride, whose ingenious treatise on the sea-scurvy can never be sufficiently commended.   For my own part I should be inclined to believe that the salubrious qualities of the wort which arise from fermentation might in some degree at least be communicated to the wheat when thoroughly saturated with its particles, which would consequently acquire a virtue similar to that of fresh vegetables, the greatest resisters of sea-scurvy known.

3rd. We got fast on to the westward, but the compass showed that the hearts of our people hanging that way caused a considerable north variation, which was sensibly felt by our navigators, who called it a current, as they do usually everything which makes their reckonings and observations disagree.

5th. The captain told me that he had during this whole voyage observed that between the degrees of 40° and 37° south latitude the weather becomes suddenly milder in a very great degree, not only in the temperature of the air, but in the strength and frequency of gales of wind, which increase very much in going towards 40°, and decrease in the same proportion as you approach 37°.

11th. Went out shooting and killed *Diomedea exulans* and *impavida :* saw *D. profuga; Procellaria melanopus, velox, oceanica, vagabunda,* and *longipes ; Nectris fuliginosa.*   Took up with dipping - net *Mimus volutator, Medusa pelagica, Dagysa cornuta, Phyllodoce velella,* and *Holothuria obtusata,* of which last an albatross that I had shot discharged a large quantity, incredible as it may appear that an animal should feed upon this blubber, whose innumerable stings give a much more acute pain to a hand which touches them than nettles.

12th. I again went out in my small boat and shot much the same birds as yesterday : took up also chiefly the same animals, to which was added *Actinia natans.* I again saw undoubted proofs that the albatrosses eat *Holothuriæ* or *Portuguese men-of-war*,[1] as the seamen call them. I had also an opportunity of observing the manner in which this animal stings. The body consists of a bladder, on the upper side of which is fixed a kind of sail, which he erects or depresses at pleasure : the edges of this he also at pleasure gathers in, so as to make it concave on one side and convex on the other, varying the concavity or convexity to which-ever side he pleases, for the conveniency of catching the wind which moves him slowly upon the surface of the sea in any direction he wishes. Under the bladder hang down two kinds of strings, one smooth, transparent and harm-less, the other full of small round knobs, having much the appearance of small beads strung together : these he contracts or extends sometimes to the length of four feet. Both these and the others are in this species of a lovely ultramarine blue, but in the more common one, which is many times larger than this, being nearly as large as a goose's egg, they are of a fine red. With these latter, however, he does his mischief, stinging, or burning, as it is called. If touched by any substance they immediately throw out millions of exceedingly fine white threads, about a line in length, which pierce the skin and adhere to it, giving very acute pain. When the animal thrusts them out of the little knobs or beads which are not in contact with some substance they can pierce, they appear very visibly to the naked eye like small fibres of snow-white cotton.

13th. Shooting as usual, but saw no new bird except a gannet, which came not near me. Of these for four or five days past I have killed a good many ; indeed, during the whole time they have been tame and appeared unknowing and unsuspicious of men, the generality of them flying to the boat as soon as they saw it, which is generally the case at great distances from land. Took up *Dagysa vitrea* and *gemma, Medusa radiata* and *porpita, Helix ianthina,* very large *Doris complanata,* and *Beroe biloba :* saw a large shoal

---

[1] See footnote, p. 15.

of *Esox scomboides* leaping out of the water in a very extra-ordinary manner, pursued by a large fish, which I saw but could not strike, though I did two of the former. In the evening saw several fish much resembling bonitos.

The weather we have had for these nine days past, and the things we have seen upon the sea, are so extraordinary that I cannot help recapitulating a little. The weather, in the first place, which till the fifth was cool, or rather cold, became at once troublesomely hot, bringing with it a mouldy dampness such as we experienced between the tropics : the thermometer, although it showed a considerable difference in the degree of heat, was not nearly so sensible of it as our bodies, which I believe is generally the case when a damp air accompanies warmth. During the continuance of this weather the inhabitants of the tropical seas appeared : the tropic bird, flying fish, and *Medusa porpita* are animals very rarely seen out of the influence of trade winds. Several others also I have never before seen in so high a latitude, and never before in such perfection as now, except between the tropics. All these uncommon appearances I myself can find no other method of accounting for than the uncommon length of time that the wind had remained in the eastern quarter before this, which possibly had all that time blown home from the trade wind ; and at the same time, as it kept the sea in a quiet and still state, had brought with it the produce of the climate from which it came.

19*th*. With the first daylight this morning the land[1] was seen ; it made in sloping hills covered in part with trees or bushes, but interspersed with large tracts of sand. At noon we were sailing along shore, five or six leagues from it, with a brisk breeze of wind and cloudy unsettled weather, when we were called upon deck to see three water-spouts which made their appearance at the same time in different places, but all between us and the land. Two,

---

[1] To the southward of Cape Howe. The most southerly land seen was by Captain Cook called Point Hicks. It is not a point, but a hill, still called Point Hicks Hill (Wharton's *Cook*, p. 237, note).

which were very distant, soon disappeared; but the third, which was about a league from us, lasted fully a quarter of an hour. It was a column which appeared of the thickness of a mast or a middling tree, and reached down from a smoke-coloured cloud about two-thirds of the way to the surface of the sea. Under it the sea appeared to be much troubled for a considerable space, and from the whole of that space arose a dark-coloured thick mist reaching to the bottom of the pipe, where it was at its greatest distance from the water. The pipe itself was perfectly transparent, and much resembled a tube of glass or a column of water, if such a thing could be supposed to be suspended in the air: it very frequently contracted and dilated, lengthened and shortened itself, and that by very quick motions. It very seldom remained in a perpendicular direction, but generally inclined either one way or the other in a curve, as a light body acted upon by the wind is observed to do. During the whole time that it lasted, smaller ones seemed to attempt to form in its neighbourhood; at last one almost as thick as a rope formed close by it, and became longer than the old one, which at that time was in its shortest state; upon this they joined together in an instant, and gradually contracting into the cloud, disappeared.

22*nd.* We stood in with the land, near enough to discern five people, who appeared through our glasses to be enormously black: so far did the prejudices which we had built on Dampier's account influence us, that we fancied we could see their colour when we could scarce distinguish whether or not they were men.

Since we have been on the coast, we have not observed those large fires which we so frequently saw in the islands and New Zealand, made by the natives in order to clear the ground for cultivation: we thence concluded not much in favour of our future friends. It has long been an observation among us, that the air in this southern hemisphere was much clearer than in our northern: these last few days at least it has appeared remarkably so.

23*rd.* Took with the dipping-net *Cancer erythrophthalmus,*

Medusa radiata, pelagica ; Dagysa gemma, strumosa, cornuta ; Holothuria obtusata ; Phyllodoce velella and *Mimus volutator.* The master to-day, in conversation, made a remark on the variation of the needle, which struck me much. As to me it was new, and appeared to throw much light on the theory of that phenomenon. The variation is here very small : he says that he has three times crossed the line of no variation, and that at all those times, as well as at this, he has observed the needle to be very unsteady, moving very easily and scarcely at all fixing. This he showed me ; he also told me that in several places he had been in, the land had a very remarkable effect upon the variation, as in the place we were in now : at one or two leagues distant from the shore, the variation was two degrees less than at eight leagues distance.

27th. Some bodies, three feet long and half as broad, floated very buoyantly past the ship : they were supposed to be cuttle bones, which indeed they a good deal resembled, but for their enormous size.

28th. An opening appearing like a harbour was seen, and we stood directly in for it : a small smoke arising from a very barren place directed our glasses that way, and we soon saw ten people who, on our approach, left the fire, and retired to a little eminence, whence they could conveniently see the ship. Soon after this two canoes carrying two men each landed on the beach under them : the men hauled up their boats, and went to their fellows upon the hill. Our boat, which had been sent ahead to sound, now approached the place, and they all retired higher up the hill. We saw, however, that at the beach or landing-place one man at least was hidden among some rocks, and never, so far as we could see, left that place. Our boat proceeded along shore, and the Indians followed her at a distance ; when she came back the officer who was in her told me that in a cove, a little within the harbour, they came down to the beach and invited our people to land by many signs and words which he did not at all understand. All, however, were armed with long pikes and a wooden weapon made like a short scimitar.[1]

[1] A boomerang.

During this time, a few of the Indians who had not followed
the boat remained on the rocks opposite the ship, threatening and menacing with their pikes and swords: two in
particular, who were painted with white, their faces seemingly only dusted over with it, their bodies painted with
broad strokes drawn over their breasts and backs, resembling
much a soldier's cross-belt, and their legs and thighs also
with broad strokes drawn round them, like broad garters or
bracelets.   Each of these held in his hand a wooden weapon
about $2\frac{1}{2}$ feet long, in shape much resembling a scimitar;
the blades of these looked whitish, and some thought shining,
insomuch that they were almost of opinion that they were
made of some kind of metal; but I thought they were
only wood smeared over with the white pigment with
which they paint their bodies.   These two seemed to talk
earnestly together, at times brandishing their crooked
weapons at us, as in token of defiance.   By noon we were
within the mouth of the inlet,[1] which appeared to be very
good.   Under the south head of it were four small canoes,
each containing one man, who held in his hand a long
pole, with which he struck fish, venturing with his little
embarkation almost into the surf.   These people seemed to
be totally engaged in what they were about: the ship passed
within a quarter of a mile of them, and yet they scarcely
lifted their eyes from their employment.   I was almost
inclined to think that, attentive to their business and
deafened by the noise of the surf, they neither saw nor
heard her go past.

    We came to an anchor abreast of a small village con-
sisting of six or eight houses.   Soon after this an old woman,
followed by three children, came out of the wood: she
carried several pieces of stick, and the children also had
their little burthens.   When she came to the houses, three
younger children came out of one of them to meet her.   She
often looked at the ship, but expressed neither surprise nor
concern: she then lighted a fire, and the four canoes came

---

[1] Botany Bay.   It was Banks who, on his return to England, recommended
the Government to form a penal settlement at this spot.

in from fishing, the people landed, hauled up their boats and began to dress their dinner, to all appearance totally unmoved by us, though we were within little more than half a mile of them. On all these people whom we had seen so distinctly through our glasses, we had been unable to observe the least signs of clothing; myself, to the best of my judgment, plainly discerned that the women did not copy our mother Eve even in the fig-leaf.

After dinner the boats were manned, and we set out from the ship, intending to land at the place where we saw these people, hoping that as they regarded the ship's coming into the bay so little, they would as little regard our landing. We were in this, however, mistaken; for as soon as we approached the rocks two of the men came down, each armed with a lance about 10 feet long, and a short stick, which he seemed to handle as though it was a machine to throw the lance. They called to us very loudly in a harsh sounding language, of which neither we nor Tupia understood a word, shaking their lances and menacing; in all appearance resolved to dispute our landing to the utmost, though they were but two, and we thirty or forty at least. In this manner we parleyed with them for about a quarter of an hour, they waving to us to be gone; we again signing that we wanted water, and that we meant them no harm. They remained resolute: so a musket was fired over them, the effect of which was that the younger of the two dropped a bundle of lances on the rock the instant he heard the report. He, however, snatched them up again, and both renewed their threats and opposition. A musket loaded with small shot was now fired at the elder of the two, who was about forty yards from the boat; it struck him on the legs, but he minded it very little, so another was immediately fired at him. On this he ran up to the house, about a hundred yards distant, and soon returned with a shield. In the meantime we had landed on the rock. The man immediately threw a lance at us and the young man another, which fell among the thickest of us, but hurt nobody; two more muskets with small shot were then fired at them, whereupon the elder threw one more lance and ran away, as did the other. We went up to the houses, in one of which we found the children hidden behind the shield, and a piece of bark.

We were conscious, from the distance the people had been from us when we fired, that the shot could have done them no material harm; we therefore resolved to leave the children upon the spot without even opening their shelter; we therefore threw into the house to them some beads, ribbons, cloth, etc., as presents, and went away. We, however, thought it no improper measure to take away with us all the lances which we could find about the houses, amounting in number to forty or fifty. They varied in length from 6 to 15 feet. Both those which were thrown at us, and all we found, except one, had four prongs headed with very sharp fish bones, which were besmeared with a greenish-coloured gum, that at first gave me some suspicion of poison.

The people were blacker than any we have seen on the voyage, though by no means negroes; their beards were thick and bushy, and they seemed to have a redundancy of hair upon those parts of the body where it commonly grows. The hair of their heads was bushy and thick, but by no means woolly like that of a negro. They were of a common size, lean, and seemed active and nimble; their voices were coarse and strong. Upon examining the lances we had taken from them, we found that most of them had been used in striking fish; at least we concluded so from the seaweed which was found stuck in among the four prongs.

At night many moving lights were seen at different parts of the bay; such we had been used to see at the Islands, from hence we supposed that the people here strike fish in the same manner.

29th. The fishing fires, as we supposed them to be, were seen during the greater part of the night. In the morning we went ashore at the houses, but found not the least good effect from our presents yesterday. No signs of people were to be seen; and in the house where the children were yesterday, was left everything which we had thrown to them.

1st May. The captain, Dr. Solander, and myself, and some of the people, making in all ten muskets, resolved to make an excursion into the country. We accordingly did so, and walked till we completely tired ourselves, which was in the evening; seeing by the way only one Indian, who ran from us as soon as he saw us. The soil, wherever we saw it, consisted of either swamps or light sandy soil, on which grew very few species of trees, one,[1] which was large, yielding a gum much like *Sanguis draconis;* but every place was covered with vast quantities of grass. We saw many Indian houses, and places where they had slept upon the grass without the least shelter. In these we left beads, ribbons, etc. We saw one quadruped about the size of a rabbit. My greyhound just got sight of him, and instantly lamed himself against a stump which lay concealed in the long grass. We saw also the dung of a large animal that had fed on grass, much resembling that of a stag; also the footprints of an animal clawed like a dog or wolf, and as large as the latter, and of a small animal whose feet were like those of a polecat or weasel. The trees overhead abounded very much with loryquets and cockatoos, of which we shot several.

2nd. The morning was rainy, and we had already so many plants that we were well contented to find an excuse for staying on board to examine them a little. In the afternoon, however, it cleared up, and we returned to our old occupation of collecting, in which we had our usual good success. Tupia, who strayed from us in pursuit of parrots, of which he shot several, told us on his return that he had seen nine Indians, who ran from him as soon as they perceived him.

3rd. Our collection of plants was now grown so immensely large that it was necessary that some extraordinary care should be taken of them, lest they should spoil in the books. I therefore devoted this day to that business, and carried ashore all the drying paper, nearly 200 quires, of which the larger part was full, and spreading them upon a

---

[1] A species of *Eucalyptus*, or gum tree.

sail in the sun, kept them in this manner exposed the whole day, often turning them, and sometimes turning the quires in which were plants inside out. By this means they came on board at night in very good condition. During this time eleven canoes, in each of which was one Indian, came towards us: we soon saw that the people in them were employed in striking fish. They came within about half a mile of us, intent upon their own employments, and not at all regarding us. Opposite the place where they were several of our people were shooting: one Indian, prompted maybe by curiosity, landed, hauled up his canoe, and went towards them. He stayed about a quarter of an hour, and then launched his boat and went off. Probably that time had been spent behind the trees in watching to see what our people did. I could not find, however, that he was seen by anybody.

When the damp of the evening made it necessary to send my plants and books on board, I made a short excursion to shoot anything I could meet with, and found a large quantity of quails, much resembling our English ones, of which I might have killed as many almost as I pleased, had I given my time up to it; but my business was to kill variety, and not too many individuals of any one species. The captain and Dr. Solander employed the day in going in the pinnace into various parts of the harbour. They saw fires at several places, and people who all ran away at their approach with the greatest precipitation, leaving behind the shell-fish which they were cooking. Of this our gentlemen took advantage, eating what they found and leaving beads, ribands, etc., in return. They found also several trees which bore a fruit of the *Jambosa* kind, in colour and shape much resembling cherries. Of these they ate plentifully, and brought home also abundance, which we ate with pleasure, though they had little to recommend them but a slight acid.

4th. Myself in the woods, botanising as usual: now quite devoid of fear, as our neighbours have turned out such rank cowards. One of our midshipmen, straying by himself a long way from any one else, met by accident with a very old man and woman and some children. They were sitting under a tree, and neither party saw the other till they were close together. They showed signs of fear, but did not attempt to run away. The midshipman had nothing about him to give them but some parrots which he had shot. These they refused, drawing away when he offered them, in token either of extreme fear or disgust. The people were very old and gray-headed, the children young. The hair of the man was bushy about his head, and his beard long and rough : the woman's hair was cropped short round her head. They were very dark-coloured, but not black, nor was their hair woolly.

On our return to the ship we found also that our second lieutenant, who had gone out striking, had met with great success. He had observed that the large sting-rays, of which there are abundance in the bay, followed the flowing tide into very shallow water ; he therefore took the opportunity, and struck several in not more than two or three feet of water. One that was larger than the rest weighed, when his guts were taken out, 239 lbs.

Our surgeon, who strayed a long way from the others, with one man in his company, in coming out of a thicket observed six Indians standing about sixty yards from him. One of these gave a signal by a word, whereupon a lance was thrown out of the wood at him, which, however, did not come very near him. The six Indians, on seeing that it had not taken effect, ran away in an instant, but on turning about towards the place from whence the lance came, he saw a young lad, who had undoubtedly thrown it, come down from a tree where he had been stationed, probably for that purpose. He descended, however, and ran away so quickly that it was impossible even to attempt to pursue him.

6th. Went to sea this morning with a fair breeze of wind. The land we sailed past during the whole forenoon appeared broken and likely for harbours. We dined to-day upon a sting-ray weighing 336 lbs., which was caught yesterday, and his tripe. The fish itself was not quite so good as a skate, nor was it much inferior. The tripe everybody thought excellent. We had it with a dish of the boiled leaves of *Tetragonia cornuta*, which eat as well, or very nearly as well, as spinach.

17*th*. About ten we were abreast of a large bay,[1] the bottom of which was out of sight. The sea here suddenly changed from its usual transparency to a dirty clay colour, appearing much as if charged with freshes, from whence I was led to conclude that the bottom of the bay might open into a large river. About it were many smokes, especially on the northern side near some remarkable conical hills.[2] At sunset the land made in one bank, over which nothing could be seen. It was very sandy, and carried with it no signs of fertility.

18*th*. Land this morning very sandy. We could see through our glasses that the sands, which lay in great patches of many acres each, were movable. Some of them had been lately moved, for trees which stood up in the middle of them were quite green. Others of a longer standing had many stumps sticking out of them, which had been trees killed by the sand heaping about their roots. Few fires were seen. Two water snakes swam by the ship. They were beautifully spotted, and in all respects like land snakes, except that they had broad flat tails, which probably serve them instead of fins in swimming.

22*nd*. In the course of the night the tide rose very considerably. We plainly saw with our glasses that the land was covered with palm-nut trees, *Pandanus tectorius*, which we had not seen since we left the islands within the tropics. Along shore we saw two men walking, who took no kind of notice of us.

23*rd*. Wind blew fresh off the land, so cold that our cloaks were very necessary in going ashore. When we landed, however, the sun soon recovered its influence, and made it sufficiently hot; in the afternoon intolerably so. We landed near the mouth of a large lagoon,[3] which ran a good way

---

[1] Moreton Bay.   [2] The Glass Houses.   [3] Bustard Bay.

into the country, and sent out a strong tide. Here we found a great variety of plants, several, however, the same as those we ourselves had before seen in the islands between the tropics, and others known to be natives of the East Indies, a sure mark that we were upon the point of leaving the southern temperate zone, and that for the future we must expect to meet with plants some of which, at least, had been before seen by Europeans. The soil in general was very sandy and dry; though it produced a large variety of plants, yet it was never covered with a thick verdure. Fresh water we saw none, but several swamps and bogs of salt water. In these, and upon the sides of the lagoons, grew many mangrove trees, in the branches of which were many nests of ants, of which one sort were quite green. These, when the branches were disturbed, came out in large numbers, and revenged themselves very sufficiently upon their disturbers, biting more sharply than any I have felt in Europe. The mangroves had also another trap which most of us fell into. This was a small kind of caterpillar, green and beset with many hairs, numbers of which sat together upon the leaves, ranged by the side of each other, like soldiers drawn up; twenty or thirty, perhaps, on one leaf. If these wrathful militia were touched ever so gently, they did not fail to make the person offending sensible of their anger, every hair in them stinging much as nettles do, but with a more acute, though less lasting, smart.

Upon the sides of the hills were many of the trees yielding a gum like *Sanguis draconis.*[1] They differed, however, from those seen on the 1st of May, in having their leaves longer, and hanging down like those of the weeping willow. Notwithstanding that, I believe that they were of the same species. There was, however, much less gum upon them. Only one tree that I saw had any, contrary to all theory which teaches that the hotter a climate is the more gums exude. The same observation, however, held good in the plant yielding the yellow gum,[2] of which, though we saw vast numbers, we did not see any that showed signs of gum

---

[1] *Eucalypti.*   [2] *Xanthorrhœa:* it has not been mentioned before.

On the shoals and sandbanks near the shore of the bay were many large birds, far larger than swans, which we judged to be pelicans; but they were so shy that we could not get within gun-shot of them. On the shore were many birds; one species of bustard, of which we shot a single bird, was as large as a good turkey. The sea seemed to abound in fish, but unfortunately, at the first haul, we tore our seine to pieces. On the mud-banks, under the mangrove trees, were innumerable oysters, hammer-oysters, and many more sorts, among which were a large proportion of small pearl-oysters. Whether the sea in deeper water might abound with as great a proportion of full-grown ones, we had not an opportunity to examine; but if it did, a pearl fishery here must turn out to immense advantage.

24th. At daybreak we went to sea. At dinner we ate the bustard we shot yesterday. It turned out an excellent bird, far the best, we all agreed, that we had eaten since we left England; and as it weighed fifteen pounds, our dinner was not only good but plentiful.

26th. We tried in the cabin to fish with hook and line, but the water was too shoal (three fathoms) for any fish. This want was, however, in some degree supplied by crabs, of which vast numbers were on the ground, who readily took our baits, and sometimes held them so fast with their claws, that they suffered themselves to be hauled into the ship. They were of two sorts, *Cancer pelagicus*, Linn., and another much like the former, but not so beautiful. The first was ornamented with the finest ultramarine blue conceivable, with which all his claws, and every joint, were deeply tinged. The under part was of a lovely white, shining as if glazed, and perfectly resembling the white of old china. The other had a little of the ultramarine on his joints and toes, and on his back three very remarkable brown spots.

In examining a fig which we had found at our last going ashore, we found in the fruit a *Cynips*, very like, if not exactly the same species as *Cynips sycomori*, Linn., described by Hasselquist in his *Iter Palestinum*, a strong proof of the fact that figs must be impregnated by means of insects, though indeed that fact wanted not any additional proofs.

29th. We went ashore and found several plants which we had not before seen; among them, however, were still more East Indian plants than in the last harbour; one kind of grass which we had also seen there was very troublesome to us. Its sharp seeds were bearded backwards, and whenever they stuck into our clothes were by these beards pushed forward till they got into the flesh. This grass was so plentiful that it was hardly possible to avoid it, and, with the mosquitos that were likewise innumerable, made walking almost intolerable. We were not, however, to be repulsed, but proceeded into the country. The gum-trees were like those in the last bay, both in leaf and in producing a very small proportion of gum; on the branches of them and other trees were large ants' nests, made of clay, as big as a bushel, something like those described in Sir Hans Sloane's *History of Jamaica*, vol. ii. pp. 221 to 258, but not so smooth. The ants also were small, and had white abdomens. In another species of tree, *Xanthoxyloides mite*, a small sort of black ant had bored all the twigs, and lived in quantities in the hollow part where the pith should be; the tree nevertheless flourishing and bearing leaves and flowers upon those very branches as freely and well as upon others that were sound. Insects in general were plentiful, butterflies especially. With one sort of these, much like *P. Semele*, Linn., the air was for the space of three or four acres crowded to a wonderful degree; the eye could not be turned in any direction without seeing millions, and yet every branch and twig was almost covered with those that sat still. Of these we took as many as we chose, knocking them down with our caps, or anything that came to hand. On the leaves of the gum-tree we found a pupa or chrysalis, which shone as brightly as if it had been silvered over with the most burnished silver, which it perfectly resembled. It was brought on board, and the next day came out into a butterfly of a velvet black changeable to blue; the wings, both upper and under, were marked near the edges with

T

many brimstone-coloured spots, those of his under wings being indented deeply at each end.

We saw no fresh water, but several swamps of salt overgrown with mangroves; in these we found some species of shells, among them *Trochus perspectivus*, Linn. Here also was a very singular phenomenon in a small fish of which there were great abundance. It was about the size of an English minnow, and had two very strong breast fins; we often found it in quite dry places, where maybe it had been left by the tide. Upon seeing us it immediately fled from us, leaping as nimbly as a frog by means of the breast fins; nor did it seem to prefer water to land, for if seen in the water he often leaped out and proceeded on dry land, and when the water was filled with small stones standing above its surface, would leap from stone to stone rather than go into the water. In this manner I observed several pass over puddles of water and proceed on the other side leaping as before.

In the afternoon we went to the other side of the bay; if anything, the soil was rather better. In neither morning nor evening were there any traces of inhabitants ever having been where we were, except that here and there trees had been burnt down.

8th June. We passed within a quarter of a mile of a small islet or rock, on which we saw with our glasses about thirty men, women, and children standing all together, and looking attentively at us; the first people we have seen show any signs of curiosity at the sight of the ship.

10th. Just without us as we lay at anchor was a small sandy island lying upon a large coral shoal much resembling the low islands to the eastward of us, but the first of the kind we had met with in this part of the South Sea. Early in the morning we weighed and sailed as usual with a fine breeze along shore. While we were at supper she went over a bank of seven or eight fathoms of water, which she came upon very suddenly; this we concluded to be the tail of the shoals we had seen at sunset, and therefore went to bed in perfect security; but scarcely were we warm in our beds

when we were called up with the alarming news of the
ship being fast upon a rock, of which she in a few moments
convinced us by beating very violently against it.   Our
situation became now greatly alarming; we had stood off
shore three hours and a half with a pleasant breeze, so knew
we could not be very near it.   We were little less than
certain that we were upon sunken coral rocks, the most
dreadful of all, on account of their sharp points and
grinding quality, which cut through a ship's bottom almost
immediately.   The officers, however, behaved with inimitable
coolness, free from all hurry and confusion.   A boat was got
out in which the master went, and after sounding round the
ship found that she had run over a rock, and consequently
had shoal water all round her.   All this time she continued
to beat very much, so that we could hardly keep our legs
upon the quarter-deck.   By the light of the moon we could
see her sheathing-boards, etc., floating thickly around her,
and about twelve her false keel came away.

11th. In the meanwhile all kind of preparations were
making for carrying out anchors, but by reason of the time it
took to hoist out boats, etc., the tide ebbed so much that we
found it impossible to attempt to get her off till next high water,
if she would hold together so long.   We now found to add
to our misfortune that we had got ashore nearly at the top
of high water; and as night tides generally rise higher than
the day ones we had little hopes of getting off even then.
For our comfort, however, the ship as the tide ebbed settled
to the rocks, and did not beat nearly so much as she had
done.   A rock, however, under her starboard bow kept
grating her bottom, making a noise very plainly to be heard
in the fore store-rooms; this we doubted not would make
a hole; we only hoped that it might not let in more water
than we could clear with our pumps.

In this situation day broke upon us and showed us the
land about eight leagues off, as we judged; nearer than that
was no island or place where we could set foot.   Day, however, brought with it a decrease of wind, and soon after that
a flat calm, the most fortunate circumstance that could

possibly attend people in our circumstances.   The tide we
found had fallen two feet and still continued to fall ; anchors
were, however, got out and laid ready for heaving as soon
as the tide should rise, but to our great surprise we could
not observe it to rise in the least.

Orders were now given for lightening the ship, which
was begun by starting our water and pumping it up; the
ballast was then got up and thrown overboard as well as
six of our guns (all that we had upon deck).   The seamen
worked with surprising cheerfulness and alacrity : no
grumbling or growling was to be heard throughout the
ship, not even an oath (though the ship was in general as
well furnished with them as most in His Majesty's service).
By about one o'clock the water had fallen so low that the
pinnace touched ground as it lay under the ship's bows ready
to take in an anchor.   After this the tide began to rise, and
as it rose the ship worked violently upon the rocks, so that
by two she began to make water, which increased very fast.
At night the tide almost floated her, but she made water so
fast that three pumps hard worked could only just keep her
clear, and the fourth absolutely refused to deliver a drop of
water.   Now, in my opinion, I entirely gave up the ship,
and packing up what I thought I might save prepared
myself for the worst.

The most critical part of our distress now approached ;
the ship was almost afloat and everything ready to get her
into deep water, but she leaked so fast that with all our
pumps we could only just keep her free.   If (as was probable)
she should make more water when hauled off she must sink,
and we well knew that our boats were not capable of carrying us all ashore, so that some, probably most of us, must be
drowned.   A better fate, maybe, than those would have who
should get ashore without arms to defend themselves from
the Indians or provide themselves with food, in a country
where we had not the least reason to hope for subsistence,
so barren had we always found it, and, had they even met
with good usage from the natives and food to support them,
debarred from the hope of ever again seeing their native

country or conversing with any but savages, perhaps the most uncivilised in the world.

The dreadful time now approached, and the anxiety in everybody's countenance was visible enough. The capstan and windlass were manned, and they began to heave; the fear of death now stared us in the face; hopes we had none but of being able to keep the ship afloat till we could run her ashore on some part of the main where out of her materials we might build a vessel large enough to carry us to the East Indies. At ten o'clock she floated, and was in a few minutes hauled into deep water, where to our great satisfaction she made no more water than she had done, which was indeed full as much as we could manage, though there was no one in the ship but who willingly exerted his utmost strength.

The people who had been twenty-four hours at exceedingly hard work now began to flag; I myself, unused to labour, was much fatigued, and had lain down to take a little rest when I was awakened about twelve with the alarming news of the water having gained so much upon the pumps that the ship had four feet of water in her hold. Add to this that a regular land breeze blew off the coast, so that all hopes of running her ashore were totally cut off. This, however, acted upon every one like a charm : rest was no more thought of, but the pumps went with unwearied vigour till the water was all out, which was done in a much shorter time than was expected; and upon examination it was found that she never had half so much water in her as was thought, the carpenter having made a mistake in sounding the pumps.

We now began to have some hopes, and talked of getting the ship into some harbour when we could spare hands from the pumps to get up our anchors; one bower, however, we cut away, but got up the other and three small anchors, far more valuable to us than the bowers, as we were obliged immediately to warp her to windward that we might take advantage of the sea breeze to run in-shore.

One of our midshipmen now proposed an expedient which

no one else in the ship had seen practised, though all had heard of it by the name of fothering a ship, by means of which he said he had come home from America in a ship which made more water than we did. Nay, so sure was the master of that ship of his expedient that he took her out of harbour knowing how much water she had made, and trusting entirely to it. The midshipman immediately set to work with four or five assistants to prepare his fother, which he did thus. He took a lower studding sail, and having mixed together a large quantity of finely chopped oakum and wool, he stitched it down upon the sail as loosely as possible in small bundles about as big as his fist; these were ranged in rows four or five inches from each other. This was to be sunk under the ship. The theory of it was that wherever the leak was there must be a great suction which would probably catch hold of one or other of these lumps of oakum and wool and, drawing it in, either partly or entirely stop up the hole. While this work was going on the water rather gained on those who were pumping, which made all hands impatient for the trial. In the afternoon the ship was got under way with a gentle breeze of wind, and stood in for the land. Soon after the fother was finished, and applied by fastening ropes to each corner, then sinking the sail under the ship, and with these ropes drawing it as far backwards as we could. In about a quarter of an hour, to our great surprise, the ship was pumped dry, and upon letting the pumps stand she was found to make very little water, so much beyond our most sanguine expectations had this singular expedient succeeded. At night we came to an anchor, the fother still keeping her almost clear, so that we were in an instant raised from almost despondency to the greatest hopes. We were now almost too sanguine, talking of nothing but of getting her into some harbour where we might lay her ashore and repair her, or if we could not find such a place we little doubted of being able by repeated fotherings to carry her quite to the East Indies.

During the whole time of this distress, I must say for the credit of our people that I believe every man exerted his utmost for the preservation of the ship, contrary to what I have universally heard to be the behaviour of seamen, who commonly, as soon as a ship is in a desperate situation, begin to plunder and refuse all command. This was no doubt owing to the cool and steady conduct of the officers, who, during the whole time, never gave an order which did not show them to be perfectly composed and unmoved by the circumstances, however dreadful they might appear.

14*th*. The captain and I went ashore to view a harbour, and found it indeed beyond our most sanguine wishes. It was the mouth of a river,[1] the entrance of which was, to be sure, narrow enough and shallow, but when once in, the ship might be moved afloat so near the shore, that by a stage from her to it all her cargo might be got out and in again in a very short time. In this same place she might be hove down with all ease, but the beach showed signs of the tides rising in the springs six or seven feet, which was more than enough to do our business without that trouble.

16*th*. Tupia had for the last few days bad gums, which were very soon followed by livid spots on his legs and every symptom of inveterate scurvy. Notwithstanding acid, bark, and every medicine our surgeon could give him, he became now extremely ill. Mr. Green, the astronomer, was also in a very poor way, which made everybody in the cabin very desirous of getting ashore, and impatient at our tedious delays.

17*th*. Weather a little less rough than it had been the last few days; weighed and brought the ship in, but in doing so ran her ashore twice by the narrowness of the channel; the second time she remained till the tide lifted her off. In the meantime Dr. Solander and I began our plant-gathering. In the evening the ship was moored within twenty feet of the shore, afloat, and before night much lumber was got out of her.

18*th*. A stage built from the ship much facilitated our undertakings. In walking about the country I saw the old frames of Indian houses, and places where they had dressed

---

[1] Endeavour River.

shell-fish in the same manner as the islanders, but no signs
that they had been at the place for six months at least.
The country in general was sandy between the hills, and
barren, which made walking very easy. Mosquitos there
were but few, a piece of good fortune in a place where we
were likely to remain some time. Tupia, who had employed
himself since we were here in angling, and had lived entirely
on what he caught, was surprisingly recovered; poor Mr.
Green still very ill. Weather blowing hard with showers;
had we not got in yesterday we certainly could not have
done so to-day.

CHAPTER XII

AUSTRALIA (ENDEAVOUR RIVER) TO TORRES STRAITS

JUNE 20—AUGUST 26, 1770

Pumice-stone—Ship laid ashore—Kangooroos seen—White ants—Preserving plants—*Chama gigas*—Fruits thrown up on the beach—Excursion up the country—Making friends with the Indians—A kangooroo killed—Turtle—Indians attempt to steal turtle and fire the grass—*Didelphis*—Among the shoals and islands—Lizard Island—Signs of natives crossing from the mainland—Ship passes through Cook's passage—Outside the grand reef—Ship almost driven on to the reef by the tides—Passes inside the reef again—Corals—Straits between Australia and New Guinea.

June 20th. Observed that in many parts of the inlet, a good way above the high-water mark, were large quantities of pumice-stones probably carried there by freshes or extra-ordinarily high tides, as they certainly came from the sea. Before night the ship was lightened, and we observed with great pleasure that the springs, which were now beginning to lift, rose as high as we could wish.

21st. Fine clear weather; began to-day to lay plants in sand.[1] By night the ship was quite clear, and in the night's tide (which we had constantly observed to be much higher than the day's) we hauled her ashore.

22nd. In the morning I saw her leak, which was very large: in the middle was a hole large enough to have sunk a ship with twice our pumps, but here Providence had most visibly worked in our favour, for it was in a great measure plugged up by a stone as big as a man's fist. Round the edges of this stone had all the water come in, which had so

[1] A mode of preserving for herbarium purposes.

nearly overcome us, and here we found the wool and oakum, or fothering, which had relieved us in so unexpected a manner.

The effect of this coral rock upon her bottom is difficult to describe, but more to believe; it had cut through her plank and deep into one of her timbers, smoothing the gashes still before it, so that the whole might easily be imagined to have been cut with an axe.[1]

Myself employed all day in laying in plants; the people who were sent to the other side of the water to shoot pigeons, saw an animal as large as a greyhound, of a mouse colour, and very swift;[2] they also saw many Indian houses, and a brook of fresh water.

24th. Gathering plants, and hearing descriptions of the animal, which is now seen by everybody. A seaman who had been out in the woods brought home the description of an animal he had seen, composed in so seamanlike a style that I cannot help mentioning it; "it was (says he) about as large and much like a one-gallon cagg, as black as the devil, and had two horns on its head; it went but slowly, but I dared not touch it."

25th. In gathering plants to-day I had the good fortune to see the beast so much talked of, though but imperfectly; he was not only like a greyhound in size and running, but had a tail as long as any greyhound's; what to liken him to I could not tell, nothing that I have seen at all resembles him.

26th. Since the ship has been hauled ashore, the water has, of course, all gone backwards; and my plants, which for safety had been stowed in the bread room, were this day found under water. Nobody had warned me of this danger, which never once entered my head. The mischief, however, was now done, so I set to work to remedy it to the best of my power. The day was scarcely long enough to get them

---

[1] "The manner these planks were damaged—or cut out, as I may say—is hardly credible ; scarce a Splinter was to be seen, but the whole was cut away as if it had been done by the Hands of Man with a blunt-edge Tool."—Wharton's *Cook*, p. 280.   [2] A kangaroo.

all shifted, etc.; many were saved, but some were entirely spoiled.

28th. We have ever since we have been here observed the nests of a kind of ant, much like the white ant in the East Indies, but to us perfectly harmless: they were always pyramidal, from a few inches to six feet in height, and very much resembled the Druidical monuments which I have seen in England. To-day we met with a large number of them of all sizes ranged in a small open place, which had a very pretty effect. Dr. Solander compared them to the runic stones on the plains of Upsala in Sweden; myself to all the smaller Druidical monuments I had seen.

1st July. Our second lieutenant found the husk of a cocoanut full of barnacles cast up on the beach;[1] it had probably come from some island to windward.

2nd. The wild plantain trees, though their fruit does not serve for food, are to us of a most material benefit. We made baskets of their stalks (a thing we had learned from the islanders), in which our plants, which would not otherwise keep, have remained fresh for two or three days; indeed, in a hot climate it is hardly practicable to manage without such baskets, which we call by the island name of *papa mija.* Our plants dry better in paper books than in sand, with the precaution that one person is entirely employed in attending them. He shifts them all once a day, exposes the quires in which they are to the greatest heat of the sun, and at night covers them most carefully up from any damp, always being careful, also, not to bring them out too soon in the morning, or leave them out too late in the evening.

3rd. The pinnace, which had been sent out yesterday in search of a passage, returned to-day, having found a way by which she passed most of the shoals that we could see, but not all. This passage was also to windward of us, so that we could only hope to get there by the assistance of a land breeze, of which we have had but one since we lay in the

---

[1] The absence of the cocoanut palm on the Australian coasts is one of the most singular facts in botanical geography.

place; so this discovery added but little comfort to our situation. The crew of the pinnace had, on their return, landed on a dry reef, where they found great plenty of shell-fish, so that the boat was completely loaded, chiefly with a large kind of cockle (*Chama gigas*), one of which was more than two men could eat; many, indeed, were larger. The coxswain of the boat, a little man, declared that he saw on the reef a dead shell of one so large that he got into it, and it fairly held him. At night the ship floated and was hauled off. An alligator was seen swimming alongside of her for some time. As I was crossing the harbour in my small boat, we saw many shoals of garfish leaping high out of the water, some of which leaped into the boat and were taken.

5th. Went to the other side of the harbour, and walked along a sandy beach open to the trade-wind. Here I found innumerable fruits, many of plants I had not seen in this country. Among them were some cocoanuts that had been opened (as Tupia told us) by a kind of crab called by the Dutch Boers *krabba* (*Cancer latro*) that feeds upon them. All these fruits were incrusted with sea productions, and many of them covered with barnacles, a sure sign that they have come far by sea, and as the trade-wind blows almost right on shore must have come from some other country, probably that discovered by Quiros, and called Terra del Espiritu Santo [New Hebrides], as the latitudes according to his account agree pretty well with ours here.

6th. Set out to-day with the second lieutenant, resolved to go a good way up the river, and see if the country inland differed from that near the shore. We went for about three leagues among mangroves: then we got into the country, which differed very little from what we had already seen. The river higher up contracted much, and lost most of its mangroves: the banks were steep and covered with trees of a beautiful verdure, particularly what is called in the West Indies *mohoe* or bark-tree (*Hibiscus tiliaceus*). The land was generally low, thickly covered with long grass, and seemed to promise great fertility, were the people to plant and improve it. In the course of the day Tupia saw a wolf, so

at least I guess by his description, and we saw three of the
animals of the country, but could not get one; also a kind
of bat as large as a partridge, but these also we were not
lucky enough to get. At night we took up our lodgings
close to the banks of the river, and made a fire; but the
mosquitos, whose peaceful dominions it seems we had invaded,
spared no pains to molest us as much as was in their power:
they followed us into the very smoke, nay, almost into the
fire, which, hot as the climate was, we could better bear the
heat of than their intolerable stings. Between the hardness
of our bed, the heat of the fire, and the stings of these indefatigable insects, the night was not spent so agreeably but
day was earnestly wished for by all of us.

7th. At last it came, and with its first dawn we set out
in search of game. We walked many miles over the flats
and saw four of the animals, two of which my greyhound
fairly chased; but they beat him owing to the length and
thickness of the grass, which prevented him from running,
while they at every bound leaped over the tops of it. We
observed, much to our surprise, that instead of going upon
all fours, this animal went only upon two legs, making vast
bounds just as the jerboa (*Mus jaculus* [1]) does.

We observed a smoke, but when we came to the place the
people were gone. The fire was in an old tree of touchwood.
Their houses were there, and branches of trees broken down,
with which the children had been playing, were not yet
withered; their footsteps, also, on the sands below high-water
mark proved that they had very lately been there. Near their
oven, in which victuals had been dressed since noon, were the
shells of a kind of clam, and the roots of a wild yam which
had been cooked in it. Thus were we disappointed of the
only good chance we have had of seeing the people since we
came here, by their unaccountable timidity. Night soon
coming on, we repaired to our quarters, which were upon a
broad sand-bank under the shade of a bush, where we hoped
the mosquitos would not trouble us. Our beds of plantain
leaves spread on the sand, as soft as a mattress, our cloaks

[1] *Dipus jaculus.*

for bed-clothes, and grass pillows, but above all the entire absence of mosquitos, made me and, I believe, all of us sleep almost without intermission. Had the Indians come they would certainly have caught us all napping; but that was the last thing we thought of.

8th. The tide serving at daylight, we set out for the ship. On our passage down we met several flocks of whistling ducks, of which we shot some. We saw also an alligator about seven feet long come out of the mangroves and crawl into the water. By four o'clock we arrived at the ship.

10th. Four Indians appeared on the opposite shore; they had with them a canoe made of wood with an outrigger, in which two of them embarked, and came towards the ship, but stopped at the distance of a long musket shot, talking much and very loud to us. We called to them, and waving, made them all the signs we could to come nearer. By degrees they ventured almost insensibly nearer and nearer till they were quite alongside, often holding up their lances as if to show us that if we used them ill they had weapons and would return our attack. Cloth, nails, paper, etc. etc., were given to them, all which they took and put into the canoe without showing the least signs of satisfaction. At last a small fish was by accident thrown to them, on which they expressed the utmost joy imaginable, and instantly putting off from the ship, made signs that they would bring over their comrades, which they very soon did, and all four landed near us, each carrying in his hand two lances, and his stick to throw them with. Tupia went towards them; they stood all in a row in the attitude of throwing their lances; he made signs that they should lay them down and come forward without them; this they immediately did, and sat down upon the ground. We then came up to them and made them presents of beads, cloth, etc., which they took, and soon became very easy, only jealous if any one attempted to go between them and their arms. At dinner-time we made signs to them to come with us and eat, but they refused; we left them, and they going into their canoe, paddled back to where they came from.

11*th*. The Indians came over again to-day; two that were with us yesterday, and two new ones, whom our old acquaintance introduced to us by their names, one of which was Yaparico. Though we did not yesterday observe it, they all had the septum or inner part of the nose bored through with a very large hole, in which one of them had stuck the bone of a bird as thick as a man's finger, and four or six inches long, an ornament no doubt, though to us it appeared rather an uncouth one. They brought with them a fish which they gave to us, in return I suppose for the fish we had given them yesterday. Their stay was but short, for some of our gentlemen being rather too curious in examining their canoe, they went directly to it, and pushing it off, went away without saying a word.

12*th*. The Indians came again to-day and ventured down to Tupia's tent, where they were so pleased with their reception that three stayed, while the fourth went with the canoe to fetch two others. They introduced their strangers (which they always made a point of doing) by name, and had some fish given them; they received it with indifference, signed to our people to cook it for them, which was done, ate part and gave the rest to my dog. They stayed the best part of the morning, but never ventured to go above twenty yards from their canoe. The ribbons by which we had tied medals round their necks on the first day we saw them, were covered with smoke; I suppose they lay much in the smoke to keep off the mosquitos.

14*th*. Our second lieutenant had the good fortune to kill the animal that had so long been the subject of our speculations. To compare it to any European animal would be impossible, as it has not the least resemblance to any one I have seen. Its fore-legs are extremely short, and of no use to it in walking; its hind again as disproportionally long; with these it hops seven or eight feet at a time, in the same manner as the jerboa, to which animal indeed it bears much resemblance, except in size, this being in weight 38 lbs., and the jerboa no larger than a common rat.

15*th*. The beast which was killed yesterday was to-day

dressed for our dinner, and proved excellent meat. In the evening the boat returned from the reef, bringing four turtles; so we may now be said to swim in plenty. Our turtles are certainly far preferable to any I have eaten in England, which must be due to their being eaten fresh from the sea before they have either wasted away their fat, or, by the unnatural food which they receive in the tubs where they are kept, acquired a fat of not so delicious a flavour as it is in their wild state. Most of those we have caught have been green turtle from two to three hundred pounds in weight; these, when killed, were always found to be full of turtle-grass (a kind of *Conferva* I believe). Two only were loggerheads, which made but indifferent meat; in their stomachs were nothing but shells.

16*th.* As the ship was now ready for her departure, Dr. Solander and I employed ourselves in winding up our botanical bottoms,[1] examining what we wanted and making up our complement of specimens of as many species as possible. The boat brought three turtles again to-day, one of which was a male, who was easily to be distinguished from the female by the vast size of his tail, which was four times longer and thicker than hers; in every other respect they were exactly alike. One of our people on board the ship, who had been a turtler in the West Indies, told me that they never sent male turtles home to England from thence, because they wasted in keeping much more than the females, which we found to be true.

17*th.* Tupia, who was over the water by himself, saw three Indians, who gave him a kind of longish root about as thick as a man's finger and of a very good taste.

18*th.* The Indians were over with us to-day and seemed to have lost all fear of us, becoming quite familiar. One of them, at our desire, threw his lance, which was about eight feet in length; it flew with a degree of swiftness and steadiness that really surprised me, never being above four feet from the ground, and stuck deep in at a distance of fifty paces. After this they ventured on board the ship and

---

[1] *i.e.* affairs.

soon became our very good friends, so the captain and I left
them to the care of those who stayed on board, and went to
a high hill about six miles from the ship; here we over-
looked a great deal of sea to leeward, which afforded a
melancholy prospect of the difficulties we were to encounter
when we came out of our present harbour. In whatever
direction we turned our eyes shoals innumerable were to be
seen, and no such thing as a passage to the sea, except through
the winding channels between them, dangerous to the last
degree.

19th. The Indians visited us to-day, and brought with
them a larger quantity of lances than they had ever done
before. These they laid up in a tree, leaving a man and a
boy to take care of them, and came on board the ship.
They soon let us know their errand, which was by some
means or other to get one of our turtles, of which we had
eight or nine lying upon the decks. They first by signs
asked for one, and on being refused showed great marks of
resentment. One who asked me, on my refusal, stamping
with his foot, pushed me from him with a countenance full
of disdain and applied to some one else. As, however, they
met with no encouragement in this, they laid hold of a
turtle and hauled it to the side of the ship where their
canoe lay. It was, however, soon taken from them and
replaced ; they nevertheless repeated the experiment two or
three times, and after meeting with so many repulses, all in
an instant leaped into their canoe and went ashore, where I
had got before them, just ready to set out plant-gathering.
They seized their arms in an instant, and taking fire from
under a pitch kettle which was boiling, they began to set
fire to the grass to windward of the few things we had left
ashore, with surprising dexterity and quickness. The grass,
which was four or five feet high and as dry as stubble,
burnt with vast fury. A tent of mine, which had been put
up for Tupia when he was sick, was the only thing of any
consequence in the way of it, so I leaped into a boat to
fetch some people from the ship in order to save it, and
quickly returning, hauled it down to the beach just in time.

The captain in the meanwhile followed the Indians to prevent their burning our linen and the seine which lay upon the grass just where they had gone. He had no musket with him, so soon returned to fetch one, for no threats or signs would make them desist. Mine was ashore, and another loaded with shot, so we ran as fast as possible towards them and came up just in time to save the seine by firing at an Indian who had already fired the grass in two distinct places just to windward of it. On the shot striking him, though he was full forty yards away, he dropped his fire and ran nimbly to his comrades, who all ran off pretty fast.

I had little idea of the fury with which the grass burnt in this hot climate, nor of the difficulty of extinguishing it when once lighted. This accident will, however, be a sufficient warning for us, if ever we should again pitch tents in such a climate, to burn everything around us before we begin.

22nd. One of our people who had been sent out to gather Indian kale, straying from his party, met with three Indians, two men and a boy. He came upon them suddenly as they were sitting among some long grass. At first he was much afraid, and offered them his knife, the only thing he had which he thought might be acceptable to them ; they took it, and after handing it from one to another returned it to him. They kept him about half an hour, behaving most civilly to him, only satisfying their curiosity in examining his body, which done, they made him signs that he might go away, which he did, very well pleased. They had hanging on a tree by them, he said, a quarter of the wild animal, and a cockatoo ; but how they had been clever enough to take these animals is almost beyond my conception, as both of them are most shy, especially the cockatoos.

23rd. In botanising to-day on the other side of the river we accidentally found the greater part of the clothes which had been given to the Indians left all in a heap together, doubtless as lumber not worth carriage. Maybe

had we looked further we should have found our other
trinkets, for they seemed to set no value on anything we
had except our turtle, which of all things we were the least
able to spare them.

24*th*. While travelling in a deep valley, the sides of
which were steep almost as a wall, but covered with trees and
plenty of brushwood, we found marking-nuts (*Anacardium
orientale*) lying on the ground. Desirous as we were to
find the tree on which they had grown, a thing that I
believe no European botanist has seen, we were not with all
our pains able to find it, so after cutting down four or five
trees, and spending much time, we were obliged to give
over our hopes.

26*th*. While botanising to-day I had the good fortune to
take an animal of the opossum (*Didelphis*) tribe ; it was a
female, and with it I took two young ones. It was not
unlike that remarkable one which De Buffon has described
by the name of *Phalanger* as an American animal. It was,
however, not the same. M. de Buffon is certainly wrong in
asserting that this tribe is peculiar to America, and in all
probability, as Pallas has said in his *Zoologia*, the *Phalanger*
itself is a native of the East Indies, as my animals and that
agree in the extraordinary conformation of their feet, in
which particular they differ from all the others.

27*th*. This day was dedicated to hunting the wild animal.
We saw several, and had the good fortune to kill a very
large one weighing 84 lbs.

28*th*. Botanising with no kind of success, the plants
were now entirely completed, and nothing new to be found,
so that sailing is all we wish for, if the wind would but
allow us.

10*th August*. Fine weather, so the anchor was got up,
and we sailed down to leeward, hoping there might be a
passage that way. In this we were much encouraged by
the sight of some high islands where we hoped the shoals
would end. By twelve we were among these, and fancied
that the grand or outer reef ended on one of them, so were
all in high spirits ; but about dinner-time the people who

were at the mast-head saw, as they thought, land all round us, on which we immediately came to an anchor, resolved to go ashore, and from the hills see whether it was so or not.

The point we went on[1] was sandy and very barren, so it afforded very few plants or anything else worth our observation. The sand itself, indeed, with which the whole country in a manner was covered, was infinitely fine and white, but until a glass-house is built here that could be turned to no account. We had the satisfaction, however, to see that what was taken for land round us proved only a number of islands.

11*th.* The captain went to-day to one of the islands,[2] which proved to be five leagues from the ship. I went with him. We passed over two very large shoals, on which we saw great plenty of turtle, but we had too much wind to strike any. The island itself was high; we ascended the hill, and from the top saw plainly the grand reef still extending itself parallel with the shore at about the distance of three leagues from us, or eight from the main. Through it were several channels exactly similar to those we had seen in the islands; through one of these, which seemed most easy, we determined to go. To ascertain, however, the practicability of it, we resolved to stay upon the island all night, and at daybreak send a boat to sound one of them, which was accordingly done. We slept under the shade of a bush that grew upon the beach very comfortably.

12*th.* Great part of yesterday and all this morning till the boat returned I employed in searching the island. On it I found some few plants which I had not before seen. The island itself was small and barren; there was, however, one small tract of woodland which abounded very much with large lizards, some of which I took. Distant as this isle was from the main, the Indians had been here in their poor embarkations, a sure sign that some part of the year must have very settled fine weather. We saw seven or eight frames of their huts, and vast piles of shells, the fish of which had, I suppose, been their food. All the houses

<hr />

[1] Cape Flattery.   [2] Lizard Island.

were built upon the tops of eminences, exposed entirely to
the S.E., contrary to those of the main, which are commonly
placed under some bushes or hillside to break the wind.
The officer who went in the boat returned with an account
that the sea broke vastly high upon the reef, and that the
swell was so great in the opening that he could not go into
it to sound; this was sufficient to assure us of a safe passage
out; so we got into the boat to return to the ship in high
spirits, thinking our dangers now at an end, as we had a
passage open for us to the main sea. On our return we
went ashore on a low island,[1] where we shot many birds:
on it was the nest of an eagle, the young ones of which we
killed; and another I knew not of what bird, built on the
ground, of a most enormous magnitude: it was in circumference 26 feet, and in height 2 feet 8 inches, built of sticks.[2]
The only bird I have seen in this country capable of building such a nest seems to be the pelican. The Indians had
been here likewise and lived upon turtle, as we could plainly
see by the heaps of callipashes [carapaces] piled up in many
parts of the island. Our master, who had been sent to leeward
to examine that passage, went ashore upon a low island, where
he slept; such great plenty of turtle had the Indians had
when there, that they had hung up the fins with the meat
left on them on trees, where the sun had dried them so well
that our seamen eat them heartily. He saw also two spots
clear of grass, which had lately been dug up; they were
about seven feet long and shaped like a grave, for which
indeed he took them.

13th. Ship stood out for the opening[3] we had seen in
the reef, and about two o'clock passed through it; it was
about half a mile wide. As soon as the ship was well within
it, we had no ground with 100 fathoms of line, so became in
an instant quite easy, being once more in the main ocean,
and subsequently freed from all fears of shoals, etc.

14th. For the first time these three months we were this

---

[1] Eagle Island.
[2] No doubt the nest of the Jungle bird, a species of *Megapodium*.
[3] Cook's passage.

day out of sight of land, to our no small satisfaction. A reef such as we have just passed is a thing scarcely known in Europe, or indeed anywhere but in these seas. It is a wall of coral rock, rising almost perpendicularly out of the unfathomable ocean, always covered at high-water, commonly by seven or eight feet, and generally bare at low-water. The large waves of the vast ocean meeting with so sudden a resistance make here a most terrible surf, breaking mountains high, especially when, as in our case, the general trade-wind blows directly upon it.

16*th*. At three o'clock this morning it dropped calm, which did not better our situation, for we were not more than four or five leagues from the reef, towards which the swell drove us. By six o'clock we were within a cable length of the reef, so fast had we been driven on it, without our being able to find ground with 100 fathoms. The boats were got out, to try if they could tow the ship off, but we were within forty yards when a light air sprang up, and moved the ship off a little. The boats being now manned tried to tow her away, but, whenever the air dropped, they only succeeded in keeping the ship stationary. We now found what had been the real cause of our escape, namely, the turn of the tide. It was the flood that had hurried us so unaccountably fast to the reef, which we had almost reached just at high-water. The ebb, however, aided by the boats' crews, only carried us about two miles from the reef, when the tide turned again, so that we were in no better situation. No wind would have been of any use, for we were so embayed by the reef that with the general trade-wind it would have been impossible to get out. Fortunately a narrow opening in the reef was observed, and a boat sent to examine it reporting that it was practicable—the other boats meanwhile struggling against the flood—the ship's head was turned towards it, and we were carried through by a stream like a mill-race. By four o'clock we came to an anchor, happy once more to encounter those shoals which but two days before we had thought ourselves supremely happy to have escaped from.

As we were now safe at an anchor, the boats were sent upon
the nearest shoal to search for shell-fish, turtle, or whatever
else they could get; Dr. Solander and I accompanied them
in my small boat.   On our way we met with two water-
snakes, one five and the other six feet long: we took them
both.   They much resembled land snakes, only their tails
were flattened sideways, I suppose, for the convenience of
swimming, and they were not venomous.   The shoal we
went upon was the very reef we had so nearly been lost
upon yesterday, now no longer terrible to us.   It afforded
little provision for the ship, no turtle, only 300 lbs. of great
cockles; some of an immense size.   We had in the way of
curiosity much better success, meeting with many curious
fish and mollusca, besides corals of many species, all alive,
among which was the *Tubipora musica.*   I have often
lamented that we had not time to make proper observations
upon this curious tribe of animals; but we were so entirely
taken up with the more conspicuous links of the chain of
creation, as fish, plants, birds, etc. etc., that it was impossible.

21st.   We observed both last night and this morning that
the main looked very narrow,[1] so we began to look out for
the passage we expected to find between New Holland and
New Guinea.   At noon one was seen, very narrow but
appearing to widen; we resolved to try it, so stood in.   The
anchor was dropped, and we went ashore[2] to examine whether
the place we stood into was a bay or a passage; for as we
sailed right before the trade-wind, we might find difficulty
in getting out, should it prove to be the former.   The hill
gave us the satisfaction of seeing a strait, at least as far
as we could see, without any obstructions: in the evening
a strong tide made us almost certain.[3]

26th.   Fine weather and clear fresh trade: stood to the
W. and deepened our water from 13 to 27 fathoms.

---

[1] York Peninsula.   [2] On Possession Island.

[3] Banks does not allude to Cook having here hoisted English colours
and taken possession of the whole east coast of Australia from 38° S. to
Cape York in the name of the king, as he had of several other places along
the coast (Wharton's *Cook*, p. 312).   Neither Cook nor Banks was aware that
Torres had sailed through these straits in 1606 (see p. li.)

CHAPTER XIII

SOME ACCOUNT OF THAT PART OF NEW HOLLAND NOW CALLED NEW SOUTH WALES [1]

General appearance of the coast—Dampier's narrative—Barrenness of the country—Scarcity of water—Vegetables and fruits—Timber—Palms—Gum trees—Quadrupeds—Birds—Insects—Ants and their habitations—Fish—Turtle—Shell-fish—Scarcity of people—Absence of cultivation—Description of natives—Ornaments—Absence of vermin—Implements for catching fish—Food—Cooking—Habitations—Furniture—Vessels for carrying water—Bags—Tools—Absence of sharp instruments—Native method of procuring fire—Weapons—Throwing-sticks—Shield—Cowardice of the people—Canoes—Climate—Language.

HAVING now, I believe, fairly passed through between New Holland and New Guinea, and having an open sea to the westward, so that to-morrow we intend to steer more to the northwards in order to make the south coast of New Guinea, it seems high time to take leave of New Holland, which I shall do by summing up the few observations I have been able to make on the country and people. I much wished, indeed, to have had better opportunities of seeing and observing the people, as they differ so much from the account that Dampier (the only man I know of who has seen them besides us) has given of them: he indeed saw them on a part of the coast very distant from where we were, and consequently the people might be different; but I should rather conclude them to be the same, chiefly from having observed an universal conformity in such of their

---

[1] This chapter is thus entitled by Banks. The name "New Wales" was bestowed by Cook on the whole eastern coast from lat. 38 S. to Cape York: the Admiralty copy of Cook's *Journal*, and that belonging to Her Majesty, call it "New South Wales" (Wharton's *Cook*, p. 312).

customs as came under my observation in the several
places we landed upon during the run along the coast.
Dampier in general seems to be a faithful relater; but in
the voyage in which he touched on the coast of New
Holland he was in a ship of pirates; possibly himself not a
little tainted by their idle examples, he might have kept no
written journal of anything more than the navigation of the
ship, and when upon coming home he was solicited to publish
an account of his voyage, may have referred to his memory
for many particulars relating to the people, etc. These
Indians, when covered with their filth, which I believe they
never wash off, are, if not coal black, very near it. As negroes,
then, he might well esteem them, and add the woolly hair
and want of two front teeth in consequence of the similitude
in complexion between these and the natives of Africa; but
from whatever cause it might arise, certain it is that
Dampier either was very much mistaken in his account,
or else saw a very different race of people from those we
have seen.

In the whole length of coast which we sailed along, there
was a very unusual sameness to be observed in the face of
the country. Barren it may justly be called, and in a very
high degree, so far at least as we saw. The soil in general
is sandy and very light; on it grow grass, tall enough but
thin set, and trees of a tolerable size; never, however, near
together, being in general 40, 50, and 60 feet apart.
This, and spots of loose sand, sometimes very large, con-
stitute the general face of the country as you sail along it,
and indeed the greater part even after penetrating inland
as far as our situation would allow us to do. The banks of
the bays were generally clothed with thick mangroves, sometimes for a mile or more in breadth. The soil under these
is rank mud, always overflowed every spring tide. Inland
you sometimes meet with a bog upon which the grass grows
rank and thick, so that no doubt the soil is sufficiently
fertile. The valleys also between the hills, where runs of
water come down, are thickly clothed with underwood; but
they are generally very steep and narrow, so that upon the

whole the fertile soil bears no kind of proportion to that which seems by nature doomed to everlasting barrenness.

Water is a scarce article, or at least was so while we were there, which I believe to have been in the very height of the dry season. At some places we were in we saw not a drop, and at the two places where we filled for the ship's use it was done from pools, not brooks. This drought is probably owing to the dryness of a soil almost entirely composed of sand, in which high hills are scarce. That there is plenty, however, in the rainy season is sufficiently evinced by the channels we saw cut even in rocks down the sides of inconsiderable hills : these were in general dry, or if any of them contained water, it was such as ran in the woody valleys, and they seldom carried water above half-way down the hill. Some, indeed, we saw that formed brooks, and ran quite down to the sea; but these were scarce and in general brackish a good way up from the beach.

A soil so barren, and at the same time entirely void of the help derived from cultivation, could not be supposed to yield much to the support of man. We had been so long at sea with but a scanty supply of fresh provisions, that we had long been used to eat everything we could lay our hands upon, fish, flesh, and vegetables, if only they were not poisonous. Yet we could only now and then procure a dish of bad greens for our own table, and never, except in the place where the ship was careened, did we meet with a sufficient quantity to supply the ship. There, indeed, palm cabbage, and what is called in the West Indies Indian kale, were in tolerable plenty ; as also was a sort of purslane. The other plants which we ate were a kind of bean (very bad), a kind of parsley, and a plant something resembling spinach, which two last grew only to the southward. I shall give their botanical names, as I believe some of them were never eaten by Europeans before : Indian kale (*Arum esculentum*), red-flowered purslane (*Sesuvium portulacastrum*), beans (*Glycine speciosa*), parsley (*Apium*), spinach (*Tetragonia cornuta*).

We had still fewer fruits; to the southwards was one somewhat resembling a heart cherry (*Eugenia*), only the stone was soft: it had nothing but a slight acid to recommend it. To the northward, we had a kind of very indifferent fig (*Ficus caudiciflora*) growing from the stalk of a tree, a fruit we called plums—like them in colour, but flat like a little cheese—and another much like a damson both in appearance and taste. Both these last, however, were so full of a large stone, that eating them was but an unprofitable business. Wild plantains we had also, but so full of seeds that they had little or no pulp.

For the article of timber there is certainly no want of trees of more than the middling size, and some in the valleys are very large, but all of a very hard nature. Our carpenters, who cut them down for firewood, complained much that their tools were damaged by them. Some trees there are also to the northward, whose soft bark, which easily peels off, is in the East Indies used for caulking ships in lieu of oakum.

Palms here are of three different sorts: the first,[1] which grew plentifully to the southward, has leaves plaited like a fan; the cabbage of these is small, but exquisitely sweet, and the nuts which it bears in great abundance make a very good food for hogs. The second is very like the real cabbage tree of the West Indies, bearing pinnated leaves like those of a cocoanut: this also yields cabbage, which, if not so sweet as the other sort, yet makes ample amends in quantity. The third,[2] which like the second is found only in the northern parts, is low, seldom 10 feet in height, with small pinnated leaves resembling those of some kinds of fern. Cabbage it has none, but generally bears a plentiful crop of nuts, about the size of a large chestnut, and rounder. By the hulls of these, which we found plentifully near the Indian fires, we were assured that these people ate them, and some of our gentlemen tried to do the same, but were deterred from a second experiment by a hearty fit of vomiting. The hogs, however, which were still shorter of

[1] *Livistona australis*, Mart.   [2] *Cycas media*, Br.

provision than we were, ate them heartily, and we considered their constitutions stronger than ours, until after about a week they were all taken extremely ill of indigestion ; two died, and the rest were saved with difficulty.

Other useful plants we saw none, except perhaps two, which might be found so, yielding resin in abundance. The one,[1] a tree tolerably large, with narrow leaves not unlike a willow, was plentiful in every place into which we went, and yielded a blood-red resin or rather gum-resin, very nearly resembling *Sanguis draconis;* indeed, as *Sanguis draconis* is the produce of several different plants, this may be perhaps one of the sorts. This I should suppose to be the gum mentioned by Dampier in his voyage round the world, and by him compared with *Sanguis draconis,* as possibly also that which Tasman saw upon Van Diemen's Land, where he says he saw gum on the trees, and gum lac on the ground. (See his voyage in a collection published at London in 1694, p. 133.) The other[2] was a small plant with long narrow grassy leaves and a spike of flowers resembling much that kind of bulrush which is called in England cat's tail : this yielded a resin of a bright yellow colour perfectly resembling gamboge, only that it did not stain ; it had a sweet smell, but what its properties are the chemists may be able to determine.

Of plants in general the country affords a far larger variety than its barren appearance seemed to promise : many of these no doubt possess properties which might be useful for physical and economical purposes, which we were not able to investigate. Could we have understood the Indians, or made them by any means our friends, we might perchance have learnt some of these ; for though their manner of life, but one degree removed from brutes, does not seem to promise much, yet they had some knowledge of plants, as we could plainly perceive by their having names for them.

Thus much for plants. I have been rather particular in mentioning those which we ate, hoping that such a record might be of use to some or other into whose hands

---

[1] *Eucalyptus.*   [2] *Xanthorrhœa.*

these papers fall. For quadrupeds, birds, fish, etc., I shall say no more than that we had some time ago learned to eat every single species which came in our way; a hawk or a crow was to us as delicate, and perhaps a better-relished meal, than a partridge or pheasant to those who have plenty of dainties. We wanted nothing to recommend any food but its not being salt; that alone was sufficient to make it a delicacy. Shags, sea-gulls, and all that tribe of sea-fowl which are reckoned bad from their trainy or fishy taste, were to us an agreeable food: we did not at all taste the rankness, which no doubt has been and possibly will again be highly nauseous to us, whenever we have plenty of beef and mutton, etc.

Quadrupeds we saw but few, and were able to catch but few of those we did see. The largest was called by the natives *kangooroo;* it is different from any European, and, indeed, any animal I have heard or read of, except the jerboa of Egypt, which is not larger than a rat, while this is as large as a middling lamb. The largest we shot weighed 84 lbs. It may, however, be easily known from all other animals by the singular property of running, or rather hopping, upon only its hinder legs, carrying its fore-feet close to its breast. In this manner it hops so fast that in the rocky bad ground where it is commonly found, it easily beat my greyhound, who, though he was fairly started at several, killed only one, and that quite a young one. Another animal was called by the natives *je-quoll;* it is about the size of, and something like, a pole-cat, of a light brown, spotted with white on the back, and white under the belly. The third was of the opossum kind, and much resembled that called by De Buffon *Phalanger.* Of these two last I took only one individual of each. Bats here were many: one small one was much if not identically the same as that described by De Buffon under the name of *Fer de cheval.* Another sort was as large as, or larger than, a partridge; but of this species we were not fortunate enough to take one. We supposed it, however, to be the *Rousette* or *Rougette* of the same author. Besides these, wolves were, I believe, seen by several of our people, and some other animals described; but from the unintelligible style of the describers, I could not even determine whether they were such as I myself had seen, or of different kinds. Of these descriptions I shall insert one, as it is not unentertaining.

A seaman who had been out on duty declared that he had seen an animal about the size of, and much like a one-gallon cagg. " It was," says he, " as black as the devil, and had wings, indeed I took it for the devil, or I might easily have catched it, for it crawled very slowly through the grass." After taking some pains, I found out that the animal he had seen was no other than the large bat.

Of sea-fowl there were several species: gulls, shags, solan geese or gannets of two sorts, boobies, etc., and pelicans of an enormous size; but these last, though we saw many thousands of them, were so shy that we never got one, as were the cranes also, of which we saw several very large and some beautiful species. In the rivers were ducks which flew in very large flocks, but were very hard to come at; and on the beach were curlews of several sorts, some very like our English ones, and many small beach birds. The land birds were crows, very like if not quite the same as our English ones, most beautiful parrots and parroquets, white and black cockatoos, pigeons, beautiful doves, bustards and many others which did not at all resemble those of Europe. Most of these were extremely shy, so that it was with difficulty that we shot any of them. A crow in England, though in general sufficiently wary, is, I must say, a fool to a New Holland crow, and the same may be said of almost all if not all the birds in the country. The only ones we ever got in any plenty were pigeons, of which we met large flocks, and of which the men who were sent out on purpose would sometimes kill ten or twelve a day. They were beautiful birds, crested differently from any other pigeon I have seen. What can be the reason of this extraordinary shyness in the birds is difficult to say, unless perhaps the Indians are very clever in deceiving them, which we have very little reason to suppose, as we never saw any instrument with them with which a bird could be killed or taken, except their lances, and these must be very improper tools for the purpose. Yet one of our people saw a white cockatoo in their possession, which very bird we looked upon to be one of the wariest of them all.

Of insects there were but few sorts, and among them only the ants were troublesome to us. Mosquitos, indeed, were in some places tolerably plentiful, but it was our good fortune never to stay any time in such places. The ants, however, made ample amends for the want of the mosquitos; two sorts in particular, one green as a leaf, and living upon trees, where it built a nest, in size between that of a man's head and his fist, by bending the leaves together, and gluing them with a whitish papery substance which held them firmly together. In doing this their management was most curious: they bend down four leaves broader than a man's hand, and place them in such a direction as they choose. This requires a much larger force than these animals seem capable of; many thousands indeed are employed in the joint work. I have seen as many as could stand by one another, holding down such a leaf, each drawing down with all his might, while others within were employed to fasten the glue. How they had bent it down, I had not an opportunity of seeing, but that it was held down by main strength, I easily proved by disturbing a part of them, on which the leaf, bursting from the rest, returned to its natural situation, and I had an opportunity of trying with my finger the strength that these little animals must have used to get it down. But industrious as they are, their courage, if possible, excels their industry; if we accidentally shook the branches on which such a nest was hung, thousands would immediately throw themselves down, many of which falling upon us made us sensible of their stings and revengeful dispositions, especially if, as was often the case, they got possession of our necks and hair. Their stings were by some esteemed not much less painful than those of a bee; the pain, however, lasted only a few seconds.

Another sort there were, quite black, whose manner of living was most extraordinary. They inhabited the inside of the branches of one sort of tree, the pith of which they hollowed out almost to the very end of the branches, nevertheless the tree flourished as well to all appearance as if no such accident had happened to it. When first we found the tree, we of course gathered the branches, and were surprised to find our hands instantly covered with legions of these small animals, who stung most intolerably; experience, however, taught us to be more careful for the future. Rumphius mentions a similar instance to this in his *Herbarium Amboinense*, vol. ii. p. 257; his tree, however, does not at all resemble ours.

A third sort nested inside the root of a plant which grew upon the bark of trees in the same manner as mistletoe.[1] The root was the size of a large turnip, and often much larger; when cut, the inside showed innumerable winding passages in which these animals lived. The plant itself throve to all appearance not a bit the worse for its numerous inhabitants. Several hundreds have I seen, and never one but what was inhabited; though some were so young as not to be much larger than a hazel nut. The ants themselves were very small, not above half as large as our red ants in England; they sting indeed, but so little that it was scarcely felt. The chief inconvenience in handling the roots came from the infinite number; myriads would come in an instant out of many holes, and running over the hand tickle so as to be scarcely endurable. Rumphius has an account of this very bulb and its ants in vol. vi. p. 120, where he describes also another sort, the ants of which are black.

The fourth kind were perfectly harmless, at least they proved so to us, though they resembled almost exactly the white ants of the East Indies, the most mischievous insect I believe known in the world. Their architecture was, however, far superior to that of any other species. They had two kinds of houses, one suspended on the branches of trees, the other standing upright on the

---

[1] Species of *Myrmecodia* or *Hydnophytum*.

ground. The first sort were generally three or four times as large as a man's head; they were built of a brittle substance, seemingly made of small parts of vegetables kneaded together with some glutinous matter, probably afforded by themselves. On breaking this outer crust innumerable cells appeared, full of inhabitants, winding in all directions, communicating with each other, as well as with divers doors which led from the nest. From each of these an arched passage led to different parts of the tree, and generally one large one to the ground. This I am inclined to believe communicated with the other kind of house, for as the animals inhabiting both were precisely the same, I see no reason why they should be supposed, contrary to every instance that I know in nature, to build two different kinds of houses, unless, according to the season, prey, etc., they inhabited both equally.

This second kind of house was very often built near the foot of a tree, on the bark of which their covered ways, though but seldom the first kind of house, were always to be found. It was formed like an irregularly sided cone, and was sometimes more than six feet high, and nearly as much in diameter. The smaller ones were generally flat-sided, and resembled very much the old stones which are seen in many parts of England, and supposed to be remains of Druidical worship. The outer coat of these was 2 inches thick at least, of hard, well-tempered clay, under which were their cells; to these no doors were to be seen. All their passages were underground, where probably they were carried on till they met the root of some tree, up which they ascended, and so up the trunks and branches by the covered way before mentioned. These I should suppose to be the houses to which they retire in the winter season, as they are undoubtedly able to defend them from any rain that can fall, while the others, though generally built under the shelter of some overhanging branch, must, from the thinness of the covering, be but a slight defence against a heavy rain.

Thus much for the ants, an industrious race which in all countries have for that reason been admired by man, though

x

probably in no country more admirable than in this. The few observations I have written down concerning them are chiefly from conjecture, and therefore are not at all to be depended upon. Were any man, however, to settle here who had time and inclination to observe their economy, I am convinced that it would far exceed that of any insects we know, not excepting our much-admired bees.

The sea, however, made some amends for the barrenness of the land. Fish, though not so plentiful as they generally are in the higher latitudes, were far from scarce; when we had an opportunity of hauling the seine we generally caught from 50 to 200 lbs. of fish in a tide. The kinds were various, none I think but mullets being known in Europe. In general, however, they were sufficiently palatable, and some very delicate food. The sting-rays, indeed, which were caught on the southern part of the coast were very coarse; so that, as little else was caught there, we were obliged to be satisfied with the comforts of plenty, and enjoy more pleasure in satiety than in eating. To the northward again, when we were entangled within the great reef, was a quantity of turtle hardly to be credited, every shoal swarmed with them. The weather indeed was generally so boisterous, that our boats could not row after them as fast as they could swim, so that we got but few; but they were excellent, and so large that a single turtle always served for the whole ship. Had we been there either at the time of laying or in a more moderate season, we might doubtless have taken any quantity. All the shoals that were dry at half ebb afforded plenty of fish, left dry in small hollows of the rocks, and a profusion of large shell-fish (*Chama gigas*) such as Dampier describes, vol. iii. p. 191. The largest of these had ten or fifteen pounds of meat in them; it was indeed rather strong, but I believe a very wholesome food, and well relished by the people in general. On different parts of the coast were also found oysters, which were said to be very well tasted; the shells also of good-sized lobsters and crabs were seen, but these it was never our fortune to catch.

Upon the whole, New Holland, though in every respect the most barren country I have seen, is not so bad but that between the productions of sea and land, a company who had the misfortune to be shipwrecked upon it might support themselves, even by the resources that we have seen : undoubtedly a longer stay and a visit to different parts would discover many more.

This immense tract of land, the largest known which does not bear the name of a continent, as it is considerably larger than all Europe, is thinly inhabited, even to admiration, at least that part of it that we saw. We never but once saw so many as thirty Indians together, and that was a family, men, women, and children, assembled upon a rock to see the ship pass by. At Sting-ray's Bay,[1] where they evidently came down several times to fight us, they never could muster above fourteen or fifteen fighting men, indeed in other places they generally ran away from us, whence it might be concluded that there were greater numbers than we saw, but their houses and sheds in the woods, which we never failed to find, convinced us of the smallness of their parties. We saw, indeed, only the sea coast ; what the immense tract of inland country may produce is to us totally unknown. We may have liberty to conjecture, however, that it is totally uninhabited. The sea has, I believe, been universally found to be the chief source of supplies to Indians ignorant of the arts of cultivation. The wild produce of the land alone seems scarcely able to support them at all seasons, at least I do not remember to have read of any inland nation who did not cultivate the ground more or less : even the North Americans, who are so well versed in hunting, sow their maize. But should a people live inland, who supported themselves by cultivation, these inhabitants of the sea coast must certainly have learned to imitate them in some degree at least, otherwise their reason must be supposed to hold a rank little superior to that of monkeys.

What may be the reason of this absence of people is

[1] Afterwards called Botany Bay.

difficult to guess, unless it be the barrenness of the soil and the scarcity of fresh water. But why should not mankind increase here as fast as in other places, unless their small tribes have frequent wars in which many are destroyed? They were indeed generally furnished with plenty of weapons, whose points of the stings of sting-rays seemed intended for use against none but their own species.

That their customs are nearly the same throughout the whole length of the coast along which we sailed, I should think very probable, though we had connections with them at only one place. Yet we saw them with our eyes or glasses many times, and at Sting-ray's Bay had some experience of their manners. Their colour, arms, and method of using them were the same as those we afterwards had a nearer view of. They likewise in the same manner went naked, and painted themselves, their houses were the same, they notched large trees in the same manner, and even the bags they carried their furniture in were of exactly the same manufacture, something between netting and knitting, which I have nowhere else seen. In the intermediate places our glasses might deceive us in many things, but their colour and want of clothes we certainly did see, and whenever we came ashore the houses and sheds, places where they had dressed victuals with heated stones, and trees notched for the convenience of climbing them, sufficiently evinced them to be the same people.

The tribe with which we had connections consisted of twenty-one people, twelve men, seven women, a boy and a girl; so many at least we saw, and there might have been more, especially women, whom we did not see. The men were remarkably short and slenderly built in proportion; the tallest we measured was 5 feet 9 inches, the shortest 5 feet 2 inches; the average height seemed to be about 5 feet 6 inches. What their absolute colour is, is difficult to say, they were so completely covered with dirt, which seemed to have stuck to their hides from the day of their birth, without their once having attempted to remove it. I tried indeed by spitting upon my finger and rubbing, but altered the colour very little, which as nearly as might be resembled chocolate. The beards of several were bushy and thick; their hair, which as well as their beards was black, they wore close cropped round their ears. In some it was as lank as an European's, in others a little crisped, as is common in the South Sea Islands, but in none of them at all resembling the wool of the negroes. They had also all their fore teeth, in which two points they differ chiefly from those seen by Dampier, supposing him not to be mistaken. As for colour they would undoubtedly be called black by any one not used to consider attentively the colours of different nations. I myself should never have thought of such distinctions, had I not seen the effect of sun and wind upon the natives of the South Sea Islands, where many of the better sort of people, who keep themselves close at home, are nearly as white as Europeans; while the poorer sort, obliged in their business of fishing, etc., to expose their naked bodies to all the inclemencies of the climate, are in some cases but little lighter than the New Hollanders. They were all to a man lean and clean-limbed, and seemed very light and active. Their countenances were not without some expression, though I cannot charge them with much, their voices in general shrill and effeminate.

Of clothes they had not the least part, but were naked as ever our general father was before his fall, whether from idleness or want of invention is difficult to say. In the article of ornaments, however, useless as they are, neither has the one hindered them from contriving, nor the other from making them. Of these the chief, and that on which they seem to set the greatest value, is a bone 5 or 6 inches in length, and as thick as a man's finger, which they thrust into a hole bored through that part which divides the nostrils, so that it sticks across the face, making in the eyes of Europeans a most ludicrous appearance, though no doubt they esteem even this as an addition to their beauty, which they purchase by hourly inconvenience; for when this bone was in its place, or, as our seamen termed it, when their spritsail-yard was rigged across, it completely stopped up both nostrils, so that they spoke in the nose in a manner one would think scarcely intelligible. Besides these extraordinary bones, they had necklaces of shells neatly cut and strung together; bracelets also, if one may call by that name four or five rings of small cord worn round the upper part of the arm ; and a belt or string tied round the waist about as thick as worsted yarn, which last was frequently made of either human hair or that of the beast called by them kangooroo.

They paint themselves with red and white. The former they commonly lay on in broad patches on their shoulders or breasts ; the white in strips, some of which are narrow and confined to small parts of their bodies, others broad and carried with some degree of taste across their bodies, round their legs and arms, etc. They also lay it on in circles round their eyes, and in patches in different parts of their faces. The red seems to be red ochre, but what the white was we could not find out, it was heavy and close-grained, almost as white lead, and had a saponaceous feel; possibly it might be a kind of steatite. We lamented not being able to procure a bit to examine.

These people seemed to have no idea of traffic, nor could we teach them ; indeed, it seemed that we had no one thing upon which they set a value sufficient to induce them to part with the smallest trifle, except one fish which weighed about half a pound. That they brought as a kind of peace token. No one in the ship procured, I believe, from them the smallest article ; they readily received the things we gave them, but never would understand our signs, when we asked for returns. This, however, must not be forgotten, that whatever opportunities they had they never once attempted to take anything in a clandestine manner ; whatever they wanted they openly asked for, and in almost all cases bore the refusal, if they met with one, with much indifference, except in the case of turtles.

Dirty as these people are, they seem to be entirely free from lice, a circumstance rarely observed among the most cleanly Indians, and which is here the more remarkable, as their hair was generally matted, and filthy enough. In all of them, indeed, it was very thin, and seemed as if seldom disturbed by the combing even of their fingers, much less to have any oil or grease put into it. Nor did the custom of oiling their bodies, so common among most uncivilised nations, seem to have the least footing here.

On their bodies we observed very few marks of cutaneous disorders, such as scurf, scars of sores, etc. Their spare thin bodies indicate a temperance in eating, the consequence either of necessity or inclination, equally productive of health, particularly in this respect. On the fleshy parts of their arms and thighs, and some of their sides, were large scars in regular lines, which by their breadth and the convexity with which they had healed, showed plainly that they had been made by deep cuts of some blunt instrument, possibly a shell or the edge of a broken stone. These, as far as we could understand the signs they made use of, were the marks of their lamentations for the deceased, in honour of whose memory, or to show the excess of their grief, they had in this manner wept in blood.

For food they seemed to depend very much, though not entirely, upon the sea. Fish of all kinds, turtle, and even crabs, they strike with their lances very dexterously. These are generally bearded with broad beards, and their points smeared over with a kind of hard resin, which makes them pierce a hard body far more easily than they would without it. In the southern parts these fish-spears had four prongs, and besides the resin were pointed with the sharp bone of a fish. To the northward their spears had only one point, yet both, I believe, struck fish with equal dexterity. For the northern ones I can witness, who several times saw them through a glass throw a spear from ten to twenty yards, and generally succeed. To the southward again the quantity of fish bones we saw near their fires proved them to be no indifferent artists.

In striking turtle they use a peg of wood well bearded, and about a foot long; this fastens into the socket of a staff of light wood as thick as a man's wrist, and eight or nine feet long, besides which it is tied to a loose line of three or four fathoms. The use of this is undoubtedly to enable the staff to serve as a float to show where the turtle is when struck, as well as to assist in tiring it till they can with their canoes overtake and haul it in. That they throw this dart with great force we had occasion to observe while we lay in Endeavour's river, where a turtle which we killed had one of these pegs entirely buried in his body just across its breast; it seemed to have entered at the soft place where the fore-fin works, but not the least outward mark of the wound remained.

We saw near their fire-places plentiful remains of lobsters, shell-fish of all kinds, and to the southward the skins of those sea animals which, from their property of spouting out water when touched, are commonly called sea-squirts. These last, however disgustful they may seem to an European palate, we found to contain, under a coat as tough as leather, a substance like the guts of a shell-fish, of a taste, though not equal to an oyster, yet by no means to be despised by a hungry man.

Of land animals they probably eat every kind that they can kill, which probably does not amount to any large number, every species being here shy and cautious in a high degree. The only vegetables which we saw them use were yams of two sorts, the one long and like a finger, the other round and covered with stringy roots; both sorts very small but sweet. They were so scarce where we were that we never could find the plants that produced them, though we often saw the places where they had been dug up by the Indians very recently. It is very probable that the dry season, which was at its height when we were there, had destroyed the leaves of the plants, so that we had no guide, while the Indians, knowing well the stalks, might find them easily. Whether they knew or ever made use of the cocos, I cannot tell; the immense sharpness of every part of this vegetable before it is dressed makes it probable that any people who have not learned the uses of it from others may remain for ever ignorant of them. Near their fires were great abundance of the shells of a kind of fruit resembling a pine-apple, though its taste was disagreeable enough. It is common to all the East Indies, and called by the Dutch *Pyn appel Boomen* (*Pandanus*). We found also the fruits of a low palm [1] called by the Dutch *Moeskruidige Callapus* (*Cycas circinalis*), which they certainly eat, though this fruit is so unwholesome that some of our people, who, though forewarned, followed their example and ate one or two of them, were violently affected by them ; and our hogs, whose constitutions we thought might be as strong as those of the Indians, literally died after having eaten them. It is probable, however, that these people have some method of preparing them by which their poisonous quality is destroyed, as the inhabitants of the East Indian Isles are said to do ,by boiling them, steeping them twenty-four hours in water, then drying them, and using them to thicken broth, from whence it would seem that the poisonous quality lies entirely in the juices, as it does in the roots of the mandihoca or cassada of the West Indies, and that when thoroughly cleared of them, the pulp remaining may be a wholesome and nutritious food.

Their victuals they generally dress by broiling or toasting them upon the coals, so we judged by the remains we saw ; they understood, however, the method of baking or stewing with hot stones, and sometimes practised it, as we now and then saw the pits and burned stones which had been used for that purpose.

We observed that some, though but few, held constantly in their mouths the leaves of a herb which they chewed as a European does tobacco, or an East Indian betel ; what sort of a plant it was we had no opportunity of learning, as we never saw anything but the chaws, which they took from their mouth to show us. It might be of the betel kind, and so far as we could judge from the fragments was so ; but whatever it was, it was used without any addition, and seemed to have no kind of effect upon either the teeth or lips of those who used it.

[1] *Cycas media*, Br., closely allied to *C. circinalis*. See pp. 299 and 421.

Naked as these people are when abroad, they are scarcely at all better defended from the injuries of the weather when at home; if that name can with propriety be given to their houses, as I believe they never make any stay in them, but wandering like the Arabs from place to place, set them up whenever they meet with a spot where sufficient supplies of food are to be met with. As soon as these are exhausted they remove to another, leaving the houses behind, which are framed probably with less art, or rather less industry, than any habitations of human beings that the world can show. At Sting-ray's Bay, where they were the best, each was capable of containing within it four or five people, but not one of all these could extend himself his whole length in any direction; he might just sit upright, but if inclined to sleep, must coil himself up in some crooked position, as the dimensions were in no direction enough to receive him otherwise. They were built in the form of an oven, of pliable rods about as thick as a man's finger, the ends of which were stuck into the ground, and the whole covered with palm leaves and broad pieces of bark. The door was a fairly large hole at one end, opposite to which there seemed from the ashes to be a fire kept pretty constantly. To the northward, where the warmth of the climate made houses less necessary, they were in proportion still more slight: a house there was nothing but a hollow shelter about three or four feet deep, built like the former, and like them covered with bark. One side of this was entirely open; it was always the side sheltered from the course of the prevailing wind, and opposite to this door was always a heap of ashes, the remains of a fire, probably more necessary to defend them from mosquitos than cold. In these it is probable that they only sought to protect their heads and the upper part of their bodies from the draught of air, trusting their feet to the care of the fire. So small they were that even in this manner not above three or four people could possibly crowd into them, but small as the trouble of erecting such houses must be, they did not always do it: we saw many places in the woods where they had slept with no other shelter than a few bushes and grass a foot or two high to shelter them from the wind This probably is their custom while they travel from place to place, and sleep upon the road, in situations where they do not intend to make any stay.

The only furniture belonging to these houses, that we saw at least, was oblong vessels of bark made by the simple contrivance of tying up the ends of a longish piece with a withe, which not being cut off serves for a handle : these we imagined served as buckets to fetch water from the springs, which may sometimes be distant. We have reason to suppose that when they travel these are carried by the women from place to place ; indeed, during the few opportunities we had of seeing the women they were generally employed in some laborious occupation, as fetching wood, gathering shell-fish, etc. The men, again, maybe constantly carry their arms in their hands, three or four lances in the one, and the machine with which they throw them in the other. These serve the double object of defending them from their enemies and striking any animal or fish they may meet with. Each has also a small bag about the size of a moderate cabbage-net hanging loose upon his back and fastened to a small string which passes over the crown of his head. This seems to contain all their earthly treasures : a lump or two of paint, some fish-hooks and lines, shells to make the fish-hooks of, points of darts, resin, and their usual ornaments, were the general contents.

Thus live these, I had almost said happy, people, content with little, nay, almost nothing ; far enough removed from the anxieties attending upon riches, or even the possession of what we Europeans call common necessaries : anxieties intended, maybe, by Providence to counterbalance the pleasure arising from the possession of wished-for attainments consequently increasing with increasing wealth, and in some measure keeping up the balance of happiness between the rich and the poor. From them appear how small are the real wants of human nature, which we Europeans have increased to an excess which would certainly appear incredible to these people could they be told it ; nor shall we cease to increase them as long as luxuries can be invented and riches found for the purchase of them.   How soon these luxuries degenerate into necessaries may be sufficiently evinced by the universal use of strong liquors, tobacco, spices, tea, etc. In this instance, again, Providence seems to act the part of a leveller, doing much towards putting all ranks into an equal state of wants, and consequently of real poverty : the great and magnificent want as much, and maybe more, than the middle classes : they again in proportion more than the inferior, each rank looking higher than its station, but confining itself to a certain point above which it knows not how to wish, not knowing at least perfectly what is there enjoyed.

Tools among these people we saw almost none, indeed, having no arts which require any, it is not to be expected that they should have many.   A stone sharpened at the edge and a wooden mallet were the only ones that we saw formed by art : the use of these we supposed to be to make the notches in the bark of high trees by which they climb them for purposes unknown to us ; and for cutting and perhaps driving in wedges to take off the bark which they must have in large pieces for making canoes, shields, and water-buckets, and also for covering their houses.   Besides these they use shells and corals to scrape the points of their darts, and polish them with the leaves of a kind of wild fig-tree (*Ficus radula*), which bites upon wood almost as keenly as our European shave-grass, used by the joiners. Their fish-hooks are very neatly made of shell, and some are exceedingly small : their lines are also well twisted, and they have them from the size of a half-inch rope to almost the fineness of a hair, made of some vegetable.

Of netting they seem to be quite ignorant, but make their bags, the only thing of the kind we saw among them, by laying the threads loop within loop, something like knitting, only very coarse and open, in the very same manner as I have seen ladies make purses in England. That they had no sharp instruments among them we ventured to guess from the circumstance of an old man coming to us one day with a beard rather longer than his fellows : the next day he came again, and his beard was then almost cropped close to his chin, and upon examination we found the ends of the hairs all burned, so that he had certainly singed it off. Their manner of hunting and taking wild animals we had no opportunity of seeing; we only guessed that the notches which they had everywhere cut in the bark of the large trees, which certainly seems to make climbing more easy to them, might be intended to allow them to ascend these trees in order either to watch for any animal unwarily passing under them which they might pierce with their darts, or to take birds which might roost in them at night. We guessed also that the fires which we saw so frequently as we passed along shore, extending over a large tract of country, and by which we could constantly trace the passage of Indians who went from us in Endeavour's river up into the country, were intended in some way or other for taking the animal called by them kangooroo, which we found to be so much afraid of fire that we could hardly force it with our dogs to go over places newly burnt.

They get fire very expeditiously with two pieces of stick : the one must be round and eight or nine inches long, and both it and the other should be dry and soft : the round they sharpen a little at one end, and pressing it upon the other turn it round with the palms of their hand, just as Europeans do a chocolate-mill, often shifting their hands up and running them down quickly to make the pressure as hard as possible : in this manner they will get fire in less than two minutes, and when once possessed of the smallest spark increase it in a manner truly wonderful. We often admired a man running along shore and apparently carrying nothing in his hand, yet as he ran along just stooping down every 50 or 100 yards; smoke and fire were seen among the drift-wood and dirt at that place almost the instant he had left it. This we afterwards found was done by the infinite readiness every kind of rubbish, sticks, withered leaves, or dry grass, already almost like tinder by the heat of the sun and dryness of the season, would take fire. He took, for instance, when he set off a small bit of fire, and wrapping it up in dry grass ran on: this soon blazed; he then laid it down on the most convenient place for his purpose that he could find, and taking up a small part of it, wrapped that in part of the dry rubbish in which he had laid it, proceeding in this manner as long as he thought proper.

Their weapons, offensive at least, were precisely the same wherever we saw them, except that at the very last view we had of the country we saw through our glasses a man who carried a bow and arrows. In this we might have been, but I believe were not, mistaken. Their weapons consisted of only one species, a pike or lance from eight to fourteen feet long: this they threw short distances with their hands, and longer (forty or more yards), with an instrument made for the purpose. The upper part of these lances was made either of cane or the stalk of a plant resembling a bulrush,[1] which was very straight and light: the point was made of very heavy and hard wood, the whole artfully balanced for throwing, though very clumsily made, in two, three, or four joints, at each of which the parts were let into each other. Besides being tied round, the joint was thickly smeared with thin resin, which made it larger and more clumsy than any other part. The points were of several sorts: those which we concluded to be intended to be used against men were most cruel weapons; they were all single pointed, either with the stings of sting-rays, a large one of which served for the point and three or four smaller ones tied the contrary way for barbs, or simply of wood made very sharp and smeared over with resin, into which were stuck many broken bits of sharp shells, so that if such a weapon pierced a man it could scarcely be drawn out without leaving several of those unwelcome guests in his flesh, certain to make the wound ten times more difficult to cure than it otherwise would be. Those lances which we supposed to be used merely for striking fish, birds, etc.,

---

[1] *Xanthorrhœa.*

had generally simple points of wood; or if they were barbed, it was with only one splinter of wood. The instrument with which they threw them was a plain stick or piece of wood $2\frac{1}{2}$ or 3 feet in length, at one end of which was a small knob or hook, and near the other a kind of cross-piece

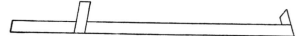

to hinder it from slipping out of their hands. With this contrivance, simple as it is, and ill-fitted for that purpose, they throw the lances forty yards or more with a swiftness and steadiness truly surprising. The knob being hooked into a small dent made in the top of the lance, they hold it over their shoulder, and shaking it an instant, as if balancing it, throw it with the greatest ease imaginable. The neatest of these throwing sticks that we saw was made of a hard reddish wood, polished and shining: the sides were flat and about two inches in breadth, and the handle, or part to keep it from dropping out of the hand, covered with thin layers of very white polished bone. These I believe to be the things which many of our people were deceived by, imagining them to be wooden swords, clubs, etc., according to the direction in which they happened to see them. Defensive weapons we saw only in Sting-ray's Bay and there only a single instance: a man who attempted to oppose our landing came down to the beach with a shield of an oblong shape about 3 feet long and $1\frac{1}{2}$ broad, made of the bark of a tree. This he left behind when he ran away, and we found upon taking it up that it had plainly been pierced through with a single-pointed lance near the centre. That such shields were frequently used in that neighbourhood we had, however, sufficient proof, often seeing upon trees the places from whence they had been cut, and sometimes the shields themselves cut out but not yet taken from the tree, the edges of the bark only being a little raised with wedges. This shows that these people certainly know how much thicker and stronger bark becomes by being suffered to remain upon the tree some time after it is cut round.

That they are a very pusillanimous people we had reason to suppose from their conduct in every place where we were, except at Sting-ray's Bay, and then only two people opposed the landing of our two boats full of men for nearly a quarter of an hour, and were not to be driven away until several times wounded with small shot, which we were obliged to do, as at that time we suspected their lances to be poisoned, from the quantity of gum which was about their points. But upon every other occasion, both there and everywhere else, they behaved alike, shunning us, and giving up any part of the country we landed upon at once. That they use stratagems in war we learnt by the instance in Sting-ray's Bay, where our surgeon with another man was walking in the woods and met six Indians: they stood still, but directed another who was up a tree how and when he should throw a lance at them, which he did, and on its not taking effect they all ran away as fast as possible.

Their canoes were the only things in which we saw a manifest difference between the southern and northern people. Those to the southward were little better contrived or executed than their houses; a piece of bark tied together in plaits at the ends, and kept extended in the middle by small bows of wood, was the whole embarkation which carried one or two people, nay, we once saw three, who moved it along in shallow water with long poles, and in deeper with paddles about eighteen inches long, one of which they held in each hand. In the middle of these canoes was generally a small fire upon a heap of seaweed, for what purpose intended we did not know, except perhaps to give the fisherman an opportunity of eating fish in perfection, by broiling it the moment it is taken. To the northward their canoes, though exceedingly bad, were far superior to these; they were small, but regularly hollowed out of the trunk of a tree, and fitted with an outrigger to prevent them from upsetting. In these they had paddles large enough to require both hands to work them. Of this sort we saw few, and had an opportunity of examining only one of them, which might be about ten or eleven feet long, but was extremely narrow. The sides of the tree were left in their natural state untouched by tools, but at each end they had cut away from the under part, and left part of the upper side overhanging. The inside also was not badly hollowed, and the sides tolerably thin. We had many times an opportunity of seeing what burthen it was capable of carrying. Three people, or at most four, were as many as dare venture in it; and if any others wanted to cross the river, which in that place was about half a mile broad, one of these would take the canoe back and fetch them.

This was the only piece of workmanship which I saw among the New Hollanders that seemed to require tools. How they had hollowed her out or cut the ends I cannot guess, but upon the whole the work was not ill done. Indian patience might do a good deal with shells, etc., without the use of stone axes, which, if they had them, they would probably have used to form her outside. That such a canoe takes much time and trouble to make may be concluded from our seeing so few, and still more from the moral certainty which we have that the tribe which visited us, consisting to our knowledge of twenty-one people, and possibly of several more, had only one such belonging to them. How tedious it must be for these people to be ferried over a river a mile or two wide by threes and fours at a time; how well, therefore, worth the pains for them to stock themselves better with boats if they could do it.

I am inclined to believe that, besides these canoes, the northern people make use of the bark canoe of the south. I judge from having seen one of the small paddles left by them upon a small island where they had been fishing for turtle: it lay upon a heap of turtle shells and bones, trophies of the good living they had had when there. With it lay the broken staff of a turtle peg and a rotten line, tools which had been worn out, I suppose, in the service of catching them. We had great reason to believe that at some season of the year the weather is much more moderate than we found it, otherwise the Indians could never have ventured in any canoes that we saw half so far from the mainland as were islands on which we saw evident marks of their having been, such as decayed houses, fires, the before-mentioned turtle bones, etc.   Maybe, at this more moderate time, they make and use such canoes, and when the bluster-ing season comes on, may convert the bark of which they were made to the purposes of covering houses, water-buckets, etc., well knowing that when the next season returns they will not want for a supply of bark to rebuild their vessels.   Another reason we have to imagine that such a moderate season exists, and that the winds are [not] then upon the eastern board as we found them is, that whatever Indian houses or sleeping places we saw on these islands were built upon the summit of small hills, if there were any, or if not, in places where no bushes or wood could intercept the course of the wind, and their shelter was always turned to the eastward.   On the main, again, their houses were universally built in valleys or under the shelter of trees which might defend them from the very winds, which in the islands they exposed themselves to.

Of their language I can say very little ; our acquaint-ance with them was of so short a duration that none of us attempted to use a single word of it to them, conse-quently words could be learned in no other manner than by signs, inquiring of them what in their language signified such a thing, a method obnoxious as leading to many mis-takes.   For instance, a man holds in his hand a stone and asks the name of it, the Indian may return him for answer either the real name of a stone, or one of the properties of it, as hardness, roughness, smoothness, etc., or one of its uses, or the name peculiar to some particular species of stone, which name the inquirer immediately sets down as that of a stone.   To avoid, however, as much as possible this inconvenience, myself and two or three others got from them as many words as we could, and having noted down those which we thought from circumstances we were not mistaken in, we compared our lists ; those in which all agreed, or rather were contradicted by none, we thought ourselves morally certain not to be mistaken in.   They very often use the article *ge*, which seems to answer to our English a, as *ge gurka*—a rope.

Wageegee	the head	Meanang	fire
Morye	the hair	Walba	a stone
Melœa	the ears	Yowall	sand
Yembe	the lips	Gurká	a rope
Bonjoo	the nose	Bāmā	a man
Unjar	the tongue	Poinja	a male turtle
Wallar	the beard	Mameingo	a female turtle
Doomboo	the neck	Maragan	a canoe
Cayo	the nipples	Pelango	to paddle
Soolpoor	the navel	Takai	set down
Mangal	the hands	Mierbarrar	smooth
Coman	the thighs	Garmbe	blood
Pongo	the knees	Yo-core	wood
Edamal	the feet	Tapool	bone in nose
Kniorror	the heel	Charngala	a bag
Chumal	the sole	Cherr	
Chongain	the ankle	Cherco	Expressions maybe of admiration which they continually used while in company.
Kulke	the nails	Yarcaw	
Gallan	the sun	Tut tut tut tut	

CHAPTER XIV

AUSTRALIA TO SAVU ISLAND

AUG. 27—SEPT. 21, 1770

"Sea-sawdust"—New Guinea—Landing—Vegetation—Natives throw fire-darts—Home-sickness of the crew—Coast along Timor—Rotte—Aurora—Savu Island—Signs of Europeans—A boat sent ashore to trade—Anchor—Reception by natives—Their Radja—Mynheer Lange—House of Assembly—Native dinner—Obstacles to trading—Mynheer Lange's covetousness—Trading—Dutch policy concerning spices.

27th August. Lay to all night; in the morning a fresh trade and fine clear weather made us hope that our difficulties were drawing to an end. It was now resolved to haul up to the northward in order to make the coast of New Guinea, so as to assure ourselves that we had really got clear of the South Sea, which was accordingly done. At dinner-time we were alarmed afresh by the usual report of a shoal just ahead; it proved, however, to be no more than a band or regular layer of a brownish colour, extending upon the sea, having very much the appearance of a shoal while at a distance. It was formed by innumerable small atoms, each scarcely half a line in length, yet, when looked at under a microscope, consisting of thirty or forty tubes, each hollow and divided throughout the whole length into many cells by small partitions, like the tubes of *Confervæ.* To which of the three kingdoms of nature they belong I am totally ignorant. I only guess that they are of a vege-table nature, because on burning them I could perceive no animal smell. We have before this during this voyage seen them several times on the coast of Brazil and of New

Holland, but never that I recollect at any considerable distance from the land. In the evening a small bird of the noddy (*Sterna*) kind hovered about the ship, and at night settled on the rigging, where it was taken, and proved exactly the same bird as Dampier has described, and given a rude figure of, under the name of a noddy from New Holland (see his *Voyages*, vol. iii. p. 98, table of birds, Fig. 5).

28th. Still standing to the northward, the water shoaling regularly; vast quantities of the little substances mentioned yesterday floating upon the water in large lines, a mile or more long, and fifty or a hundred yards wide, all swimming either immediately upon the surface of the water, or not many inches below it. The seamen, who were now convinced that it was not as they had thought the spawn of fish, began to call it sea-sawdust, a name certainly not ill adapted to its appearance. One of them, a Portuguese, who came on board the ship at Rio de Janeiro, told me that at St. Salvador on the coast of Brazil, where the Portuguese have a whale fishery, he had often seen vast quantities of it taken out of the stomachs of whales or grampuses.

29th. During the whole night our soundings were very irregular, but never less than seven fathoms, and never so shoal for any time. In the morning the land[1] was seen from the deck. It was uncommonly low, but very thickly covered with wood. At eight o'clock it was not more than two leagues from us, but the water had gradually shoaled since morn to five fathoms, and was at this time as muddy as the river Thames, so that it was not thought prudent to go any nearer at present. We accordingly stood along shore, seeing fires and large groves of cocoanut trees, in the neighbourhood of which we supposed the Indian villages to be situated.

1st September. Distant as the land was, a very fragrant smell came off from it early in the morning, with the little breeze that blew right off shore. It resembled much the smell of gum Benjamin. As the sun gathered power it died

[1] Coast of New Guinea, near Cape Valsche.

away, and was no longer perceived. All the latter part of the day we had calms or light winds all round the compass, the weather at the same time being most intolerably hot.

3rd. We stood right in-shore, and at half-past eight had less than three fathoms water five or six miles from the shore. The captain, Dr. Solander, and I, with the boat's crew and my servants, consisting in all of twelve men, well armed, rowed directly towards the shore, but could not get nearer than about 200 yards on account of the shallowness of the water. We quickly, however, got out of the boat, and waded ashore, leaving two men to take care of her. We had no sooner landed than we saw the print of naked feet upon the mud below high-water mark, which convinced us that the Indians were not far off, though we had yet seen no signs of any. The nature of the country made it necessary for us to be very much upon our guard. The close, thick wood came down to within less than 100 yards of the water, and so near therefore might the Indians come without our seeing them, and should they by numbers overpower us, a retreat to the boat would be impossible, as she was so far from the shore. We proceeded, therefore, with much caution, looking carefully about us, the doctor and I looking for plants at the edge of the wood, and the rest walking along the beach.

About 200 yards from our landing, we came to a grove of cocoanut trees of very small growth, but well hung with fruit, standing upon the banks of a small brook of brackish water. Near them was a small shed, hardly half covered with cocoanut leaves, in and about which were numberless cocoanut shells, some quite fresh. We stayed under these trees some time, admiring and wishing for the fruit, but as none of us could climb, it was impossible to get even one, so we left them, and proceeded in search of anything else which might occur. We soon found plantains and a single bread-fruit tree, but neither of these had any fruit upon them, so we proceeded, and had got about a quarter of a mile from the boat when three Indians suddenly rushed out of the woods, with a hideous shout, about a hundred yards beyond us, and running towards us, the foremost threw something out of his hand which flew on one side of him and burned exactly like gunpowder. The other two immediately threw two darts at us, on which we fired. Most of our guns were loaded with small shot, which, at the distance they were from us, I suppose they hardly felt, for they moved not at all, but immediately threw a third dart, on which we loaded and fired again. Our balls, I suppose, this time fell near them, but none of them were materially hurt, as they ran away with great alacrity. From this specimen of the people we immediately concluded that nothing was to be got here but by force, which would, of course, be attended with the destruction of many of these poor people, whose territories we certainly had no right to invade, either as discoverers or people in real want of provisions. We therefore resolved to go into our boat and leave this coast to some after-comer who might have either more time or better opportunities of gaining the friendship of its inhabitants. Before we had got abreast of her, however, we saw the two people in her make signals to us that more Indians were coming along shore, and before we had got into the water we saw them come round a point about 500 yards from us. They had probably met the three who first attacked us, for on seeing us they halted and seemed to wait till the main body should come up, nor did they come nearer us while we waded to the boat. When we were embarked and afloat, we rowed towards them and fired some muskets over their heads into the trees, on which they walked gradually off, continuing to throw abundance of their fires, whatever they might be designed for. We guessed their numbers to be about 100. After we had watched them and their behaviour as long as we chose, we returned to the ship, where our friends had suffered much anxiety for our sakes, imagining that the fires thrown by the Indians were real muskets, so much did they resemble the fire and smoke made by the firing of one. These " fire-arms " were also seen by Torres (see p. li.)

The place where we landed we judged to be near *Cabo de*

la Colta de Santa Bonaventura, as it is called in the French
charts, about nine or ten leagues to the southward of *Keer
Weer*.[1] We were not ashore altogether more than two hours,
so cannot be expected to have made many observations.

The soil had all the appearance of the highest fertility,
being covered with a prodigious quantity of trees, which
seemed to thrive luxuriantly. Notwithstanding this, the
cocoanut trees bore very small fruit, and the plantains did
not seem very thriving. The only bread-fruit tree that we
saw was, however, very large and healthy. There was very
little variety of plants; we saw only twenty-three species,
every one of which was known to us, unless two may prove
upon comparison to be different from any of the many
species of *Cyperus* we have still undetermined from New
Holland. Had we had axes to cut down the trees, or
could we have ventured into the woods, we should doubtless
have found more, but we had only an opportunity of examining the beach and edge of the wood. I am of opinion, however, that the country does not abound in variety of species,
as I have been in no one before where I could not, on a
good soil, have gathered many more with the same time and
opportunity.

The people, as well as we could judge, were nearly of the
same colour as the New Hollanders; some thought rather
lighter. They were certainly stark naked. The arms which
they used against us were very light, ill-made darts of
bamboo cane, pointed with hard wood, in which were many
barbs. They perhaps shot them with bows, but I am of
opinion that they threw them with a stick something in the
manner of the New Hollanders. They came about sixty
yards beyond us, but not in a point-blank direction.
Besides these, many among them, maybe a fifth part of the
whole, had in their hands a short piece of stick, perhaps a
hollow cane, which they swing sideways from them, and
immediately fire flew from it perfectly resembling the flash
and smoke of a musket, and of no longer duration. For

---

[1] Cook and Banks landed "on a part of the coast scarcely known to this
day."—Wharton's *Cook*.

what purpose that was done is far beyond my guessing. They had with them several dogs, who ran after them in the same manner as ours do in Europe.

The house or shed that we saw was very mean and poor. It consisted of four stakes driven into the ground, two being longer than the others. Over these cocoanut leaves were loosely laid; not half enough to cover it. By the cutting of these stakes, as well as of the arrows or darts which they threw at us, we concluded that they had no iron.

As soon as ever the boat was hoisted in we made sail, and steered away from this land, to the no small satisfaction of, I believe, three-fourths of our company. The sick became well and the melancholy looked gay. The greater part of them were now pretty far gone with the longing for home, which the physicians have gone so far as to esteem a disease under the name of nostalgia. Indeed I can find hardly anybody in the ship clear of its effects but the captain, Dr. Solander, and myself, and we three have ample constant employment for our minds, which I believe to be the best, if not the only remedy for it.

4th. The altered countenances of our common people were still more perceptible than they were yesterday. Two-thirds allowance had, I believe, made the chief difference with them, for our provisions were now so much wasted by keeping, that that allowance was little more than was necessary to keep life and soul together.

12th. As soon as the light was pretty clear, land was seen five or six leagues off, and we stood in for it. It was very high, rising in gradual slopes from the hills, which were in great measure covered with thick woods. Among them, however, we could distinguish bare spots of large extent, which looked as if made by art. Many fires were also seen on all parts of the hills, some very high up. At nightfall we were within a mile and a half off the beach, just abreast of a little inlet. The country seemed to answer very well to the description which Dampier has given of Timor, the land close to the beach being covered with high tapering trees, which he likens to pines (*Casuarina*), behind which was a great appearance of salt-water creeks and many mangroves. In parts, however, were many cocoanut trees. Close down to the beach the flat land seemed to extend in some places two or three miles before the rise of the first hill. We saw no appearance of plantations or houses near the sea, but the land looked most fertile, and from the many fires we saw in different parts we could not help having a good opinion of its population.

14*th*. Infinite albecores and bonitos were about the ship, attended, as they always are when near land, by some species of *Sterna*. These were Dampier's New Holland noddies, which flew in large flocks, hovering over the shoals of fish. Many man-of-war birds also attended, and entertained us by very frequently stooping at albecores so large that twenty times their strength could not have lifted them, had they been dexterous enough to seize them, which they never once effected.

15*th*. About a mile up from the beach began the plantations, and houses almost innumerable standing under the shade of large groves of palms, appearing like the fan-palm (*Borassus*). The plantations, which were in general enclosed with some kind of fence, reached almost to the top of the hills, but near the beach were no certain marks of habitations seen. But what surprised us most was that, notwithstanding all these indisputable marks of a populous country, we saw neither people nor any kind of cattle stirring all the day, though our glasses were almost continually employed.

16*th*. Soon after breakfast the small island of Rotte was in sight, and a little later the opening appeared plainly, which at last convinced our old unbelievers that the island we had so long been off was really Timor. Soon after dinner we passed the straits. Rotte was not mountainous or high like Timor, but consisted of hills and vales. On the east end of it some of our people saw houses, but I did not. The north side had many sandy beaches, near which grew some of the fan-palms, but the greater part was covered with a kind of bushy tree which had few or no leaves. The straits between Timor and the island called by Dampier *Anabao* we plainly saw; they appeared narrow. Anabao itself looked much like Timor, but was not quite so high. We saw on it no signs of cultivation, but as it was misty, and we were well on the other side of the straits, which we judged to be five leagues across, we saw it but very indifferently.

About ten o'clock a phenomenon appeared in the heavens, in many things resembling the aurora borealis, but differing materially in others. It consisted of a dull reddish light, reaching in height about twenty degrees above the horizon. Its extent varied much at different times, but was never less than eight or ten points of the compass. Through and out of this passed rays of a brighter-coloured light, tending directly upwards. These appeared and vanished nearly in the same time as those of the aurora borealis, but were entirely without the trembling or vibratory motion observed in that phenomenon. The body of it bore from the ship S.S.E. It lasted as bright as ever till nearly midnight, when I went down to sleep, and how much longer I cannot tell.

17*th.* In the morning an island [1] was in sight, very imperfectly, if at all, laid down in the charts. By ten we were very near the east end of it. It was not high, but composed of gently sloping hills and vales almost entirely cleared and covered with innumerable palm trees. Near the beach were many houses, but no people were seen stirring. Soon after we passed the N.E. point, we saw on the beach a large flock of sheep, but still no people. The north side of the isle appeared scarcely at all cultivated, but, like that of Rotte, was covered with thick brushwood, almost or quite destitute of leaves. Among these, as we passed, we saw numerous flocks of sheep, but no houses or plantations. At last, however, one was discovered in a grove of cocoanut trees, and it was resolved to send a boat in charge of a lieutenant to attempt to establish a commerce with people who seemed so well able to supply our many necessities. We saw on the hills two men on horseback, who seemed to ride for their amusement, looking often at the ship, a circumstance which

---

[1] Savu Island, belonging to the Dutch.

made us at once conclude that there were Europeans among
the islanders, by whom we should be received at least more
politely than we were used to be by uncivilised Indians.

After a very short stay the lieutenant returned, bringing
word that he had seen Indians, in all respects, as colour,
dress, etc., much resembling the Malays; that they very
civilly invited him ashore, and conversed with him by signs,
but neither party could understand the other. They were
totally unarmed, except for the knives which they wore in
their girdles, and had with them a jackass, a sure sign that
Europeans had been among them.

It was resolved to go to the lee side of the island in hopes
there to find anchoring ground; in the meanwhile, however,
the boat with some truck was sent ashore at the cocoanut
grove, in hopes of purchasing some trifling refreshment for
the sick, in case we should be disappointed later on.   Dr.
Solander went in it.   Before it reached the shore we saw
two fresh horsemen, one of whom had on a complete European
dress, blue coat, white waistcoat, and laced hat; these as the
boat lay ashore, seemed to take little notice of her, but only
sauntered about, looking much at the ship.   Many more
horsemen, however, and still more footmen gathered round
our people, and we had the satisfaction of seeing several
cocoanuts brought into the boat, a sure sign that peace and
plenty reigned ashore.

After a stay of an hour and a half the boat made a
signal of having had intelligence of a harbour to leeward,
and we in consequence bore away for it; the boat following
soon came on board and told us that the people had behaved
in an uncommonly civil manner, that they had seen some of
their principal people, who were dressed in fine linen, and
had chains of gold round their necks, that they had not been
able to trade, the owner of the cocoanut trees not being
there, but had got about two dozen cocoanuts given as a
present by these principal people who accepted linen in
return, and made them understand by drawing a map upon
the sand, that on the lee side of the island was a bay in
which we might anchor near a town and buy sheep, hogs,

fruit, fowls, etc. They talked much of the Portuguese and of Larntuca on the Island of Ende,[1] from which circumstance it was probable that the Portuguese were somewhere on the island, though none of the natives could speak more than a word or two of the language. Our conclusion was strengthened as one of the Indians, in speaking of the town, made a sign of something we should see there by crossing his fingers, which a Portuguese, who was in the boat, immediately interpreted into a cross, a supposition which appeared very probable. Just before they put off the man in an European dress came towards them, but the officer in the boat, not having his commission about him, thought proper to put off immediately without staying to speak to him, or know what countryman he was.

We sailed along shore, and after having passed a point of land found a bay sheltered from the trade wind, in which we soon discovered a large Indian town or village, on which we stood in, hoisting a Jack. To our no small surprise Dutch colours were hoisted in the town, and three guns fired ; we, however, proceeded, and just at dark got soundings, and anchored about one and a half miles from the shore.

18th. In the morning the boat with the second lieutenant went ashore and was received by a guard of twenty or thirty Indians armed with muskets, who conducted them to the town, about a mile in the country, marching without any order or regularity, and carrying away with them the Dutch colours, which had been hoisted upon the beach opposite to where the ship lay. Here he was introduced to the Radja or Indian king, whom he told through a Portuguese interpreter that we were an English man-of-war, which had been long at sea and had many sick on board, for whom we wanted to purchase such refreshments as the island provided. He answered that he was willing to supply us with everything that we should want, but being in alliance with the Dutch East India Company, he was not allowed to trade with any other people without their consent, which, however, he would immediately apply for to a Dutchman belonging to

---

[1] Now better known as Flores.

that company, who was the only white man residing upon
that island. A letter was accordingly despatched immediately, and after some hours' waiting, answered by the man
in person, who assured us with many civilities that we
were at liberty to buy of the natives whatever we pleased.
He, as well as the king and several of his attendants, expressed a desire of coming on board, provided, however, that
some of our people might stay on shore; on which two were
left.

About two o'clock they arrived; our dinners were ready,
and they soon agreed to dine with us. On sitting down,
however, the king excused himself, saying that he did
not imagine that we who were white men would suffer him
who was black to sit down in our company. A compliment,
however, removed his scruples, and he and his prime
minister sat down and ate sparingly. During all dinner-
time we received many professions of friendship from both
the king and the European, who was a native of Saxony, by
name Johan Christopher Lange. Mutton was our fare: the
king expressed a desire to have an English sheep, and as we
had one left it was presented to him. Mynheer Lange then
hinted that a spying-glass would be acceptable, and was immediately presented with one. We were told that the
island abounded in buffaloes, sheep, hogs, and fowls, all
which should be next day driven down to the beach, and we
might buy any quantity of them. This agreeable intelligence put us all into high spirits, and the liquor went about
fully as much as Mynheer Lange or the Indians could bear.
They, however, expressed a desire of going away before they
were quite drunk. They were received upon deck, as they
had been when they came on board, by the marines under
arms. The king wished to see them exercise, which they
accordingly did, and fired three rounds much to his Majesty's
satisfaction, who expressed great surprise, particularly at
their so quickly cocking their guns. Dr. Solander and I
went ashore in the boat with them: as soon as we put off
they saluted the ship with three cheers, which the ship
answered with five guns.

We landed and walked up to the town, which consisted of a good many houses, some tolerably large, each being a roof of thatch supported by pillars three or four feet from the ground, and covering a boarded floor. Before we had been long there it began to grow dark, and we returned on board, having only just tasted their palm wine, which had a very sweet taste, and suited all our palates very well, giving us hopes at the same time that it might be serviceable to our sick, as, being the fresh and unfermented juice of the tree, it promised antiscorbutic virtues.

19*th*. We went ashore, and proceeded immediately to the house of assembly, a large house which we had yesterday mistaken for the king's palace; this, as well as two or three more in the town, or *nigrie*, as the Indians call it, have been built by the Dutch East India Company. They are distinguished from the rest by two pieces of wood, one at each end of the ridge of the house, resembling cows' horns; undoubtedly the thing designed by the Indian, who on the 17th made a sign of the mark by which we were to know the town by crossing his fingers, and which our Catholic Portuguese interpreted into a cross, making us believe that the settlement was originally Portuguese. In this house of assembly we met Mynheer Lange, and the Radja, *Madocho Lomi Djara*, attended by many of the principal people. We told them that we had in the boat an assortment of what few goods we had to truck with, and desired leave to bring them ashore, which was immediately granted, and orders given accordingly. We then attempted to settle the price of buffaloes, sheep, hogs, etc., which were to be paid in money, but here Mynheer Lange left us, and told us that we must settle that with the natives, who would bring down large quantities to the beach. By this time the morning was pretty far advanced, and we, resolving not to go on board, and eat salt meat, when such a profusion of flesh was continually talked of, petitioned his Majesty that we might have liberty to purchase a small hog, some rice, etc., and employ his subjects to cook them for dinner. He answered that if we could eat victuals dressed by his subjects, which he could hardly suppose, he would do himself the honour of entertaining us ; we expressed our gratitude, and sent immediately on board for liquors.

About five o'clock dinner was ready, consisting of thirty-six dishes, or rather baskets, containing alternately rice and boiled pork, and three earthenware bowls of soup, which was the broth in which the pork had been boiled. These were ranged on the floor, and mats laid round for us to sit upon. We were now conducted by turns to a hole in the floor, near which stood a man with a basket of water in his hand : here we washed our hands, and then ranged ourselves in order round the victuals, waiting for the king to sit down. We were told, however, that the custom of the country was that the entertainer never sits down to meat with his guests, but that if we suspected the victuals to be poisoned, he would willingly do it. We suspected nothing, and therefore desired that all things might go on as usual. We ate with good appetites, the Prime Minister and Mynheer Lange partaking with us. Our wine passed briskly about, the Radja alone refusing to drink with us, saying that it was wrong for the master of the feast to be in liquor. The pork was excellent, the rice as good, the broth not bad, but the spoons, which were made of leaves, were so small that few of us had patience to eat it. Every one made a hearty dinner, and as soon as we had done, removed, as it seems the custom was, to let the servants and seamen take our places. These could not despatch all, but when the women came to take away, they forced them to take away with them all the pork that was left.

Before dinner Mynheer Lange mentioned to us a letter which he had in the morning received from the Governor of Timor : the particulars of it were now discussed. It acquainted him that a ship had been seen off that island, and had steered from thence towards that which we were now upon. In case such ship was to touch there in any distress, she was to be supplied with what she wanted, but was not to be allowed to make any longer stay than was necessary, and was particularly required not to make any large presents to the inferior people, or to leave any with the principal ones to be distributed among them after she was gone. This we were told did not at all extend to the beads or small pieces of cloth which we gave the natives in return for their small civilities, as bringing us palm wine, etc. Some of our gentlemen were of opinion that the whole of this letter was an imposition, but whether it was or not I shall not take upon myself to determine.

In the evening we had intelligence from our trading place that no buffaloes or hogs had been brought down; but only a few sheep, which were taken away before our people, who had sent for money, could procure it. Some few fowls, however, were bought, and a large quantity of a kind of syrup made from the juice of the palm tree, which, though infinitely superior to molasses or treacle, sold at a very small price. We complained to Mynheer Lange: he said that as we had not ourselves been down upon the beach, the natives were afraid to take money from any one else, lest it should be false. On this, the captain went immediately down, but could see no cattle: while he was gone, Mr. Lange complained that our people had not yet offered gold for anything: this he said the islanders were displeased at, as they had expected to have had gold for their stock.

20th. In the morning early the captain went ashore himself to purchase buffaloes: he was shown two, one of which they valued at five guineas, the other a musket: he offered three guineas for the one, and sent for a musket to give for the other. The money was flatly refused, and before the musket could be brought off, Dr. Solander, who had been up in the town in order to speak to Mr. Lange, returned, followed by eighty spearmen and twenty musketeers sent by the king, to tell us that this day and no more would be allowed us to trade, after which we must be gone. This was the message that Dr. Solander had from the Radja by Mr. Lange's interpretation, but a Portuguese Indian who came from Timor, probably next in command to Mr. Lange, carried it much further, telling us that we might stay ashore till night if we pleased, but none of the Indians would be

allowed to trade with us, after which he began to drive
away those who had brought hens, syrup, etc.   To remedy
this an old sword which lay in the boat was given to the
Prime Minister, as I have called him, *Mannudjame*, who in
an instant restored order, and severely chid the officer of the
guard, an old Portuguese Indian, for having gone beyond
his orders.   Trade now was as brisk as ever; fowls and
syrup were bought cheap, and in vast plenty.   The state
of the case now appeared plain: Mr. Lange was to have a
share of what the buffaloes were sold for, and that was to
be paid in money.   The captain, therefore, though sore
against his will, resolved to pay five guineas apiece for one
or two buffaloes, and try to buy the rest for muskets.   Accordingly, no sooner had he hinted his mind to the Portuguese Indian, than a buffalo, but a very small one, was
brought down, and five guineas given for it: two larger ones
followed immediately, for one of which a musket, and for
the other five guineas was given.   There was now no more
occasion for money, we picked them just as we chose for a
musket apiece.   We bought nine, as many as we thought
would last us to Batavia, especially as we had little or no
victuals, but so ill were we provided with cords that three
of the nine broke from us; two of these the Indians recovered, but the third got quite off, though our people,
assisted by the Indians, followed it for three hours.

In the evening Mr. Lange came down to the beach,
softened by the money which, no doubt, he had received,
and took frequent occasions of letting us know that if we
pleased we might come ashore the next day.   Our business
was, however, quite done, so to fulfil a promise which we
had made, he was presented with a small cag of beer, and
we took our leave as good friends as possible.

I have been very diffuse and particular in mentioning
every trifling circumstance which occurred in this transaction, as this may perhaps be the only opportunity I shall
ever have of visiting an island of great consequence to the
Dutch, and scarcely known to any other Europeans, even
by name.   I can find it in only one of the draughts, and

that an old one printed by Mount and Page, the Lord
knows when, which has it by the name of Sau, but con-
founds it with Sandel Bosch, which is laid down quite
wrong. Rumphius mentions an island by the name of
Saow, and says it is that which is called by the Dutch
Sandel Bosch, but no chart that I have seen lays either that,
Timor, Rotte, or indeed any island that we have seen hereabouts, in anything near its right place.

While we were here an accident happened by the im-
prudence of Mr. Parkinson, my draughtsman, which might
alone have altered our intended and at first promised reception very much; indeed, I am of opinion that it did. He,
desirous of knowing whether or not this island produced
spices, carried ashore with him nutmegs, cloves, etc., and
questioned the inhabitants about them without the least
precaution, so that it immediately came to Mr. Lange's ears.
He complained to the doctor that our people were too inquisitive, particularly, says he, " in regard to spices, concerning which they can have no reason to wish for any information unless you are come for very different purposes than
those you pretend." The doctor, not well versed in the
German language, in which they conversed, immediately
conceived that Mr. Lange meant only some questions which
he himself had asked concerning the cinnamon; nor did we
ever know the contrary till the day after we had left the
place, when Mr. Parkinson boasted of the information we
had obtained of these people certainly having a knowledge
of the spices, as they had in their language names for them.

CHAPTER XV

DESCRIPTION OF SAVU

I SHALL now proceed to give such an account of the island as I could get together during our stay, which, short as it was, was so taken up with procuring refreshments, in which occupation every one was obliged to exert himself, that very little, I confess, is from my own observation. Almost everything is gathered from the conversation of Mr. Lange, who at first and at the end was very free and open, and, I am inclined to believe, did not deceive us in what he told us, how much soever he might conceal; except, perhaps, in the strength and warlike disposition of the islanders, which account seems to contradict itself, as one can hardly imagine these people to be of a warlike disposition who have continued in peace time out of mind. As for the other islands in this neighbourhood, his information was all we had to go upon. I would not, however, neglect to set it down, though in general it was of little more consequence than to confirm the policy of the Dutch in confining their spices to particular isles, which, being full of them, cannot supply themselves with provisions.

The little island of Savu, which, trifling as it is, appears to me to be of no small consequence to the Dutch East India Company, is situate in lat. 10° 35′ S. and long. 122° 30′ E.[1] from the meridian of Greenwich : its length and breadth are nearly the same, viz. about 6 German or 24 English miles. The whole is divided into five principalities, *nigries* as they are called by the Indians, *Laai, Seba, Regeeua, Timo,* and *Massara,* each governed by its respective radja or king. It has three harbours, all good; the best is *Timo,* situate somewhere round the S.E. point of the isle; the next, *Seba,* where we anchored, situate round the N.W. point: of the third we learnt neither the name nor situation, only guess it to be somewhere on the south side. Off the west end of the island is another called *Pulo,* with an additional name, which in the hurry of business was forgotten, and never again asked for.

The appearance of the island, especially on the windward side where we first made it, was allowed by us all to equal in beauty, if not excel, anything we had seen, even parched up as it was by a drought, which, Mr. Lange informed us, had continued for seven months without a drop of rain, the last rainy season having entirely failed them. Verdure, indeed, there was at this time no sign of, but the gentle sloping of the hills, which were cleared quite to the top, and planted in every part with thick groves of the fan-palm, besides woods almost of cocoanut trees, arecas which grew near the seaside, filled the eye so completely that it hardly looked for or missed the verdure of the earth, a circumstance seldom seen in any perfection so near the line. How beautiful it must appear when covered with its springing crops of maize, millet, indigo, etc., which cover almost every foot of ground in the cultivated parts of the island, imagination can hardly conceive. The verdure of Europe, set off by those stately pillars of India, palms—I mean especially the fan-palm, which for straightness and proportion, both of the stem itself and of the head to the stem, far excels all the

---

[1] The latitude and longitude were left blank: they have been filled in from Cook's Journal.

palms that I have seen—requires a poetical imagination to describe, and a mind not unacquainted with such sights to conceive.

The productions of this island are buffaloes, sheep, hogs, fowls, horses, asses, maize, guinea corn, rice, calevances, limes, oranges, mangroves, plantains, water-melons, tamarinds, sweet sops (*Annona*), blimbi (*Averrhoa bilimbi*), besides cocoanuts and fan-palms, which last are in sufficient quantity, should all other crops fail, to support the whole island, people, stock, and all, who have at times been obliged to live upon its sugar, syrup, and wines for some months. We saw also a small quantity of European garden herbs, as celery, marjoram, fennel, and garlic, and one single sugar-cane. Besides these necessaries, it has for the supply of luxury betel and areca, tobacco, cotton, indigo, and a little cinnamon, only planted for curiosity, said Mr. Lange ; indeed, I almost doubt whether or not it was genuine cinnamon, as the Dutch have been always so careful not to trust any spices out of their proper islands. Besides these were probably other things which we had not an opportunity of seeing, and which Mr. Lange forgot or did not choose to mention.

All their produce is in amazing abundance, so we judged at least from the plantations we saw, though this year every crop had failed for want of rain. Most of them are well known to Europeans: I shall, however, spend a little ink in describing such only as are not, or as differ at all in appearance from those commonly known. To begin then with buffaloes, of which they have got good store ; these beasts differ from our cattle in Europe in their ears, which are considerably larger, in their skins, which are almost without hair, and in their horns, which, instead of bending forwards as ours do, bend directly backwards, and also in their total want of dewlaps. We saw some of these as big as well-sized European oxen, and some there must be much larger ; so at least I was led to believe by a pair of horns which I measured : they were from tip to tip 3 feet $9\frac{1}{2}$ inches, across their widest diameter 4 feet $1\frac{1}{2}$ inch ; the whole sweep of their semicircle in front 7 feet 6½ inches. One caution is, however, exceedingly necessary in buying these beasts, which is that one of them of any given size does not weigh half as much as an ox of the same size in England; in this we, who were ignorant of the fact, were very much deceived. The larger animals which we guessed to be 400 lbs. did not weigh more than 250, and the smaller which we guessed to be 250 not more than 160; this vast difference proceeded first from a total want of fat, of which there was not the least sign, but more especially from the thinness of the flanks, and thin pieces which were literally nothing but skin and bone. Their flesh, notwithstanding this, was not bad; it was well tasted and full of gravy : not that I can put it on a footing with the leanest beef in England, yet I should suppose it better than a lean ox would be in this burnt-up climate.

Mr. Lange told us that when the Portuguese first came to this island there were horses upon it, an opinion from which I confess I rather apostatise; but, to waive the dispute, horses are now very plentiful. They are small, generally eleven or twelve hands high, but very brisk and nimble, especially in pacing, which is their common step. The inhabitants appear to be tolerable horsemen, riding always without a saddle, and generally with only a halter instead of a bridle. This is not, however, the only benefit that these islanders receive from them, for they use them as food, and prefer their flesh to that of buffaloes and every other sort but swine's flesh, which holds the highest rank in their opinion.

Their sheep are of the kind that I have seen in England under the name of Bengal sheep; they differ from ours in having hair instead of wool, in their ears being very large and flapping down, their horns almost straight, and in their noses, which are much more arched than those of our European kind. These sheep are, I believe, very frequently called *cabritos*, from their resemblance to goats, which, though I cannot say it appeared to me at all striking, yet had such an effect on the whole ship's company, officers and seamen, that not one would believe them to be sheep till they heard their voices, which are precisely the same as those of European ones.   Their flesh was like that of the buffaloes, lean and void of flavour, to me the worst mutton I have ever eaten.

Their fowls are chiefly of the game breed and large; but the eggs are the smallest I have ever seen.

Besides these animals there are great plenty of dogs, some cats and rats, and a few pigeons, of which I saw three or four pair.   Nor are any of these animals exempted from furnishing their part towards the support of polyphagous man, except the rats, which alone they do not eat.

Fish appeared to us to be scarce, indeed it was but little valued by these islanders, none but the very inferior people ever eating it, and these only at the time when their duties or business required them to be down upon the sea beach. In this case every man was provided with a light casting-net, which was girt round him and served as part of his dress; with this he took any small fish which might happen to come in his way.   Turtles are scarce; they are esteemed a good food, but are very seldom taken.

Of the vegetables most are well known.   The sweet sop is a pleasant fruit well known to the West Indians.   Blimbi alone is not mentioned by any voyage-writer I have met with : it is a small oval fruit, thickest in the middle and tapering a little to each end, three or four inches in length, and scarcely as large as a man's finger; the outside is covered with very thin skin of a light green colour, and in the inside are a few seeds disposed in the form of a star; its flavour is a light, but very clean and pleasant acid.   It cannot be eaten raw, but is said to be excellent in pickles; we stewed it and made sour sauce to our stews and bouilli, which was very grateful to the taste, and doubtless possessed no small share of anti-scorbutic virtues.   But what seems to be the genuine natural production of the island, and which they have in the greatest abundance and take the most care of, is the fan-palm or toddy-tree (*Borassus flabellifer*).   Large groves of these trees are to be seen in all parts of the island, under which other crops, as maize, indigo, etc., are planted, so that in reality they take up no room, though they yield the treble advantage of fruit, liquor, and sugar, all, but especially the two last, in great profusion. The leaves also serve to thatch their houses, and to make baskets, umbrellas (or rather small conical bonnets), caps, tobacco pipes, etc. etc. The fruit, which is least esteemed, is also in the least plenty; it is a nut about as big as a child's head, covered like a cocoanut with a fibrous coat under which are three kernels which must be eaten before they are ripe, otherwise they become too hard to chew. In their proper state they a good deal resemble in taste the kernel of an unripe cocoanut, and like them probably afford but a watery nutriment. The excellence of the palm wine or toddy which is drawn from this tree makes, however, ample amends for the poorness of its fruit. It is got by cutting the buds, which should produce flowers, soon after their appearance, and tying under them a small basket made of the leaves of the same tree; into this the liquor drips, and must be collected by people who climb the trees for that purpose every morning and evening. This is the common drink of every one upon the island, and a very pleasant one it was so to us, even at first, only rather too sweet; its anti-scorbutic virtues, as the fresh unfermented juice of a tree, cannot be doubted.

Notwithstanding that this liquor is the common drink of both rich and poor, who in the morning and evening drink nothing else, a much larger quantity is drawn off daily than is sufficient for that use. Of this they make a syrup and a coarse sugar, both which are far more agreeable to the taste than they appear to the sight. The liquor is called in the language of the island *dua* or *duac*, the syrup and sugar by one and the same name, *gula*; it is exactly the same as the *jagara* sugar on the continent of India, and prepared by simply boiling down the liquor in earthenware pots until it is sufficiently thick. In appearance it exactly resembles molasses or treacle, only it is considerably thicker; in taste, however, it much excels it, having, instead of the abominable twang which treacle leaves in the mouth, only a little burnt flavour, which was very agreeable to our palates. The sugar is reddish brown, but more clear tasted than any un-refined cane-sugar, resembling mostly brown sugar candy. The syrup seemed to be very wholesome, for though many of our people ate enormous quantities of it, it hurt nobody.

Firewood is very scarce here; to remedy, therefore, that inconvenience as much as possible, they make use of a con-trivance which is not unknown in Europe, though seldom practised but in camps. It is a burrow or pipe dug in the ground as long as convenient, generally about two yards, and open at each end; the one opening of this, into which they put the fire, is large; the other, which serves only to cause a draught, is much smaller. Immediately over this pipe circular holes are dug which reach quite down into it: in these the earthen pots are set (about three to such a fire); they are large in the middle and taper towards the bottom, by which means the fire acts upon a large part of their surface. It is really marvellous to see with how small a quantity of fire they will keep these pots boiling, each of which contains eight or ten gallons; a palm leaf or a dry stalk now and then is sufficient; indeed, it seemed in that part of the island, at least, where we were, that the palms alone supplied sufficient fuel, not only for boiling the sugar, but for dressing all their victuals, besides those which are cooked by this con-trivance. How many parts of England are there where this contrivance would be of material assistance to not only the poor, but the better sort of people, who daily complain of the dearness of fuel, a charge which this contrivance alone would doubtless diminish by at least one-third. But it is well known how averse the good people of England, especially of that class that may be supposed to be not above want, are to adopt any new custom which savours of parsimony. I have been told that this very method was proposed in the *Gentle-man's Magazine* many years ago, but have not the book on board. Frézier, in his voyage to the South Sea, describes a contrivance of the Peruvian Indians upon the same principles, plate 31, p. 273, but his drawing and plan are difficult to understand, if not actually very faulty, and his description is

nothing; the drawing may serve, however, to give an idea to
a man who has never seen a thing of the kind.

The syrup or *gula* which they make in this manner is so
nourishing that Mr. Lange told us that it alone fed and
fattened their hogs, dogs, and fowls, and that men themselves
could and had sometimes lived upon it alone for a long time,
when by bad seasons, or their destructive feasts, which I
shall mention by and by, they have been deprived of all other
nourishment. We saw some of the swine, whose uncommon
fatness surprised us much, which very beasts we saw one
evening served with their suppers, consisting of nothing but
the outside husks of rice and this syrup dissolved in water.
This they told us was their constant and only food; how far
it may be found consonant to truth that sugar alone should
have such nourishing qualities I shall leave to others to
determine; I have only accounts, not experience, to favour
that opinion.

The people of this island are rather under than over the
middling size, the women especially, most of whom are remarkably short and generally squat built. Their colour is well
tinged with brown, and in all ranks and conditions nearly the
same, in which particular they differ much from the inhabitants of the South Sea Isles, where the better sort of people
are almost universally whiter than their inferiors. The men
are rather well made, and seem to be active and nimble;
among them we observed a greater variety of features than
usual. The women on the other hand are far from handsome,
and have a kind of sameness of features among them which
might well account for the chastity of the men, for which
virtue this island is said to be remarkable. The hair of both
sexes is universally black and lank; the men wear it long,
and fastened upon the tops of their heads with a comb; the
women have theirs also long, and tied behind into a kind of
not very becoming club.

Both men and women dress in a kind of blue and white
clouded cotton cloth, which they manufacture themselves:
of this two pieces, each about two yards long, serve for a
dress. One of these is worn round the middle; this the

men wear pretty tight, but it makes a kind of loose belt, in which they carry their knives, etc., and often many other things, so that it serves entirely the purpose of pockets. The other piece is tucked into this girdle, and reaching over the shoulders, passes down to the girdle on the other side, so that by opening or folding it they can cover more or less of their bodies as they please.   The arms, legs, and feet of both sexes are consequently bare, as are the heads of the women, which is their chief distinction by which they are at once known from the men, who always wear something wrapped round theirs, which, though small, is of the finest material they can procure; many we saw had silk handkerchiefs, which seemed to be much in fashion.

The distinction of the women's dress, except only the head, consists merely in the manner of wearing their clothes, which are of the same materials and the same quality as the men's.   Their waist-cloths reach down below the knees, and their body-cloths are tied under their arms and over their breasts.   Both sexes eradicate the hair from under their armpits, a custom in these hot climates almost essential to cleanliness ; the men also pluck out their beards, for which purpose the better sort carry always a pair of silver pincers hanging round their necks : some, however, wear a little hair on their upper lips, but they never suffer it to grow long.

Ornaments they have many; some of the better sort wear gold chains round their necks, but these were chiefly made of plated wire of little value ; others had rings which, by their appearance, seemed to have been worn out some generations ago.   One had a silver-headed cane, on the top of which was engraved ᚨᚷ, so that it had probably been a present from the East India Company.   Besides these, beads were worn, chiefly by the men of distinction, round their necks in the form of a solitaire ; others had them round their wrists, etc., but the women had the largest quantity, which they wore round their waists in the form of a girdle, serving to keep up their waist-cloths.   Both sexes universally had their ears bored, but we never saw any ornaments in them,

indeed, we never saw any one man dressed the whole time
we were there in anything more than his ordinary clothes.
Some boys of twelve or fourteen years of age wore circles of
thick brass wire, passed screw-fashion three or four times
round their arms above the elbow : and some men wore
convex rings of ivory, two inches in breadth, and above an
inch in thickness, in the same manner above the joint of the
elbow. These we were told were the sons of Radjas, who
alone had the privilege of wearing these cumbersome badges
of high birth.

Almost all the men had their names traced upon their
arms in indelible characters of black ; the women had a
square ornament of flourished lines on the inner part of each
arm, just under the bend of the elbow ; on inquiring into
the antiquity of this custom, so consonant with that of
tattowing in the South Sea Islands, Mr. Lange told us that
it had been among these people long before the Europeans
came here, but was less used in this than in most islands
in the neighbourhood, in some of which the people marked
circles round their necks, breasts, etc.

Both sexes are continually employed in chewing betel
and areca ; the consequence is that their teeth, as long as
they have any, are dyed of that filthy black colour which
constantly attends the rottenness of a tooth, for it appears
to me that from their first use of this custom, which they
begin very young, their teeth are affected and continue by
gradual degrees to waste away till they are quite worn to
the stumps, which seems to happen before old age. I have
seen men, in appearance between twenty and thirty, whose
fore teeth were almost entirely gone, no two being of the
same length or the same thickness, but every one eaten to
unevenness as iron is by rust. This loss of the teeth is
attributed by all whose writings on the subject I have read,
to the tough and stringy coat of the areca nut, but in my
opinion is much more easily accounted for by the well-
known corrosive quality of the lime, which is a necessary
ingredient in every mouthful, and that too in no very
insignificant quantity. This opinion seems to me to be

almost put out of dispute by the manner in which their
teeth are destroyed; they are not loosened or drawn out as
they would be by the too frequent labour of chewing tough
substances, but melt away and decay as metals in strong
acids; the stumps always remaining firmly adhering to the
jaws, just level with the gums.   Possibly the ill-effects
which sugar is believed by us Europeans to have upon the
teeth may proceed from the same cause, as it is well known
that refined or loaf-sugar contains in it a large quantity of
lime.

To add flavour, I suppose, to the betel and areca, some
use with it a small quantity of tobacco, adding the nauseous
smell of that herb to the not less disagreeable look of the
other, as if they were resolved to make their mouths disgustful to the sense of smell as well as that of sight.
They also smoke, rolling up a small quantity of tobacco in
one end of a palm leaf, about as thick as a quill and six
inches long; of this not above one inch is filled with tobacco,
so that the quantity is very small.   To make amends for
this the women especially often swallow the smoke, which
no doubt increases its effects in no small degree.

Their houses are all built upon one and the same plan,
differing only in size according to the rank and riches of
the proprietors, some being 300 or 400 feet in length, and
others not 20.   They consist of a well-boarded floor, raised
upon posts three or four feet from the ground; over this is
raised a roof shelving like ours in Europe, and supported by
pillars of its own, independent of the floor.   The eaves of
this reach within two feet of the floor, but overhang it by
as much; this arrangement serves to let in air and light,
and makes them very cool and agreeable.   The space within
is generally divided into two by a partition, which takes off
one-third: in front of this partition is a loft, shut up
close on all sides, raised about six feet from the ground, and
occupying the centre of the house.   There are sometimes
one or two small rooms on the sides of the house.   The use
of these different apartments we did not learn, we only were
told that the loft was appropriated to the women.

The shortness of our stay and the few opportunities we had of going among these people, gave us no opportunity of seeing what arts or manufactures they might have among them. That they spin, weave, and dye their cloth we, however, made shift to learn, for though we never saw them practise any of these arts, yet the instruments accidentally fell in our way; first, a machine for clearing cotton of its seeds, which was in miniature much upon the same principles as ours in Europe. It consisted of two cylinders about as thick as a man's thumb, one of which was turned round by a plain winch handle, and that turned the other round by an endless worm at their extremities ; the whole was not above seven inches high and about twice as long. How it answered, I know not, but do know that it had been much worked, and that there were many pieces of cotton hanging on different parts of it, which alone induced me to believe it a real machine, otherwise, from its slightness, I should have taken it for no more than a Dutch toy of the best sort. Their spinning gear I also once saw ; it consisted of a bobbin on which a small quantity of thread was wound, and a kind of distaff filled with cotton, from whence I conjecture that they spin by hand, as our women in Europe did before wheels were introduced, and I am told still do in some parts of Europe where that improvement is not received. Their loom I also saw ; it had this merit over ours, that the web was not stretched on a frame, but only extended by a piece of wood at each end, round one of which the cloth was rolled as the threads were round the other. I had not an opportunity of seeing it used, so cannot at all describe it ; I can say only that it appeared very simple, much more so than ours, and that the shuttle was as long as the breadth of the web, which was about half a yard. From this circumstance, and the unsteadiness of a web fixed to nothing, the work must in all probability go on very slowly. That they dyed their own cloth we first guessed by the indigo which we saw in their plantations, which guess was afterwards confirmed by Mr. Lange. We likewise saw them dye women's girdles of a dirty, reddish colour ; their cloth itself was universally dyed in the yarn with blue, which, being unevenly and irregularly done, gave the cloth a clouding or waving of colour, not inelegant even in our eyes.

One chirurgical operation of theirs Mr. Lange mentioned to us with great praise, and indeed it appears sensible. It is a method of curing wounds, which they do by first washing the wound in water in which tamarinds have been steeped, then plugging it up with a pledget of the fat of fresh pork. In this manner the wound is thoroughly cleansed, and the pledget renewed every day. He told us that by this means they had a very little while ago cured a man in three weeks of a wound from a lance which had pierced his arm and half through his body. This is the only part of their medicinal or chirurgical art which came to our knowledge; indeed, they did not seem to outward appearance to have much occasion for either, but on the contrary appeared healthy, and did not show, by scars of old sores or any scurviness upon their bodies, a tendency to disease. Some, indeed, were pitted with the smallpox, which Mr. Lange told us had been now and then among them; in which case all who were seized by the distemper were carried to lonely places, far from habitations, where they were left to the influence of their distemper, meat only being daily reached to them by the assistance of a long pole.

Their religion, according to the account of Mr. Lange, is a most absurd kind of paganism, every man choosing his own god, and also his mode of worshipping him, in which hardly any two agree, notwithstanding which their morals are most excellent, Mr. Lange declaring to us that he did not believe that during his residence of ten years upon the island a single theft had been committed. Polygamy is by no means permitted, each man being allowed no more than one wife, to whom he is to adhere during life; even the Radja himself has no more.

The Dutch boast that they make many converts to Christianity; Mr. Lange said that there were 600 in the

township of Seba, where we were.   What sort of Christians
they are I cannot say, as they have neither clergymen nor
church among them ; the Company have, however, certainly
been at the expense of printing versions of the New Testa-
ment, catechisms, etc. etc., in this and several other languages,
and actually keep a half-bred Dutchman, whose name is
Frederick Craig, in their service, who is paid by them for
instructing the youth of the island in reading, writing, and
the principles of the Christian religion.   Dr. Solander was
at his house, and saw not only the Testaments and
catechisms before mentioned, but also the copy-books of the
scholars.

The island is divided into five principalities, each of which
has its respective radja or king ; what his power may be we
had no opportunity of learning.   In outward appearance
he had but little recognition shown to him, yet every kind
of business seemed to centre in him and his chief councillor,
so that in reality he seemed to be more regarded in essentials
than in showy useless ceremonies.   The reigning Radja, while
we were there, was called *Madocho Lomi Djara*, he was
about thirty-five, the fattest man we saw upon the whole
island, and the only one upon whose body grew any quantity
of hair, a circumstance very unusual among Indians.   He
appeared of a heavy, dull disposition, and I believe was
governed almost entirely by a very sensible old man called
Mannudjame, who was beloved by the whole principality.
Both these were distinguished from the rest of the natives
by their dress, which was always a night-gown, generally of
coarse chintz ; once, indeed, the Radja received us in form
in one of Black Prince's stuff, which I suppose may be
looked upon as more grave and proper to inspire respect.
If any differences arise between the people, they are settled
by the Radja and his councillors without the least delay or
appeal, and, says Mr. Lange, always with the strictest
justice.   So excellent is the disposition of these people that
if any dispute arise between any two of them, they never,
if it is of consequence, more than barely mention it to
each other, never allowing themselves to reason upon it lest

2 A

heat should beget ill-blood, but refer it immediately to this court.

After the Radja we could hear of no ranks of people but landowners, respectable according to the quantity of their land; and slaves, the property of the former, over whom, however, they have no other power than that of selling them for what they will fetch, when convenient; no man being able to punish his slave without the concurrence and approbation of the Radja. Of these slaves some men have 500, others only two or three; what was their price in general we did not learn, only heard by accident that a very fat hog was of the value of a slave, and often bought and sold at that price. When any great man stirs out he is constantly attended by two or more of these slaves, one of whom carries a sword or hanger, commonly with a silver hilt, and ornamented with large tassels of horse hair; the other carries a bag containing betel, areca, lime, tobacco, etc. In these attendants all their idea of show and grandeur seems to be centred, for we never saw the Radja himself with any more.

The pride of descent, particularly of being sprung from a family which has for many generations been respected, is by no means unknown here; even living in a house which has been for generations well attended is no small honour. It is a consequence of this that few articles, either of use or luxury, bear so high a price as those stones which by having been very much sat upon by men have contracted a bright polish on their uneven surfaces; those who can purchase such stones, or who have them by inheritance from their ancestors, place them round their houses, where they serve as benches for their dependents, I suppose to be still more and more polished.

Every Radja during his lifetime sets up in his capital town, or *nigrie*, a large stone, which serves futurity as a testimony of his reign. In the *nigrie Seba*, where we lay, were thirteen such stones, besides many fragments, the seeming remains of those which had been devoured by time. Many of these were very large, so much so that it would be difficult to conceive how the strength of man alone, unassisted by engines, had been able to transport them to the top of the hill where they now stand, were there not in Europe so many far grander instances of the perseverance as well as the strength of our own forefathers. These stones serve for a very peculiar use ; upon the death of a Radja a general feast is proclaimed throughout his dominions, and in consequence all his subjects meet about the stones. Every living creature that can be caught is now killed, and the feast lasts a longer or shorter number of weeks or months according to the stock of provisions the kingdom happens to be furnished with at the time. The stones serve for tables, on which whole buffaloes are served up. After this madness is over, the whole kingdom is obliged to fast and live upon syrup and water till the next crop ; nor are they able to eat any flesh till some years after, when the few animals which have escaped the general slaughter and been preserved by policy, or which they have acquired from neighbouring kingdoms, have sufficiently increased their species.

The five kingdoms, says Mr. Lange, of which this island consists, have been from time immemorial not only at peace, but in strict alliance with each other ; notwithstanding which they are of a warlike disposition,—constant friends but implacable enemies,—and have always courageously defended themselves against foreign invaders. They are able to raise on a very short notice 7300 men, armed with muskets, lances, spears, and targets : of these the different kingdoms bear their different proportions — *Laai* 2600, *Seba* 2000, *Regeeua* 1500, *Timo* 800, and *Massara* 400. Besides the arms before mentioned, every man is furnished with a large chopping-knife, like a straightened wood-bill, but much heavier, which must be a terrible weapon, if these people should have spirit enough to come to close quarters. Mr. Lange upon another occasion took an opportunity of telling us that they heave their lances with surprising dexterity, being able at the distance of sixty feet to strike a man's heart and pierce him through. How far these dreadful accounts of their martial prowess might be true I dare not take upon myself to determine; all I shall say is that during our stay we saw no signs either of a warlike disposition or such formidable arms. Of spears and targets, indeed, there were about a hundred in the Dutch house, the largest of which spears served to arm the people who came down to intimidate us; but so little did these doughty heroes think of fighting, or indeed keeping up appearances, that instead of a target each was furnished with a cock, some tobacco, or something of that kind, which he took this opportunity of bringing down to sell. Their spears seem all to have been brought to them by Europeans, the refuse of old armouries, no two being anything near the same length, varying in that particular from six feet to sixteen. As for their lances, not one of us saw one. Their muskets, though clean on the outside, were honeycombed with rust on the inside. Few or none of their cartridge-boxes had either powder or ball in them. To complete all, the swivels and patereroes at the Dutch house were all lying out of their carriages; and the one great gun which lay before it on a heap of stones was not only more honeycombed with rust than any piece of artillery I have ever seen, but had the touch-hole turned downwards, probably to conceal its size, which might not be in all probability much less than the bore of the gun itself. The Dutch, however, use these islanders as auxiliaries in their wars against the inhabitants of Timor, where they do good service; their lives at all events not being nearly so valuable as those of the Dutchmen.

This island was settled by the Portuguese almost as soon as they went into these seas. When the Dutch first came here the Portuguese, however, were very soon wormed out by the machinations of the artful new-comers, who not only attempted to settle themselves in the island, but also sent sloops occasionally to trade with the natives, by whom they were often cut off; as often, I suppose, as they cheated them in too great a degree. This, however, and the probably increasing value of the island, at last tempted them to try some other way of securing it, and running less risk. This

took place about ten years ago, when a treaty of alliance
was signed between the five Radjas and the Dutch Company; in consequence of which the Company is yearly to
furnish each of these kings with a certain quantity of fine
linen and silk, cutlery ware, etc., in short, of any kind of
goods which he wants, all which is delivered in the form of
a present accompanied with a certain cask of arrack, which
the Radja and his principal people never cease to drink as
long as a drop of it remains.   In return for this, each Radja
agrees that neither he nor his subjects shall trade with any
person except the Company, unless they have the permission
of their resident, that they shall yearly supply so many
sloop-loads of rice, maize, and calevances, the maize and
calevances being sent off to Timor in sloops, which are kept
on the island for that purpose.   Each sloop is navigated by
ten Indians.   The rice is taken away by a ship, which at the
time of the harvest comes to the island annually, bringing
the Company's presents, and anchoring by turns in each of
the three bays.

In consequence of this treaty, Mr. Lange, a Portuguese
Indian, who seems to be his second, and a Dutch Indian,
who serves for schoolmaster, are permitted to live among
them.

Mr. Lange himself is attended by fifty slaves on
horseback, with whom he every two months makes the
tour of the island, visiting all the Radjas, exhorting those
to plant who seem idle; and, observing where the crops are
got in, he immediately sends sloops for them, navigated by
these same slaves, so that the crop proceeds immediately
from the ground to the Dutch storehouses at Timor.   In
these excursions he always carries certain bottles of arrack,
which he finds of great use in opening the hearts of the
Radjas with whom he has to deal.   Notwithstanding the
boasted honesty of these people, it requires his utmost
diligence to keep the arrack from his slaves, who, in spite of
all his care, often ease him of a great part of it.   During
the ten years that he has resided on this island no European
but himself has ever been here, except at the time of the

arrival of the Dutch ship which had sailed about two months before we came. He is indeed distinguishable from the Indians only by his colour; like them he sits upon the ground and chews his betel, etc. He has been for some years married to an Indian woman of the island of Timor, who keeps his house in the Indian fashion, and he excused himself to us for not asking us to his house, telling us he was not able to entertain us in any other way than the rest of the Indians whom we saw. He speaks neither German, his native language, nor Dutch, without frequent hesitations and mistakes; on the other hand, the Indian language seems to flow from him with the utmost facility. As I forgot to mention this language in its proper place, I shall take this opportunity to write down the few observations I had an opportunity of making during our short stay. The genius of it seems much to resemble that of the South Sea Isles; in several instances the words are exactly the same, and the numbers are undoubtedly derived from the same source. I give here a list of words :——

Momonne	a man	Wurroo	the moon
Mobunnea	a woman	Aidassec	the sea
Catoo	the head	Ailei	water
Row Catoo	the hair	Aee	fire
Matta	the eyes	Maate	to dye
Rowna Matta	the eyelashes	Tabudje	to sleep
Swanga	the nose	Ta teetoo	to rise
Cavaranga	the cheeks	Tooga	the thighs
Wodecloo	the ears	Rootoo	the knees
Vaio	the tongue	Baibo	the legs
Lacoco	the neck	Dunceala	the feet
Soosoo	the breasts	Kissovei yilla	the toes
Caboo Soosoo	the nipples	Camacoo	the arms
Dulloo	the belly	Wulaba	the hand
Assoo	the navel	Cabaou	a buffalo
Carow	the tail	Djara	a horse
Pangoutoo	the beak	Vavee	a hog
Ica	the fish	Doomba	a sheep
Unjoo	a turtle	Kesavoo	a goat
Nicu	cocoanut	Guaca	a dog
Braceree	fan-palm	Maio	a cat
Calella	areca	Mannu	a fowl
Canana	betel	Usse	1
Aou	lime	Lhua	2
Maanadoo	a fish-hook	Tullu	3
Tata	tattoo	Uppah	4
Lodo	the sun	Lumme	5

Unna	6	Lhuangooroo, etc.	20
Pedu	7	Sing Assu, etc.	100
Arru	8	Setuppah, etc.	1000
Saou	9	Selacussa, etc.	10,000
Singooroo	10	Serata, etc.	100,000
Singooring Usse, etc.	11	Sereboo, etc.	1,000,000

In the course of conversation Mr. Lange gave us little
accounts of the neighbouring islands; these I shall set down
just as he gave them, merely upon his authority.

The small island to the westward of Savu, he said,
produces nothing of consequence except areca nuts, of which
the Dutch annually receive two sloop-loads in return for
their presents to the islanders.

Timor is the chief island in these parts belonging to the
Dutch, all the others in the neighbourhood being subject to
it in so far as that the residents on them go there once a
year to pass their accounts. It is now nearly in the same
state that it was in Dampier's time. The Dutch have their
fort of *Concordia*, where are storehouses, which, according
to Mr. Lange's account, would have supplied our ship with
every article we could have got at Batavia, even salt provisions and arrack. The Dutch, however, are very frequently
at war with the natives, even of *Copang*,[1] their next neighbours, in which case they are themselves obliged to send to
the neighbouring isles for provisions. The Portuguese still
possess their towns of *Laphao* and *Sesial* on the north side
of the island.

About two years ago a French ship was wrecked upon
the east coast of Timor. She lay some days upon the shoal,
when a sudden gale of wind coming on broke her up at
once and drowned most of the crew, among whom was the
captain. Those who got ashore, among whom was one of
the lieutenants, made the best of their ways towards
Concordia, where they arrived in four days, having left
several of their party upon the road. Their number was
above eighty; they were supplied with every necessary, and
had assistance given them in order to go back to the
wreck and fish up what they could. This they did, and

[1] Part of Timor, near Concordia.

recovered all their bullion, which was in chests, and several of their guns, which were large. Their companions which they had left upon the road were all missing; the Indians it was supposed had either by force or persuasion kept them among them, as they are very desirous of having Europeans among them to instruct them in the art of war. After a stay of two months at *Concordia*, their company was diminished more than half by sickness, chiefly in consequence of the great fatigues they had endured in the days when they got ashore, and travelled to that place. These were then furnished with a small ship, in which they sailed for Europe.

We inquired much for the island of *Anabao* or *Anambao*, mentioned by Dampier; he assured us that he knew of no island of that name anywhere in these seas. I since have observed that it is laid down in several charts by the name of *Selam*,[1] which is probably the real name of it. *Rotte* is upon much the same footing as *Savu*: a Dutchman resides upon it to manage the natives; its produce is also much like that of *Savu*. It has also some sugar, which was formerly made by simply bruising the canes and boiling the juice to a syrup, as they do the palm wine; lately, however, they have made great improvements in that manufacture. There are three islands of the name of *Solar* lying to the eastward of *Ende* or *Flores*: they are flat and low, abounding with vast quantity of provisions and stock: they are also managed in the same manner as *Savu*. On the middlemost of them is a good harbour, the other two are without shelter. *Ende* is still in the hands of the Portuguese, who have a town and good harbour called *Larntuca* on the northeast corner of it: the old harbour of *Ende*, situated on the south side of it, is not nearly so good, and therefore now entirely neglected.

The inhabitants of each of these different islands speak different languages, and the chief policy of the Dutch is to prevent them from learning each other's language, as by this means the Dutch keep them to their respective

[1] The real name is Semau. (Note by Banks.)

islands, preventing them from entering into traffic with each other, or learning from mutual intercourse to plant such things as would be of greater value to themselves than their present produce, though less beneficial to the Dutch East India Company. The Dutch at the same time secure to themselves the benefit of supplying all their necessities at their own rates, no doubt not very moderate. This may possibly sufficiently account for the expense they must have been at in printing prayer-books, catechisms, etc., and teaching them to each island in its own language rather than in Dutch, which in all probability they might have as easily done, but at the risk of Dutch becoming the common language of the islands, and consequently of the natives by its means gaining an intercourse with each other.

CHAPTER XVI

SAVU ISLAND TO BATAVIA

SEPT. 21—DEC. 24, 1770

Leave Savu—Arrive off Java—European and American news—Formalities required by Dutch authorities—Mille Islands—Batavia road—Land at Batavia—Prices and food at the hotel—Tupia's impressions of Batavia—Introduction to the Governor—Malarious climate—Bougainville's visit to Batavia—Orders given to heave down the ship—Illness of Tupia, Dr. Banks, Dr. Solander, etc.—Death of Mr. Monkhouse, Tayeto, and Tupia—Remove to a country-house—Malay women as nurses—Critical state of Dr. Solander—Ship repaired—Captain Cook taken ill—Heavy rains—Frogs and mosquitos—Return to the ship.

21st. Notwithstanding that our friend Mr. Lange invited us very kindly last night to come ashore again in the morning, and that we saw divers jars of syrup, a sheep, etc., waiting for us upon the beach, a sure sign that the Radja's prohibition was not intended to prejudice trade in the least, we, who had now got plenty of all the refreshments which the isle afforded, thought it most prudent to weigh and sail directly for Batavia; all our fears of westerly winds being dissipated by Mr. Lange assuring us that the easterly monsoon would prevail for two months longer. Accordingly we did so, and soon passed by the small island lying to the west about a league from Savu; its name I have unluckily forgotten (*Pulo Samiri*, or something like it, maybe). One of the buffaloes which was killed weighed only 166 lbs., which was a great drawback on our expectations, as we had thought that even that, though much the smallest of our stock, would not weigh less than 300 lbs.

1st October. About midnight land was seen, which in the

morning proved to be Java Head and Prince's Island. At
night we had passed Cracatoa.

2nd. We espied two large ships lying at anchor behind
Anger Point; we came to an anchor, and sent a boat on
board the ships for news. They were Dutch East Indiamen; one bound for Cochin and the coast of Coromandel;
the other for Ceylon. Their captains received our officer
very politely, and told him some European news; as,
that the government in England were in the utmost disorder, the people crying up and down the streets "Down
with King George, King Wilkes for ever," that the Americans
had refused to pay taxes of any kind, the consequence of
which being that a large force had been sent there, both of
sea and land forces; that the party of Polanders, who had
been forced into the late election by the Russians inter-
fering, had asked assistance of the Grand Signior, who had
granted it, in consequence of which the Russians had sent
twenty sail of the line, and a large army by land to besiege
Constantinople, etc. etc. etc. With regard to our present
circumstances, they told us that our passage to Batavia
was likely to be very tedious, as we should have a strong
current constantly against us, and at this time of the year
calms and light breezes were the only weather we had to
expect. They said also that near where they lay was a
Dutch packet boat, whose business it was to go on board all
ships coming through the straits to inquire of them their
news, and carry or send their letters to Batavia with the
utmost despatch, which business they said her skipper was
obliged to do even for foreigners, if they desired it. This
skipper, if we wanted refreshments, would furnish us with
fowls, turtle, etc., at a very cheap rate.

3rd. The Dutch packet of which we had been told yesterday, and which proved to be a sloop of no inconsiderable size,
had been standing after us all the morning, and still continued
to do so, gaining however but little, till a foul wind sprang
up, on which she bore away. At night an Indian proa
came on board, bringing the master of the sloop. He
brought with him two books, in one of which he desired

that any of our officers would write down the name of the
ship, commander's name, where we came from, and where
bound, with any particulars we chose relating to ourselves,
for the information of any of our friends who might come
after us, as we saw that some ships, especially Portuguese,
had done. This book, he told us, was kept merely for the
information of those who might come through these straits.
In the other, which was a fair book, he entered the names
of the ships and commanders, which only were sent to the
Governor and Council of the Indies.   On our writing
down Europe as the place we had come from, he said :
" Very well, anything you please, but this is merely for
the information of your friends."   In the proa were
some small turtle, many fowls and ducks, also parrots,
parroquets, rice-birds and monkeys, some few of which we
bought, paying a dollar for a small turtle, and the same, at
first for ten, afterwards for fifteen large fowls, two monkeys,
or a whole cage of paddy-birds.

4th. Calm with light breezes, not sufficient to stem the
current, which was very strong.   To make our situation as
tantalising as possible, innumerable proas were sailing about
us in all directions.   A boat was sent ashore for grass, and
landed at an Indian town, where by hard bargaining
some cocoanuts were bought at about three halfpence
apiece, and rice in the straw at about five farthings a gallon.
Neither here, nor in any other place where we have had
connections with them, would they take any money but
Spanish dollars.   Large quantities of that floating substance
which I have mentioned before under the name of sea-
sawdust, had been seen ever since we came into the straits,
and particularly to-day.   Among it were many leaves, fruits,
old stalks of plantain trees, plants of *Pistia stratiotes*, and
such like trash, from whence we almost concluded that it
came out of some river.

5th. Early in the morning a proa came on board, bringing a Dutchman, who said that his post was much like
that of the man who was on board on the 3rd.   He
presented a printed paper, of which he had copies in

English, French, and Dutch, regularly signed in the name of the Governor. These he desired we would give written answers to, which he told us would be sent express to Batavia, where they would arrive to-morrow at noon. He had in the boat turtle and eggs, of which latter he sold a few for somewhat less than a penny apiece, and then went away.

The day was spent as usual in getting up and letting down the anchor. At night, however, we were very near Bantam Point.

8th. At eight Dr. Solander and I went ashore on a small islet belonging to the *Mille* Isles, not laid down in the draught, lying five miles N. by E. from *Pulo Bedroe.* The whole was not above 500 yards long, and 100 broad, yet on it was a house and a small plantation, in which, however, at this time was no plant from whence any profit could be derived, except *Ricinus palma Christi,* of which castor-oil is made in the West Indies. Upon the shoal, about a quarter of a mile from the island, were two people in a canoe, who seemed to hide themselves as if afraid of us ; we supposed them to be the inhabitants of our island. We found very few species of plants, but shot a bat, whose wings measured three feet when stretched out (*Vesp. vam-pyrus*), and four plovers exactly like our English golden plover (*Charadrius pluvialis*). With these and the few plants we returned, and very soon after a small Indian boat came alongside, having in her three turtles, some dried fish, and pumpkins. We bought his turtles, which weighed altogether 146 lbs., for a dollar, with which bargain he seemed well pleased, but could scarce be prevailed upon to take any other coin for his pumpkins, after desiring that we would cut a dollar and give him a part. At last, however, a petack, shining and well-coined, tempted him to part with his stock, which consisted of twenty-six. He told us that the island, called in most draughts *Pulo Babi,* was really called *Pulo Sounda,* and that called *Pulo Bedroe, Pulo Payon.* At parting he made signs that we should not tell at Batavia that any boat had been on board us.

9th. Before four we were at anchor in Batavia road. A boat came immediately on board us from a ship which had a broad pendant flying ; the officer on board inquired who we were, etc., and immediately returned. Both he and his people were pale almost as spectres, no good omen of the healthiness of the country we had arrived at. Our people, however, who might truly be called rosy and plump (for we had not a sick man among us), jeered and flaunted much at their brother seamen's white faces. By this time our boat was ready and went ashore with the first lieutenant, who had orders to acquaint the commanding officer ashore of our arrival. At night he returned, having met with a very civil reception from the *Shabandar*, who, though no military officer, took cognizance of all these things. I forgot to mention before that we found here the *Harcourt* Indiaman, Captain Paul, and two English private traders from the coast of India.

10th. After breakfast this morning we all went ashore in the pinnace, and immediately went to the house of Mr. Leith, the only Englishman of any credit in Batavia. We found him a very young man, under twenty, who had lately arrived here, and succeeded his uncle, a Mr. Burnet, in his business, which was pretty considerable, more so, we were told, than our new-comer had either money or credit to manage. He soon gave us to understand that he could be of very little service to us either in introducing us, as the Dutch people, he said, were not fond of him, or in money affairs, as he had begun trade too lately to have any more than what was employed in getting more. He, however, after having kept us to dine with him, offered us his assistance in showing us the method of living in Batavia, and in helping us to settle in such a manner as we should think fit. We had two alternatives. We could go to the hotel, a kind of inn kept by order of the Government, where it seems all merchant strangers are obliged to reside, paying $\frac{1}{2}$ per cent for warehouse room for their goods, which the master of the house is obliged to find for them. We, however, having come in a king's ship, were free from that obligation, and might live wherever we pleased. After having asked leave of the Council, which was never refused, we might therefore, if we chose it, take a house in any part of the town, and bringing our own servants ashore, might keep it, which would be much cheaper than living at the hotel, provided we had anybody on whom we could depend to buy our provisions. As this was not the case, having none with us who understood the Malay language, we concluded that the hotel would be the best for us, certainly the least trouble-some, and maybe not much the most expensive; accordingly, we went there, bespoke beds, and slept there at night.

The next day we agreed with the keeper of the house, whose name was Van Heys, as to the rates we should pay for living, as follows (for this he agreed, as we were five of us, who would probably have many visitors from the ship, to keep us a separate table). For ourselves we were to pay two rix-dollars a day each; and for each stranger we were to pay one rix-dollar (4s.) for dinner, and another for supper and bed if he stayed ashore. We were to have also for ourselves and friends, tea, coffee, punch, pipes and tobacco, as much as we could consume; in short, everything the house afforded, except wine and beer, which we were to pay for at the following rates :—

					s.	d.
Claret	.	.	.	39 stivers	3	3
Hock	.	.	.	1 rix̃.	4	0
Lisbon	.	.	.	39 stivers	3	3
Sweet wine	.	.	39 ,,	3	3
Madeira	.	.	.	1 rupee	2	6
Beer	.	.	.	1 ,,	2	6
Spa water .	.	.	.	1 rix̃.	4	0

Besides this we were to pay for our servants ½ a rupee (1s. 3d.) a day each.

For these rates, which we soon found [1] to be more than double the common charges of boarding and lodging in the town, we were furnished with a table which under the appearance of magnificence was wretchedly covered; indeed,

---

[1] The Journal at Batavia, until the 21st at least, was evidently not written up day by day.

our dinners and suppers consisted of one course each, the
one of fifteen, the other of thirteen dishes, of which, when
you came to examine them, seldom less than nine or ten
were of bad poultry, roasted, boiled, fried, stewed, etc. etc.
So little conscience had they in serving up dishes over and
over again, that I have seen the same identical duck appear
upon the table three times as roasted duck, before he found
his way into the fricassee, from whence he was again to pass
into forcemeat.

This treatment, however, was not without remedy; we
found that it was the constant custom of the house to supply
strangers at their first arrival with every article as bad as
possible; if through good nature or indolence they put up
with it, it was so much the better for the house, if not
it was easy to mend their treatment by degrees, till they
were satisfied. On this discovery we made frequent remon-
strances, and mended our fare considerably, so much so that
had we had any one among us who understood this kind of
wrangling, I am convinced we might have lived as well as
we could have desired.

Being now a little settled, I hired a small house next
door to the hotel, for which I payed 10 rix! (£2) a month.
Here our books, etc., were lodged, but here we were far from
private, almost every Dutchman that came by running in
and asking what we had to sell; for it seems that hardly
any individual had ever been at Batavia before who had not
something or other to sell. I also hired two carriages, which
are a kind of open chaise made to hold two people and
driven by a man on a coach-box. For each of these I paid
2 rix! (8s.) a day, by the month. We sent for Tupia, who
had till now remained on board on account of his illness,
which was of the bilious kind, and for which he had all
along refused to take any medicine. On his arrival, his
spirits, which had long been very low, were instantly raised
by the sights which he saw, and his boy Tayeto, who had
always been perfectly well, was almost ready to run mad;
houses, carriages, streets, and everything, were to him sights
which he had often heard described but never well under-

stood, so he looked upon them with more than wonder, almost mad with the numberless novelties which diverted his attention from one to the other. He danced about the streets examining everything to the best of his abilities. One of Tupia's first observations was the various dresses which he saw worn by different people; on his being told that in this place every different nation wore their own country dress, he desired to have his, on which South Sea cloth was sent for on board, and he clothed himself according to his taste. We were now able to get food for him similar to that of his own country, and he grew visibly better every day, so that I doubted not in the least of his perfect recovery, as our stay at this place was not likely to be very short.

Ever since our arrival at this place, Dr. Solander and I had applied to be introduced to the General, or Governor, on one of his Public or Council days; we had been put off by various foolish excuses, and at last were told plainly that as we could have no business with him, we could have no reason to desire that favour. This did not satisfy us, so I went myself to the *Shabandar*, who is also master of the ceremonies, in order to ask his reasons for refusing so trifling a request, but was surprised at being very politely received, and told that the very next day he would attend us, which he did, and wè were introduced, and had the honour of conversing for a few minutes with his high mightiness, who was very polite to us.

Ever since our first arrival here we had been universally told of the extreme unwholesomeness of the place, which we, they said, should severely feel on account of the freshness and healthiness of our countenances. This threat, however, we did not much regard, thinking ourselves too well seasoned to variety of climates to fear any, and trusting more than all to an invariable temperance in everything, which we had as yet unalterably kept during our whole residence in the warm latitudes. Before the end of the month, however, we were made sensible of our mistake. Poor Tupia's broken constitution felt it first, and he grew

worse and worse every day. Then Tayeto, his boy, was
attacked by a cold and inflammation in his lungs ; then my
servants, Peter and James, and I myself had intermittent
fevers, and Dr. Solander a constant nervous one. In short,
every one on shore, and many on board, were ill, chiefly of
intermittents, occasioned no doubt by the lowness of the
country, and the numberless dirty canals, which intersect
the town in all directions.

Some days before this, as I was walking the streets with
Tupia, a man totally unknown to me ran out of his house,
and eagerly accosting me, asked if the Indian whom he saw
with me had not been at Batavia before. On my declaring
that he had not, and asking the reason of so odd a question,
he told me that a year and a half before, Mr. De Bougainville had been at Batavia with two French ships, and that
with him was an Indian so like this that he had imagined
him to be the identical same person, until I informed
him of the contrary. On this I inquired, and found that
Mr. De Bougainville was sent out by the French to the
Malouine or Falkland Isles (in order, as they said here, to
sell them to the Spaniards), had gone from thence to the
River Plate, and afterwards having passed into the South Seas,
—maybe to other Spanish parts, where he and all his people
had got an immense deal of money in new Spanish dollars,—
came here across the South Seas, in which passage he discovered divers lands unknown before, and from one of them
he brought the Indian in question.

This at once cleared up the account given us by the
Otahite Indians of the two ships which had been there
ten months before us (p. 96 of this journal) ; these were undoubtedly the ships of Mr. De Bougainville, and the Indian
was *Otourrou*, the brother of *Rette*, chief of *Hidea*. Even
the story of the woman was known here ; she, it seems, was
a Frenchwoman, who followed a young man sent out in the
character of botanist, in men's clothes.[1] As for the article
of the colours, the Indians might easily be mistaken, or Mr.
De Bougainville, if he had traded in the South Seas under

[1] See note on Bougainville, p. xliii.

Spanish colours, might choose to go quite across with them. The iron, which most misled us, had undoubtedly been bought in Spanish America. Besides the botanist mentioned above, these ships were furnished with one or more draughtsmen, so that they have probably done some of our work for us.

21st. After petitioning and repetitioning the Council of the Indies, our affairs were at last settled, and orders given to heave down the ship with all expedition; so she this day went down to *Kuyper*, called by the English *Cooper's Island*, where a warehouse was allotted for her to lay up her stores, etc.

We now began sensibly to feel the ill effects of the unwholesome climate we were in. Our appetites and spirits were gone, but none were yet really sick except poor Tupia and Tayeto, both of whom grew worse and worse daily, so that I began once more to despair of poor Tupia's life. At last he desired to be moved to the ship, where, he said, he should breathe a freer air clear of the numerous houses, which he believed to be the cause of his disease, by stopping the free draught. Accordingly on the 28th I went down with him to Kuyper, and on his liking the shore had a tent pitched for him in a place he chose, where both sea and land breezes blew right over him, a situation in which he expressed great satisfaction.

The seamen now fell ill fast, so that the tents ashore were always full of sick. After a stay of two days I left Tupia well satisfied in mind, but not at all better in body, and returned to town, where I was immediately seized with a tertian, the fits of which were so violent as to deprive me entirely of my senses, and leave me so weak as scarcely to be able to crawl downstairs. My servants, Peter and James, were as bad as myself, and Dr Solander now felt the first attacks of the fever, but never having been in his lifetime once ill, resisted it, resolved not to apply to a physician. But the worst of all was Mr. Monkhouse, the ship's surgeon; he was now confined to his bed by a violent fever, which grew worse and worse notwithstanding all the efforts of the physician.

4th November. At last, after many delays caused by
Dutch ships which came alongside the wharfs to load
pepper, the *Endeavour* was this day got down to *Onrust*,
where she was to be hove down without delay, most welcome
news to us all, now heartily tired of this unwholesome
country.

Poor Mr. Monkhouse became worse and worse without
the intervention of one favourable symptom, so that we now
had little hopes of his life.

6th. In the afternoon of this day poor Mr. Monkhouse
departed, the first sacrifice to the climate, and the next day
was buried. Dr. Solander attended his funeral, and I should
certainly have done the same, had I not been confined to my
bed by my fever. Our case now became melancholy, neither
of my servants were able to help me, no more than I was
them, and the Malay slaves, whom alone we depended on,
naturally the worst attendants in nature, were rendered less
careful by our incapacity to scold them on account of our
ignorance of the language. When we became so sick that
we could not help ourselves, they would get out of call, so
that we were obliged to remain still until able to get up
and go in search of them.

9th. This day we received the disagreeable news of the
death of Tayeto, and that his death had so much affected
Tupia, that there were little hopes of his surviving him
many days.

10th. Dr. Solander and I still grew worse and worse,
and the physician who attended us declared that the country
air was necessary for our recovery ; so we began to look out
for a country house, though with a heavy heart, as we knew
that we must there commit ourselves entirely to the care of
the Malays, whose behaviour to sick people we had all the
reason in the world to find fault with. For this reason we
resolved to buy each of us a Malay woman to nurse us,
hoping that the tenderness of the sex would prevail even
here, which indeed we found it to do, for they turned out
by no means bad nurses.

11th. We received the news of Tupia's death ; I had

quite given him over ever since the death of his boy, whom I well knew he sincerely loved, though he used to find much fault with him during his lifetime.

12th. Dr. Solander, who had not yet entirely taken to his bed, returned from an airing this evening extremely ill. He went to bed immediately. I sat by him, and soon observed symptoms which alarmed me very much. I sent immediately for our physician, Dr. Jaggi, who applied sinapisms to his feet, and blisters to the calves of his legs, but at the same time gave me little or no hopes of even the possibility of his living till morning. Weak as I was I sat by him till morning, when he changed very visibly for the better. I then slept a little, and on waking found him still better than I had any reason to hope.

13th. As Dr. Jaggi had all along insisted on the country air being necessary for our recovery, I at once agreed with my landlord, Van Heys, for his country house, which he immediately furnished for us; agreeing to supply us with provisions, and give us the use of five slaves who were there, as well as three we were to take with us, for a dollar a day (4s.), more than our common agreement. This country house, though small and very bad, was situated about two miles out of the town, in a situation that prepossessed me much in its favour, being upon the banks of a briskly running river, and well open to the sea breeze, two circumstances which must much contribute to promote circulation of the air, a thing of the utmost consequence in a country perfectly resembling the low part of my native Lincolnshire. Accordingly, Dr. Solander being much better, and in the doctor's opinion not too bad to be removed, we carried him to it this day, and also received from the ship Mr. Sporing (our writer), a seaman, and the captain's own servant, whom he had sent on hearing of our melancholy situation, so that we were now sufficiently well attended, having ten Malays and two whites, besides Mr. Sporing. This night, however, Dr. Solander was extremely ill, so much so that fresh blisters were applied to the inside of his thighs, which he seemed not at all sensible of; nevertheless in the

morning he was something better, and from that time recovered, though by extremely slow degrees, till his second
attack. I myself, either by the influence of the bark of
which I had all along taken quantities, or by the anxiety I
suffered on Dr. Solander's account, missed my fever, nor
did it return for several days, until he became better.

14th. We had the agreeable news of the repairs of the
ship being completely finished, and that she had returned
to Cooper's Island, where she proved to be no longer leaky.
When examined she had proved much worse than anybody
expected; her main plank being in many places so cut by
the rocks that not more than one-eighth of an inch in
thickness remained; and here the worm had got in and
made terrible havoc. Her false keel was entirely gone, and
her main keel much wounded. The damages were now,
however, entirely repaired, and very well too in the opinion
of everybody who saw the Dutch artificers do their work.

Dr. Solander grew better, though by very slow degrees.
I soon had a return of my ague, which now became quotidian;
the captain also was taken ill on board, and of course we
sent his servant to him. Soon after both Mr. Sporing and
our seaman were seized with intermittents, so that we were
again reduced to the melancholy necessity of depending
entirely upon the Malays for nursing us, all of whom were
often sick together.

24th. We had for some nights now had the wind on the
western board, generally attended with some rain, thunder
and lightning; this night it blew strong at S.W. and rained
harder than ever I saw it before for three or four hours.
Our house rained in every part, and through the lower part
of it ran a stream almost capable of turning a mill. In the
morning I went to Batavia, where the quantities of bedding
that I everywhere saw hung up to dry, made a very
uncommon sight, for I was told almost every house in
the town and neighbourhood suffered more or less. This
was certainly the shifting of the monsoon; for the winds,
which had before been constantly to the eastward, remained
constantly on the western board. The people here, however,

told us that it did not commonly shift so suddenly, and were loth to believe that the westerly winds were really set in for several days after.

Dr. Solander had recovered enough to be able to walk about the house, but gathered strength very slowly. I myself was given to understand that curing my ague was of very little consequence while the cause remained in the badness of the air. The physician, however, bled me, and gave me frequent gentle purges, which he told me would make the attacks less violent, as was really the case. They came generally about two or three in the afternoon, a time when everybody in these climates is always asleep, and by four or five I had generally recovered sufficiently to get up and walk in the garden. The rainy season had now set in, and we had generally some rain in the night; the days were more or less cloudy, and sometimes wet; this, however, was not always the case, for we once had a whole week of very clear weather.

The frogs in the ditches, whose voices were ten times louder than those of European ones, made a noise almost intolerable on nights when rain was to be expected; and the mosquitos or gnats, who had been sufficiently troublesome even in the dry time, were now breeding in every splash of water, and became innumerable, especially in the moonlight nights. Their stings, however, though painful and troublesome enough at the time, never continued to itch above half an hour; so that no man in the daytime was troubled with the bites of the night before. Indeed, I never met with any whose bites caused swellings remaining twenty-four hours, except the midges or gnats of Lincolnshire (which are identically the same insect as is called mosquito in most parts of the world) and the sand flies of North America.[1]

1st December. About this time Dr. Solander had a return of his fever, which increased gradually for four or five days, when he became once more in imminent danger.

7th. We received the agreeable news of the ship's arrival in the road, having completed all her rigging, etc., and having

---

[1] Alluding to his experience in Newfoundland in 1766.

now nothing to take in but provisions and a little water. The people on board, however, were extremely sickly, and several had died, a circumstance necessarily productive of delays; indeed, had they been strong and healthy we should have been before now at sea.

Dr. Solander had changed much for the better within these two last days, so that our fears of losing him were entirely dissipated, for which much praise is due to his ingenious physician, Dr. Jaggi, who at this juncture especially was indefatigable.

16th. Our departure being now very soon to take place, I thought it would be very convenient to cure the ague, which had now been my constant companion for many weeks. Accordingly I took decoction of bark plentifully, and in three or four days missed it. I then went to town, settled all my affairs, and remained impatient to have the day fixed.

24th. The 25th, Christmas Day by our account, being fixed for sailing, we this morning hired a large country proa, which came up to the door and took in Dr. Solander, now tolerably recovered, and carried him on board the ship, where in the evening we all joined him.

CHAPTER XVII

DESCRIPTION OF BATAVIA

BATAVIA, the capital of the Dutch dominions in India, and
generally esteemed to be by much the finest town in the
possession of Europeans in these parts, is situated in a low
fenny plain, where several small rivers, which take their
rise in mountains called *Blaen Berg*, about forty miles inland,
empty themselves into the sea. The Dutch (always true to
their commercial interests) seemed to have pitched upon this
situation entirely for the convenience of water-carriage, which
indeed few, if any, towns in Europe enjoy in a higher degree.
Few streets in the town are without canals of considerable
breadth, running through or rather stagnating in them.
These canals are continued for several miles round the town,
and with five or six rivers, some of which are navigable
thirty or forty or more miles inland, make the carriage of
every species of produce inconceivably cheap.

It is very difficult to judge of the size of the town: the
size of the houses, in general large, and the breadth of the

streets increased by their canals, make it impossible to compare it with any English town. All I can say is that when seen from the top of a building, from whence the eye takes it in at one view, it does not look nearly so large as it seems to be when you walk about it. Valentijn, who wrote about and before the year 1726, says that in his time there were within the walls 1242 Dutch houses, and 1200 Chinese; without, 1066 Dutch and 1240 Chinese, besides twelve arrack houses. This number, however, appeared to me to be very highly exaggerated, those within the walls especially. But of all this I confess myself a very indifferent judge, having enjoyed so little health, especially towards the latter part of my stay, that I had no proper opportunity of satisfying myself in such particulars.

The streets are broad and handsome, and the banks of the canals in general planted with rows of trees. A stranger on his first arrival is very much struck with these, and often led to observe how much the heat of the climate must be tempered by the shade of the trees and coolness of the water. Indeed, as to the first, it must be convenient to those who walk on foot; but a very short residence will show him that the inconveniences of the canals far over-balance any convenience he can derive from them in any but a mercantile light. Instead of cooling the air, they contribute not a little to heat it, especially those which are stagnant, as most of them are, by reflecting back the fierce rays of the sun. In the dry season these stink most abominably, and in the wet many of them overflow their banks, filling the lower storeys of the houses near them with water. When they clean them, which is very often, as some are not more than three or four feet deep, the black mud taken out is suffered to lie upon the banks, that is, in the middle of the street, till it has acquired a sufficient hardness to be conveniently laden into boats. This mud stinks intolerably. Add to this that the running water, which is in some measure free from the former inconveniences, has every now and then a dead horse or hog stranded in the shallow parts, a nuisance which I was informed no particular person was appointed to remove. I am inclined to believe this, as I remember a dead buffalo lying in one of the principal thoroughfares for more than a week, until it was at last carried away by a flood.

The houses are in general large and well built, and conveniently enough contrived for the climate. The greater part of the ground-floor is always laid out in one large room with a door to the street and another to the yard, both which generally stand open. Below is the ground-plan of one.

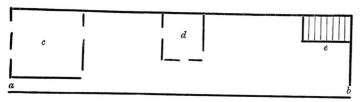

In this plan *a* is the front door, *b*, the back door, *c*, a room where the master of the house does his business, *d*, a court to give light to the rooms as well as increase the draught, and *e*, the stairs for going upstairs, where the rooms are generally large though few in number. Such, in general, are their town houses, differing in size very much, and sometimes in shape; the principles, however, on which they are built are universally the same, two doors opposite each other, and one or more courts between them to cause a draught, which they do in an eminent degree, as well as dividing the room into alcoves, in one of which the family dine, while the female slaves (who on no occasion sit anywhere else) work in another. Showy, however, as these large rooms are to the stranger on his first seeing them, he is soon sensible of the small amount of furniture which is universal in all of them. The same quantity of furniture is sufficient for them as is necessary for our smaller rooms in Europe, as in those we entertain fully as many guests at a time as is ever done in these; consequently the chairs, which are spread at even distances from each other, are not very easily collected into a circle if four or five visitors arrive at once.

Public buildings they have several, most of them old and executed in rather a clumsy taste. Their new church, however, built with a dome (which is seen very far out at sea), is certainly far from an ugly building on the outside, though rather heavy, and in the inside is a very fine room. Its organ is well proportioned, being large enough to fill it, and it is so well supplied with chandeliers that few churches in Europe are as well lighted.

From buildings I should make an easy transition to fortifications, were it not a subject of which I must confess myself truly ignorant. I shall attempt, however, to describe what I have seen in general terms. The city of Batavia is enclosed by a stone wall of moderate height, old, and in many parts not in the best repair; besides this, a river in different places from fifty to one hundred paces broad, whose stream is rather brisk but shallow, encircles it without the walls, and within again is a canal of very variable breadth, so that in passing their gates you cross two draw-bridges. This canal, useless as it seems, has, however, this merit, that it prevents all walking on the ramparts, as is usual in fortified towns, and consequently all idle examination of the number or condition of the guns. With these they seem to be very ill provided, all that are seen being of very light metal; and the west side of the town, where alone you have an opportunity of examining them, being almost totally unprovided.

In the north-east corner of the town stands the castle or citadel, the walls of which are higher and larger than those of the town, especially near the boats' landing-place, which it completely commands, and where are mounted several very large and well-looking guns. The neighbourhood, however, of the north-east corner seems sufficiently weak on both sides, especially on the east.

Within this Castle, as it is called, are apartments for the Governor-General and all the members of the Council of India, to which they are enjoined to repair in case of a siege; here are also large storehouses, where are kept great quantities of the Company's goods, especially European goods, and where all their writers, etc., do their business. Here are also stored a large quantity of cannon, but whether to mount on the walls or furnish their shipping in case of the approach of an enemy, I could not learn; from their appearance I should judge them to be intended for the latter. As for powder, they are said to be well supplied with it, dispersed in various magazines on account of the frequency of lightning.

Besides the fortifications of the town, there are numerous forts up and down the country, some between twenty and thirty miles from the town. Most of these seem very poor defences, and are probably intended to do little more than keep the natives in awe. They have also a kind of house mounting about eight guns apiece, which seem to me to be the best defences against Indians I have ever seen. They are generally placed in such situations as will command three or four canals, and as many roads upon their banks. Some there are in the town itself, and one of these it was which, in the time of the Chinese rebellion (as the Dutch call it), quickly levelled all the best Chinese houses to the ground. Indeed, I was told that the natives are more afraid of these than of any other kind of defences. There are many of them in all parts of Java, and on the other islands in the possession of the Dutch. I lamented much not being able to get a drawing and plan of one, which, indeed, had I been well, I might easily have done, as I suppose they never could be jealous of a defence which one gun would destroy in half an hour.

Even if the Dutch fortifications are as weak and defence-less as I suppose, they have, nevertheless, some advantages in their situation among morasses, where the roads, which are almost always a bank thrown up between a canal and a ditch, might easily be destroyed. This would very much delay the bringing up of heavy artillery, unless this could be shipped upon some canal, and a sufficient number of proper boats secured to transport it. There are plenty of these, but they all muster every night under the guns of the Castle, from whence it would be impossible to take them. Delays, however, from whatever cause they might happen, would be inevitably fatal. In less than a week we were sensible of the unhealthiness of the climate, and in a month's time one half of the ship's company were

unable to perform their duty; but could a very small body
of men get quickly to the walls of Batavia, bringing with them
a few battering cannon, the town must inevitably yield on
account of the weakness of its defence.

We were told that of a hundred soldiers, who arrive here
from Europe, it is a rare thing for fifty to outlive the first
year; and that of those fifty half will by that time be in the
hospitals, and of the other half not ten in perfect health.
Whether this account may not be exaggerated I cannot say,
but will venture to affirm that it seemed to me probable
from the number of pale faces, and limbs hardly able to
support a musket, which I saw among the few soldiers to
be seen upon duty. The white inhabitants indeed are all
soldiers, and those who have served five years are liable to
be called out on any occasion; but as they are never
exercised or made to do any kind of duty, it is impossible
to expect much from men more versed in handling pens
than guns. The Portuguese are generally good marksmen,
as they employ themselves much in shooting wild hogs and
deer; as for the *Mardykers*, who are certainly numerous—
being Indians of all nations who are, or whose ancestors
have been, freed slaves—few, either of them or of the
Chinese, know the use of firearms. Their numbers, however,
might be troublesome, as some of them are esteemed brave
with their own weapons, lances, swords, daggers, etc.

Thus much for the land. By sea it is impossible to
attack Batavia, on account of the shallowness of the water,
which will scarcely suffer even a long-boat to come within
cannon-shot of the walls, unless she keep a narrow channel
walled in on both sides by strong piers, and running about
half a mile into the harbour, which channel terminates
exactly under the fire of the strongest part of the Castle.
At this point there is a large wooden boom, which is shut
every night at six o'clock, and not opened again till morning under any pretence. It is said that before the earth-
quake in [1699] ships of large burthen used to come up to
this place, and be stopped by the boom, but at present only
boats attempt it.

The harbour of Batavia is generally accounted the finest in India; and indeed it answers that character, being large enough to contain any number of ships, and having such good holding ground that no ships ever think of mooring, but ride with one anchor, which always holds as long as the cable. How it is sheltered is difficult to say, the islands without it not being by any means sufficient, but so it is that there is never any sea running at all troublesome to shipping. Its greatest inconvenience is the shoal water between the ships and the mouth of Batavia river, which, when the sea breeze has blown pretty freshly, as it often does, makes a cockling sea very dangerous to boats. Our long-boat, in attempting to come off, struck two or three times and with difficulty regained the river's mouth; the same evening a Dutch boat loaded with sails and rigging for one of their Indiamen was entirely lost.

Round the outside of the harbour are many small islands, some of which the Dutch make use of; as *Edam*, to which they transport all Europeans who have been guilty of crimes not worthy of death. Some of these are sentenced to remain there 99, others 40, 20, 5 years, etc., according to their deserts, during which time they work as slaves, making ropes, etc. etc. At *Purmerent* they have a hospital in which people are said to recover much more quickly than at Batavia. On *Kuyper* are warehouses in which are kept many things belonging to the Company, chiefly such as are of small value, as rice, etc.; here also all foreign ships who are to be hove down at *Onrust* discharge their cargoes at wharves very convenient for the purpose. Here the guns, sails, etc., of the "Falmouth," a gun-ship which was condemned here on her return from Manilla, were kept, and she herself remained in the harbour with only two warrant officers on board, who had remittances most regularly from home, but no notice ever taken of the many memorials they sent, desiring to be recalled. The Dutch, however, for reasons best known to themselves, thought fit about six months before our arrival to sell her and all her stores by public auction, and send her officers home in their ships.

The next island, which is indeed of more consequence to the Dutch than all the rest, is *Onrust ;* here they heave down and repair all their shipping, and consequently keep a large quantity of naval stores. On this island are artificers of almost all kinds employed in the shipbuilding way, and very clever ones, so at least all our most experienced seamen allowed, who said they had seen ships hove down in most parts of the world, but never saw that business so cleverly done as here. The Dutch do not seem to think this island of so much consequence as they perhaps would do if all their naval stores were here (the greater part are at Batavia) ; it seems to be so ill defended, that one 60-gun ship would blow it up without a possibility of failure, as she might go alongside the wharfs as near as she pleased.

It is generally said in Europe that the Dutch keep a strong fleet in the East Indies, ready and able to cope with any European Power which might attack them there. This is true thus far and no farther : their Indiamen, which are very large ships, are pierced for 50 or 60 guns each. Should they be attacked when all these were in India, or indeed a little before the sailing of the Europe fleet, they might, if they had sufficient warning to get in their guns, etc., raise 40 or 50 sail ; but how it would be possible for them to man this fleet, if they kept anybody at all on shore, is to me a mystery. Again, should they be attacked after the fleet had sailed, they have very few ships, and those terribly out of condition ; for they keep no ships even in tolerable repair in India, except those employed to go to Ceylon and the coast, which places indeed are generally taken in the way to or from Europe. As for the eastern islands, no ships of any force are employed there ; but all the trade is carried on in small vessels, many of which are brigs and sloops.

The country round about Batavia for some miles is one continued range of country houses and gardens, some of which are very large, and all universally planted with trees as close as they can stand by each other, so that the country enjoys little benefit from being cleared, the woods standing now nearly as thick as when they grew there originally, with only this difference, that they are now of useful, whereas they were formerly of useless trees. But, useful as these trees are to their respective owners, who enjoy their fruits, to the community they are certainly highly detrimental in preventing the sea breeze from penetrating into the country as it ought; or at best loading it with unwholesome vapours collected and stagnating under their branches. This, according to our modern theory, should be the reason why thunder and lightning are so frequent and mischievous here that scarcely a month passes in which either ships or houses do not feel the effects of it. While we stayed three accidents happened; the first, a few days after our arrival, dismasted a large Dutch Indiaman which lay next to us, and wounded two or three of her people: nor were we exempt from the consequences of that flash, which, according to the belief of those on board, came down the lightning chain, and certainly struck down the sentry who stood near it.

Besides these frugiferous forests, the country has all the appearance of unhealthiness imaginable. I may venture to call it for some miles round the town one universal flat, as I know few exceptions to it. This flat is intersected in many directions by rivers, in still more by canals navigable for small vessels; but worst of all are the ditches, which, as in the marshes of Lincolnshire, are the universal fences of fields and gardens, hedges being almost totally absent. Nor are filthy, fenny bogs and morasses, fresh as well as salt, wanting even in the near neighbourhood of the town to add their baneful influence to the rest, and complete the unhealthiness of the country, which, much as I have said of it, I believe I have not exaggerated. The people themselves speak of it in as strong terms as I do, while the pale faces and diseased bodies of those who are said to be inured to it, as well as the preventive medicines, etc., and the frequent attacks of disease they are subject to, abundantly testify to the truth of what they assert. The very churchyards show it by the number of graves constantly open in them, far disproportionate to the number of people. The inhabitants themselves talk of death with the same indifference as people in a camp; it is hardly a piece of news to tell any one of the death of another, unless the dead man is of high rank, or somehow concerned in money matters with the other. If the death of any acquaintance is mentioned, it commonly produces some such reflexion as, "Well, it is very well he owed me nothing, or I should have had to get it from his executors."

So much for the neighbourhood of Batavia and as far round it as I had an opportunity of going. I saw only two exceptions to this general description, one where the General's country house is situated. This is a gradually rising hill of tolerable extent, but so little raised above the common level that you would be hardly sensible of being upon it were it not that you have left the canals, and that the ditches are replaced by bad hedges. The Governor himself has, however, strained a point so as to enclose his own garden with a ditch, to be in the fashion I suppose. The other exception is the place where a famous market called *Passar Tanabank* is held. Here, and here only during my whole stay, I had the satisfaction of mounting a hill of about ten yards perpendicular height, and tolerably steep. About forty miles inland, however, are some pretty high hills, where, as we were informed, the country is healthy in a high degree, and even at certain heights tolerably cool. There European vegetables flourish in great perfection, even strawberries, which bear heat very ill. The people who live there also have colour in their cheeks, a thing almost unknown at Batavia, where the milk-white faces of all the inhabitants are unstained by any colour; especially the women, who never go into the sun, and are consequently free from the tan, and have certainly the whitest skins imaginable. From what cause it proceeds is difficult to say, but in general it is observed that they keep their health much better than the men, even if they have lately arrived from Europe.

On these hills some of the principal people have country houses, which they visit once a year; the General especially has one, said to be built upon the plan of Blenheim House, near Oxford, but never finished. Physicians also often send

people here for the recovery of their health lost in the low
country, and say that the effects of such a change of air is
almost miraculous, working an instant change in favour of
the patient, who during his stay there remains well, but no
sooner returns to his necessary occupations at Batavia than
his complaints return in just the same degree as before his
departure.

Few parts of the world, I believe, are better furnished
with the necessaries as well as the luxuries of life, than the
island of Java. The unhealthiness of the country about
Batavia is in that particular rather an advantage to it; for
the very cause of it, a low flat situation, is likewise the
cause of a fruitfulness of soil hardly to be paralleled, which
is sufficiently testified by the flourishing condition of the
immense quantities of fruit-trees all round the town, as well
as by the quantity and excellence of their crops of sugar-
cane, rice, Indian corn, etc. etc. Indeed, the whole island is
allowed to be uncommonly fruitful by those who have seen
it, and in general as healthy as fruitful, excepting only such
low fenny spots as the neighbourhood of Batavia, far fitter
to sow rice upon than to build towns.

The tame quadrupeds are horses, cattle, buffaloes, sheep,
goats, and hogs. The horses are small, never exceeding in
size what we call a stout Galloway, but nimble and spirited:
they are said to have been found here when the Europeans
first came round the Cape of Good Hope. The cattle are
said to be the same as those in Europe, but differ from them
in appearance so much that I am inclined to doubt. They
have, however, the *palearia*, which naturalists make to be
the distinguishing mark of our species. On the other hand,
they are found wild, not only on Java, but on several of
the eastern islands. The flesh of those that I ate at
Batavia was rather finer-grained than European beef, but
much drier, and always terribly lean. Buffaloes are very
plentiful, but the Dutch are so much prejudiced against
them, that they will not eat their flesh at all, nor even drink
their milk, affirming that it causes fevers. The natives,
however, and the Chinese do both, and have no such opinion

concerning them. Their sheep, of that sort whose ears hang down and have hair instead of wool, are most intolerably bad, lean, and tough to the last degree. They have, however, a few Cape sheep, which are excellent, though intolerably dear. We gave £2 : 5s. a piece for four, which we bought for sea stock, the heaviest of which weighed only 45 lbs. Their goats are much of a par with their sheep, but their hogs are certainly excellent, especially the Chinese, which are so immensely fat that nobody thinks of buying the fat with the lean. The butcher, when you buy it, cuts off as much as you please, and sells it to his countrymen, the Chinese, who melt it down and eat it instead of butter with their rice. Notwithstanding the excellence of this pork, the Dutch are so prejudiced in favour of everything which comes from the Fatherland, that they will not eat it at all, but use entirely the Dutch breed, which are sold as much dearer than the Chinese here, as the Chinese are dearer than them in Europe.

Besides these domestic animals, their woods afford some wild horses and cattle, but only in the distant mountains, and even there they are very scarce. Buffaloes are not found wild upon Java, though they are upon Macassar, and are numerous in several of the eastern islands. The neighbourhood of Batavia, however, is pretty plentifully supplied with deer of two kinds, and wild hogs, both which are very good meat, and often shot by the Portuguese, who sell them tolerably cheap. Monkeys also there are, though but few in the neighbourhood of Batavia.

On the mountains and in the more desert part of the island are tigers, it is said, in too great abundance, and some rhinoceroses ; but neither of these animals are ever heard of in the neighbourhood of Batavia, or indeed any in well-peopled part of the island.

Fish are in immense plenty ; many sorts of them very excellent and inconceivably cheap ; but the Dutch, true to the dictates of luxury, buy none but those which are scarce. We, who in the course of our long migration in the warm latitudes had learned the real excellence of many of the cheapest sorts, wondered much at seeing them the food of none but slaves. On inquiry, however, of a sensible house-keeper, he told us that he, as well as we, knew that for one shilling he could purchase a better dish of fish than he did for ten. "But," said he, "I dare not do it, for should it be known that I did so, I should be looked upon in the same light as one in Europe who covered his table with offal fit for nothing but beggars or dogs." Turtle is here also in abundance, but despised by Europeans; indeed, for what reason I know not, it is neither so sweet nor so fat as our West Indian turtle, even in England. They have also a kind of large lizard or iguana, some of which are said to be as thick as a man's thigh. I shot one about five feet long, and it proved very good meat.

Poultry is prodigiously plentiful; very large fowls, ducks, and geese are cheap; pigeons are rather dear and turkeys extravagant. In general, those we ate at Batavia were lean and dry, but this I am convinced proceeds from their being ill-fed, as I have eaten every kind there as good or better than commonly met with in Europe.

Wild fowl are in general scarce. I saw during my stay one wild duck in the fields, but never one to be sold. Snipe, however, of two kinds, one exactly the same as in Europe, and a kind of thrush, are plentifully sold every day by the Portuguese, who, for I know not what reason, seem to monopolise the wild game.

Nor is the earth less fruitful of vegetables than she is of animals. Rice, which everybody knows is to the inhabitants of these countries the common corn, serving instead of bread, is very plentiful: one kind of it is planted here, and in many of the eastern islands, which in the western parts of India is totally unknown. It is called by the natives *paddy gunang*, that is, *mountain rice;* this, unlike the other sort, which must be under water three parts of the time of its growth, is planted upon the sides of hills, where no water but rain can possibly come. They take, however, the advantage of planting it in the beginning of the rainy season, by which means they reap it in the beginning of the dry. How far this kind of rice might be useful in our West Indian islands, where they grow no bread corn at all, I leave to the judgment of those who know their respective interests, as also the question whether the cassava, or manioc, their substitute for bread, is not as wholesome and cheaper than anything else which could be introduced among them.

Besides rice they grow also Indian corn or maize, which they gather when young and toast in the ear. They have also a vast variety of kidney beans and lentils, called *cadjang*, which make a great part of the food of the common people. They have millet, yams, both wet and dry, sweet potatoes and some European potatoes, not to be despised, but dear. Their gardens produce cabbage, lettuce, cucumbers, radishes, China white radishes, which boil almost as well as turnips, carrots, parsley, celery, pigeon-pease (*Cytissus cajan*), kidney beans of two sorts (*Dolichos chinensis* and *lignosus*), egg plants (*Solanum melongena*), which eat delicately when boiled with pepper and salt, a kind of greens much like spinach (*Convulvulus reptans*), very small but good onions, and asparagus, scarce and very bad. They had also some strong-smelling European plants, as sage, hyssop and rue, which they thought smelt much stronger here than in their native soils, though I cannot say I was sensible of it. But the produce of the earth from which they derive the greatest advantage is sugar; of it they grow immense quantities, and with little care have vast crops of the finest, largest canes imaginable, which I am inclined to believe contain in an equal quantity a far larger proportion of sugar than our West Indian ones. White sugar is sold here for about $2\frac{1}{4}$d. a pound. The molasses makes their arrack, of which, as of rum, it is the chief ingredient; a small quantity of rice only, and some cocoanut wine, being added, which I suppose gives it its peculiar flavour. Indigo they also grow a little, but I believe no more than is necessary for their own use.

The fruits of the East Indies are in general so much cried up by those who have eaten of them, and so much preferred to our European ones, that I shall give a full list of all the sorts which were in season during our stay, and my judgment of each, which I confess is not so much in their favour, as is that of the generality of Europeans after their return home; though while here I did not find that they were more fond of them, or spoke more in their praise, when compared with European fruits, than I did.

(1) The *pine-apples* (*Bromelia ananas*), called here *nanas*, are very large, and so plentiful that in cheap times I have been told that a man who buys them first hand may get them for a farthing apiece. When we were there we could without much haggling get two or three for twopence halfpenny at the common fruit shops. In quality they are certainly good and well flavoured, as good, but not a bit better, than those which are called good in England. So luxuriant are they in their growth that most of them have two or three crowns, and a large number of suckers from the bottom of the fruit: I have counted nine. These are so forward, that they often, while still adhering to the mother, shoot out their fruit, which by the time the large one is ripe, are of a tolerable size. Of these I have seen three upon one apple, and have been told that nine have been seen; but this was esteemed so great a curiosity, that it was preserved in sugar and sent to the Prince of Orange.

(2) *Oranges* (*Citrus aurant. sinensis*) are tolerably good, but while we were here were very dear, seldom less than sixpence apiece. (3) *Pumplemouses* (*Citrus decumanus*), called in the West Indies shaddocks, were well flavoured, but had no juice in them, which we were told depended upon the season. (4) *Lemons* (*Citrus medica*) were very scarce, but the want of them was amply made up by the plenty of (5) *limes*, of which the best were to be bought for about twelvepence a hundred. Of Seville oranges I saw two or three only, and they were almost all peel. There are many other sorts of oranges and lemons; none of which are at all esteemed by the Europeans, or indeed by the natives themselves. (6) *Mango* (*Mangifera indica*): this fruit during our stay was so infested with maggots, which bred inside them, that scarcely four out of ten would be free; nor were those

which were by any means so good as those of Brazil. Europeans commonly compare this fruit to a melting peach, to which in softness and sweetness it certainly approaches, but in flavour as certainly falls much short of any that can be called good. The climate, as I have been told, is here too hot and damp for them; and on the coast of India they are much better. Here are almost as many sorts of them as of apples in England; some much inferior to others; some of the worst sorts are so bad that the natives themselves can hardly eat them when ripe, but use them as an acid when just full grown. One sort, called by them *mangha cowani*, has so strong a smell that a European can scarce bear one in the room; these, however, the natives are fond of. The best kinds for eating are first *mangha doodool*, incomparably better than any other, then *mangha santock* and *mangha gure*; and besides these three I know no other which a European would be at all pleased with.

(7) Of *bananas* (*Musa*) here are likewise innumerable kinds: three only of which are good to eat as fruit, viz. *pisang mas, pisang radja*, and *pisang ambou*; all of which have a tolerably vinous taste; the rest, however, are useful in their way. Some are fried with butter, others boiled in place of bread (which is here a dearer article than meat), etc. One of the sorts, however, deserves to be taken notice of by botanists, as it is, contrary to the nature of the rest of its tribe, full of seeds, from whence it is called *pisang batu* or *pisang bidjis*. It has, however, no excellence to recommend it to the taste or any other way, unless it be, as the Malays think, good for the flux.

(8) *Grapes* (*Vitis vinifera*) are here to be had, but in no great perfection: they are, however, sufficiently dear, a bunch about the size of a fist costing about a shilling or eighteen-pence. (9) *Tamarinds* (*Tamarindus indica*) are prodigiously common and as cheap; the people, however, either do not know how to put them up, as the West Indians do, or do not practise it, but cure them with salt, by which means they become a black mass so disagreeable to the sight and taste that few Europeans choose to meddle with them. (10)

Water melons (*Cucurbita citrullus*) are plentiful and good, as are also (11) *pumpkins* (*Cucurbita pepo*), which are certainly almost or quite the most useful fruit which can be carried to sea, keeping without any care for several months, and making, with sugar and lemon-juice, a pie hardly to be distinguished from apple-pie, or with pepper and salt, a substitute for turnips not to be despised. (12) *Papaws* (*Carica papaia*): this fruit when ripe is full of seeds, and almost without flavour; but while green, if pared, the core taken out, and boiled, is also as good or better than turnips. (13) *Guava* (*Psidium pomiferum*) is a fruit praised much by the inhabitants of our West Indies, who, I suppose, have a better sort than we met with here, where the smell of them alone was so abominably strong, that Dr. Solander, whose stomach is very delicate, could not bear them even in the room, nor did their taste make amends, partaking much of the goatish rankness of their smell. Baked in pies, however, they lost much of this rankness, and we, less nice, ate them very well. (14) *Sweet sop* (*Annona squamosa*), also a West Indian fruit, is nothing but a vast quantity of large kernels, from which a small proportion of very sweet pulp, almost totally devoid of flavour, may be sucked. (15) *Custard apple* (*Annona reticulata*) is likewise common to our West Indies, where it has got its name, which well enough expresses its qualities; for certainly it is as like a custard, and a good one too, as can be imagined. (16) *Casshew apple* (*Anacardium occidentale*) is seldom or never eaten on account of its astringency; the nut which grows on the top of it is well known in Europe, where it is brought from the West Indies. (17) *Cocoanut* (*Cocos nucifera*) is well known everywhere between the tropics; of it are infinite different sorts: the best we met with for drinking is called *calappa edjou*, and easily known by the redness of the flesh between the skin and the shell.

(18) *Mangostan* (*Garcinia mangostana*). As this, and some more, are fruits peculiar to the East Indies, I shall give short descriptions of them. This is about the size of a crab apple, and of a deep red wine colour: at the top of it is a mark

made by five or six small triangles joined in a circle, and at the bottom several hollow green leaves, the remains of the flower.   When they are to be eaten, the skin, or rather flesh, which is thick, must be taken off, under which are found six or seven white kernels placed in a circle.   The pulp with which these are enveloped is what is eaten, and few things I believe are more delicious, so agreeably is acid mixed with sweet in this fruit, that without any other flavour, it competes with, if not excels, the finest flavoured fruits. So wholesome also are these mangostans, that they, as well as sweet oranges, are allowed without stint to people in the highest fevers.   (19) *Jambu* (*Eugenia malaccensis*) is esteemed also a most wholesome fruit; it is deep red, of an oval shape, the largest as big as a small apple; it has not much flavour, but is certainly very pleasant on account of its coolness.   There are several sorts of it, but, without much reference to kinds, the largest and reddest are always the best.   (20) *Jambu ayer* (*Eugenia*).   Of these are two sorts, alike in shape resembling a bell, but differing in colour, one being red and the other white; in size they a little exceed a large cherry; in taste they are totally devoid of flavour, or even sweetness, being nothing more than a little acidulated water, and yet their coolness recommends them very much. (21) *Jambu ayer mauwar* (*Eugenia jambos*) is more pleasant to the smell than the taste; in the latter resembling something the conserve of roses, as in the former, the fresh scent of those flowers.   (22) *Pomegranate* (*Punica granatum*) is the same fruit as in England, and everywhere else that I have met with it, in my opinion but ill repaying any one who takes the trouble of breaking its tough hide.   (23) *Durian* in shape resembles much a small melon, but has a skin covered over with sharp conical spines, whence its name, *dure* signifying in the Malay language a spine.   This fruit when ripe divides itself longitudinally into seven or eight compartments, each of which contains six or seven nuts, not quite so large as chestnuts, coated over with a substance both in colour and consistence very much resembling thick cream.   This is the delicate part of the fruit, which the

natives are vastly fond of; but few Europeans, at first, however, can endure its taste, which resembles sugared cream
mixed with onions. The smell also prejudices them much
against it, being most like that of rotten onions. (24)
Nanca (*Sitodium cauliflorum*), called in some parts of India
jack,[1] has like the durian a smell very disagreeable to
strangers, resembling very mellow apples with a little
garlic. The taste, however, in my opinion makes amends
for the smell, though I must say that amongst us English
I was, I believe, single in that opinion. Authors tell
strange stories about the immense size to which this
fruit grows in some countries which are favourable to it.
Rumphius says that they are sometimes so large that a man
cannot easily lift one of them : the Malays told me that at
Madura they were so large that two men could but carry
one of them ; at Batavia, however, they never exceed the
size of a large melon, which in shape they resemble, but are
coated over with angular spines like the shootings of some
crystals : they are, however, soft, and do not at all prick any
one who handles them. (25) *Tsjampada* (*Sitodium*) differs
from *nanca* in little else than size. (26) *Rambutan*[2] is a
fruit seldom mentioned by Europeans ; it is in appearance
much like a chestnut with the husk on, being like it covered
with soft prickles, but smaller and of a deep red colour:
when eaten, this skin must be cut, and under it is a fruit,
the flesh of which indeed bears but a small proportion to the
stone, but makes rich amends for the smallness of its quantity by the elegance of its acid, superior to any other (maybe)
in the whole vegetable kingdom. (27) *Jambolan* (*Myrtus*)
is in size and appearance not unlike an English damson, but
has always rather too astringent a flavour to allow it to be
compared even with that fruit. (28) *Boa bidarra* (*Rhamnus
jujuba*) is a round yellow fruit, about the size of a musket
bullet ; its flavour is compared to an apple, but like the
former has too much astringency to be compared with any
thing but a crab. (29) *Nam nam* (*Cynometra cauliflora*) is
shaped something like a kidney, very rough and rugged on

[1] *Artocarpus integrifolia*, Linn. f.   [2] *Nephelium lappaceum*, Linn.

the outside and about three inches long: it is seldom eaten raw, but when fried with butter makes very good fritters. (30) *Catappa* (*Terminalia catappa*) and (31) *canari* (*Canarium commune*) are both nuts, the kernels of which are compared to almonds, and indeed are fully as sweet, but the difficulty of getting at their kernels out of their tough rinds and hard shells is so great that they are nowhere publicly sold, nor did I taste any others than those which for curiosity's sake I gathered from the tree and had opened under it. (32) *Madja* (*Limonia*), under a hardish brittle shell, contains a slightly acid pulp, which is only eaten mixed with sugar, nor is it then to be called pleasant. (33) *Sunbul* (*Trichilia*) is by far the worst fruit of any I have to mention: it is in size and shape much like the madja, as large as a middling apple, but rounder; it has a thick hide, containing within it kernels like the mangostan; its taste is both acid and astringent, without one merit to recommend it, indeed I should not have thought it eatable, had I not seen it often publicly exposed for sale upon the fruit stalls. (34) *Blimbing* (*Averrhoa bilimbi*), (35) *blimbing-bessi* (*Averrhoa carambola*), and (36) *cherrema* (*Averrhoa acida*) are all three species of one genus, which, though they differ much in shape, agree in being equally acid, too much so to be used without dressing, except only blimbing-bessi, which is sweeter than the other two; they make, however, excellent sour sauce, and as good pickles. (37) *Salack*[1] (*Calamus rotang-zalacca*) is the fruit of a most prickly bush; it is as big as a walnut, and covered over with scales like a lizard or snake; these scales, however, easily strip off, and leave two or three soft and yellow kernels, in flavour resembling a little, I thought, strawberries: in this, however, I was peculiar, for no one but myself liked them. In short, I believe I may say that bad as the character is that I have given of these fruits, I ate as many of them as any one, and at the time thought I spoke as well of them as the best friends they had. My opinions were then as they are now; whether my shipmates may change theirs between here and home I cannot tell.

---

[1] A species of rattan cane.

Besides these they have several fruits eaten only by the natives, as *Kellor Guilandina, Moringa, Soccum* of two or three kinds, the same as is called bread-fruit in the South Seas. All the kinds here, however, are so incomparably inferior to the South Sea ones, that were it not for the great similitude of the outward appearance of both tree and plant, they would scarcely deserve that name. There are also *bilinju (Gnetum gnemon), boa bune,* etc. etc., all which I shall pass over in silence as not deserving to be mentioned to any but hungry people.

They no doubt have many more which were not in season during our stay : we were told also that several kinds of European fruits, as apples, strawberries, etc., had been planted up in the mountains, where they came to great perfection ; but this I can only advance upon the credit of report. Several other fruits they have also, which they preserve in sugar, as *kumquit, boa, atap,* etc., but these require to be prepared in that way before they are at all eatable.

Batavia consumes an almost incredible quantity of fruits, generally over-ripe, or otherwise bad, before they are sold : nor can a stranger easily get any that are good, unless he goes to a street called *Passar Pisang,* which lies north from the great church, and very near it. Here there live none but Chinese who sell fruit: they are in general supplied from gentlemen's gardens in the neighbourhood of the town, and consequently have the best always fresh. For this excellence of their goods, however, they are well paid, for they will not take less for any kind than three or four times as much as the market price ; nor did we ever grudge to give it, as their fruit was always ten times better than any in the market. The chief supplies of Batavia come from a pretty considerable distance, where great quantities of land are cultivated merely for the sake of the fruits. The country people, to whom these lands belong, meet the town's people at two great markets ; one on Mondays, called *Passar Sineen,* and the other on Saturdays, called *Passar Tanabank,* held at very different places ; each however, about five miles from Batavia. Here the best of fruits may be got at the cheapest rates. The sight of these

markets is to a European very entertaining.   The immense
quantities of fruit exposed is almost beyond belief: forty or
fifty cart-loads of pine-apples, packed as carelessly as we do
turnips in England, is nothing extraordinary ; and everything
else is in the same profusion.   The time of holding these
markets, however, is so ill-contrived, that, as all the fruit for
the ensuing week, both for retailers and housekeepers, must
be bought on Saturday and Monday, there is afterwards no
good fruit in the hands of any but the Chinese in *Passar
Pisang*.

Thus much for meat : in the article of drink, nature has
not been quite so bounteous to the inhabitants of this island
as she has to some of us, sons of the less abundant North.
They are not, however, to-day devoid of strong liquors, though
their religion, Mahometanism, forbids them the use of such ;
by this means driving them from liquid to solid intoxicants,
as opium, tobacco, etc. etc.

Besides their arrack, which is too well known in Europe
to need any description, they have palm wine, made from a
species of palm.   This liquor is extracted from the branches
which should have borne flowers, but are cut by people who
make it their business.   Joints of bamboo cane are hung
under them, into which liquor intended by nature for the
nourishment of both flowers and fruit, distils in tolerable
abundance ; and so true is nature to her paths, that so long
as the fruit of that branch would have remained unripe, so
long, but no longer, does she supply the liquor or sap.   This
liquor is sold in three states, the first almost as it comes
from the tree, only slightly prepared by some method
unknown to me, which causes it to keep thirty-six or
forty-eight hours instead of only twelve : in this state it is
sweet and pleasant, tasting a little of smoke, which, though
at first disagreeable, becomes agreeable by use and not at all
intoxicating.   It is called *tuackmanise*, or sweet palm-wine.
The other two, one of which is called *tuack oras*, and the
other *tuack cuning*, are prepared by placing certain roots in
them, and then fermenting ; so that their taste is altered from
a sweet to a rather astringent and disagreeable taste, and

they have acquired the property of intoxicating in a pretty
high degree. Besides this they have tuack from the cocoanut tree, but very little of this is drunk as a liquor; it being
mostly used to put into the arrack, of which, when intended
to be good, it is a necessary ingredient.

Next to eating and drinking, the inhabitants of this part
of India seem to place their chief delight in a more delicious
as well as less blameable luxury, namely, in sweet smells of
burning rosins, etc., and sweet-scented woods, but more than
all in sweet flowers, of which they have several sorts, very
different from ours in Europe. Of these I shall give a short
account, confining myself to such as were in season during
our stay here.

All these were sold about the streets every night at
sunset, either strung in wreaths of about two feet (a Dutch
ell) long, or made up into different sorts of nosegays, either
of which cost about a halfpenny apiece. (1) *Champacka*
(*Michelia champacka*) grows upon a tree about as large as an
apple tree, and like it spreading. The flower itself consists
of fifteen longish narrow petals, which give it the appearance
of being double, though in reality it is not. Its colour is
yellow, much deeper than that of a jonquil, which flower,
however, it somewhat resembles in scent, only is not so
violently strong. (2) *Cananga* (*Uvaria cananga*) is a green
flower, not at all resembling any European flower, either in
its appearance, which is more like a bunch of leaves than a
flower, or smell, which, however, is very agreeable. (3)
Mulatti (*Nyctanthes sambac*) is well known in English hot-
houses under the name of Indian jasmine; it is here in
prodigious abundance, and certainly as fragrant as any flower
they have; but of this as well as all the Indian flowers it
may be said that, though fully as sweet as any European,
even of the same kinds, they have not that overpowering
strength; in short, their smell, though very much the same,
is much more delicate and elegant than any we can boast
of. (4) *Combang caracnassi* and (5) *Combang tonquin*
(*Pergularia glabra*) are much alike in shape and smell: small
flowers of the dog's-bane kind, hardly to be compared to any

in our English gardens, but like all the rest most elegant in their fragrance. (6) *Sundal malam* (*Polianthes tuberosa*), our English tuberose; this flower is considerably smaller, as well as more mildly fragrant than ours in Europe. The Malay name signifies "intriguer of the night," from a rather pretty idea. The heat of the climate here allows few or no flowers to smell in the day; and this especially from its want of smell and modest white array, seems not at all desirous of admirers; but when night comes its fragrance is diffused around and attracts the attention as well as gains the admiration of every passer-by. (7) *Bonga tanjong* (*Mimusops elengi*) is shaped exactly like a star of seven or eight rays, about half an inch in diameter; it is of a yellowish colour, and like its fellows has a modest agreeable smell; but it is chiefly used to make a contrast with the mulatti in the wreaths which the ladies here wear in their hair, and this it does very prettily.

Besides these there are in private gardens many other sweet flowers, which are not in sufficient plenty to be brought to market, as Cape jasmine, several sorts of Arabian jasmine, though none so sweet as the common, etc. etc. They also make a mixture of several of these flowers and leaves of a plant called *pandang* (*Pandanus*), chopped small, with which they fill their hair and clothes, etc. But their great luxury is in strewing their beds full of this mixture and flowers; so that you sleep in the midst of perfumes, a luxury scarcely to be expressed or even conceived in Europe.

Before I leave the productions of this country I cannot help saying a word or two about spices, though in reality none but pepper is a native of the island of Java, and but little even of that. Of pepper, however, I may say that, large as the quantities of it are that are annually imported into Europe, little or none is used in this part of the Indies. Capsicum or cayenne pepper, as it is called in Europe, has almost totally supplied its place. As for cloves and nutmegs, the monopoly of the Dutch has made them too dear to be plentifully used by the Malays, who are otherwise very fond of them. Cloves, though said to be originally the produce of *Machian* or *Bachian*,[1] a small island far to the eastward, and fifteen miles north of the line, from whence they were when the Dutch came here disseminated over most or all of the eastern isles, are now entirely confined to *Amboyna* and the neighbouring small islets; the Dutch having by different treaties of peace with the conquered kings of all the other islands, stipulated that they should have only a certain number of trees in their dominions; and in future quarrels, as a punishment, lessened their quantity, till at last they left them no right to have any. Nutmegs have been in the same manner extirpated in all the islands, except their native *Banda*, which easily supplies this world, and would as easily supply another, if the Dutch had but another to supply. Of nutmegs, however, there certainly are a few upon the eastern coast of New Guinea, a place on which the Dutch hardly dare set their feet, on account of the treachery and warlike disposition of the natives. There may be also both cloves and nutmegs upon the other islands far to the eastward; for those I believe neither the Dutch nor any other nation seem to think it worth while to examine at all.

The town of Batavia, though the capital of the Dutch dominions in India, is so far from being peopled with Dutchmen, that I may safely affirm that of the Europeans inhabiting it and its neighbourhood, not one-fifth part are Dutch. Besides them are Portuguese, Indians and Chinese, the two last many times exceeding the Europeans in number. Of each of these I shall speak separately, beginning with Europeans, of which there are some, especially in the troops, of almost every nation in Europe. The Germans, however, are so much the most numerous, that they two or three times exceed in number all other Europeans together. Fewer English are settled here than of any other nation, and next to them French; the politic Dutch (well knowing that the English and French, being maritime powers, must often have ships in the East Indies, and will demand and obtain from them the subjects of their

---

[1] *Bachian*, off the south-west coast of Gilolo, is really south of the equator.

2 D

respective kings) will not enter either English or Frenchmen into their service, unless they state that they were born in some place out of their own country. This trick, foolish as it is, was played with us in the case of an Irishman, whom we got on board, and whom they demanded as a Dane, offering to prove by their books that he was born at Elsinore; but our captain, convinced by the man's language, refused to give him up so resolutely, that they soon ceased their demands. Notwithstanding the very great number of other Europeans, the Dutch are politic enough to keep all or nearly all the great posts, as Raads of India, Governors, etc., in their own hands.   Other nations may make fortunes here by traffic if they can, but not by employments. No man can come over here in any other character than that of a soldier in the Company's service; in which, before he can be accepted, he must agree to remain five years. As soon, however, as ever he arrives at Batavia, he, by applying to the Council, may be allowed to absent himself from his corps, and enter immediately into any vocation in which he has any money or credit to set up in.

Women may come out without any of these restrictions, be they of what nation they will.   We were told that there were not in Batavia twenty women born in Europe; the rest of the white women, who were not very scarce, were born of white parents, possibly three or four generations distant from their European mothers.   These imitate the Indians in every particular; their dress, except in form, is the same; their hair is worn in the same manner, and they chew betel as plentifully as any Indian; notwithstanding which I never saw a white man chew it during my whole stay.

Trade is carried on in an easier and more indolent way here, I believe, than in any part of the world.   The Chinese carry on every manufacture of the place, and sell the produce to the resident merchants; for, indeed, they dare not sell to any foreigner.   Consequently when a ship comes in, and bespeaks 100 leggers of arrack, or anything else, the seller has nothing to do but to send orders to his China-man to deliver them on board such a ship; which done, the latter brings the master of the ship's receipt for the goods to his employer, who does nothing but receive money from the stranger, and, reserving his profit, pay the Chinaman his demands. With imports, however, they must have a little more trouble; for they must examine, receive, and preserve them in their own warehouses, as other merchants do.

To give a character of them in their dealings, I need only say that the jewel known to English merchants by the name of fair dealing is totally unknown here: they have joined all the art of trade that a Dutchman is famous for to the deceit of an Indian. Cheating by false weights and measures, false samples, etc. etc., are looked upon only as arts of trade: if you do not find them out, 'tis well; if you do, "well," they say, "then we must give what is wanting," and refund without a blush or the least wrangle, as I myself have seen in matters relating to the ship. But their great forte is asking one price for their commodities and charging another; so that a man who has laid in 100 peculs of sugar, at five dollars a pecul as he thinks, will, after it has been a week or ten days on board, have a bill brought him in at seven; nor will the merchant go from his charge unless a written agreement or witnesses be brought to prove the bargain. For my own part I was fortunate enough to have heard this character of them before I came here; and wanting nothing but daily provision, agreed immediately in writing for every article at a certain price, which my landlord could consequently never depart from. I also, as long as I was well, constantly once a week, looked over my bill, and took it into my possession, never, however, without scratching out the charges of things which I had never had to a considerable amount, which was always done without a moment's hesitation.

Next to the Dutch are the Portuguese, who are called by the natives *Oran Serane*, that is Nazarenes, to distinguish them from the Europeans, notwithstanding which, they are included in the general name of *Capir* or *Cafir*, an opprobrious term given by the Mahometans to all those who have not entered into their faith, of whatsoever religion they may be. These, though formerly they were Portuguese, have no longer any pretensions to more than the name; they have all changed their religion and become Lutherans, and have no communication with or even knowledge of the country of their forefathers. They speak, indeed, a corrupt dialect of the Portuguese language, but much oftener Malay : none of them are suffered to employ themselves in any but mean occupations ; many make their livelihood by hunting, taking in washing, and some by handicraft trades. Their customs are precisely the same as those of the Indians, like them they chew betel, and are only to be distinguished from them by their noses being sharper, their skins considerably blacker, and their hair dressed in a manner different from that of Indians.

The Dutch, Portuguese, and Indians here are entirely waited upon by slaves, whom they purchase from Sumatra, Malacca, and almost all their eastern islands. The natives of Java only have an exemption from slavery, enforced by strong penal laws, which, I believe, are very seldom broken. The price of these slaves is from ten to twenty pounds sterling apiece; excepting young girls, who are sold on account of their beauty ; these sometimes go as high as a hundred, but I believe never higher. They are a most lazy set of people, but contented with a little ; boiled rice, with a little of the cheapest fish, is the food which they prefer to all others. They differ immensely in form of body, disposition, and consequently in value, according to the countries they come from. African negroes, called here *Papua*, are the cheapest and worst disposed of any, being given to stealing and almost incorrigible by stripes. Next to them are the Bougis and the Macassars, both inhabitants of the island of Celebes. They are lazy and revengeful in the highest degree, easily giving up their lives to satisfy their revenge. The island of Bali sends the most honest and faithful, consequently the dearest slaves, and Nias, a small island on the coast of Sumatra, the handsomest women, but of tender, delicate constitutions, ill able to bear the unwholesome climate of Batavia. Besides these are many more sorts, whose names and qualifications I have entirely forgotten.

The laws and customs regarding the punishment of slaves are these. A master may punish his slaves as far as he thinks proper by stripes, but should death be the consequence, he is called to a very severe account; if the fact is proved, very rarely escaping with life. There is, however, an officer in every quarter of the town called *marineu*, who is a kind of constable. He attends to quell all riots, takes up all people guilty of crimes, etc., but is more particularly utilised for apprehending runaway slaves, and punishing them for that or any other crime for which their master thinks they deserve a greater punishment than he chooses to inflict. These punishments are inflicted by slaves bred up to the business : on men they are inflicted before the door of their master's house : on women, for decency's sake, within it. The punishment is stripes, in number according to custom and the nature of the crime, with rods made of split rattans, which fetch blood at every stroke. Consequently they may be, and sometimes are, very severe. A common punishment costs the master of the slave a rix-dollar (4s.), and a severe one about a ducatoon (6s. 8d.) For their encouragement, however, and to prevent them from stealing, the master of every slave is obliged to give him three dubblecheys (7½d.) a week.

Extraordinary as it may seem, there are very few Javans, that is descendants of the original inhabitants of Java, who live in the neighbourhood of Batavia, but there are as many sorts of Indians as there are countries the Dutch import slaves from; either slaves made free or descendants of such. They are all called by the name of *oran slam*, or *Isalam*, a name by which they distinguish themselves from all other religions, the term signifying believers of the true faith. They are again subdivided into innumerable divisions, the people from each country keeping themselves in some degree distinct from the rest. The dispositions generally observed in the slaves are, however, visible in the freemen, who completely inherit the different vices or virtues of their respective countries.

Many of these employ themselves in cultivating gardens,

and in selling fruit and flowers; all the betel and areca, called here *siri* and *pinang*, of which an immense quantity is chewed by Portuguese, Chinese, Slams, slaves, and freemen, is grown by them.   The lime that they use here is, however, slaked, by which means their teeth are not eaten up in the same manner as those of the people of Savu who use it unslaked.   They mix it also with a substance called *gambir*, which is brought from the continent of India, and the better sort of women use with their chew many sorts of perfumes, as cardamoms, etc., to give the breath an agreeable smell. Many also get a livelihood by fishing and carrying goods upon the water, etc.   Some, however, there are who are very rich and live splendidly in their own way, which consists almost entirely in possessing a number of slaves.

In the article of food no people can be more abstemious than they are.   Boiled rice is of rich, as well as of poor, the principal part of their subsistence : this with a small proportion of fish, buffalo or fowl, and sometimes dried fish and dry shrimps, brought here from China, is their chief food. Everything, however, must be highly seasoned with cayenne pepper.   They have also many pastry dishes made of rice flour and other things I am totally ignorant of, which are very pleasant : fruit also they eat much of, especially plantains.

Their feasts are plentiful, and in their way magnificent, though they consist more of show than meat : artificial flowers, etc., are in profusion, and meat plentiful, though there is no great variety of dishes.   Their religion of Mahometanism denies them the use of strong liquors : nor do I believe that they trespass much in that way, having always tobacco, betel, and opium wherewith to intoxicate themselves. Their weddings are carried on with vast form and show : the families concerned borrowing as many gold and silver ornaments as possible to adorn the bride and bridegroom, so that their dresses are always costly.   The feasts and ceremonies relating to them last in rich men's families a fortnight or more ; during all which time the man, though married on the first day, is by the women kept from his wife.

The language spoken among them is entirely Malay, or at least so called, for I believe it is a most corrupt dialect. Notwithstanding that Java has two or three languages, and almost every little island besides its own, distinct from the rest, yet none use, or I believe remember, their own language, so that this *Lingua Franca* Malay is the only one spoken in this neighbourhood, and, I have been told, over a very large part of the East Indies.

Their women, and in imitation of them the Dutch also, wear as much hair as ever they can nurse up on their heads, which by the use of oils, etc., is incredibly great. It is universally black, and they wear it in a kind of circular wreath upon the tops of their heads, fastened with a bodkin, in a taste inexpressibly elegant. I have often wished that one of our ladies could see a Malay woman's head dressed in this manner, with her wreath of flowers, commonly Arabian jasmine, round that of hair; for in that method of dress there is certainly an elegant simplicity and unaffected show of the beauties of nature incomparably superior to anything I have seen in the laboured head-dresses of my fair country-women. Both sexes bathe themselves in the river constantly at least once a day, a most necessary custom in hot climates. Their teeth also, disgustful as they must appear to a European from their blackness, occasioned by their continued chewing of betel, are a great object of attention: every one must have them filed into the fashionable form, which is done with whetstones by a most troublesome and painful operation. First, both the upper and under teeth are rubbed till they are perfectly even and quite blunt, so that the two jaws lose not less than half a line each in the operation. Then a deep groove is made in the middle of the upper teeth, crossing them all, and itself cutting through at least one-fourth of the whole thickness of the teeth, so that the enamel is cut quite through, a fact which we Europeans, who are taught by our dentifricators that any damage done to the enamel is mortal to the tooth, find it difficult to believe. Yet among these people, where this custom is universal, I have scarce seen even in old people a rotten tooth : much may be attributed to what they chew so continually, which they themselves, and indeed every one else, agree is very beneficial to the teeth. The blackness, however, caused by this, of which they are so proud, is not a fixed stain, but may be rubbed off at pleasure, and then their teeth are as white as ivory, but very soon regain their original blackness.

No one who has ever been in these countries can be ignorant of the practice here called *amoc*, which means that an Indian intoxicated with opium rushes into the street with a drawn dagger in his hand, and kills everybody he meets, especially Europeans, till he is himself either killed or taken. This happened at Batavia three times while we were there to my knowledge, and much oftener I believe ; for the *marineu*, or constable, whose business it is to apprehend such people, himself told me there was scarcely a week when either he himself or some of his brethren was not called upon to seize or kill them. So far, however, from being an accidental madness which drove them to kill whomsoever they met without distinction of persons, the three people that I knew of, and I have been told all others, had been severely injured, chiefly in love affairs, and first revenged themselves on the party who had injured them. It is true that they had made themselves drunk with opium before they committed this action ; and when it was done rushed out into the streets, foaming at the mouth like mad dogs, with their drawn *criss* or dagger in their hands : but they never attempted to hurt any one except those who tried or appeared to them to try to stop or seize them. Whoever ran away or went on the other side of the street was safe. To prove that these people distinguish persons, mad as they are with opium, there is a famous story in Batavia of one who ran amoc on account of stripes and ill-usage which he had received from his mistress and her elder daughter, but who on the contrary had always been well used by the younger. He stabbed first the eldest daughter; the youngest hearing the bustle, ran to the assistance of her mother, and placed herself between him and her, attempting to persuade him from his design; but he repeatedly pushed her on one side before he could get at her mother, and when he had killed the latter, ran out as usual. These people are generally slaves, who indeed are by much the most subject to insults, which they cannot revenge. Freemen, however, sometimes do it: one of them who did it while I was there was free and of some substance. The cause was jealousy of his own brother, whom he killed, with two more that attempted to oppose him before he was taken. He, however, never came out of his house, which he attempted to defend; but so mad was he with the effects of the opium, that out of three muskets which he tried to use against the officers of justice, not one was either loaded or primed.

The *marineu* has also these *amocs* committed to his charge. If he takes them alive his reward is great: if he kills them that reward is lost; notwithstanding which three out of four are killed, so resolute and active is their resistance when attacked. They have contrivances like large tongs or pincers to catch them, and hold them till disarmed: those who are taken are generally wounded severely; for the *marineu's* assistants, who are all armed with hangers, know how to lame the man if once they can get within reach. The punishment of this crime is always breaking upon the wheel; nor is that ever relaxed, but so strictly adhered to, that if an amoc when taken is judged by the physician to be in danger from his wounds, he is executed the very next day, as near as possible to the place where he committed his first murder.

Among their absurd opinions proceeding from their original idolatry, which they still retain to some extent, is certainly the custom of consecrating meat, money, etc., to the devil, whom they call Satan. This is done, either in cases of dangerous sickness, when they by these means try to appease the devil, whom they believe to be the cause of all sickness, and make him spare the diseased man's life, or in consequence of dreams. If any man is restless and dreams much for two or three nights, he immediately concludes that Satan has taken that method of laying his commands upon him, and that if he neglects to fulfil them, he will certainly suffer sickness or death as a punishment for his inattention. Consequently he begins to labour over in his brains all the circumstances of his dream, and try his utmost to put some explanation or other upon them. In this, if he fails, he sends for the *cawin* or priest, who assists him to interpret them. Sometimes Satan orders him to do this thing or that, but generally he wants either meat or money, which is always sent him, and hung upon a little plate made of cocoanut leaves on the boughs of a tree, near the river. I have asked them what they thought the devil did with money, and whether or no they thought that he ate the victuals. As for the money, they said, so that the man ordered to do so did but part with it, it signified not who took it, therefore it was generally a prey to the first stranger who found it; and the meat he did not eat, but bringing his mouth near it, he at once sucked all the savour out of it, without disturbing its position in the least, but rendering it as tasteless as water.

But what is more difficult to reconcile to the rules of human reason, is the belief that these people have, that women who bring forth children sometimes bring forth at the same time young crocodiles as twins to the children. These creatures are received by the midwives most carefully, and immediately carried down to the river, where they are turned loose, but have victuals supplied them constantly from the family, especially the twin, who is obliged to go down to the river every now and then, and give meat to this *sudara*, as it is called. The latter, if he is deprived of such attendance, constantly afflicts his relation with sickness. The existence of an opinion so contrary to human reason, and which seemed totally unconnected with religion, was with me long a subject of doubt, but the universal testimony of every Indian I ever heard speak of it was not to be withstood. It seems to have taken its rise in the islands of Celebes and Bouton, very many of the inhabitants of which have crocodiles in their families; from thence it has spread all over the eastern islands, even to Timor and Ceram, and

west again as far as Java and Sumatra; on which islands,
however, such instances are very scarce among the natives.
To show how firmly this prejudice has laid hold of the
minds of ignorant people, I shall repeat one story out of
the multitude I have heard, confirming it from ocular
demonstration.

A slave girl who was born and bred up among the
English at Bencoulen on the island of Sumatra, by which
means she had learnt a little English, told me that her
father when on his deathbed told her that he had a crocodile
for his *sudara*, and charged her to give him meat, etc., after
he was gone, telling her in what part of the river he was to
be found. She went, she said, constantly, and calling him
by his name *Radja pouti* (White King), he came out of the
water to her, and ate what she brought. He was, she said,
not like other crocodiles, but handsomer, his body being
spotted, and his nose red; moreover, he had bracelets of gold
on his feet, and earrings of the same metal in his ears. I
heard her out patiently, without finding fault with the
absurdity of her giving ears to a crocodile. While I am
writing this, my servant, whom I hired at Batavia, and is a
mongrel, between a Dutchman and a Java woman, tells me
that he has seen at Batavia a crocodile of this kind: it was
about two feet long, being very young. Many, both Malays
and Dutch, saw it at the same time; it had gold bracelets on.
"Ah!" said I, "why such a one at Batavia told me of one
which had earrings likewise, and you know that a crocodile
has no ears." "Ah! but," said he, "these *sudara* are different
from other crocodiles, they have five toes on each foot, and
a large tongue which fills the mouth, and they have ears
also, but they are very small." So far will a popular error
deceive people unused to examine into the truth of what
they are told. The Bougis, Macassars, and Boutons, many
of whom have such relations left behind in their own
country, make a kind of ceremonial feast in memory of
them: a large party go in a boat furnished with plenty of
provisions of all kinds and music, and row about in places
where crocodiles or alligators are most common, singing and

crying by turns, each invoking his relation. In this manner they go on till they are fortunate enough to see, or fancy at least that they see, one, when their music at once stops, and they throw overboard provisions, betel, tobacco, etc., imagining, I suppose, that their civility to the species will induce their kindred at home to think well of them, though unable to pay their proper offerings.

Next come the Chinese, who in this place are very numerous, but seem to be people of small substance. Many of them live within the walls, and keep shops, some few of which are furnished with a pretty rich show of European as well as Chinese goods; but by far the greater number live in a quarter by themselves, without the walls, called *Campon China.* Besides these, there are others scattered everywhere about the country, where they cultivate gardens, sow rice and sugar, or keep cattle and buffaloes, whose milk they bring daily to town. Nor are the inhabitants of the town and Campon China less industrious: you see among them carpenters, joiners, smiths, tailors, slipper-makers, dyers of cottons, embroiderers, etc.; in short, the general character of industry given to them by all authors who have written on them is well exemplified here, although the more genteel of their customs cannot, on account of the want of rich and well-born people, be found among them: those can be shown in China alone; here nothing can be found but the native disposition of the lowest class of people. There is nothing, be it of what nature it will, clean or dirty, honest or dishonest (provided there is not too much danger of a halter), which a Chinese will not readily do for money. They work diligently and laboriously, and, loth to lose sight of their main point, money getting, no sooner do they leave off work than they begin to game, either with cards, dice, or some one of the thousand games they have, which are unknown to us in Europe. In this manner they spend their lives, working and gaming, scarcely allowing themselves time for the necessary refreshments of food and sleep; in short, it is as extraordinary a sight to see a Chinaman idle as it is to see a Dutchman or Indian at work.

In manner they are always civil, or rather obsequious; in dress always neat and clean in a high degree, from the highest to the lowest. To attempt to describe either their dresses or persons would be only to repeat some of the many accounts of them that have already been published, as every one has been written by people who had much better opportunities of seeing them, and more time to examine them than I have had. Indeed, a man need go no farther to study them than the China paper, the better sorts of which represent their persons, and such of their customs, dresses, etc., as I have seen, most strikingly like, though a little in the *caricatura* style. Indeed, some of the plants which are common to China and Java, as bamboo, are better figured there than in the best botanical authors that I have seen. In eating, they are easily satisfied, not but that the richer have many savoury dishes. Rice, however, is the chief food of the poor, with a little fish or flesh, as they can afford it. They have a great advantage over the Malays, not being taught by their laws or religion to abstain from any food that is wholesome, so that, besides pork, dogs, cats, frogs, lizards and some kinds of snakes, as well as many sea animals looked upon by other people to be by no means eatable, are their constant food. In the vegetable way, they also eat many things which Europeans would never think of, even if starving with hunger; as the young leaves of many trees, the lump of *bracteæ* and flowers at the end of a bunch of plantains, the flowers of a tree called by the Malays *combang ture* (*Aeschinomine grandiflora*), the pods of *kellor* (*Guilandina moringa*), two sorts of blites (*Amaranthus*), all which are boiled or stewed; also the seeds of *taratti* (*Nymphea Nelumbo*), which indeed are almost as good as hazel nuts. All these, however, the Malays also eat, as well as many more whose names I had not an opportunity of learning, as my illness rendering me weak and unable to go about prevented me from mixing with these people as I should otherwise have done.

In their burials the Chinese have an extraordinary superstition, which is that they will never more open the ground where a man has been buried. Thus their burying-grounds in the neighbourhood of Batavia cover many hundred acres, on which account the Dutch, grudging the quantity of ground laid waste by this method, will only sell them land for it at enormous prices; notwithstanding which they will always raise money to purchase grounds, whenever they can find the Dutch in a humour to sell them; and actually had while we were there a great deal of land intended for that purpose, but not yet begun upon. Their funerals are attended with much purchased and some real lamentations; the relations of the deceased attending as well as women hired to weep. The corpse is nailed up in a large thick wooden coffin, not made of planks, but hollowed out of a trunk of a tree. This is let down into the grave and then surrounded with eight or ten inches of their mortar or *chinam* as it is called, which in a short time becomes as hard as a stone, so that the bones of the meanest among them are more carefully preserved from injury than those of our greatest and most respected people.

Of the Government here I can say but very little, only that a great subordination is kept up; every man who is able to keep house having a certain rank acquired by the length of his services to the Company, which ranks are distinguished by the ornaments of the coaches and dresses of the coachman; for instance, one must ride in a plain coach, another paints his coach with figures and gives his driver a laced hat, another gilds his coach, etc.

The Governor-General who resides here is superior over all the Dutch Governors and other officers in the East Indies, who, to a man, are obliged to come to him at Batavia to have their accounts passed. If they are found to have been at all negligent or faulty, it is a common practice to delay them here one, two or three years, according to the pleasure of the Governor; for no one can leave the place without his consent. Next to the Governor-General are the *Raaden van Indie*, or members of the Council, called here *Edele Heeren*, and by the corruption of the English *Idoleers*, in respect to whom every one who meets them in a carriage is obliged to drive on one side of the road, and stop there till they have passed, which distinction is expected by their wives and even children, and commonly paid to them. Nor can the hired coachman be restrained from paying this slavish mark of respect by anything but the threats of instant death, as some of our captains have experienced, who thought it beneath the dignity of the rank they held in his Britannic Majesty's service to submit to any such humiliating ceremony.

Justice is administered here by a parcel of gentlemen of the law, who have ranks and dignities among themselves as in Europe. In civil matters I know nothing of their proceedings, but in criminal they are rather severe to the natives, and too lenient to their countrymen, who, whatever crime they have committed, are always allowed to escape if they choose; and, if brought to trial, very rarely punished with death. The poor Indians, on the other hand, are flogged, hanged, broken upon the wheel, and even impaled without mercy. While we were there three remarkable crimes were committed by Christians, two duellists each killed his antagonist, and both fled; one took refuge on board our ship, bringing with him so good a character from the Batavians, that the captain gave him protection, nor was he ever demanded. The other, I suppose, went on board some other ship, as he was never taken. The third was a Portuguese, who by means of a false key had robbed an office to which he belonged of 1400 or 1500 pounds; he, however, was taken, but instead of death condemned to a public whipping, and banishment to Edam for ninety-nine years.

The Malays and Chinese have each proper offices of their own, a captain and lieutenants as they are called, who administer justice among them in civil cases, subject to an appeal to the Dutch court, which, however, rarely occurs. Before the Chinese rebellion, as the Dutch, or the massacre, as the Chinese themselves and most Europeans, call it, in 1740 (when the Dutch, upon, maybe, too slight information, massacred no man knows how many thousand unresisting Chinese, for a supposed rebellion which the latter to this day declare they never so much as thought of), the Chinese had two or three of their body in the Council, and had many more privileges than now. From that time to this they have by no means recovered either their former opulence or numbers. Every one now who has got anything considerable prefers to retire with it either to China or anywhere, rather than remain in the power of a people who have behaved so ill to them.

The taxes paid by these people to the Company are very considerable; among which that commonly said to be paid for the liberty of wearing their hair is not inconsiderable. It is, however, no other than a kind of head-money or poll-tax, for no Chinese can wear his hair who has ever been in China, it being a principle of their religion never to let their hair grow again when once it has been shaved off. These taxes are paid monthly, when a flag is hoisted at a house in the middle of the town appointed for that purpose.

The coins current here are ducats, worth 11s. sterling, ducatoons (6s. 8d.), Imperial rix-dollars (5s.), rupees (2s. 6d.), scellings (1s. 6d.), dubblecheys (2½d.) and doits (¼d.) Spanish dollars were when we were there at 5s. 5d., and we were told were never lower than 5s. 4d. Even at the Company's warehouse I could get no more than 19s. for English guineas, for though the Chinamen would give 20s. for some of the brightest, they would for those at all worn give no more than 17s. Strangers must, however, be cautious in receiving money, as there are several kinds, of two sorts, milled and unmilled; ducatoons, for example, when milled are worth 6s. 8d., unmilled only 6s. All accounts are kept in rix-dollars and stivers, both imaginary coins, at least here; the first worth 4s., the other 1d. It must also be remarked that this valuation of their coin is rated on the supposition of a stiver being worth a penny, while it is really more; a current rix-dollar of 48 stivers being worth 4s. 6d.

CHAPTER XVIII

BATAVIA TO CAPE OF GOOD HOPE

DECEMBER 25, 1770

Leave Batavia—Cracatoa—Mosquitos on board ship—Prince's Island—Visit the town—Account of Prince's Island—Produce—Religion—Nuts of *Cycas circinalis*—Town—Houses—Bargaining—Language—Affinity of Malay, Madagascar and South Sea Islands languages—Leave Prince's Island—Sickness on board—Deaths of Mr. Sporing, Mr. Parkinson, Mr. Green, and many others—Coast of Natal—Dangerous position of the ship—Cape of Good Hope—Dr. Solander's illness—French ships—Bougainville's voyage.

25th December 1770. There was not, I believe, a man in the ship but gave his utmost aid to getting up the anchor, so completely tired was every one of the unhealthy air of this place. We had buried here eight people. In general, however, the crew were in rather better health than they had been a fortnight before.[1]

While we were at work a man was missed, and as it was supposed that he did not intend to stay ashore, a boat was sent after him; its return delayed us so long that we entirely lost the sea breeze, and were obliged to come to again a few cables' lengths only from where we lay before.

1st January 1771. Worked all night, and to-day likewise: at night anchored under a high island, called in the draughts *Cracatoa* and by the Indians *Pulo Racatta*. I had been unaccountably troubled with mosquitos ever since we

---

[1] At the time of sailing the number of sick on board amounted to forty or more, and the rest were in a weakly condition, having every one been sick except the sailmaker, an old man about seventy or eighty years of age; and what was more extraordinary about this man was his being more or less generally drunk every day.—Wharton's *Cook*, p. 362.

left Batavia, and still imagined that they increased instead
of decreasing, although my opinion was universally thought
improbable.   To-day, however, the mystery was discovered,
for on getting up water Dr. Solander, who happened to
stand near the scuttle-cask, observed an infinite number
of them in their water-state, which, as soon as the sun had
a little effect upon the water, began to come out in real
effective mosquitos incredibly fast.

2nd. We saw that there were many houses and much
cultivation upon Cracatoa, so that probably a ship which
chose to touch here in preference to Prince's Island might
meet with refreshments.

4th. Soon after dinner-time to-day we anchored under
Prince's Island and went ashore.   The people who met us
carried us immediately to a man who they told us was their
king, and with whom, after a few compliments, we proceeded
to business.   This was to settle the price of turtle, in which
we did not well agree.   This, however, did not at all discourage us, as we doubted not but that in the morning we
should have them at our own price.   So we walked a little
way along shore and the Indians dispersed.   One canoe,
however, remained, and, just as we went off, sold us three
turtle on a promise that we should not tell the king.

5th. Ashore to-day trading: the Indians dropped their
demands very slowly, but were very civil.   Towards noon,
however, they came down to the offered price, so that before
night we had bought up a large supply of turtle.   In the
evening I went to pay my respects to his Majesty the king,
whom I found in his house in the middle of a rice-field, cooking his own supper; he received me, however, very politely.

11th. My servant, Sander, whom I had hired at Batavia,
having found out that these people had a town somewhere
along shore to the westward, and not very far off, I resolved
to visit it; but knowing that the inhabitants were not at all
desirous of our company, kept my intentions secret from
them.   In the morning I set out, accompanied by our second
lieutenant, and went along shore, telling all whom I met
that I was in search of plants, which indeed was also the

case. In about two hours we arrived at a place where were four or five houses. Here we met an old man, and ventured to ask him questions about the town. He said it was very distant; but we, not much relying on his information, proceeded on our way, as did he in our company, attempting, however, several times to lead us out of the pathway which we were now in. We remained firm to our purpose, and soon got sight of our desired object; the old man then turned our friend, and accompanied us to the houses, I suppose nearly 400 in number, divided into the old and new town, between which was a brackish river. In the old town we met with several old acquaintances, one of whom at the rate of 2d. a head undertook to transport us over the river, which he did in two very small canoes, which we prevented from oversetting by laying them alongside each other, and holding them together. In this manner we safely went through our navigation, and arrived at the new town, where were the houses of the king and all the nobilities. These the inhabitants very freely showed to us, though most of them were shut up, the people in general at this time of the year living in their rice-fields, to defend the crop from monkeys, birds, etc. When our curiosity was satisfied, we hired a large sailing boat, for which we gave two rupees (4s.),[1] and which carried us home again in time to dine upon a deer we had bought the day before. It proved very good and savoury meat.

In the evening, when we went ashore, we were acquainted that an axe had been stolen from one of our people : this, as the first theft, we thought it not proper to pass over, so immediate application was made to the king, who after some time promised that it should be returned in the morning.

12th. The hatchet was brought down according to promise ; the thief, they said, afraid of conviction, had in the night conveyed it into the house of the man who brought it. Myself was this day seized with a return of my Batavia fever, which I attributed to having been much exposed to a burning sun in trading with the natives.

[1] At Batavia the rupee was stated to be worth 2s. 6d.

13*th.* My fever returned, but I resolved not to attempt to cure it till in the main ocean I should meet with a better air than this uncleared island could possibly have. In the evening after my fit I went ashore to the king, to whom time after time I had made small presents, altogether not of five shillings value, carrying two quires of paper, which, like everything else, he most thankfully received. We had much conversation, the purport of which was his asking why the English ships did not touch here, as they used to do. I told him that as they had not on the island turtle enough to supply one ship, they could not expect many; but advised him to breed cattle, sheep, and buffaloes, which advice, however, he did not seem much to approve of.

Some account of Prince's Island.

Prince's Island, as it is called by the English, in Malay *Pulo Selan*, and in the language of the inhabitants *Pulo Paneitan*, is a small island situated at the western entrance to the straits of Sunda. It is woody and has no remarkable hill upon it, though the English call the small one which is just over the anchoring place the Pike. This island was formerly much frequented by India ships of many nations, but especially English, who have of late forsaken it, on account, it is said, of the badness of its water, and stop either at North Island, a small island on the Sumatra coast outside the east entrance of the straits, or at New Bay, a few leagues only from Prince's Island, at neither of which places, however, can any quantity of refreshments be procured.

Its chief produce is water, which is so situated that if you are not careful in taking it high enough up the brook, it will inevitably be brackish, from which circumstance alone I believe it has got a bad name with almost all nations. It also produces turtle, of which, however, its supplies are not great; so that if a ship comes second or third in the season she must be contented with small ones, and no great plenty of them, as indeed was in some measure our case. We bought at very various prices, according to the humour of the people;

but, altogether, I believe, they came to about a halfpenny or
three farthings a pound. They were of the green kind, but
not fat nor well flavoured in any degree, as they are in most
other parts. This I believe is in great measure owing to the
people keeping them, sometimes for a very long time, in crawls
of brackish water, where they have no kind of food given to
them. Fowls are tolerably cheap, a dozen large ones sold
when we were there for a Spanish dollar, which is 5d.
apiece. They have also plenty of monkeys and small deer
(*Moschus pygmœus*), the largest of which are not quite so big
as a new fallen lamb, and another kind of deer, called by
them *munchack*, about the size of a sheep. The monkeys
were about half a dollar (2s. 6d.), the small deer 2d.; the
larger, of which they brought down only two, a rupee, or 2s.
Fish they have of various kinds, and we always found
them tolerably cheap. Vegetables they have : cocoanuts—
a dollar for 100, if you choose them, or 130 if you take
them as they come,—plantains in plenty, some water melons,
pine-apples, jaccas (jack fruit), pumpkins ; also rice, chiefly of
the mountain sort which grows on dry land, yams, and
several other vegetables: all which are sold reasonably enough.

The inhabitants are Javans, whose Radja is subject to
the Sultan of Bantam, from whom they receive orders, and
to whom they possibly pay a tribute, but of that I am not
certain. Their customs, I believe, are very much like those
of the Indians about Batavia, only they seem much more
jealous of their women, so much so that I never saw one
during the whole time of our stay, unless she was running away
at full speed to hide herself in the woods. Their religion is
Mahometanism, but I believe they have not a mosque upon
the island : they were, however, very strict in the observance
of their fast (the same as the Ramadan of the Turks), during
which we happened to come. Not one would touch victuals
until sunset, or even chew their betel ; but half an hour
before that time all went home to cook the kettle, nor would
they stay for any time but in the hope of extraordinary profit.

The food was nearly the same as the Batavian Indians,
adding only to it the nuts of the palm *Cycas circinalis*, with

which on the coast of New Holland some of our people were made ill, and some of our hogs poisoned outright. Their method of preparing them to get rid of their deleterious qualities they told me were, first to cut the nuts into thin slices and dry them in the sun, then to steep them in fresh water for three months, afterwards pressing the water from them, and drying them in the sun once more. They, however, were so far from being a delicious food that they never used them but in times of scarcity, when they mixed the preparation with their rice.

Their town, which they called *Samadang*, consisted of about 400 houses; great part of the old town, however, was in ruins. Their houses were all built upon pillars four or five feet above the ground. The plan of that of *Gundang*, a man who seemed to be next in riches and influence to the king, will give an idea of them all. It was walled with boards, a luxury which none but the king and he himself had, but in no other respect differed from those of the middling people except in being a little larger. The walls

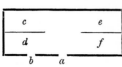

a, door; *b*, window; *c*, part where the master and his wife sleep; *d*, part where the children sleep; *e*, where the victuals are cooked; *f*, where strangers or visitors sleep.

were made of bamboo, platted on small perpendicular sticks fastened to the beams. The floors were also of bamboo, each stick, however, laid at a small distance from the next; so that the air had a free passage from below, by which means these houses were always cool. The thatch, of palm leaves, was always thick and strong, so that neither rain nor sunbeams could find entrance through it. When we were at the town there were very few inhabitants there: the rest lived in occasional houses built in the rice-fields, where they watched the crop to prevent the devastations of monkeys, birds, etc. These occasional houses are smaller than those of the town; the posts which support them also, instead of being four or five feet in height, are eight or ten: otherwise the divisions, etc., are exactly the same.

Their dispositions, as far as we saw them, were very

good; at least they dealt very fairly with us upon all occasions, Indian-like, however, always asking double what they would take for whatever they had to dispose of. But this produced no inconvenience to us, who were used to this kind of traffic. In making bargains they were very handy, and supplied the want of small money reasonably well by laying together a quantity of anything, and when the price was settled dividing it among each other according to the proportion each had brought to the general stock. They would sometimes change our money, giving 240 doits for a Spanish dollar, that is 5s. sterling, and 92, that is 2s. sterling, for a Bengal rupee. The money they chose, however, was doits in all small bargains; dubblecheys they had, but were very nice in taking them.

Their language is different both from the Malay and Javan: they all, however, speak Malay.

Prince's Island.	Java.	Malay.	English.
Jalma	Oong Lanang	Oran Lacki Lacki	A man
Becang	Oong Wadong	Parampuan	A woman
Oroculatacke	Lari	Anack	A child
Holo	Undass	Capalla	The head
Erung	Erung	Edung	The nose
Mata	Moto	Mata	The eyes
Chole	Cuping	Cuping	The ears
Cutock	Untu	Ghigi	The teeth
Beatung	Wuttong	Prot	The belly
Pimping	Poopoo	Paha	The thigh
Hullootoor	Duncul	Loutour	The knee
Metis	Sickil	Kauki	The leg
Cucu	Cucu	Cucu	A nail
Langan	Tangan	Tangan	A hand
Ramo Langan	Jari	Jaring	A finger

These specimens of languages, so near each other in situation, I choose to give together, and select the words without any previous choice, as I had written them down, that the similar and dissimilar words might equally be seen. As for the parts of the body which I have made the subject of this and all my specimens of language, I chose them in preference to all others, as the names of them are easily got from people of whose language the inquirer has not the least idea. What I call the Javan is the language spoken at Samarang, a day's journey from the seat of the Emperor of Java. I have been told that there are several other languages upon the island, but I had no opportunity of collecting words of any of these, as I met with no one who could speak them.

The Prince's Islanders call their language *Catta Gunung*, that is, the *mountain language*, and say that it is spoken upon the mountains of Java, from whence their tribe originally came, first to New Bay, only a few leagues off, and from thence to Prince's Island, driven there by the quantity of tigers.

The Malay, Javan, and Prince's Island languages all have words in them, either exactly like, or else plainly deriving their origin from the same source with others in the language of the South Sea Islands. This is particularly visible in their numbers, from whence one would at first be inclined to suppose that their learning, at least, had been derived originally from one and the same source. But how that strange problem of the numbers of the black inhabitants of Madagascar being vastly similar to those of Otahite could have come to pass, surpasses, I confess, my skill to conjecture. The numbers that I give below in the comparative table I had from a negro slave, born at Madagascar, who was at Batavia with an English ship, from whence he was sent for merely to satisfy my curiosity in the language.

That there are much fewer words in the Prince's Island language similar to South Sea words, is owing in great measure to my not having taken a sufficient quantity of words upon the spot to compare with them.

The Madagascar language has also some words similar to Malay words, *ouron*, the nose, in Malay, *erung; lala*, the tongue, *lida; tang*, the hand, *tangan; taan*, the ground, *tanna.*

From this similitude of language between the inhabitants of the Eastern Indies and the islands in the South Sea, I should have ventured to conjecture much did not Madagascar interfere: and how any communication can ever have been

SPECIMENS OF LANGUAGES

South Sea.	Malay.	Java.	Prince's Island.	English.
Matta	Mata	Moto	Mata	An eye
Maa	Macan	Mangan	...	To eat
Inoo	Menum	Gnumbe	...	To drink
Matte	Matte	Matte	...	To kill
Outou	Coutou	...	...	A louse
Euwa	Udian	Udan	...	Rain
Owhe	...	...	Awe	Bamboo cane
Ooma	Sousou	Sousou	...	A breast
Mannu	...	Mannu	Mannuk	A bird
Eyea	Ican	Iwa	...	A fish
Uta	Utan	...	...	Inland
Tapao	...	Tapaan	...	The foot
Tooura	Udang	Urang	...	A lobster
Eufwhe	Ubi	Uwe	...	Yams
Etannou	Tannam	Tandour	...	To bury
Enammou	Gnammuck	...	...	A muscheto
Hearu	Garru	Garu	...	To scratch
Taro	Tallas	Talas	...	Cocos roots
Outou	...	...	Surgoot	The mouth
Eto	...	...	Tao	Sugar-cane

	South Sea.	Malay.	Java.	Prince's Island.	Madagascar.
1.	Tahie	Satou	Sigi	Hegie	Issa
2.	Rua	Dua	Lorou	Dua	Rove
3.	Torou	Tiga	Tullu	Tollu	Tello
4.	Haa	Ampat	Pappat	Opat	Effat
5.	Ruma	Lima	Limo	Limath	Limi
* 6.	Whene	Annam	Nunnam	Gunnap	Enning
7.	Hetu	Tudju	Petu	Tudju	Fruto
8.	Waru	Delapan	Wolo	Delapan	Wedo
9.	Heva	Sembilan	Songo	Salapan	Sidai
10.	Ahourou	Sapoulou	Sapoulou	Sapoulou	Scula
11.	Matahie	Sabilas	Suvalas	...	...
12.	Marua	Dubilas	Roalas	...	...
20.	Tahie taou	Duapoulou	Rompoulon	...	...
100.	Rima taou	Saratus	Satus	Satus	...
200.	Mannu	Duaratus	Rongatus	...	...
1000.	Lima mannu	Sereboo	Seavo	Seavo	...
2000.	Mannu tiné	...	...	...	...

* N.B.—In the island of Ulhietea 6 is called *ono*. [Note by Banks.]

carried between Madagascar and Java to make the brown, long-haired people of the latter speak a language similar to that of the black, woolly-headed natives of the other, is, I confess, far beyond my comprehension : unless the Egyptian learning running in two courses, one through Africa, the other through Asia, might introduce the same words, and, what is still more probable, numerical terms into the languages of people who never had communicated with each other.   But this point, requiring a depth of knowledge of antiquities, I must leave to antiquarians to discuss.

14th January. Weighed ; our breeze, though favourable, was, however, so slack, that by night we had got no further than abreast of the town, where we anchored.

20th. Myself, who had begun with the bark yesterday, missed my fever to-day ; the people, however, in general grew worse, and many had now the dysentery or bloody flux.

22nd. Almost all the ship's company were now ill, either with fluxes or severe purgings ; myself far from well, Mr. Sporing very ill, and Mr. Parkinson very little better : his complaint was a slow fever.

23rd. Myself was too ill to-day to do anything—one of our people died of the flux in the evening.

24th. My distemper this day turned out to be a flux, attended (as that disease always is) with excruciating pains in my bowels, on which I took to my bed : in the evening Mr. Sporing died.

25th. One more of the people died to-day.   Myself endured the pain of the damned almost.   The surgeon of the ship thought proper to order me the hot bath, into which I went four times at the intervals of two hours and felt great relief.

26th. Though better than yesterday my pains were still almost intolerable.   In the evening Mr. Parkinson died, and one more of the ship's crew.

28th. This day Mr. Green, our astronomer, and two of the people died, all of the very same complaint as I laboured under, no very encouraging circumstance.

29th. Three more of the people died this day.

30th. For the first time I found myself better and slept some time, which my continual pains had never suffered me to do before notwithstanding the opiates which were constantly administered. One person only died to-day, but so weak were the people in general that, officers and men included, there were not more than eight or nine could keep the deck; so that four in a watch were all they had.

31st. This day I got out of my bed in good spirits and free from pain, but very weak; my recovery had been as rapid as my disease was violent; but to what cause to attribute either the one or the other we were equally at a loss. The wind, which went to E. and S.E. yesterday, blew to-day in the same direction, so we had little reason to doubt its being the true trade, a circumstance which raised the spirits of even those who were most afflicted with the tormenting disease which now raged with its greatest violence.

1st February. Fine brisk trade kept up our spirits and helped to raise me fast: two of the people died to-day, nevertheless.

2nd. Breeze continued to-day: the surgeon began to think that the rapid progress of the disease was checked by it, but declared at the same time that several people were still almost without hopes of recovery.

3rd. Some of the people who were least affected began now to show signs of amendment, but two of the worst died notwithstanding.

6th. One more died to-day. Those of our people who were not very bad before the 1st of this month had now almost universally recovered; but there were still several in the ship who at that time were very bad. These remained unalterably the same, neither becoming better nor worse. Throughout the whole course of this distemper medicine has been of little use, the sick generally proceeding gradually to their end without a favourable symptom, till the change of weather instantaneously stopped in a manner the malignant quality of the disease.

11th. One more of our people died.

12th. Another died.

14th. A third died to-day: neither of these people had grown either better or worse for many days.

20th. Lost another man.

26th. Lost three more people to-day.

3rd March. In the evening some of the people thought they saw land, but that opinion was rejected almost without examination, as by the journals which had been kept by the log, we were still above a hundred leagues from land, and by observations of sun and moon, full 40. The night was chiefly calms and light breezes, with fog and mist.

4th. Day broke and showed us at its earliest dawn how fortunate we had been in the calms of last night. What was then supposed to be land proved really so, and not more than five miles from us, so that another hour would have infallibly have carried us upon it. But fortunate as we might think ourselves to be yet unshipwrecked, we were still in extreme danger. The wind blew right upon the shore and with it ran a heavy sea, breaking mountains high upon the rocks, with which it was everywhere lined, so that, though some in the ship thought it possible, the major part did not hope to be able to get off. Our anchors and cables were accordingly prepared, but the sea ran too high to allow us a hope of the cables holding should we be driven to the necessity of using them, and should we be driven ashore the breakers gave us little hope of saving even our lives. At last, however, after four hours spent in the vicissitudes of hope and fear, we found that we got gradually off, and before night we were out of danger. The land from whence we so narrowly escaped is part of Terra de Natal, lying between the rivers Sangue and Fourmis, about twenty leagues to the southward of the Bay of Natal.

7th. For these some days past the seamen have found the ship to be driven hither and thither by currents[1] in a manner totally unaccountable to them.

The surface of the water was pretty thickly strewed with

---

[1] The Agulhas currents.

the substance that I have before often mentioned under the name of sea-sawdust; the water likewise emitted a strong smell like that of sea-weeds rotting on the shore.

12*th.* In the morning saw Cape Falso,[1] and soon after the Cape of Good Hope, off which we observed a rock not laid down in the charts. The breeze was fresh and fair; it carried us as far as Table Bay, off which we anchored. In coming along shore we saw several smokes upon the next hill before the Lion's rump, and when at anchor fires upon the side and near the top of the Table Mountain. In the bay were several ships, four French, two Danes, one English, viz. the *Admiral Pocock*, Indiaman, and several Dutch.

13*th.* Wind so fresh at S.E. that we could not attempt to go ashore; no boat, indeed, in the whole harbour attempted to stir; the Dutch Commodore hauled down his broad pennant, a signal for all boats belonging to him to keep on board. Jno. Thomas died.

14*th.* The ship was got under way and steered into the harbour to her proper berth. A Dutch boat came on board to know from whence we came, and brought with her a surgeon, who examined our sick, and gave leave for them and us to come ashore, which we accordingly did at dinner-time.

17*th.* Dr. Solander, who had been on board the Indiaman last night, was taken violently ill with a fever and a pain in his bowels. A country physician was immediately sent for, who declared on hearing his case that it was the common consequence of Batavian fevers, that the Doctor would be much worse, and would for some time suffer very much by his bowel complaint, but upon the whole he declared that there was no danger. I could not, however, help being a good deal alarmed in my own opinion.

31*st.* Dr. Solander, after having been confined to his bed or chamber ever since the 17th of this month, this day came downstairs for the first time, very much emaciated by his tedious illness.

[1] This appears to have been Cape Agulhas.

3rd April. Theodosio[1] . . . a seaman, died very suddenly; he had enjoyed an uninterrupted state of good health during all our times of sickness.

7th. Of the four French vessels which we found in this harbour, three have now sailed, and the fourth is ready for sea, two were 64-gun ships, the third a large snow, and the fourth a frigate. All these came from the Isle de France[2] for provisions, of which they carry away hence a prodigious quantity, and consequently must have many mouths to feed. It is probable they meditate some stroke from this island at our East India settlements in the beginning of a future war, which, however, our Indian people are not at all alarmed at, trusting entirely to the vast armies which they constantly keep up, the support of which in Bengal alone costs £840,000 a year.

Mr. De Bougainville, pleased with the beauty of the ladies of Otahite, gave that island the name of Cypre. On his return home he touched at Isle de France, where the person who went out with him in the character of natural historian was left, and still remains. *Otourrou*, the Indian, whom he brought from thence, was known on board his ship by the name of *Tootavu*, a plain corruption of Bougainville, with whom it may be supposed he meant to change names according to his custom. This man is now at Isle de France, from whence a large ship is very soon to sail and carry him back to his own country, where she is to make a settlement. In doing this she must necessarily follow the track of Abel Jansen Tasman, and consequently, if she does not discover Cook's Straits, which in all probability she will do, must make several discoveries on the coast of New Zealand. Thus much the French who were here made no secret of. How necessary then will it be for us to publish an account of our voyage as soon as possible after our arrival, if we mean that our own country shall have the honour

---

[1] This is clearly Jeh. Dozey, A.B., who is stated, in the "Introduction" to Wharton's *Cook* (p. liii.), to have died on April 7, 1771, but his death is not alluded to in Cook's Journal.

[2] The more usual name now is Mauritius.

of our discoveries. Should the French have published an account of Mr. De Bougainville's voyage before that of the second *Dolphin*,[1] how infallibly will they claim the discovery of Cypre, or Otahite, as their own, and treat the *Dolphin's* having seen it as a fiction, which we are enabled to set forth with some show of truth, as the *Endeavour* really did see it, a twelvemonth, however, after Mr. De Bougainville. If England choose to assert her prior claim to it, as she may hereafter do if the French settle, it may be productive of very disagreeable consequences.

---

[1] *i.e.* the second voyage of the *Dolphin*, under Wallis (*q.v.* p. li.) No important discoveries were made on the *Dolphin's* first voyage under Byron.

CHAPTER XIX

CAPE OF GOOD HOPE TO ENGLAND

Account of the Cape of Good Hope—Its settlement by the Dutch—Cape Town—Dutch customs—Government—Climate—General healthiness— Animals—Wines—Cost of living—Botanical garden—Menagerie—Settle- ments in the interior—Barrenness of the country—Hottentots: their appearance, language, dancing, customs, etc.— Money — Leave Table Bay — Robben Island — St. Helena —Volcanic rocks — Cultivation— Provisions—Introduced plants—Natural productions—Ebony—Specula- tions as to how plants and animals originally reached so remote an island—Leave St. Helena—Ascension Island—Ascension to England— Land at Deal.

NOTWITHSTANDING that hydrographers limit the Cape of Good Hope to a single point of land on the S.W. end of Africa, which is not the southernmost part of that immense continent, I shall under this name speak of the southern parts of Africa in general, as far as latitude 30° at least. The country was originally inhabited by the Hottentots alone, but is now settled by the Dutch, and from the convenience of its situation as a place of refreshment for ships sailing to and from India, is perhaps visited by Europeans oftener than any other distant part of the globe.

The Dutch, if their accounts can be credited, have also people much farther inland. They have upon the whole of this vast tract, however, only one town, which is generally known by the name of Cape Town: it is situated on the Atlantic side about twenty miles to the north of the real Cape, on the banks of a bay sheltered from the S.E. wind by a large mountain level at the top, from whence both itself and the bay have got the name of Tafel or Table. It has of late years very much increased in size, and consists of about a thousand houses, neatly built of brick, and in general whitened over. The streets in general are broad and commodious, all crossing each other at right angles. In the chief of them is a canal, on each side of which is a row of oak trees, which flourish tolerably well, and yield an agreeable shade to walkers. Besides this there is another canal running through the town, but the slope of the ground is so great that both have to be furnished with sluices, at intervals of little more than fifty yards.

In houses the same poverty of inventions exists here as at Batavia. They are almost universally built upon one and the same plan, whether small or large. In general they are low, and universally covered with thatch ; precautions said to be necessary against the violence of the S.E. winds, which at some seasons of the year came down from the Table Mountain with incredible violence.

Of the inhabitants, a far larger proportion are real Dutch than of those of Batavia ; but as the whole town is in a manner supported by entertaining and supplying strangers, each man in some degree imitates the manners and customs of the nation with which he is chiefly concerned. The ladies, however, do not follow their husbands in this particular, but so true are they to the customs of the fatherland, that scarcely one of them will stir without a *sooterkin* or *chauffette* ready to place under her feet, whenever she shall sit down. The younger ones, though, do not in general put any fire in them, but seem to use them merely for show. In general they are handsome, with clear skins and high complexions, and when married (no reflections upon my country-women) are the best housekeepers imaginable, and great child-bearers. Had I been inclined for a wife, I think this is the place of all others I have seen, where I could have best suited myself.

Their servants are in general Malay slaves, who are brought here from Batavia; to these they behave much better than the Batavians, in consequence of which these

Malays are much quieter, honester, and more diligent, and less wicked than in that place : in instance of which I need only say that there has never been a case of running amoc here.

The town is governed by a Governor and Council who are quite independent of Batavia. The present Governor is Ryck Tulback. He is very old, and has long enjoyed his present station with a most universal good character, which is easily explained in this manner : he is unmarried, and has no connections which may make him wish to make more money than his salary furnishes him with ; consequently, not entering into trade, he interferes with no man, and not wishing to be bribed, does strict justice on all occasions to the best of his abilities.

The climate, though not at all too hot for those who come from India, would doubtless appear sufficiently warm could any one be transported immediately from England to this place. Upon the whole it seems much of the temperature as the island of Madeira, though scarcely quite so hot. This I judge from the productions. In general, during the whole summer, the air is frequently fanned by S.E. winds, which come off the hills above the town with vast violence, and during the time of their blowing, especially at first, are very troublesome to such as are obliged to be abroad in them, by raising the sand with which the whole country abounds, and filling their eyes with it. Nor are the houses quite free from its effects ; however closely they are shut up, the sand will find an entrance, and in a short time cover every kind of furniture with a thick dust.

Inconvenient as this certainly is, it, however, does not seem to have any effect beyond the present moment, though the inhabitants must in the course of a summer inhale an immense quantity of this sand, which has been thought by some physicians to be productive of ulcers in the lungs, etc. etc. Yet consumptions are diseases scarcely known here, and the healthy countenances, fresh complexions, and above all, the number of children with which all ranks of people here are blessed, abundantly prove that the climate in general is very friendly to the human constitution.

Diseases brought here from Europe are said to be almost immediately cured, but those of the Indies not so easily, which latter we ourselves experienced: our sick recovering very little for the first fortnight, and after that very slowly, so that after a month's stay several of them were far from recruited.

The industry of the Dutch, so well known, and so constantly exerted in all foreign settlements, has supplied this place with a profusion of all kinds of European provisions. Wheat and barley are as good here as in Europe; hops, however, will not grow, so that they cannot make beer, even tolerably. Cattle are in great plenty, and beef is very fair; sheep likewise are in great plenty. Both these the native Hottentots had before the Dutch settled the place, so that they differ a little in appearance from those of other places: the oxen are lighter, more neatly made, and have vast spreading horns; the sheep, instead of wool, are covered with a kind of substance between hair and wool. Their tails also are very large: I have seen some which could not weigh less than ten or twelve pounds, and was told that they are often much larger. Of the milk of their cows they make very good butter, but cheese they know not how to make in any degree of perfection. Besides these they have goats in plenty, which, however, they never eat; and hogs, but these are less plentiful. Poultry, as fowls, ducks, geese, etc., are in tolerable plenty. They have also wild game, as hares exactly like ours in Europe, partridges of two kinds, quails, antelopes of many kinds, and bustards, in general very well flavoured, but rather drier than those of the same kinds in Europe.

As their fields produce European wheat and barley, so their gardens produce the same kinds of vegetables as we have in Europe. Cabbages, turnips, potatoes, asparagus, broccoli, etc., are all plentiful and excellent of their kind. Their fruits are also the same, apples, pears, oranges, peaches, apricots, figs, etc. Of Indian fruits, they have plantains, guavas, and jambus; but neither of these in any kind of perfection. Their vineyards produce a great quantity of wines, which they class into many sorts, calling one Madeira, another Frontinac, etc. None of these are comparable to the wines which we commonly drink in Europe, yet they are all light, well cured, and far from unpalatable; in taste not unlike some of the light French and Portuguese white wines. The famous Constantia, so well known in Europe, is made genuine only at one vineyard about ten miles distant from Cape Town. Near that, however, is another vineyard, which is likewise called Constantia, where a wine not much inferior to it is made, which is always to be had at a lower price.

The common method of living is to lodge and board with some one of the inhabitants, many of whose houses are always open for the reception of strangers. The prices are 5, 4, 3, and 2 shillings a day, for which all necessaries are found you, according as your situation leads you to choose a more or less expensive method of living, in what may truly be called profusion in proportion to the price you give. Besides this there is hardly an expense in the place. Coaches are seldom or never used, but may be hired at the rate of 6 rix-dollars or £1 : 4s. a day. Horses are 6s. a day, but the country is not tempting enough to induce any one often to make use of them. Public entertainments there are none, nor were there any private ones owing to the measles, which broke out about the time of our arrival: at other times I was told there were, and that strangers were always welcome to them if of any rank.

At the farther end of the High Street is the Company's garden, which is nearly two-thirds of an English mile in length. The whole is divided by walks, intersecting each other at right angles, and planted with oaks, which are clipped into wall hedges, except in the centre walk, where they are suffered to grow to their full size. This walk, therefore, at all times of the day furnishes an agreeable shade, no doubt highly beneficial to the sick, as the country has not the least degree of shade, nor has nature made the soil capable of producing a single tree, at least within several miles round the town. By far the largest part of this garden is utilised for producing cabbages, carrots, etc.; two small squares, however, are set apart for botanical plants, which are well taken care of and neatly kept. At the time we were there the greater part of the plants, as the annuals, bulbs, etc., were underground. Upon the whole, I am of opinion that the number now to be found there will not amount to above half of what they were when Oldenland wrote his Catalogue; indeed, at that time it is possible that more ground was employed for the purpose.

At the farther end of the garden is a vivarium or menagerie, supported also at the expense of the Company, where rare beasts and birds are kept. Here were ostriches, cassowaries, antelopes of several kinds, zebras and several other animals seldom or never seen in Europe; particularly that called by the Hottentots *coedoe*, whose beautiful spiral horns are often brought over to Europe. This animal, which was as large as a horse, died while we were there, but not before I had time to get a description and drawing of him.

Near this enclosure is another for birds, in which were the crowned pigeons of Banda, and several more rare birds, especially of the Dutch kind, of which there was indeed a very fine collection. Both birds and beasts were very carefully and well taken care of.

It remains now, after having described the town and its environs, to say a little of the country about it. Of this, indeed, I can say but little, and even for that little am obliged to depend entirely upon hearsay, not having had an opportunity of making even one excursion, owing in great measure to Dr. Solander's illness.

The Dutch say that they have settled the country as far as 2000 miles inland, at least that is the distance to the furthest habitations of Europeans: how far it may be, however, in a straight line north and south, is hard to say, nor do they pretend to guess. Supposing it, however, the shortest distance possible, it is sufficient to prove the infinite, and indeed to a European almost inconceivable, barrenness of the country in general, that the mere supply of food should make it necessary for men to spread themselves over such an immense tract of country, in order to find fertile spots capable of producing it. How far distant such spots are from each other may be concluded from what one farmer told us while there. On being asked why he brought his young children with him to the Cape, from whence he lived fifteen days' journey, and told that he had better have left them with his next neighbour : "neighbour," said he, "my nearest neighbour lives five days' journey from me."

Nor does the country in the immediate neighbourhood of the Cape give any reason to contradict the idea of immense barrenness which must be formed from what I have said. The country in general is either bare rock, shifting sand, or grounds covered with heath, etc., like the moors of Derbyshire and Yorkshire, except the very banks of the few rivulets, where are a few plantations chiefly utilised, if well sheltered, for raising garden stuff, and if rather less sheltered as vineyards ; but if exposed nothing can stand the violence of the wind, which blows here through the whole summer or dry season. During my whole stay I did not see a tree in its native soil as tall as myself ; indeed housekeepers complain of the dearness of firewood, as almost equal to that of provisions, nothing being burnt here but roots, which must be dug out of the ground. What, indeed, proves the influence of the wind in prejudice to vegetation is that a stem not thicker than my thumb (and thicker they never are) will have a root as thick as my arm or leg.

As their distant settlements are directly inland, and the whole coast either is, or is thought to be, totally destitute of harbours, their whole communication is carried on by land carriage. Waggons drawn by oxen are employed in that service : they are, however, very light, and the cattle so much more nimble than ours in Europe, that they assured us that they sometimes travelled at the rate of eight miles an hour. Travelling is also very cheap. As there are no inns upon the roads, every one must carry his own provisions with him, and the oxen must live upon the heath or ling

which they meet with upon the road. Great as these
conveniences are, the people who come from afar must do
little more than live, as there is no trade here, but in a few
articles of provisions, which are sent to the East Indies, and
curiosities. They can bring nothing to market but a little
butter, such skins of wild beasts as they have been able to
procure, and perhaps a few kinds of drugs.

There remains nothing but to say a word or two concerning the Hottentots, so frequently spoken of by travellers,
by whom they are generally represented as the outcast of
the human species, a race whose intellectual faculties are so
little superior to those of beasts, that some have been
inclined to suppose them more nearly related to baboons
than to men.

Although I very much desired it, I was unable to see
any of their habitations, there being none, as I was
universally informed, within less than four days' journey
from the Cape, in which they retained their original customs.
Those who come to the Cape, who are in number not a few,
are all servants of the Dutch farmers, whose cattle they
take care of, and generally run before their waggons: these
no doubt are the lowest and meanest of them, and these
alone I can describe.

They were in general slim in make, and rather lean
than at all plump or fat: in size equal to Europeans,
some six feet and more; their eyes not expressive of any
liveliness, but rather dull and unmeaning; the colour of
their skins nearest to that of soot, owing in great measure to
the dirt, which, by long use, was ingrained into it, for I
believe that they never wash themselves. Their hair curled
in very fine rings like that of negroes, or a Persian lamb's
skin, but hung in falling ringlets seven or eight inches
long. Their clothes consisted of a skin, generally of a sheep,
and round their waists a belt, which in both sexes was
richly ornamented with beads and small pieces of copper.
Both sexes wore necklaces, and sometimes bracelets, likewise
of beads, and the women had round their legs certain rings
made of very hard leather, which they said served to defend

them from the thorns with which the country everywhere abounds. Under their feet some wore a kind of sandal of wood or bark, but the greater number went entirely unshod. For bodily qualifications they were strong, and appeared nimble and active in a high degree.

Their language, which appears to a European but indistinctly articulated, has this remarkable singularity, that in pronouncing a sentence they click or cluck with their tongues at very frequent intervals, so much so that these clicks do not seem to have any particular meaning, except possibly to divide words, or certain combinations of words. How this can be effected, unless they can click with their tongues without inspiring their breath, appears mysterious to a European : and yet I am told that many of the Dutch farmers understand and speak their language very fluently. Almost all the natives, however, speak Dutch, which they do without clicking their tongues, or any peculiarity whatever.

In general they have more false shame (*mauvaise honte*) than any people I have seen, which I have often had occasion to experience when I have with the greatest difficulty persuaded them to dance or even to speak to each other in their own language in my presence. Their songs and dances are in extremes ; some tolerably active, consisting of quick music and brisk motions, generally of distortions of the body with unnatural leaps, crossing the legs backwards and forwards, etc. ; others again as dull and spiritless as can be imagined. One dance consists entirely of beating the earth first with one foot and then with the other, without moving their place at all, to the cadence of a tune furnished with little more variety than the dance.

Smoking is a custom most generally used among them, in doing which they do not, as the Europeans do, admit the smoke no farther than their mouths, but like the Chinese suck it into their lungs, where they keep it for nearly a minute before they emit it. They commonly mix with their tobacco the leaves of hemp, which they cultivate for that purpose, or *Phlomis leonurus*, which they call *dacha*. Their food is the same as that of the farmers, chiefly bread and coarse cheese; but they are immensely fond of spirituous liquors, and will never fail to get drunk with them if they have an opportunity.

This little, and no more, of the customs of this much-spoken-of people I had myself an opportunity of seeing: from the Dutch I heard much, and select the following from their accounts:—

Within the boundaries of the Dutch settlements are many different nations of Hottentots, differing from each other in custom very materially. Some are far superior to others in arts. In general, however, all live peaceably with each other, seldom fighting, except those who live to the eastward, who are much annoyed by people called by the Dutch *Boschmen*. The latter live entirely upon plunder, stealing the cattle of the Hottentots, but not openly attacking them. They are armed, however, with lances or assagais, arrows (which they know how to poison, some with the juice of herbs, others with the poison of the snake called cobra di capelo [1]), and stones (which some particular tribes throw so well that they will repeatedly strike a dollar or crown-piece at the distance of a hundred paces). They train up bulls, which they place round their crawls or towns in the night: these will constantly assemble and oppose either man or beast that approaches them, nor will they desist till they hear the voice of their masters, who know how to encourage them to fight, or to make them in an instant as tame and tractable as their other cattle.

Some nations know how to melt and prepare copper, which is found among them, probably native, and make of it broad plates to ornament their foreheads. Others again, indeed most, know how to harden bits of iron, which they procure from the Dutch, and make of them knives superior to any the Dutch can sell them.

Their chief people, many of whom have a large quantity of cattle of their own, are generally clad in the skins of lions, tigers, or zebras, etc., which they adorn and fringe very

---

[1] The term *cobra di capella* is only applied to the common Indian species of the cobra.

prettily, especially the women, who, as in all other countries, are fond of dress. Both sexes grease themselves very frequently, but never use any stinking grease if they can possibly get either fresh mutton suet or sweet butter, which last, made by shaking the milk in a bag made of skin, is generally used by the richer sort.

A Table of the Value of Money, supposing a Dutch Stiver equal to a Penny Sterling

	£		
A guinea	£0	18	0
Half do.	0	9	0
A crown-piece	0	4	0
Half do.	0	2	0
A shilling	0	0	10
A louis d'or			
A French crown	0	4	6
A ducat	0	9	0
A ducatoon	0	6	0
A skilling	0	0	6
A dubblechey	0	0	2
A stiver	0	0	1
An imperial rix-dollar	0	4	0
Albert's do.	0	6	0
Dane's rix-dollar	0	4	0
Spanish dollar	0	4	6
A quarter of do.	0	1	0

14th April 1771. Sailed from the road, but having very little wind were obliged to anchor abreast of Robben Island.

15th. In the morning it was quite calm, so a boat was hoisted out in order to land on the island in hopes of purchasing some refreshments, especially of garden stuff and salletting, with which two articles it is said to abound; but as soon as the boat came near the shore the Dutch hailed her, and told the people in her at their peril to attempt landing, bringing down at the same time six men with muskets, who paraded on the beach as long as she stayed, which was but a short time, as we did not think it worth while to risk landing in opposition to them, when a few cabbages were the only reward to be expected.

The island, which is named after the seals (in Dutch *Robben*) that formerly frequented it, is low and sandy, situate in the mouth of Table Bay. Here are confined such criminals as are judged not worthy of death for terms of years proportioned to the heinousness of their crimes. They are employed as slaves in the Company's service, chiefly in digging for lime-stone, which, though very scarce upon the continent, is plentiful here. Their reason for not letting foreigners land is said to be that formerly a Danish ship, which by sickness had lost the greater part of her crew, came into the Cape and asked for assistance. When this was refused she came down to this island, and sending her boats ashore, secured the guard, and took on board as many of the criminals as she thought proper to navigate the ship home.

28th. This day we crossed our first meridian and completed the circumnavigation of the globe, in doing which we, as usual, lost a day, which I should upon this occasion have expended properly had not I lost it a second time, I know not how, in my irregular journal at the Cape.

1st May. In the morning at daybreak saw the island of St. Helena about six leagues ahead, and consequently before noon arrived in the road where were found His Majesty's ship *Portland*, Captain Elliot, sent out to convey home the Indiamen on the account of the likelihood of a breach with Spain, also His Majesty's ship *Swallow*,[1] which had the day before brought word of the pacific measures adopted by that Court, and twelve sail of Indiamen.

2nd. As the fleet was to sail immediately and our ship to accompany it, it became necessary to make as much of a short time as possible, so this whole day was employed in riding about this island, in the course of which we very nearly made the complete circuit of it, visiting all the most remarkable places that we had been told of.

3rd. Spent this day in botanising on the ridge where the cabbage-trees grow, visiting Cucold's Point and Diana's Peak, the highest in the island, as settled by the observations

---

[1] This was not the consort of the *Dolphin* in 1766.

of Mr. Maskelyne, who was sent out to this island by the Royal Society for the purpose of observing the transit of Venus in the year [1761].

Some Account of St. Helena.

This small island, which is no more than twelve miles long and seven broad, is situated in a manner in the middle of the vast Atlantic Ocean, being 400 leagues distant from the coast of Africa and above 600 from that of America. It appears to be, or rather is, the summit of some immense mountain, which towering far above the level of the earth (in this part of the globe very much depressed) elevates itself even considerably above the surface of the sea, which covers its highest neighbours with a body of water even to this time unfathomable by the researches of mankind.

The higher parts of all countries have been observed almost without exception to be the seats of volcanoes,[1] while the lower parts are much more seldom found to be so. Etna and Vesuvius have no land higher than themselves in their neighbourhood. Hecla is the highest hill in Iceland; in the highest parts of the Andes in South America volcanoes are frequent, and the Pike of Teneriffe is still on fire. These still continue to burn, but numberless others have been found to show evident marks of fire, although now extinct from the times of our earliest traditions.

That this has been the case with St. Helena, and that the great inequalities of the ground there have been originally caused by the sinking of the ground, easily appears to an observing eye, who compares the opposite ridges, which, though separated always by deep and sometimes by tolerably broad valleys, have such a perfect similarity in appearance as well as in direction as scarce leaves room for a doubt that they formerly made part of a much less uneven surface, and that this sinking in of the earth has been occasioned by sub-terraneous fires. The stones abundantly testify to this, as they universally show marks of having been at some time

---

[1] This is not accurate ; nor is Hecla the highest mountain in Iceland.

or other exposed to the effects of a great degree of heat.
Some are evidently burnt almost to a cinder, especially those
which are found near the bottoms of valleys, as may be
seen in going up Side Path, and probably Ladder Hill also.
Others show small bubbles as are seen in glass which has
been heated almost to fusion ; others again from their situation on the tops of ridges have been exposed to a far less
degree of heat, or from their own apyrous qualities show
scarcely any signs of having been on fire, yet in many of
these, when carefully examined, are found small pieces of
extraneous bodies such as mundics, etc., which have sub-
mitted to the fire, though it was not able to make any altera-
tion in the appearance of the stone containing them.

Thus much for these suggestions, fit only for those who
can believe a Babylonian chronology. I pass now to the
present state of the island, a subject which affords much
entertainment to a contemplative mind, and more food to an
inquisitive one than the shortness of my stay gave me
opportunity to collect.

Making it as we did, and as indeed most ships do, on the
windward side, it is a rude heap of rocks bounded ؛by
precipices of an amazing height composed of a kind of half-
friable rock, which, however, show not the least sign of
vegetation, nor does a nearer view appear more promising.
In sailing along the shore ships come uncommonly near it,
so that the huge cliffs seem almost to overhang and threaten
destruction by the apparent probability of their giving way ;
in this manner they sail until they open Chapel Valley, where
stands the small town. Even that valley resembles a large
trench, in the bottom of which a few plants are to be seen ;
but its sides are as bare as the cliff next the sea. Such is
the apparent bareness of the island in its present cultivated
state. Nor do you see any signs of fertility till you have
penetrated beyond the first hills, when the valleys begin to be
green, and although everywhere inconceivably steep, produce
a great deal of good herbage. Among these are the planters'
houses, near each of which is a small plantation of cocos, the
only vegetable they seem to take much trouble to cultivate.

The town, very small, and, with the exception of a few houses, ill-built, stands just by the seaside. The church, which was originally a very poor building, is now almost in ruins, and the market-house is advancing by quick steps to the same situation.

The white inhabitants are almost to a man English, who, as they are not allowed to have any trade or commerce of their own, live entirely by supplying refreshments to such ships as touch at the place. To their shame be it spoken, they appear to have a supply of refreshments by no means equal to the extent and fertility of their soil, as well as the fortunate situation that their island seems to promise, situated as it is between temperate and warm latitudes. Their soil might produce most, if not all, the vegetables of Europe, together with the fruits of the Indies, yet both are almost totally neglected. Cabbages, indeed, and garden stuff in general, are very good, but so far from being in sufficient plenty to supply the ships that touch here, a scanty allowance only of them are to be got, chiefly by favour from the greater people, who totally monopolise every article produced in the island, excepting only beef and mutton, which the Company keep in their own hands. Although there is a market-house in the town, nothing is sold publicly, nor could either of the three King's ships that were there get greens for their tables, except only Captain Elliot, the commanding officer, who was furnished by order of the Governor out of his own garden.

Here are plantains, peaches, lemons, apples, and guavas, but, I believe, scarcely any other fruit. But while their pastures lie, as they really do, as much neglected as their gardens, there can be little hopes of amendment. In short, the custom of the Indiamen's captains, who always make very handsome presents to the families where they are entertained, besides paying extravagant prices for the few refreshments they get, seems to have inspired the people with laziness. Were refreshments cheap they would probably on the whole receive not much more money for them in the year, and the presents would be the same, so, at least, they seem to think. In short, the contrast between the Cape of

Good Hope, which, though by nature a mere desert, supplies abundantly refreshments to all nations who touch there, and this island highly favoured by nature, shows not unaptly the genius of the two nations for making colonies. Nor do I think I go too far in asserting that were the Cape now in the hands of the English it would be a desert, as St. Helena in the hands of the Dutch would as infallibly become a paradise.

Small as the island is, and not raised very much above the surface of the sea, it enjoys a variety of climates hardly to be believed. The cabbage-trees,[1] as they are called, which grow on the highest ridges, can by no art be cultivated on the lower ones, where the red wood and gum wood both grow; these in their turn refuse the high ridges, and neither of the three are to be found in the valleys, which indeed are in general covered with European plants, or the more common ones of the Indies, in all probability originally brought here by ships. This is the more probable, as much the largest proportion of them are natives of England. Among them I may mention the meadow grass (*Anthoxanthum odoratum*), which is the chief covering of their pastures, and to which I am much inclined to attribute the verdure of the island, far exceeding anything I have before seen in equally low latitudes. The furze also (*Ulex Europeus*), the seeds of which were brought over in the beginning of this century, thrives wonderfully, and is highly praised by the islanders as a great improvement, though they make no use of it except for heating their rooms. Barley was sown here about forty years ago, and produced sufficient to supply the island without any being sent from home. Its cultivation has, however, suddenly dropped, for what reason I could not find out, and since that time has never again been attempted. Yams, the same as are called cocos in the West Indies, are what they chiefly depend upon to supply their numerous slaves with provisions: these, however, are not cultivated in half the perfection that I have seen in the South Sea Islands; nor have they like the Indians several sorts, many of which are very palatable; but are confined to only one, and that one of the worst.

---

[1] Small trees and shrubs allied to the aster and groundsel.

All kind of labour is here performed by man, indeed he is the only animal that works, except a few saddle-horses; nor has he the least assistance of art to enable him to perform his task. Supposing the roads to be too steep and narrow for carts, an objection which lies against only one part of the island, yet the simple contrivance of wheel-barrows would doubtless be far preferable to carrying burthens upon the head, and even that expedient is never tried. Their slaves indeed are very numerous; they have them from most parts of the world, but they appeared to me a miserable race, almost worn out with the severity of the punishments, of which they frequently complained. I am sorry to say that it appeared to me that far more frequent and more wanton cruelties were exercised by my countrymen over these unfortunate people than ever their neighbours the Dutch, famed for inhumanity, are guilty of. One rule, however, they strictly observe, which is never to punish when ships are there.

Nature has blessed this island with very few productions either useful for the support, or conducive to the luxury, of mankind. Partridges and doves are the only animals, except possibly rats and mice; the latter, however, more probably brought here by ships. Among vegetables, purslain, celery, water-cresses, wild mint, and tobacco are now common among the rocks; though I doubt much whether they were so before people came here, as none, except the last, are found in parallel latitudes.

The first, indeed, is found on Ascension, and in many parts equally unlikely to have originally produced it, but that is accounted for by the ancient custom of the Portuguese, who, finding this herb particularly beneficial in complaints contracted in long voyages, made a point of sowing it wherever they went ashore, a custom from whence all nations have since reaped no small benefit. Amongst its native products, however, ebony [1] must be reckoned, though the trees that produce it are now nearly extinct, and no one remembers the time when they were at all plentiful. Yet

---

[1] *Melhania melanoxylon*, Br., now quite extinct.

pieces of the wood are frequently found in the valleys, of a fine black colour, and of a hardness almost equal to iron; these, however, are almost always so short and so crooked that no use has yet been made of them. Whether the tree is the same as that which produces ebony on the Isle of Bourbon and the adjacent islands is impossible to know, as the French have not yet published any account of it. Other species of trees and plants, which seem to have been originally natives of the island, are few in number. Insects there are also a few, and one species of snail, which inhabits only the tops of the highest ridges, and has probably been there ever since their original creation.

Had our stay upon the island been longer, we should in all probability have discovered some more natural productions, but in all likelihood not many; secluded as this rock is from the rest of the world by seas of immense extent, it is difficult to imagine how anything not originally created in that spot could by any accident arrive at it. For my part I confess I feel more wonder at finding a little snail on the top of the ridges of St. Helena, than in finding people upon America, or any other part of the globe.

As the benefits of the land are so limited, the sea must often be applied to by the natives of this little rock; nor is she unmindful of their necessities, for she constantly supplies immense plenty, and no less variety, of fish. She would indeed be culpable did she do otherwise: she never met with a calamity equal to that of the earth in the general deluge, and her children, moreover, have the advantage of a free intercourse with all parts of the globe, habitable to them, without being driven to the necessity of tempting the dangers of an element unsuited to their natures; a fatal necessity under which too many even of us, lords of the creation, yearly perish, and of all others through the wide bounds of creation how vast a proportion must die. The seed of a thistle supported by its down, the insect by its weak, and the bird by its more able, wing, may tempt the dangers of the sea; but of these how many millions must perish for one which arrives at the distance of twelve

2 G

hundred miles from the place of its rest. It appears, indeed, far more difficult to account for the passage of one individual, than to believe the destruction of all that may ever have been by their ill fate hurried into such an attempt.

Money of all nations passes here according to its real intrinsic European value; there is therefore no kind of trouble on that head, as in all the Dutch settlements.

4th. Sailed after dinner in company with twelve India-men and His Majesty's ship *Portland.* We resolved to steer homewards with all expedition, in order (if possible) to bring the first news of our voyage, as we found that many particulars of it had transpired, and particularly that a copy of the latitudes and longitudes of most or all the principal places we had been at had been taken by the captain's clerk from the captain's own journals, and given or sold to one of the India captains. War we had no longer the least suspicion of; the Indiamen being ordered to sail immediately without waiting for the few who had not yet arrived was a sufficient proof that our friends at home were not at all ap-prehensive of it.

10th. This day we saw the Island of Ascension, which is tolerably high land : our captain, however, did not choose to anchor, unwilling to give the fleet so much start of him. Those who have been ashore upon this island say that it is little more than a heap of cinders, the remains of a volcano ever since the discovery of the Indies. Osbeck, who was ashore on it, found only five species of plants; but I am much in-clined to believe that there are others which escaped his notice, as he certainly was not on the side of the island where the French land, in which place I have been informed is a pretty wide plain covered with herbage, among which grows *Cactus opuntia,* a plant not seen by that gentleman.

11th. Saw *Holothuria physalis,* which our seamen call Portuguese man-of-war, for the first time since we left these seas in going out.

23rd. Dined on board the *Portland* with Captain Elliot :

while on board her saw a common house martin flying about the ship.

29*th*. Fresh trade, which quickly relieved everybody from the depression of spirits, etc., which is the constant companion of the damp calms we have now passed through.

1*st June*. Saw some gulph-weed to-day for the first time.

3*rd*. This day passed under the sun, and were for the last time ascii.[1]

5*th*. Less gulph-weed than yesterday, so we began to catch it by means of a pole with six large hooks fastened at the end. Out of it we took *Scyllœa pelagica*, *Medusa porpita*, *Syngnathus pelagicus*, *Lophius pelagicus*, and *Cancer minutus*.

6*th*. More gulph-weed, in which took up several individuals of the afore-mentioned species, besides which were caught *Cancer pelagicus*, and a shrimp not described. Several tropic birds were seen, all of which flew in a straight line towards the coast of Africa.

18*th*. Saw three New England schooners cruising for whales: sent a boat on board one, who told us that she had yesterday spoken to an outward-bound Englishman, who had said that all was peace in Europe, and that the Spaniards had agreed to pay the Manilla ransom with interest for one year, and a million of dollars for damages done at Falkland's Islands.

This vessel had by their own account been out five weeks and caught nothing: they had chased a whale sixty leagues into Fayal harbour, where they could not follow it, as the Portuguese suffer no whaler to go into any of their ports in the Western Islands.[2] They had, they said, no meat on board, but lived upon what they could catch. They readily sold us four large albecores, saying that they could catch more. As for American news, King George, they said, had behaved very ill for some time, but the colonists had brought him to terms at last.

---

[1] *i.e.* without a shadow (Gr. ἄσκιος).

[2] The Azores, of which Fayal is one.

23rd. Saw one shearwater: the reason of so few having been seen this passage, may be that during their breeding time they do not wander far out at sea.

4th July. My bitch "Lady" was found dead in my cabin, lying upon a stool on which she generally slept; she had been remarkably well for some days; in the night she shrieked out very loud, so that we who slept in the great cabin heard her, but becoming quiet immediately no one regarded it: whatever disease was the cause of her death, it was the most sudden that ever came under my observation.

7th. Caught *Lepas cygnifera* [1] floating upon the water in round congeries, some of which were large enough to fill a man's hat.

8th. Calm: went in boat and shot fulmar and Manx puffin, of Pennant's British Zoology.

10th. This morning the land was discovered by young Nick,[2] the same boy who first saw New Zealand: it proved to be the Lizard.

12th. At three o'clock landed at Deal.

[1] Probably *Lepas anatifera*.
[2] His real name was Nicholas Young.

APPENDIX

25th October 1768, about five miles south of the line. My machine was made by Ramsden, and worked by a flat plate 8 inches in diameter. The phial used was $6\frac{1}{2}$ inches in height and $5\frac{1}{2}$ in diameter without the neck; the distance between the stopper and the coating, 3 inches, the stopper made of wood and fastened to the glass on the inside by a red cement (probably sealing-wax). The electrometer was divided into thirty parts of $1\frac{1}{2}$ inch as nearly as possible. About nine in the morning the machine was set up, the day being rather cloudy, and the ship going between three and four knots.

When the plate was first turned round the cushions appeared to be damp, adhering to the glass so much that it was with difficulty made to move very slowly, although the cushions were screwed on as tightly as possible. After wiping them very well the plate was made to go round, and in about ten minutes electricity was excited, though but in a small degree; the motion of the ship and the shaking of the table, caused by turning the machine, made the electrometer (which was a very unsteady one) move backwards and forwards visibly, so that it was impossible to ascertain exactly at what distance it discharged the phial, it however was guessed to be about a line when at the greatest distance.

It continued to work in this manner about half an hour, in which time several attempts were made to give a shock, but they succeeded very badly, the shocks being very slight, though given with as much electricity as could be got into the phial. It then (having grown by degrees weaker and weaker) ceased to work entirely. Water was applied to the cushions, but without any effect: everything then was wiped and dried as well as could be done in our situation, the cushions being carried to the fire, but no electricity perceptible to the touch was communicated to the conductor. Whether any was excited on the surface of the plate we did not then observe. An amalgam of lead was then applied, causing a small amount of electricity, but much less than at first, and this very soon ceased also. From that time no electricity perceptible (except by Canton's electrometer) could be communicated to the conductor, though the machine was worked nearly an hour.

In the course of these experiments two things were observed, differing from the phenomena usually seen. First, the phial when filled with as much electricity as possible would not retain it more than a very few seconds, three or four by guess (for no opportunity of measuring by a watch was given, the machine stopping work without any warning); at the end of this time not the smallest quantity of electricity was left, though I tried all my five phials. Two of these phials were such as were described above; the others were smaller, made much in the same manner, but instead of being coated on the inside were filled with leaf-gold. Secondly, the floor of the cabin in which the experiments were tried was covered with a red floor-cloth of painted canvas that had been issued to the ship from His Majesty's stores at Deptford. This was usually washed with salt water every morning and allowed to dry without being taken up. This proved as good a conductor of electricity as any we could make use of, so that a man standing on one side the machine and touching the coating of the phial was shocked by another who touched the conductor, without having any other communication with the first than by the floor-cloth under his feet. Dr. Solander and myself tried this in several ways, and made more experiments afterwards with Mr. Green's machine, as noticed further on.

The ill success of these experiments seems to me to have arisen chiefly from the uncommon dampness of the circumambient air, which had been observed by everybody since we crossed the tropic, and is fully noticed in my journal. By this solution alone can all the phenomena that appeared be accounted for.

Air charged with particles of damp is well known to be of all others the greatest enemy to electricity. It immediately attracts and dissipates all the electrical matter which is collected by the machine, which therefore worked faintly for a little while, till the damp was condensed on the conductor, and chiefly on the surface of the glass phial, and then ceased entirely. A small quantity was, however, always noticeable upon the surface of the plate, even to the end of the conductor.

The phial, though charged as full as the machine would fill it, even at the time of its best working, scarcely retained the electrical matter at all, owing doubtless to the communication made by the condensed damp between the coating and the stopper of the phial; this increased every moment, so that at last it would not contain any electricity.

The situation on board ship would not allow the use of a fire to warm the whole machine, which should have been done, and which would have been a great satisfaction, but the motion of the ship, the distance of the galley from the cabin, and the number of people who are constantly busy there, made that impossible.

The dampness of the air complained of here has not been observed now for the first time. Piso, in his account of the Brazils, mentioned it, and says that victuals which have kept well before spoil immediately there. This therefore may account for the general opinion of electrical machines failing to work when near the line, as the fault could not be in my machine which worked remarkably well in London, and fully as well as I expected in Madeira.

25th October 1768, 17 miles south of the line—*Mr. Green's machine.* This was made by Watkins: the jar was of glass 8 inches high and 7 deep, coated with varnish between the lead and the stopper, which was of cork, no varnish coming between that and the neck. The electrometer was divided into thirty parts of $1\frac{1}{8}$ inch.

The plate at first refused to go round, as mine had done before, the cushions being drawn together by the glass, to which they seemed to adhere, probably from their dampness. After some time, however, this went off, and in about ten minutes electricity was excited.

The electrometer was then applied and went off at 7.

2. Electricity was kept in the phial thirty seconds without any appreciable quantity being lost.

3. A hole was struck through two cards by the discharging wire.

4. Much greater shocks were given to several people than any that could be given by my machine.

5. The phenomenon of the floor-cloth proving a conductor was tried more fully than before. A wire (*b*, see

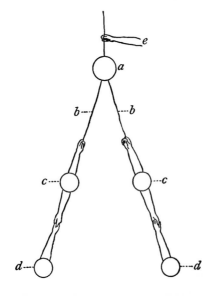

figure) was passed through the phial (*a*), the two ends of which were taken hold of by two people (*c c*), who each took hold of another person (*d d*); the operator (*e*) then touched the phial with his discharging wire, and received the shock through both arms, as did (*c c*) and (*d d*). Sometimes, however, the others (*d d*) felt it only in the arm by which they held (*c c*). The comparative force of the blows which each felt were difficult to ascertain, but we supposed that (*c c*) felt more than (*d d*), and probably the operator most of all.

The chief reason that this machine worked better than mine seems to be that the bottle was coated with varnish between the stopper and coating of lead; this probably did not condense the damp of the air so readily as glass, and consequently the machine worked well when mine refused to work at all.

Monday, 19th March 1770. The machine on being taken out of the box was found to have had the plate and one of the phials broken by some accident. The former was replaced by a spare one. Every part was perfectly dry and worked with great freedom, but a small proportion of electricity only could be excited, at most enough to strike through one card. During all our experiments the floor-cloth conducted as it had done before, though it had not been washed for some weeks. Our experiments were soon cut short by the wind, which was foul, freshening so much that we could not with safety let the machine stand. The day was rather hazy.

Friday, 23rd March 1770. All the day was clear, and the evening also very fine. At sunset the machine was set up. It at first entirely refused to work, but after about a quarter of an hour some sparks were excited. The most, however, that we could do was to obtain a slight shock. The floor-cloth conducted as usual, which we ascertained by resting upon a table or chair, in which case we did not feel the shock as we always did when standing upon the ground.

THE WORLD

A S I A

PACIFIC OCEAN

NEW ZEALAND

AUSTRALIA OR NEW HOLLAND

VAN DIEMEN'S LAND

NEW GUINEA

PHILIPPINE ISLANDS

Ladrone Is.

Samoa

Solomon

Endeavour Strait & Cook's Passage

Botany Bay

Port Jackson

Moreton Bay

C. Howe

CHINA

INDIA

Formosa

Oriental Coast

Cochin China

CEYLON

INDIAN OCEAN

MADAGASCAR

Isle de France Mauritius

NATAL

Cape Town

Saint Augustine

Cape of Good Hope

Table R. & Robben I.

False Bay

AFRICA

GUINEA

TROPIC OF CANCER

EQUATOR

TROPIC OF CAPRICORN

Ascension I.

St. Helena

ATLANTIC OCEAN

ICELAND

ENGLAND

PORTUGAL

Madeira

Teneriffe

Cape Verd I.

NEWFOUNDLAND

WEST INDIES

Jamaica

SOUTH AMERICA

BRAZIL

PERU

CHILI

PATAGONIA

Eastern

RIO JANEIRO

San Thiago

Para

R. Plate

C. San Mathias

Falkland I.

TERRA DEL FUEGO

Staten I.

Juan Fernandez I.

Concepcion

Valdivia

Port S.t Julian

Mendoza

NORTH AMERICA

UNITED STATES

Mexico

PACIFIC OCEAN

EQUATOR

Sandwich Is.

SOCIETY ISLANDS

Lagoon I.

Marquesas I.

Track of the Endeavour 1769-70

Bering Strait

Icy Cape

Bering Strait

Icy Cape

Meridian of Greenwich

North Lat.

South Lat.

East of Gr.

West of Gr.

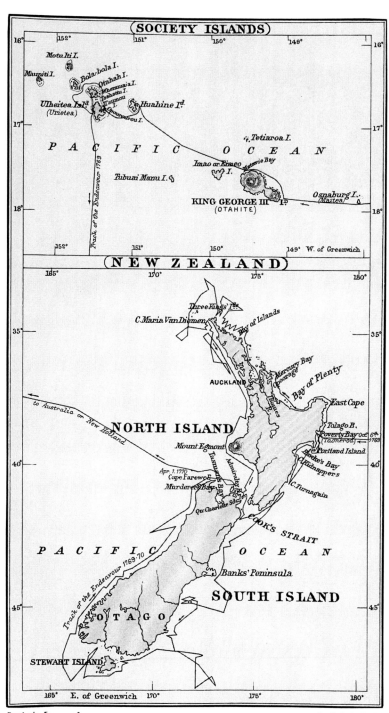

MELANESIA.

North Latitude

0°

South Latitude

Caroline Islands

Marshall Ids.

PACIFIC OCEAN

Gilbert Ids.

Palmyra I.

Fanning I.

Christmas I.

EQUATOR

Phoenix Ids.

Tokelau Ids.

Ellice Ids.

Penrhyn I.

Samoa or Navigator Ids.

Friendly Ids.

FIJI ISLANDS

NEW HEBRIDES

Santa Cruz or Queen Charlotte I.

Tierra del Espiritu Santo

Loyalty I.

New Caledonia

SOLOMON ISLANDS

New Britain

NEW GUINEA

Louisiade Ids.

TORRES STRAIT

Cape York

Possession I.

Eagle I. & Cook Passage

C. Flattery

Endeavour

Track of the Endeavour 1770

Bustard Bay

AUSTRALIA OR NEW HOLLAND

140°   150°   160°   170°   180°   170°   160°

East Greenwich   West Greenwich

TROPIC OF CAPRICORN

10°

20°

Banks's Journal.

London : Macmillan & Co. Ltd.

Stanford's Geog¹ Estab¹

EAST INDIA ARCHIPELAGO.

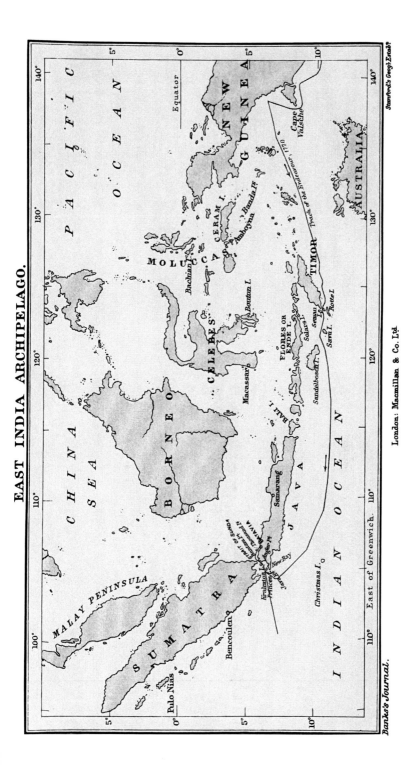

London: Macmillan & Co. Ltd.

Stanford's Geog.l Estab.t

INDEX

THE END

Printed by R. & R. CLARK, LIMITED, *Edinburgh.*

Lightning Source UK Ltd.
Milton Keynes UK
UKOW03f1954260314

228896UK00001B/23/P